PHENOMENOLOGY OF THE SACRED

PHENOMENOLOGY OF THE SACRED

FOUNDATIONS FOR A RETROPROGRESSIVE PHENOMENOLOGY

PHENOMENOLOGY OF THE SACRED
FOUNDATIONS FOR A RETROPROGRESSIVE PHENOMENOLOGY
by Prabhuji

Copyright © 2026
First edition

Printed in Round Top, New York, United States

All rights reserved. None of the information contained in this book may be reproduced, republished, or re-disseminated in any manner or form without the prior written consent of the publisher.

Published by Prabhuji Mission
Website: prabhuji.net

Avadhutashram
PO Box 900
Cairo, NY, 12413
USA

Painting on the cover by Prabhuji:
"Phenomenology of the Sacred"
Acrylic on canvas, New York, USA, 2022
Canvas Size: 12"x36"

Library of Congress Control Number: 2025920013
ISBN-13: 978-1-945894-67-1

Contents

Preface 1
Introduction 5

Section I: Being and the phenomenon

Chapter 1: The human phenomenon 19
Chapter 2: The Being as phenomenon 25
Bibliography section I 37

Section II: Phenomenology and symbolism

Chapter 3: The potentiality and actualization of Being 41
Chapter 4: From phenomenology to symbolism 53
Bibliography section II 57

Section III: Transcendental phenomenology

Chapter 5: From skepticism to realization 61
Chapter 6: The return to the Being of things 67
Chapter 7: The destruction of the concept 75
Bibliography section III 89

Section IV: Phenomenology of the manifest and the hidden

Chapter 8: Phenomenology of the unmanifested 93
Chapter 9: Criticisms of transcendental philosophy 101
Chapter 10: The mystery of givenness 107
Chapter 11: Intentionality and knowledge 113
Chapter 12: Perception and intuition according to Husserl ... 129

Chapter 13: Pure self-givenness 143
Bibliography section IV 151

SECTION V: PHENOMENOLOGY OF REVELATION

Chapter 14: The history of the religious revelation 155
Chapter 15: Revelation in Western Philosophy
　　　　　　according to Saint Augustine 165
Chapter 16: Revelation according to Schelling: a path
　　　　　　toward the Divine 181
Chapter 17: Revelation according to René Descartes 189
Chapter 18: The importance of divine revelation
　　　　　　according to Kierkegaard 215
Chapter 19: Phenomenological foundations of
　　　　　　the revelation of the sacred 225
Bibliography section V 235

SECTION VI: FROM PHENOMENOLOGY TO ONTOLOGY

Chapter 20: The phenomenological exploration of consciousness 239
Chapter 21: Heidegger's ontological turn 255
Chapter 22: The object of phenomenology: from Husserl to Heidegger .. 267
Chapter 23: The "theological turn" in phenomenology 283
Chapter 24: The method as a phenomenological criterion 295
Chapter 25: Phenomenology of the hidden 305
Chapter 26: Relationality and the appearance of Being as the sacred ... 317
Bibliography section VI 329

Section VII: From ontology to (post)phenomenology

Chapter 27: The saturated phenomenon 333
Chapter 28: The divine manifestation... 357
Chapter 29: Manifestation and concealment:
    phenomenon, time, and language...................................... 369
Bibliography section VII... 383

Section VIII: Phenomenology of time

Chapter 30: A genealogy of time.. 387
Chapter 31: Time according to Aristotle... 391
Chapter 32: Time and eternity according to Saint Augustine............. 401
Chapter 33: Time according to Kant, Husserl, and Heidegger 411
Chapter 34: The transcendence of time 417
Chapter 35: The art of waiting.. 427
Bibliography section VIII 447

Section IX: Phenomenology of the sacred

Chapter 36: The saturated phenomenon in the light of hermeneutics..451
Chapter 37: Heidegger's understanding of the sacred......................... 465
Chapter 38: Intentionality in the revelation of the sacred....................477
Chapter 39: The role of the observer.. 489
Bibliography section IX 497

Section X: In search of God

Chapter 40: Echoes of Spinoza, Hegel, and Schopenhauer on God 501
Chapter 41: A philosophical journey in the search for God................. 509
Bibliography section X..523

Section XI: Toward a Retroprogressive Phenomenology

Chapter 42: The retroprogressive inversion 527

Chapter 43: Light and consciousness: a retroprogressive exploration 535

Appendices

About Prabhuji 553

The term *prabhuji* by Swami Ramananda 565

The term *avadhūta* 567

About the Prabhuji Mission 577

About the Avadhutashram 579

The Retroprogressive Path 581

Prabhuji today 583

Titles by Prabhuji 586

ॐ अज्ञानतिमिरान्धस्य ज्ञानाञ्जनशलाकया ।
चक्षुरुन्मीलितं येन तस्मै श्रीगुरवे नमः ॥

oṁ ajñāna-timirāndhasya
jñānāñjana-śalākayā
cakṣur unmīlitaṁ yena
tasmai śrī-gurave namaḥ

Salutations unto that holy Guru who, applying the ointment [medicine] of [spiritual] knowledge, removes the darkness of ignorance of the blinded [unenlightened] and opens their eyes.

This book is dedicated, with deep gratitude and eternal respect, to the holy lotus feet of my beloved masters His Divine Grace Bhakti-kavi Atulānanda Ācārya Mahārāja (Gurudeva) and His Divine Grace Avadhūta Śrī Brahmānanda Bābājī Mahārāja (Guru Mahārāja).

Preface

The story of my life is an odyssey from what I believed myself to be to what I truly am… an inner and outer pilgrimage. A journey from the personal to the universal, from the partial to the whole, from the illusory to the real, from the apparent to the true. A wandering flight from the human to the Divine.

Everything that awakens at dawn rests at dusk; every lit flame eventually extinguishes. Only what begins, ends; only what starts, finishes. But what dwells in the present is neither born nor dies, for that which lacks a beginning never perishes.

As a simple autobiographer and narrator of significant experiences, I share my intimate story with others. My story is not public but profoundly private and intimate. It does not belong to the turmoil of social life, but is a sigh kept in the most hidden depths of the soul.

I am a disciple of seers, enlightened beings, shadows of the universe who are nobody and walk in death. I am just a whim or perhaps a joke from the heavens and the only mistake of my beloved spiritual masters. I was initiated in my spiritual childhood by the moonlight, which showed me its light and shared its being with me. My muse was a seagull that loved to fly more than anything else in life.

In love with the impossible, I traversed the universe, obsessed with the brilliance of a star. I traveled countless paths, following the traces and vestiges of those with the vision to decipher the hidden. Like the ocean that longs for water, I sought my home within my own house.

I do not claim to be a guide, coach, teacher, instructor, educator, psychologist, enlightener, pedagogue, evangelist, rabbi, *posek halacha*, healer, therapist, satsangist, psychic, leader, medium, savior, guru, or authority of any kind, whether spiritual or material. I allow myself the audacity and daring to represent nothing and no one but myself. I am only a traveler whom you can ask for directions. With pleasure, I point you to a place where everything calms upon arrival... beyond the sun and the stars, your desires and longings, time and space, concepts and conclusions, and beyond all that you believe you are or imagine you will be.

I paint sighs, hopes, silences, aspirations, and melancholies, inner landscapes, and sunsets of the soul. I am a painter of the indescribable, inexpressible, and indefinable, and unconfessable of our depths... or maybe I just write colors and paint words. Aware of the abyss that separates revelation and works, I live in a frustrated attempt to faithfully express the mystery of the spirit.

Since childhood, little windows of paper captivated my attention; through them, I visited places, met people, and made friends. Those tiny mandalas were my true elementary school, high school, and college. Like skilled teachers, these *yantras* have guided me through contemplation, attention, concentration, observation, and meditation.

Like a physician studies the human body, or a lawyer studies laws, I have dedicated my entire life to the study of myself. I can say with certainty that I know what resides and lives in this heart.

My purpose is not to persuade others. It is not my intention to convince anyone of anything. I do not offer theology or philosophy, nor do I preach or teach, I simply think out loud. The echo of these words may lead you to the infinite space of peace, silence, love, existence, consciousness, and absolute bliss.

Do not search for me. Search for yourself. You do not need me or anyone else, because the only thing that really matters is you. What you yearn for lies within you, as what you are, here and now.

I am not a merchant of rehashed information, nor do I intend to do business with my spirituality. I do not teach beliefs or philosophies. I only speak about what I see and just share what I know.

Avoid fame, for true glory is not based on public opinion but on what you really are. What matters is not what others think of you, but your own appreciation of who you are.

Choose bliss over success, life over reputation, and wisdom over information. If you succeed, you will know not only admiration but also true envy. Jealousy is mediocrity's tribute to talent and an open acceptance of one's own inferiority.

I advise you to fly freely and never be afraid of making mistakes. Learn the art of transforming your mistakes into lessons. Never blame others for your faults: remember that taking complete responsibility for your life is a sign of maturity. Flying teaches you that what matters is not touching the sky but having the courage to spread your wings. The higher you rise, the more graciously small and insignificant the world will seem. As you walk, sooner or later you will understand that every search begins and ends in you.

Your unconditional well-wisher,

Introduction

Phenomenology: consciousness and phenomenon

Phenomenology, defined as the science dedicated to the study of phenomena in their immediate manifestation, constitutes a fundamental pillar in contemporary philosophical research. This historical and conceptual study unfolds as a vast panorama that has exerted a notable impact on philosophical thought to the present day. This intellectual journey finds its roots in the eighteenth and nineteenth centuries, particularly in the work of Immanuel Kant, and spread until it became established as the predominant philosophical trend during the twentieth century. Kant was the first to outline the framework for investigating phenomena as they reveal themselves to our consciousness. He emphasized the importance of exploring the conditions that make experience itself possible. Developing this line of thought, Edmund Husserl, known as the father of phenomenology, laid out a detailed methodological approach for scrutinizing conscious experiences. He strove to authentically characterize the beings that manifest in consciousness. He coined the philosophical catchphrase "back to the things themselves" (*Zurück zu den Sachen selbst*), which permeates throughout his book *Logical Investigations*, a response to Kantian and especially neo-Kantian philosophy. Husserl played a crucial role in the development of phenomenology, especially with his work *Ideas Pertaining to a Pure Phenomenology and to a Phenomenological Philosophy*. Husserl defined phenomenology as the discipline devoted to the study of essences through eidetic intuition and the performance of phenomenological reduction. This process involves bracketing preconceptions about the objective existence of phenomena, that is, the things themselves, to focus on their appearance in front of consciousness.

Martin Heidegger, Husserl's disciple, took phenomenology further into the realm of fundamental ontology. In his seminal work *Being and Time,* Heidegger delves into the analysis of humans (*Dasein*) and their link with Being more broadly, introducing concepts such as "anguish" and "being-toward-death," which he identifies as essential aspects of human existence. Later, Merleau-Ponty enriched phenomenology with his focus on perception and embodiment. His main work, *Phenomenology of Perception,* argues that our body does not merely act as another object in the world, but as the central axis through which the world becomes accessible to us. In other words, consciousness is embodied consciousness, and phenomena are phenomena of a corporeally pulsating consciousness. Following Merleau-Ponty, Jean-Paul Sartre integrated phenomenology and existentialism. He emphasized concepts like freedom, decision, and individual subjectivity. In *Being and Nothingness,* Sartre delves into the importance of nothingness in understanding consciousness and human existence. Simultaneously, Emanuel Levinas, a disciple of both Husserl and Heidegger in his youth, took a further step in the field of phenomenology. His approach steps away from Husserl's epistemology and Heidegger's ontology; instead, he locates the origin of all experience in ethics and the "absolutely Other."

These approaches to phenomenology have had a significant influence on and intertwined with multiple philosophical currents including hermeneutics, deconstructionism, and philosophy of mind. Thinkers like Gadamer and Derrida have further extended the boundaries of phenomenology by investigating intersections between phenomenology, hermeneutics, and textual structure. Partly due to its interactions with other schools of thought, phenomenology remains immersed in a process of evolution. It addresses philosophical challenges in ethics, politics, psychology, and cognitive science, which make it relevant and versatile across diverse contexts.

Despite the differences, or sometimes even rifts, between some phenomenologists and their research lines, the genealogical trajectory of phenomenology shows a persistent effort to elucidate the dynamics between consciousness and the world. It highlights the essential role of immediate experience in the formation of meaning and knowledge. As we have seen, phenomenology focuses on analyzing how phenomena present or emerge in consciousness. It prioritizes observing their appearance within the confines of their apparent reality. According to this approach, understanding any phenomenon is inherently limited to the sphere in which it becomes evident to consciousness. This is why, first and foremost, it is important for us to briefly explore the historical genealogy of the concept of "consciousness." Its trajectory begins at the dawn of philosophical reflection and continues today.

In the origins of Western thought, it was not until the advent of Christianity that Latin employed the term *conscientia* with meanings we recognize today. Prior to this, in ancient Greek philosophy, there was no direct equivalent for the modern concept of consciousness, for either epistemological consciousness or moral conscience. However, the foundations of self-exploration and personal ethics were evident in the reflections of principal figures such as Plato and Aristotle. Plato's emblematic cave allegory outlines an initial attempt to characterize consciousness as awakening to knowledge and aspiring to Truth. Later, in the Hellenistic period, Stoic and Epicurean doctrines contributed significantly to the understanding of an intrinsic moral dimension of Being. The Stoics introduced the concept of *syneidēsis*, meaning moral consciousness and self-awareness. The Epicureans emphasized internal reflection and emotional control.

In early Christianity, the Latin term *conscientia* emerged through Saint Augustine and other theologians to describe how divinity is interwoven with the human soul, setting a moral guide and introspective knowledge. Augustine specifically highlights consciousness as an internal dialogue and the guiding presence of God. The medieval era and the scholastic system deepened the study of this consciousness, with figures such as Thomas Aquinas, who differentiated between *synderesis*, an innate understanding of ethical principles, and *conscientia*, reasoning applied to specific moral contexts.

Centuries later, modernity introduced a significant conceptual expansion of consciousness through the work of thinkers such as René Descartes and John Locke. They linked consciousness to introspection and the individual cognitive process. While Descartes places consciousness at the core of existence with his *cogito, ergo sum*, Locke conceptualizes it as the understanding of personal mental processes.

In the nineteenth century, with the emergence of psychoanalysis, figures such as Friedrich Nietzsche and Sigmund Freud complexified the notion of consciousness, exploring the underlying layers of the psyche and establishing the dichotomy between consciousness and unconsciousness. This radically transformed perceptions of the mind. In the twentieth century and contemporary philosophy, authors such as Jean-Paul Sartre and Maurice Merleau-Ponty examined consciousness from existentialist and phenomenological perspectives, emphasizing its importance in the construction of experience, freedom, and subjectivity.

As we can see from this summary, the Latin term *conscientia* can be understood in two ways in English: "conscience" and "consciousness." Conscience refers to the moral ability to distinguish between good and evil. Consciousness generally refers to the faculty that allows humans, and other forms of life, to discern their own existence, as well as the complexity of their situation; it manifests as the capacity to internally experience perceptions, sensations, thoughts, and feelings in a deeply personal way. It is distinctive for several fundamental attributes: self-recognition, the ability to capture stimuli through the senses, the thought process, the intimate experience of phenomena (the phenomenological aspect), and the capacity to decide freely.

Approached from multiple fields such as philosophy, psychology, and neuroscience, the study of consciousness is fertile ground for passionate discussions about its essence and foundations. It is one of the most provocative and enigmatic topics in contemporary academic discourse. This conceptual framework not only illustrates the richness of consciousness but also underscores the diversity of approaches and perspectives that attempt to unravel its mystery. In recent years, research on consciousness has made remarkable progress, largely driven by advances in neuroscience and cognitive psychology. Scientists such as Antonio Damasio and Daniel Dennett have delved into the relationship between neuronal activity and conscious experience. Simultaneously, the Integrated Information Theory of Consciousness, formulated by Giulio Tononi, offers a novel approach to understanding consciousness, interpreting it through the prism of the processing and integration of information. Our own definition is that consciousness is the source from which all experiences arise, the metaphysical place where they occur, and the substance of all experiences.

Now let us explore the philosophical evolution of the term "phenomenon," with a rich history that spans various philosophical periods. In ancient times, Plato and Aristotle differentiated between sensory perceptions and the underlying forms or essences but did not use the term "phenomenon" in its modern sense. They saw phenomena as direct sensory experiences. During the medieval period, this term did not play a central role. Theological issues and divine revelations predominated over empirical observation of the world. In the Renaissance and modernity, René Descartes called "phenomenon" to everything apparent and sensory, although not within a fully developed philosophical framework. It was Immanuel Kant who introduced a crucial distinction, defining phenomena as what we experience as opposed to noumena, or "things-in-themselves" (*Dinge an sich*), which are inaccessible to our direct perception. By virtue of this distinction between phenomena and noumena, Kant held that only phenomena are accessible to human knowledge. Later, in the nineteenth century, Hegel defined phenomenology as the study of the historic progress of consciousness and spirit, thus diverging from Kant's conception. Next, Edmund Husserl moved the term to the center of his philosophical thought, defining phenomenology as the analysis of phenomena in consciousness, abstracted from their "objective" existence. In the twentieth century, Heidegger and Sartre expanded Husserl's phenomenology. Heidegger considered phenomena to be whatever reveals itself in experience. In analytic philosophy, on the other hand, "phenomenon" is associated with its scientific use, referring to empirical data and observations. Currently, "phenomenon" encompasses both the phenomenological and empirical meanings. In continental philosophy, as it is often called to differentiate it from the analytic current, the term in question often retains Husserlian or Heideggerian connotations, while in general language and science, it refers to any observable event.

After presenting the historical and etymological context of the term "phenomenon," I would like to offer our own definition: it is the ability of beings to show themselves. That is, every phenomenon always reveals itself to someone, since a revelation without a receiver would be inconceivable. The phenomenon manifests itself in front of the perception of consciousness. In this way, the phenomenon and consciousness are the two facets that connect the object of observation and the observer. The role of the object is to reveal itself, while observers take on the task of interpreting what is revealed to them. However, in phenomenology, the traditional distinction between observers as passive entities and objects as active entities dissolves. Instead, we have a reciprocal interaction between observer and object, which can be described as phenomenological reduction. In this process, the notion of an autonomous observer and an isolated object gives way to the concept of the phenomenon. In these spaces of encounter and dialogue between observer and object, which Nietzsche would call "the corridors," both lose their unilateral character in order to interact.

Therefore, we understand phenomenology as the philosophical approach that focuses on examining how these phenomena manifest to consciousness, emphasizing that a thorough analysis is only feasible within the limits of their direct presentation. In this context, any inference that goes beyond what is explicitly revealed by the phenomenon is considered speculative. Thus, everything that is not immediately revealed by the phenomenon remains outside the scope of phenomenological study. It is essential to understand that the process by which phenomena reveal themselves and donating themselves to consciousness constitutes a key element of their manifestation. This process does not depend on the senses. Although we perceive through our senses, we cannot assert with certainty that the objects perceived possess an authentic and independent existence beyond consciousness—or, in other words, beyond their apprehension within consciousness. Ultimately, the reality of the observed thing remains indemonstrable. In the words of Descartes: "the senses: but I have discovered that they sometimes deceive us."[1] Hence, our task as phenomenologists is centered on describing what is manifested, regardless of whether our perception occurs in a dream or while awake, whether it is from imagination or fantasy. The crucial point is that we cannot state with certainty the nature of what we perceive.

When describing phenomena, whether from in dreams or while awake, our approach does not stop at validating whether they are based on real facts. Being a phenomenologist involves dedicating oneself to narrating what is presented in this "movie" of experience and not questioning its reality or delving into metaphysical debates. We commit to only narrate events as they unfold before us. If, when observing a tree, we begin to speculate about its real existence, we drift from the phenomenological path into metaphysics. Phenomenology urges us to remain faithful to the description of immediate experience, without mixing in with questions about the ultimate reality of what is observed. This methodological decision distinguishes phenomenology from other philosophical approaches. It is not a mere whim, but a philosophical necessity that does not allow us to take for granted the real or physical existence of what is observed, imagined, or dreamed. Husserl argues that phenomenology cannot take anything for granted, and this includes considering that objects have their own existence before we experience them. Otherwise, as Husserl warns, we would be basing our investigation on a "natural attitude," that is, on prejudices and assumptions that cloud both our investigation and understanding of reality and of the human being. Husserl's phenomenology uses the term "the phenomenological reduction," or *epoché*, to exclude real and independent dimensions of objects. Through *epoché*, we suspend all judgment about the preexistence of essence over existence, or

---

1. René Descartes, *Meditations on First Philosophy: With Selections from the Objections and Replies*, trans. Michael Moriarty (Oxford: Oxford University Press, 2008), 18.

whether Being is equivalent to essence. These are the philosophical questions that occupied thinkers like Avicenna, Duns Scotus, St. Thomas Aquinas, and Suárez.

For this reason, we propose a transcendental phenomenology that is not concerned with the nature of what is revealed, but with revelation itself. As a corollary of this approach, phenomenology, in Husserl's eyes, is the method that places all its focus on the appearance of phenomena in front of consciousness. This is a robust analytical and descriptive framework for understanding human experience. This approach enables a more direct and illuminating exploration of reality, emphasizing that the essence of any being or entity can only be apprehended within the specific context of its self-revelation, without being presupposed in advance. Phenomenology focuses exclusively on how things present themselves to consciousness and for consciousness, setting aside inquiry into the ultimate essence of the things themselves. In this framework, and using phenomenological terminology, we can define the phenomenon as "the relationship between the object and the subject through appearance (*phainómenon*)." In the immediate perception is an object-that-appears-to-consciousness and then is an object-of-consciousness. In this sense, we can say that the phenomenological task is limited to documenting and narrating phenomena as they emerge in everyday experience and manifest themselves to consciousness, without delving into other types of questions.

From the Phenomenology of Consciousness to the Phenomenology of the Sacred

The work *The Idea of Phenomenology* comprises five lectures delivered by Husserl in 1907. It marked his first public exposition on phenomenology, offering a penetrating exploration of how phenomena reveal themselves in human consciousness. This book is a milestone that outlines phenomenology as a method and a unique philosophical stance. In earlier works such as *Logical Investigations*, Husserl used phenomenology as a descriptive method for analyzing intentional experiences, rather than as a clearly defined field of study. This methodology involved a thorough breakdown and detailed description of experiences, treating them as fundamental units of analysis.

Husserl's intellectual evolution led him to a deeper and more philosophically integrated understanding of phenomenology. After *Logical Investigations*, Husserl shifted from viewing phenomenology as mere descriptive psychology to considering it to be an essential component in the architecture of philosophy. This shift was not only directed at solving specific knowledge problems but also at redefining and revitalizing the very notion of philosophical science. Husserl began his discourse by avoiding questions about the nature of Being, essence, existence, or the causes of the universe, focusing on the description of things as they present themselves to us. In later work, he did address more philosophical questions and metaphysical issues, but always stayed focused on what actually manifests. The task of the phenomenologist, in this sense, could be compared to observing a neorealist painting, where the technique and visual result are described without immediately delving into questions about the essence of art. Later, Husserl delved into other philosophical questions, following our example of art, which would be like reflecting on what art is, whether every painted work can be considered art, how art is defined, and its relationship with ethics.

This change reflects an evolution in Husserl's thought, from a descriptive and direct approach to phenomena as they present themselves, toward a deeper analysis. Without abandoning the phenomenological framework, it made it possible to explore the philosophical implications of phenomena within the limits of their manifestation. Thus, the second and third Husserl developed more complex approaches and analyzed phenomena with greater depth, but always in the context of their appearance to consciousness. During this phase of introspection and evolution of his concepts, He began to consider the critique of reason as an essential pillar for the validation of both his previous work and his ongoing philosophical project. This reorientation firmly positioned phenomenology as a central discipline dedicated to rational reflection and philosophical self-analysis.

This brief exposition on the most basic aspects of Husserl's phenomenology is our starting point for the present study. In the following chapters, we will discuss the contributions of other principal authors, especially Heidegger, Marion, and Henry. With these figures, we will show how phenomenology evolves—from Husserl's more classical position, through Heidegger's phenomenological ontology, to what we have called the (post)phenomenology of Henry and Marion. This evolution will show us how phenomenology began as a study of how phenomena appear to consciousness clearly and without dogmatism, became an ontological investigation of Being, and finally, reemerged as a study of revelation and the sacred. In this process, phenomenology transcends the exploration of consciousness and the phenomenon, and even of Being as such, to immerse itself in revelation, which is that which occurs and overflows the appearance of any object in human consciousness.

Above all, this study will show us how the very development of phenomenology as a philosophy and method contributes to outlining, defining, and explaining what it means to be human. First, we conceive of a human as a transcendental subjective consciousness that knows the world. Then this human is a being-in-the-world, that correlates with Being before even thinking about Being or the world. Finally, the human becomes a witness to the revelation of the sacred. Bringing in revelation and the sacred is not a mere whim, but rather a philosophical necessity that allows us to approach religion without dogma. This opens the door to the innermost depths of the human spirit.

Retroprogressive Phenomenology

Our two fundamental topics, phenomenology and the sacred, lead us to a preliminary formulation of Retroprogressive Phenomenology. This new current of thought, rooted in the phenomenological tradition, uses the sacred to expand the horizons of all experience. In this process, traditional limits of perception and visual intuition are transcended, as well as the established frameworks of knowledge that commonly accompany these faculties. Retroprogressive

Phenomenology observes the phenomenon of the sacred through the metaphor of light (from the Greek *phos*, the etymological root of *fainómena*). Light is not simply an agent of visibility, but a fundamental key to investigate the topic of Being. Here, Being is the primordial light that makes all forms of perception and cognition possible. Although this light illuminates the horizon of understanding, it remains opaque and inaccessible in its ultimate essence. Our phenomenological approach seeks to overcome ordinary forms of perception. It uses a new conception of meaning that does not depend on conventional channels of language, the senses, or the intellect. The suggested meaning arises directly from the sacred, understood as an emanation of the primordial light, to which consciousness opens in an act of receptivity and revelation. This new perspective transforms our relationship with the world by revealing that the authentic nature of existence is not a passive entity, but a profoundly dynamic process, in which consciousness and light intertwine in the revelation of Being. This will reveal a new reality to us. Everything around us, far from being a collection of inert objects, is endowed with life, and at its innermost core, is pure luminous consciousness.

Section I

Being and the phenomenon

Etymologically speaking, the word *phenomenology* is composed of the Greek *phainómenon* (φαινόμενον), or "phenomenon," and the term *logos*, which is translated as "science or study." Hence, phenomenology is understood as the study or science of phenomena. *Phainómenon* originates from the grammatical particle *phós*, which means "light." Therefore, phenomenon is that which "gives itself to the light," "appears," or "shows itself." In his magnum opus *Being and Time*, Heidegger argues that, due to its etymological origin, the phenomenon should be understood as "the showing itself in itself"[3] or in its "essence," and not through analogical relationship. In an analogical relationship, we make one being intelligible by means of another.

Under this precept, and as an example, phenomenology proposes describing a person without referring to what they share with others. What is shared describes their aspect as humanity, but not their particularity. For example, when I say, "I saw Henry and Paul die, and I deduce that Daniel and Sam will also die," I believe I know a person by what they have in common with others. But in this way, I will not know the most proper aspect of a person's being; instead, my knowledge will be reduced to what they share with all human beings. Therefore, we can affirm that phenomenology is born precisely as a critique of the analogical method, which, by asserting that if Paul died, then Daniel and Sam will also die, generalizes that all human beings are mortal, leading us into metaphysical questions about mortality and the meaning of life.

This leap to generality is precisely what phenomenology seeks to avoid, striving to stay focused on the specific phenomenon, without diverting attention from it. Following Duns Scotus, Heidegger refers to a haecceity, that is, a formal essence of the concrete individual, a "thisness" that must show itself and not through another. In this sense, and paraphrasing Duns Scotus, the haecceity is precisely what makes a given entity individual, meaning it is "this individual

---

3. Martin Heidegger, *Being and Time*, trans. John Macquarrie and Edward Robinson (Oxford: Blackwell, 1962), 54 (§7).

and not another."[4] However, we should not reduce this haecceity to matter, as defended by Thomas Aquinas, nor to form, as the ultimate determinants, since neither of these can singularize an entity.

Haecceity, then, is what we might call the ultimate reality of the individuated thing. Analogy and concept likewise prove incapable of grasping this "thisness." The concept can only think the universal or the abstract, while the human being is a concrete and individuated being. Although human beings are indeed living, rational, and political beings, to conceptualize them is, by default, to refer to all of them and not to any one in particular. Phenomenology seeks precisely to bring their haecceity to light. Generality—through analogy or conceptualization—prevents beings as haecceity, as phenomena, from showing themselves in their essential individuation. This book explores what means might allow the phenomenon to reveal itself as such, without analogies or concepts that distort it and conceal its being.

The symbol and the haecceity of the phenomenon

Here, we advance the proposal that we can only allow the unveiling and describe the selfhood of the phenomenon through the symbol. The symbol includes a history, biography, scent, taste, texture, image, and everything concrete that allows the phenomenon to manifest itself in its own right, without resorting to abstractions or generalities. To explain the necessity of the symbol, we turn to the distinction between what we call universal essence and individual essence.

On the one hand, universal essence is that which we all share as members of the same species, but in which—as we have already seen—the haecceity is not resolved. The haecceity, or the unique quality of being oneself, is not found in abstract or general concepts, but in singular essence, in the "thisness" of each individual. The symbol, on the other hand, possesses both a universal and a singular dimension; on the one hand, the universal would correspond to what phenomenology understands as the "image" (which in the

---

4. Philip Tonner, "*Haecceitas and the Question of Being: Heidegger and Duns Scotus,*" KRITIKE: An Online Journal of Philosophy 2, no. 2 (December 2008): 153.

field of metaphysics has been called the "form"), while the singular would be the interpretative charge that this image carries for each individual. In this sense, individuated existence fits in the symbol because it implies a way of appropriating that image. That is, the individual and concrete being appropriates that image in a manner suited to their history and existence, without that appropriation corrupting its essence.

However, there is a risk of transforming the symbol into a concept when we impose our way of appropriating the symbol as the only valid one and turning it into a rule. In the strategy of pastoral power, for example, a canon is created to declare that anyone who does not appropriate the symbol in this specific way will be committing heresy and, therefore, will be labeled as blasphemous. Obviously, that is not a strategy for truth but for the exercise of power, which consists of excluding anyone who does not appropriate the symbol as orthodoxy dictates. When that happens, the individual is forced to create a precise methodology that allows them to appropriate the symbol as imposed, rather than as it appeared before their own consciousness. The problem with conceptualizing a symbol is that a particularity is absolutized, forgetting that the symbol is, above all, a biography. That biography is dynamic, because it is alive and continues to unfold. By universalizing an image, many other experiences linked to that image are excluded. This is an attempt to totalize the experience of Being does not lend itself to totalizations.

It is unlikely that anyone would identify with the description "rational and political animal." Although this classical definition of human beings is rooted in philosophical tradition, it excludes the uniqueness and complexity of individual lived experiences. On the contrary, composing a song or painting a portrait that highlights the unique attributes of a person may resonate more intimately with their sense of identity. By detailing specific personal characteristics and lived experiences, these artistic works offer a representation that many might consider more faithful to the essence of each individual. Thus, art is associated with the realm of symbols, capable of evoking and communicating profound aspects of human experience, while conceptual definitions align with metaphysics. By approaching reality from a universal and theoretical perspective, the individual beingness slips away like water falling on a clenched fist.

However, something concrete has the capacity to reveal itself in its own essence and phenomenality through symbols. The symbol allows for revelation by means of another medium. For example, a particular human being can offer a window into their singularity and essence through expressions such as poems, paintings, and books. This same idea is clearly delineated in the New Testament, where we read:

> Jesus said to him, "Have I been with you so long, and yet you have not known Me, Philip? He who has seen Me has seen the Father; how can you say, 'Show us the Father'?"
>
> (John, 14:9)

Jesus becomes the symbol of the Father, revealing the Father Himself, showing Himself. The phenomenon of manifestation implies a desire to be revealed. Similarly, Lord Chaitanya Mahāprabhu symbolizes Kṛṣṇa, since Kṛṣṇa manifests as Lord Chaitanya Mahāprabhu. We cannot come to know someone through abstract universality. We can know them through symbols, for they reveal to us the phenomenological haecceity of what they symbolize. Concepts are ahistorical and possess no narrative of their own. For this reason, they cannot describe human beings, who are historical entities. Myth is a narrative endowed with history. We might say that our biography is a myth, for it is a story we regard as real. We conclude by affirming that the phenomenon—that is, the appearance of something in its haecceity—bears a close relation to the symbol, in that whatever reveals itself, reveals itself symbolically.

CHAPTER 2

THE BEING AS PHENOMENON

Toward a phenomenology of the Divine

In light of what was said in the previous chapter, and given our condition as historical beings, any understanding of a nation or a people also requires a symbolic approach. Judaism speaks of the God of Abraham, Isaac, and Jacob. The conception of God is not limited to a metaphysical discussion of a Being that exists by itself, but includes a phenomenological dimension that emphasizes the historical and personal relationship with the Divine. This underscores how symbolism, rather than conceptual abstraction, captures the essence of our experiential living and existence in the world, offering a richer and deeper path to human and divine understanding. This is clearly reflected in several religious texts, as we will show below:

वयं तु न वितृप्याम उत्तमश्लोकविक्रमे ।
यच्छृण्वतां रसज्ञानां स्वादु स्वादु पदे पदे ॥

> *vayaṁ tu na vitṛpyāma*
> *uttama-śloka-vikrame*
> *yac-chṛṇvatāṁ rasa-jñānāṁ*
> *svādu svādu pade pade*

We never tire of hearing the transcendental pastimes of the Personality of Godhead, who is glorified by hymns and prayers. Those who have developed a taste for transcendental relationships with Him relish hearing of His pastimes at every moment.

(*Bhāgavata Purana*, 1.1.19)

Section I: Being and the phenomenon

The devotee does not refer to God without telling a story or referring to His pastimes.

सतां प्रसङ्गान्मम वीर्यसंविदो
भवन्ति हृत्कर्णरसायना: कथा: ।
तज्जोषणादाश्वपवर्गवर्त्मनि
श्रद्धा रतिर्भक्तिरनुक्रमिष्यति ॥

satāṁ prasaṅgān mama vīrya-saṁvido
bhavanti hṛt-karṇa-rasāyanāḥ kathāḥ
taj-joṣaṇād āśv apavarga-vartmani
śraddhā ratir bhaktir anukramiṣyati

In the association of pure devotees, discussion of the pastimes and activities of the Supreme Personality of Godhead is very pleasing and satisfying to the ear and the heart. By cultivating such knowledge, one gradually becomes advanced on the path of liberation, and thereafter he is freed, and his attraction becomes fixed. Then real devotion and devotional service begin.

(*Bhāgavata Purāṇa*, 3.25.25)

In a similar way, in the Old Testament we read:

וְהִגַּדְתָּ לְבִנְךָ בַּיּוֹם הַהוּא לֵאמֹר בַּעֲבוּר זֶה עָשָׂה ה' לִי בְּצֵאתִי מִמִּצְרָיִם:
(שמות י"ג, ח')

And you shall tell your son on that day, saying: Because of this the Lord wrought for me when I went out of Egypt.

(Exodus, 13:8)

מַשְׂכִּיל לְאָסָף הַאֲזִינָה עַמִּי תּוֹרָתִי הַטּוּ אָזְנְכֶם לְאִמְרֵי־פִי:
אֶפְתְּחָה בְמָשָׁל פִּי אַבִּיעָה חִידוֹת מִנִּי־קֶדֶם:
אֲשֶׁר שָׁמַעְנוּ וַנֵּדָעֵם וַאֲבוֹתֵינוּ סִפְּרוּ־לָנוּ:
לֹא נְכַחֵד מִבְּנֵיהֶם לְדוֹר אַחֲרוֹן מְסַפְּרִים תְּהִלּוֹת ה' וֶעֱזוּזוֹ וְנִפְלְאֹתָיו אֲשֶׁר עָשָׂה:

Chapter 2: The Being as phenomenon

וַיָּקֶם עֵדוּת בְּיַעֲקֹב וְתוֹרָה שָׂם בְּיִשְׂרָאֵל אֲשֶׁר צִוָּה אֶת־אֲבוֹתֵינוּ לְהוֹדִיעָם לִבְנֵיהֶם:
לְמַעַן יֵדְעוּ דּוֹר אַחֲרוֹן בָּנִים יִוָּלֵדוּ יָקֻמוּ וִיסַפְּרוּ לִבְנֵיהֶם:

(תהילים ע"ח, א'-ו')

A maskil of Asaf. Hear, my people, my Torah. Incline your ears to the words of my mouth. I shall open my mouth in parable; I shall speak in riddles from [days of] yore. Which we heard and we knew, and which our fathers related to us. We shall not hide it from their sons to the last generation relating the praises of the Lord, and His strength, and the wonders that He wrought. He set up testimony in Jacob and placed Torah in Israel, which He commanded our fathers to make known to their sons. So that [even] the last generation know, the sons that they beget, arise, and relate it to their sons.

(Psalms, 78:1–6)

וַאֲפִילוּ כֻּלָּנוּ חֲכָמִים כֻּלָּנוּ נְבוֹנִים כֻּלָּנוּ זְקֵנִים כֻּלָּנוּ יוֹדְעִים אֶת הַתּוֹרָה מִצְוָה עָלֵינוּ לְסַפֵּר בִּיצִיאַת מִצְרָיִם. וְכָל הַמַּרְבֶּה לְסַפֵּר בִּיצִיאַת מִצְרַיִם הֲרֵי זֶה מְשֻׁבָּח.

(הגדה של פסח)

And even if we were all wise [men], all discerning, all sages, all knowledgeable about the Torah, it would be a commandment upon us to tell the story of the exodus from Egypt. And anyone who elaborates [and spends extra time] in telling the story of the exodus from Egypt, behold he is praiseworthy.

(*The Passover Haggadah*)

בִּשְׁלֹשִׁים וּשְׁתַּיִם נְתִיבוֹת פְּלִיאוֹת חָכְמָה חָקַק י-ה ה' צְבָאוֹת אֱלֹהֵי יִשְׂרָאֵל אֱלֹהִים חַיִּים וּמֶלֶךְ עוֹלָם אֵל שַׁדַּי רַחוּם וְחַנּוּן רָם וְנִשָּׂא שׁוֹכֵן עַד מָרוֹם וְקָדוֹשׁ שְׁמוֹ וּבָרָא אֶת עוֹלָמוֹ בִּשְׁלֹשָׁה סְפָרִים: בְּסֵפֶר וּסְפָר וְסִפּוּר:

(ספר יצירה, א', א')

With thirty-two wondrous paths of wisdom, Y-H, the Lord of Hosts, God of Israel, Living God and King of the World,

Section I: Being and the Phenomenon

> El Shaddai, Merciful and Compassionate, High and Lofty One Dwelling Eternally Above, Holy is His Name (Isaiah, 57:15), engraved and created His world with three S.P.Rs [i.e 3 words with the root S.P.R]: with *sefer* (scroll, book), *sefar* (enumeration), and *sippur* (story, narrative).
>
> (*Sefer Yetzirah*, 1:1)

Referring to God in abstract terms falls within the realm of metaphysics, but this approach does not necessarily nourish devotion or personal spiritual experience. What truly enriches devotion and gives meaning is speaking of God in a personal context, that is, in relation to His presence and action in the individual's life and how He manifests in their consciousness. This intimate and experiential perspective allows for a deeper and more meaningful connection with the Divine. However, the story of God is *with* the human being, and, therefore, responds to a symbolism that reintegrates the human and the Divine.

This relational context with the Divine allows us to differentiate between myth and philosophy. On the one hand, myth, whose nature lies in its genetic ability to narrate the origins of reality, focuses on unveiling the genesis of phenomena within well-defined limits of time and culture. Myths often elucidate how certain aspects of the cosmos, social structures, cultural rituals, or belief systems emerged through stories that incorporate divine figures, legendary heroes, or supernatural entities firmly anchored in a specific historical or proto-historical period.

In contrast to the mythological approach, philosophy adopts an archaeological stance, striving to discover the transhistorical foundations of the cosmos. In other words, philosophy seeks to transcend narratives confined to specific times and cultures in order to unravel the basic pillars, the primal causes, or the underlying truths that transcend temporal barriers. Through this archaeological approach, it aims to delve into the fundamental structures that form the basis of existence, aspiring to understand the quintessence of beings beyond how they manifest in specific historical episodes.

Therefore, while myth offers narratives that take root and flourish within the substrate of specific cultural traditions of the time, philosophy seeks an understanding that is universal and eternal, questioning the essence, the structure of reality, ethical principles, the nature of knowledge, and other fundamental issues, without being confined to a specific historical framework. This philosophical approach then seeks clarity and truth that are not tied to the fluctuations of historical narrative but are intended to resonate through the ages with a validity that is, in essence, timeless. In other words, in the realm of philosophy, the quest for Truth is equivalent to uncovering the Being of things, that is, allowing that which makes something what it is and how it is to be revealed or manifested in consciousness.

For this reason, the history of Western philosophy has always walked hand in hand with the matter of Being. The Greek philosophers, for their part, desacralized Being by attempting to approach it through metaphysics, without conceiving it within the horizon of history, for they defined it as immutable. In Parmenides, Being is what is always identical to itself, immovable, permanent, fixed, necessary, and stable. Parmenides, known as the philosopher of the immovable Being, distinguishes between two paths of inquiry: "there is a way that is, and a way that is not." In other words, there is a path of reality or Truth and another of mere opinions about entities. For the philosopher of Elea, it is imperative to understand the path "that is" in order to achieve a profound understanding of the foundation of life. Parmenides defends the existence of a single and perpetual Truth, rejecting any form of relativism or change. Obviously, under Parmenides' optimal view of Being, it is impossible to found a history, which might explain why the Greeks never made a philosophy of history. History and the sacred remain in the hands of mythology and art. Based on this perspective from Parmenides, and considering the meaning of phenomenon alongside that of logos, we can affirm that phenomenology consists in the study—and therefore the enabling of the vision—of that which shows itself, or of phenomena in their self-showing. Phenomenology is the study of what shows itself within the limits in which it shows.

Section I: Being and the phenomenon

Being as a saturated phenomenon

René Descartes, one of the pillars of methodology and phenomenological endeavors, especially Husserlian ones, already warns that the being of things is not what is shown to the eyes, as all appearance to the senses is inevitably illusory and, therefore, must be corrected by reason. In other words, what appears is a "semblance," insofar as the being of the thing does not present itself as it truly is. In Descartes, the concept of *phainómenon*, of "appearing," is understood as "semblance or mere appearance." From Descartes' perspective, therefore, what appears to the eyes is merely a semblance of reality, not reality itself, and only what reason shows, *cogito* through *cogitatum*, or consciousness, becomes real for the subject. In this sense, Descartes discerns that appearing consists of a "seeming." This conception of "phenomenological reality," as we might call it, does not deny or pervert the meaning of the term "phenomenon" (*phainómenon*), which can mean both "appearing" and "seeming." In fact, there are three concepts of phenomena to which we will now pay special attention:

- Appearing or showing as what one is not.
- Seeming or not showing as what one is.
- Appearing or showing as what one is.

As we mentioned earlier in an introductory way, phenomenology, in its general conception, holds that beings reveal themselves by themselves in consciousness. However, a current called hermeneutic phenomenology exists, which argues that phenomena do not manifest in their real essence, but rather present themselves under an appearance. In this spectrum, Descartes is situated, as he is associated with this perspective due to his emphasis on the need to interpret what is presented to us, since what appears does not reveal itself in its true nature. We speak of hermeneutic phenomenology precisely because of this need for interpretation in the face of the appearance of phenomena, as opposed to when an entity shows itself in its authenticity, in which case interpretation becomes unnecessary.

Chapter 2: The Being as phenomenon

That might be the case, for example, of a plant, whose presence is revealed as direct and, therefore, requires no further interpretation, not even for a child, as the plant, as a plant, presents itself as it is, without needing to decipher its essence.

Kant followed a similar line by stating that what things show when presented to us as objects of understanding is not their being. According to Kant, the being of things does not "appear" and, instead, remains beyond our "sensible intuition," and therefore, also beyond our comprehension. In fact, Kant refers to this being of things with the term "noumenon," a concept with which he establishes a clear separation between reality as it is, in its being (which, as such, does not "appear" to us), and, on the other hand, the phenomenon, that is, the dimension of reality that does appear to us through sensible intuition and which we convert into an object of our understanding. For Kant, therefore, the thing-in-itself does not appear and, hence, is not a phenomenon of human knowledge. By placing the noumenon beyond human understanding and even beyond the senses in which understanding occurs, Kant is already delimiting a phenomenal framework of "appearing," in which, however, Being has no place. In this sense, Kantian philosophy argues that, in the field of knowledge, we only have access to how things show themselves to consciousness, but we do not have access to what the thing is in itself.

However, unlike Descartes' illusory "appearing," the showing in Kant would be a "seeming." From the Kantian perspective, it "seems" to us that reality is that way, but we do not know that it is so because the thing-in-itself is unknowable to the subject, which leads us to define the Kantian phenomenon as the being that presents itself in a certain way to our perception, but not as it is, nor as itself. Under this vision of knowledge, phenomenon, and Being, the universe is configured in a specific way, although knowledge of its exact nature eludes us.

It is important to emphasize that, for Kant, our perception of phenomena is always mediated by our senses and cognitive faculties. In contrast, entities not perceived in time and space are not directly experienced or lived through the senses because they lie beyond our judgment capacity. These are classified within noumenal reality, which we introduced above, referring to a conceptual dimension that encompasses that which remains inaccessible to direct experience or that which arises from ideas or concepts we have about things that are not experienced. The limitation of the human being to understand the essence of things as they are in themselves lies in the nature of its cognitive structure, which only allows for the knowledge of things as they manifest within that framework. According to Kant, it is not that entities deliberately hide themselves, but that our capacity for knowledge is configured in a certain way, being precisely within the limits of these perceptive and cognitive faculties that scientific knowledge is possible.

In the case of Descartes, "appearance" is accompanied by a dimension of uncertainty; that is, the world does not really conform to how it appears. According to Descartes, there is a discrepancy between presentation and reality, suggesting a veil of illusion over the true nature of the world. In contrast, according to Kant, we face a limitation in our knowledge; phenomena only appear to us in a certain way, and we remain uncertain about their authentic essence. While Descartes suggests a sort of deception in appearance, affirming that knowledge shows that reality differs from how it is presented to us, in Kant, beings never fully reveal themselves, leaving us in a state of speculation about what they truly are. This difference leads us to say that, if in Kant beings hide behind their appearance, in Descartes, the appearance itself is unmasked as a falsehood. In both cases, however, and despite the established difference, it is impossible to speak of Being, whether it seems or appears.

To know the thing-in-itself, even though it is unknowable, Jean-Luc Marion proposes the concept of the "saturated phenomenon."[5] According to the French phenomenologist, the thing-in-itself is indeed unknowable to the subject, unless it can reveal itself by itself and with its own rules, as it is. The thing appears but by givenness.

---

5. Jean-Luc Marion, *Being Given: Toward a Phenomenology of Givenness*, trans. Jeffrey L. Kosky (Stanford, CA: Stanford University Press, 2002), 199–212 (§§21–22).

The thing-in-itself donates itself, but it does so phonetically, that is, before the ears and not before the eyes, as philosophical tradition had already determined since Plato. This suggests the need to attend to Being through listening, and not through seeing. According to Marion, one must participate beyond mere objectivity with which tradition had insisted on "seeing" it as image and form and thus explore the richness of experience that surpasses the evident. If vision, since the ancient Greeks, had been established as the means of all understanding, Marion now displaces this cognitive parameter from the Western philosophical tradition and reconfigures the frameworks of knowledge and epistemology through a new phenomenology, which we will later pay special attention to.

Precisely at this crossroads are Kant, Descartes, and those philosophers who long to perceive Being with the gaze. Marion picks up on that vein of hermeneutic phenomenology, which warns against the deception of the eyes in the search for Being and proposes a learning to listen to it instead. Here lies the pathos of listening, for what is heard does not require a physical presence; it does not have to be an image and likeness of the eyes that look at it, and by looking at it, drawing it without hearing it. Rather, it would be a phenomenological presence that resonates in consciousness, even beyond the physical auditory capacity. Thus, according to Marion, the ear is what connects us to the sacred text where Being dwells.

This auditory connection with the sacred scriptures can be appreciated in the yogic path toward devotion, *śrāvaṇam*, or "listening," which represents a first step in that direction. This act of listening binds us to the Holy Scriptures, which are not seen, but heard and understood through an intimate encounter with the revealed word. What is given or revealed in the "saturated phenomenon" is God. In Marion, God is nothing other than the thing-in-itself of Kant, the noumenon, the Being that does not show itself before the eyes but becomes accessible through a givenness in the symbol, which is what unites the sensible image with the auditory myth, unifying what is seen and what is heard. What is seen, then, is the sensible image that is a sign of the invisible. The meaning of the image is the myth narrated that tells us that image. For example, the flute of Kṛṣṇa is nothing but an image that becomes a symbol only when the story is told. The flute becomes a symbol when the *Vaiṣṇava* devotee tells us *Kṛṣṇa-kathā* or the "stories related to Kṛṣṇa." The same happens with the cross in Christianity. If the story of Christ's crucifixion is not narrated, the cross will be nothing more than two simple pieces of wood on top of each other. The sign is the visible image, a sign of the symbol, and the symbol is a sign of God. The symbol is the narrative that links that invisible sign with the image and allows it to be given to the individual consciousness.

Therefore, we identify the thing-in-itself of Kant with God. God eludes all human knowledge, because He does not show himself. He is imperceptible as the noumenon. However, what does not appear can also be known insofar as it is given in the word through listening, thus opening up a different way of appearing and, therefore, even of knowing. God is unlimited and, thus, cannot show himself as a limited being or object in space and time. However, this does not mean that God, Being, hides only because it does not fit within space and time. Rather, what is suggested here is that it is precisely showing itself in such a way that it always exceeds. As Heraclitus holds: "Nature loves to hide."[6] That is to say, Being hides in a permanent showing. Paradoxically, the concealment of Being consists of a constant showing, becoming what Marion calls "the saturated phenomenon," which, instead of fading away, never ceases to give itself. Although we will return to this issue much more deeply later on, we will now advance that this means that in every act of knowing the being, the known-ness of Being is revealed.

In contrast to an impoverished phenomenon, which only shows itself temporarily in the thing, this saturated phenomenon that Marion proposes—exceeding in its constant givenness—responds to a fundamental phenomenological relationality in which there is only subject for an object and vice versa, but in which the subject and object are both ontic terms, meaning that Being is both the knower and the known. The omnipresence of Being obviously does not allow

---

6. Heraclitus, in John Burnet, *Early Greek Philosophy*, 4th ed. (London: A. & C. Black, 1920), 133 (frag. 10 = DK B123).

Chapter 2: The Being as phenomenon

the existence of an independent subject or object, with their own life separate from this relationship and, therefore, lacking Being. At the same time, the saturated phenomenon, whose own Being pulses in its constant givenness and is unveiled in its own pronunciation, cannot be conceptualized because, for that purpose, we would need a genre that would allow us to delimit it and say that it is this and not that. This new phenomenological perspective makes the function of the preacher and the diffuser of creeds superfluous. Since Being manifests constantly, it is precisely because of this perpetual manifestation that it simultaneously hides itself. The essential thing is to learn to discern that which is incessantly revealed before us. The intervention of a mediator, who is listened to reveal what would otherwise remain inaudible, becomes unnecessary because he has no access to the manifestation of Being in the lived experience of the subject in whom it manifests. This approach that stems from Marion's religious phenomenology paradoxically suggests the decline of organized beliefs structured around figures of spiritual or religious authority who act as bridges between the Divine and the human. The phenomenology of religion, under Marion's guidance, helps to safeguard religion itself and the sacredness of Being from institutionalization, that is, from its traditional metaphysical chains.

As we will see later, Jean-Luc Marion's notion of the "saturated phenomenon" will signify an important turn within phenomenology itself. In the introduction, we had already said that Husserl's phenomenology was epistemological and later surpassed by Heidegger's ontology and Levinas's phenomenology of "the ethical." Now we can affirm that Marion's proposal draws a "theological turn" that exceeds the limits of phenomenology itself in order to become open to Being, to the Divine, to the sacred. This allows to describe the ways in which Being gives itself and reveals itself, manifesting in its own hiding. This will not mean the end of phenomenology but a redesign of its way of proceeding. As we have just presented, albeit only as an introductory point and in an overly generic manner, Being shows itself in many ways and can only be studied within the limits in which it shows itself. According to Marion, phenomenology deals with examining the totality of the forms in which phenomena make themselves present to consciousness, thus overcoming the limitations that would be imposed by reducing them to mere acts of revelation, concealment, or disguise. This approach encompasses a broader spectrum of modes of manifestation, which indicates that phenomenology transcends simple categorization in terms of these three processes. Consequently, attempting to confine phenomenology to these three dynamics would overlook the richness and diversity of experiences and the ways in which reality unfolds before the subject. Therefore, the essence of phenomenology lies in its capacity to explore and understand the multiple ways phenomena present themselves to us, in an effort to capture the complexity of the human experience in its totality.

Bibliography section I

- Burnet, John. *Early Greek Philosophy*. 4th ed. London: A. & C. Black, 1920.
- Descartes, René. *Meditations on First Philosophy: With Selections from the Objections and Replies*. Translated by Michael Moriarty. Oxford: Oxford University Press, 2008.
- Heidegger, Martin. *Being and Time*. Translated by John Macquarrie and Edward Robinson. Oxford: Blackwell, 1962.
- Marion, Jean-Luc. *Being Given: Toward a Phenomenology of Givenness*. Translated by Jeffrey L. Kosky. Stanford, CA: Stanford University Press, 2002.
- Manoussakis, John Panteleimon, and Neal DeRoo, eds. *Phenomenology and Eschatology: Not Yet in the Now*. Farnham: Ashgate, 2009.
- Tonner, Philip. "Haecceitas and the Question of Being: Heidegger and Duns Scotus." KRITIKE: An Online Journal of Philosophy 2, no. 2 (December 2008): 146–54.

Section II
Phenomenology and Symbolism

CHAPTER 3

THE POTENTIALITY AND ACTUALIZATION OF BEING

The relationship between Martin Heidegger and phenomenology, particularly with the approach of Husserl, has been complex, to the point that it is not always possible to say that his philosophy is simply inscribed within the phenomenological movement. At the same time, the influence he received from Husserl is undeniable, especially in Heidegger's early work. We believe that this should always be taken into account to understand the starting point and the development of Heidegger's philosophy. Despite these difficulties, we can affirm that his philosophy connects directly with the phenomenological tradition through several key conceptions that have occupied the debates of Western philosophy in general and phenomenology in particular for centuries. Specifically, and in our context, we understand Heidegger's theses from the relationship between the terms "potency" and "act," which have contributed to formulating and designing the structures of philosophical thought and Western culture since Aristotle and the origins of metaphysics. One of the key critiques that underpins Heidegger's philosophy is his response to what is called "the metaphysics of presence," that is, to that traditional metaphysical perspective which has absolutely associated Being with presence.

The word *present* can mean "time or being." If we say "I am present," we are referring to Being. Conversely, if we say "the present time is problematic," we are speaking of time. Therefore, it becomes complicated to resolve time solely as presence because the past and the future, though part of Being, unfold without being present. The notion of temporality, as displayed in this analysis, reveals a profound approach to how the past and the future influence the present despite their physical absence, operating through emotional dimensions such as guilt and fear of death, respectively. This Heideggerian reading of the question of time emphasizes the idea that the human experience of time transcends the mere sequence of present events, extending into dimensions that, though not present, exert a tangible influence on our daily lives.

By questioning the "metaphysics of presence," Heidegger introduces the perspective that time is not constituted only by what is immediately tangible or present, but rather as a field of pure possibility. In this framework, he defines the human being as *Dasein* (being-there or being-there-in-the-world)[7], characterized by its temporality and understood as the manifestation of these possibilities. In this sense, possible beings, those that have not yet come to be but could come to be, contrast with impossible beings, exemplified by figures of the imagination such as flying cats or green cows, which, although conceivable, do not find a correlation in tangible reality.

This distinction between the possible and the impossible is reflected in the human experience of Being and time. For example, the future offspring of an individual, previously non-existent but conceivable, illustrates how possibility precedes effectiveness. Temporality, then, is lived through a constant interplay between what was possible, what is possible now, and what will be possible in the future, thus marking human existence with an openness toward future realities that have not yet come to be.

This tension between the past and the future experienced in the present illustrates the ongoing dynamic in which humans find themselves, inhabiting a world full of possibilities that determine our actions, decisions, and life projects. Possibility, as such, becomes the essence of human openness to the future, defining our capacity to imagine, plan, and aspire. In this context, death presents itself

---

7. Martin Heidegger, *Being and Time*, trans. John Macquarrie and Edward Robinson (Oxford: Blackwell, 1962), 78 (§12).

as the ultimate limit of possibility, as a being that has perished no longer participates in the realm of future possibilities. Therefore, for Heidegger, human existence can be understood as a continuous unfolding of potentialities. Each present moment is saturated with the influence of both past and future times, shaping our way of being in the world.

This reflection on temporality and possibility, viewed through the prism of what we can potentially be and become, questions our traditional understanding of time and invites a reconsideration of the human condition itself. On the one hand, under the Heideggerian perspective, the time has ceased to follow the natural order established by traditional metaphysics, which stipulated that the past simply preceded the present and this, in turn, the future. As we have already sketched, the future opens up as a horizon of possibility where not only the present, but perhaps even the past, is sculpted. That is, life is not merely a concatenation of facts or acts that we commit one after another, responding to a mere cause-effect pattern under which the present rules, controls, and gives meaning to past and future, to the point of constantly "presentifying" past and future in order to give them meaning. On the contrary, Heidegger's study of time proposes an understanding of time that allows us to grasp the permanent and indissoluble tension between past, present, and future outside the framework of traditional metaphysics. With this, Heidegger "liberates" time from the traditional metaphysics of presence that conceives existence as that which is merely present before our eyes in space and time, here and now. This vision banishes from Being everything that does not inhabit the immediately present space and time.

The nature of temporality, viewed from the perspective of the traditional metaphysics of presence, is characterized by a sequentiality in which each moment follows one after the other in an exclusive and linear manner; that is, the existence of a given instant excludes the presence of the previous one. Thus, when a second moment is experienced after the first, the first would have already ceased to be, and that second moment would have vanished upon reaching a third, and so on. Under the presentist premise, this chain of moments that continues indefinitely reveals that temporality is intrinsically linked to the present in a sequence of discrete moments: one follows the other in a constant flow but is always limited to the current "now." In this sense, nothing transcends the actuality of the presence of Being.

This absolute presentification of existence that Heidegger dissects is the origin of the prejudice he himself expressed with the phrase *usía estim parousía* or "Being is presence." Under this prism, and when understood as mere and absolute presence, Being is only what is now, as Parmenides would say. This implies, however, that Being is not what is, was, and will be, nor what could be, because—from this perspective—it is impossible to affirm that Being can cease to be at any moment to be otherwise. When understood as pure presence (*parousía*), Being is only and can only permanently be what is here and now. The problem with this absolute presentification of Being is that it leads Being to be thought of only as a permanent stagnation, an absolute stillness, which would fill everything, and outside of which nothing would exist, not even nothingness. Nothing could escape the absolute stillness of Being that floods everything permanently because it already is everything.

In his *Introduction to Metaphysics*,[8] *The Age of the World Picture*[9], and other texts, Heidegger's critique is that this conception of Being reduces Being to pure act, emptying it of all potentiality. Furthermore, by emptying Being of its potentiality, the metaphysics of presence does nothing but ultimately deny Being and make it impossible. If only what is present in time and space existed, only beings would exist and not Being. If this were the case, it would be impossible to speak of the ontological difference between Being and beings, which we will later pay particular attention to. In response to this position, Heidegger suggests thinking of Being in, or even as, temporality (*Zeitlichkeit*); that is, as the tension of past, present, and

---

8. Martin Heidegger, *Introduction to Metaphysics*, trans. Gregory Fried and Richard Polt (New Haven: Yale University Press, 2000), 207.
9. Martin Heidegger, The Age of the World Picture, in *The Question Concerning Technology and Other Essays*, trans. William Lovitt (New York: Harper & Row, 1977), 28–29.

future that constantly interweave and interpenetrate in an order that does not respond to the concatenation of three impermeable units from one another.

The terms *Zeit*, *Zeitlichkeit*, and *Temporalität*, with which Heidegger dissects time, do not admit direct translation into English or other languages without loss, displacement, or reformulation. The German language, in which Heidegger thinks and writes, is not merely a vehicle for his ideas: it is the very scene in which those ideas take shape. For this reason, every translator, when choosing "temporeity," "temporality," "Temporality" (with capital T), or other variations, interprets rather than merely naming or renaming.

It is no surprise that Heidegger's conception of time diverges from the dominant view. Everyday time (*Zeit*), the time that organizes schedules, work rhythms, and domestic routines, may be useful, but its usefulness does not make it foundational. It operates with derivative schemas that impoverish temporal experience when absolutized. Heidegger's proposal does not consist in replacing one chronology with another. On the contrary, it proposes a rupture: a way of thinking that opens to a form of time that cannot be thematized as an object. Thus, the subject of time is so central to Heidegger's work and thought not because it is just another topic or chapter, but because it is the prism through which Heidegger can rethink and reinterpret Being. It is in this sense that Heidegger asserts:

> Thus neither the way time (*Zeit*) is conceived in our ordinary experience of it, nor the problematic which arises from this experience, can function without examination as a criterion for the appropriateness of an Interpretation of time.[10]

This statement underlines Heidegger's critique of traditional conceptions of time, which regard it as an objective sequence of moments. These conceptions think of time as a graph in which human beings are inscribed. This, by default, externalizes time from

---

10. Martin Heidegger, *Being and Time*, trans. John Macquarrie and Edward Robinson (Oxford: Blackwell, 1962), §61. See also the original German text *Zeiterfahrung und die ihr entwachsende Problematik können deshalb nicht unbesehen als Kriterien der Angemessenheit einer Zeitinterpretation fungieren.* en *Sein und Zeit* (Tübingen: Max Niemeyer Verlag, 1927), §61.

the human being, rather than thinking time as the temporality that is an intrinsically constitutive structure of *Dasein*. From the viewpoint of Heidegger, and of phenomenology and hermeneutics in general, this conventional representation of time, to which Heidegger opposes, cannot withstand even the slightest phenomenological analysis without collapsing into contradiction. Let us consider the present, the "now" with which Being is so easily associated. If we repeat the word "now" five times, what seemed to be there vanishes. The first "now" is no more. Nor is the second. Presence becomes flight. Thus, what is present is already past at the very moment we try to fix it. Being, if it is identified with that presence, does not endure. Here is where Heidegger intervenes most radically. He does not deny presence, but neither is he fascinated by it.

Heidegger's thought proposes a rupture with the tendency of Western metaphysics, which since Plato has identified Being with presence—with what is given, available, present before the subject. Where tradition sees constancy, Heidegger detects a forgetting: the suppression of the dynamic, open, and unstable character of Being. From this perspective, presence ceases to be an ontological guarantee and is revealed as a historically conditioned figure of appearing. Therefore, for Heidegger, instead of presenting as a simple, continuous, or linear unity, time rather emerges as a plurality of temporal modes. The essence of time consists in its internal difference, in the diversity of structures that configure it. This conception refers directly to a central matrix of Heideggerian thought: the impossibility of saying Being in a single key. Heidegger insists again and again: *Sein* is not univocal.

Fundamental ontology, then, instead of limiting itself to producing yet another theory of time—whether physical, psychological, or cosmological—opens the dimension of original experience that makes it possible for something to appear as temporal. This experience, which is neither linear nor cumulative, is nonetheless a condition. Thinking time, ultimately, is thinking from time, the very possibility of Being, the horizon that gives rise to Being itself. In other words, time is the condition of possibility for *Dasein* to think itself. When Heidegger thinks about time, he thinks about the innermost

CHAPTER 3: THE POTENTIALITY AND ACTUALIZATION OF BEING

structure of *Dasein* itself, about the dimension from which and within which *Dasein* can think itself (and think itself as time), and all else.

Temporality (*Zeitlichkeit*) as the ontological meaning of care (*Sorge*).[11]

Heidegger connects this notion of temporality (*Zeitlichkeit*) as the essence of *Dasein* with the notion of care (*Sorge*), which is the ontological structure that describes how *Dasein* is in the world—that is, the way it exists. This fundamental structure of *Dasein*'s Being is not an emotion, a moral attitude, or Husserlian intentional consciousness. Rather, care (*Sorge*) is the very structure through which *Dasein* is oriented toward Being. This structure consists of three fundamental temporal dimensions: (1) existentiality (projective anticipation toward the future), (2) facticity (openness to the weight of the unchosen past), and (3) fallenness (the ever-latent possibility of dissolving into the impersonality of the everyday). These are not phases nor dissociable components. They are vectors that, interwoven, configure the temporality (*Zeitlichkeit*) proper to *Dasein*. *Sorge* means remaining open to what is not yet, sustaining possibility as possibility without there yet being an object to categorize, to know, or to conceptualize. Therefore, in this framework, Being does not appear as a consolidated presence, but is announced as that which demands interpretation, what is still yet to be said. Thinking time, from this perspective, means questioning the assumption that schemas can represent time.

Likewise, Heidegger does not conceive the structure of care (*Sorge*) as a mechanical aggregate of parts, as if the whole could be reconstructed from an external sum. Rather, it is a living configuration, whose coherence is not exhausted in the successive arrangement of its moments. It is a unity that unfolds from the internal tension that constitutes it and whose key lies, inevitably, in temporality.

---

11. Martin Heidegger, *Being and Time*, trans. John Macquarrie and Edward Robinson (Oxford: Blackwell, 1962), §61. See also the original German text *Die Zeitlichkeit als der ontologische Sinn der Sorge* en *Sein und Zeit* (Tübingen: Max Niemeyer Verlag, 1927), §61

Section II: Phenomenology and Symbolism

In light of this notion of *Sorge*, Heidegger can view *Dasein*—that being that we are—as a being-there-in-the-world that is neither fixed in the present nor dissolved in a succession of fleeting instants. Its existential structure is traversed by a tension that overflows it: projection toward what is to come and appropriation of what has been. *Dasein* is tensional simultaneity, and therefore, it does not move between the past and the future as if they were external poles. Its mode of being consists in that articulation which holds them together, in a present that is not a point, but a horizon.

The time that traverses this structure of temporality (*Zeitlichkeit*), of the care that keeps *Dasein* open to Being as pure possibility, is not the abstract time (*Zeit*) of physics, nor the time that organizes the everyday schedule. It is not a homogeneous sequence of instants, nor a uniform chain of events. On the contrary, it is the time that *Dasein* lives from within, in the mode of its being-there. It is the manner in which *Dasein* happens, in which its existence occurs as possibility and not as a finished fact. It is the very texture of existing. That is why Heidegger says directly that the *Dasein*, conceived in its most extreme possibility of being, is not in time, but is time itself. Perhaps the most rigorous way to put it is to say that *Dasein* is temporality (*Zeitlichkeit*). More than the time that is measured, ordered, or represented, *Zeitlichkeit* is the living structure of openness in which past, future, and present are interwoven in tension: as retention, as anticipation, as presence that does not close upon itself.

In this way, Heidegger dismantles any conception of time as something external to the subject and, with that, also the notion of a subjectivity bearing a pure "now." Temporality (*Zeitlichkeit*) is not a function of the subject; it is that through which the subject is. Temporality is what gives thickness to existence as lived tension. However, to affirm that the meaning of temporality allows for the Being of existence is not a decorative formula. On the contrary, it is to assume that any understanding of the human being must be historical, because time does not simply pass—it configures, structures, and gives meaning.

Thus, Being, as Heidegger thinks it, can never be fixed nor be fixated, and that is why he uses the expression that Being is a "a future which makes present in the process of having been."[12] This expression, far from poeticism, indicates that Being is itself a dynamic structure, marked by the dislocated simultaneity of future, past, and present. Being does not stabilize at a point. It cannot be captured in presence. What appears is already slipping away, already fallen through. More than a completed being or a substantial identity, *Dasein* is a temporal totality. Being is always mine—the Being of this one who writes or thinks, the Being of each one. Heidegger reminds us:

> Furthermore, *Dasein* is an entity which in each case I myself am.[13]

This "myself" does not refer to the empirical self nor to psychological subjectivity. Nor is it an interiority accessible through introspection. Far from all that, it is an ontological structure whose concretion occurs in the existential, but which cannot be reduced to what is observable or to what others recognize. That "I" is what remains even when all masks have fallen. It is not identical with "the human being" as a general category. *Dasein* appears when the human being becomes a problem for himself, when its existence becomes a question. And in questioning his existence and becoming a problem, the human being "becomes aware" of himself and understands himself as *Dasein*, that is, as his own "potentiality-for-being," as a being whose authentic existence is inexorably open and oriented toward his own possibilities (of being), and not as a fully actualized, finished, and (en)closed being.

At this point, Heidegger introduces another notion of time in *Being and Time* that he calls *Temporalität* (often translated as "Temporality" with capital T). *Temporalität* would be the "time of Being," which

---

12. Martin Heidegger, *Being and Time*, trans. John Macquarrie and Edward Robinson (Oxford: Blackwell, 1962), §65. Heidegger analyzes the idea of temporality as a dynamic and unitary structure, where the future, the past, and the present mutually configure each other in the existence of *Dasein*.

13. Ibid., §12. See also the original German text *Dasein ist ferner Seiendes, das je ich selbst bin.* en *Sein und Zeit* (Tübingen: Max Niemeyer Verlag, 1927), §12.

should not be confused with a chronological category, much less with some kind of external container in which beings unfold, as if time passively held them. This formula is an ontological figure that compels us to revisit, from the ground up, the most basic assumptions of our understanding of time.

> Thus the fundamental ontological task of Interpreting Being as such includes working out the Temporality of Being (*Temporalität*).[14]

The distinction between *Zeitlichkeit* (temporality) and *Temporalität* (Temporality) bears profound ontological significance. Whereas *Zeitlichkeit* is the internal temporal structure of *Dasein*, *Temporalität* would be the even more fundamental structure of time itself—and this includes *Zeitlichkeit*. *Temporalität* would be the condition of possibility for Being itself. This means that *Temporalität* makes *Zeitlichkeit* possible, and thus the understanding of the meaning of Being, not only of *Dasein*. This distinction allows *Dasein* to become aware both of itself and of Being (*Sein*). That is, when human beings question existence and become self-aware, what they do is to understand themselves as a structure of *Zeitlichkeit* (temporality), while simultaneously opening themselves to thinking and understanding the meaning of Being in general. Ultimately, Heidegger seems to suggest that to understand themselves as *Dasein*, human beings must open themselves to the understanding of Being as such—something they could not do without first understanding themselves as *Dasein*.

With this inversion, Heidegger breaks with a philosophical heritage that had hitherto been rarely questioned. Traditionally, time was conceived as a neutral backdrop upon which beings appeared, persisted, and disappeared. Instead, Heidegger introduces a decisive twist: it is not time that contains *Dasein*, but *Dasein* that opens time as a horizon of possibility. There is no time (*Zeitlichkeit*)

---

14. Ibid., §5. See also the original German text *Die fundamentale ontologische Aufgabe der Interpretation von Sein als solchem begreift daher in sich die Herausarbeitung der Temporalität des Seins* en *Sein und Zeit* (Tübingen: Max Niemeyer Verlag, 1927), §5.

prior to existence, and there is no existence (of *Dasein*) without the Temporality (*Temporalität*) of Being (*Sein*) of *Da-Sein*. It is through *Dasein* that what we understand as time occurs, is constituted, and comes into being. Thus, without exaggeration, it may rightly be said that without *Dasein*, there would be no world, no history, no becoming. For becoming needs a *Da* (there) that allows *Sein* (Being) to unfold as such.

From this perspective, all becoming—of love, of language, of suffering, or even of the sacred—occurs because there is *Dasein*. Not because *Dasein* causes it, but because it sustains it as experience. Nothing happens for anyone without someone who can receive that happening as such. The world does not give itself by itself: it gives itself because there is a being capable of receiving it. And there is no becoming without an existence that inhabits, interprets, and traverses it. *Dasein* does not produce what happens, but without it, what happens would neither have happened nor be recognized as an event.

This allows us to understand why Heidegger dismisses any theory of time that excludes human existence. What happens, happens not because of an objective sequence of facts, but because there is a being who—by being time—sustains the world as horizon. There is no time without world. There is no world without *Dasein*. This is not an abstract formulation nor a decorative thesis. It is, at its core, an ontological imperative.

This revision of the notions of Being and time, and of metaphysics itself, ultimately leads us to a new vision of the human being. *Dasein*, the being-there-in-the-world, finds itself at the crossroads of these two dimensions of time and Being that we have just described. On the one hand, its corporeal existence anchors it to a life lived in terms of presence, of actuality, which subjects it to the sequence of consecutive and exclusive moments through which it inevitably experiences its factual everyday life. On the other hand, however, its ontological structure, the Being of its being, projects it toward temporality, allowing it to encompass and transcend the linear succession of time to embrace past, present, and future as an integrated and always accessible totality of meaning in which it can think and understand its authentic Being. This duality, this double life of *Dasein*, emphasizes the complexity of *Dasein*, living momentarily through the body while, in its deepest essence, extending through the vast continuum of original time.

CHAPTER 4

FROM PHENOMENOLOGY TO SYMBOLISM

The phenomenon as the power of Being

As we advanced in the previous chapter, the concept that possibility prevails over actuality is presented as a recurring theme in various interpretations of phenomenology. Furthermore, it is directly linked to the development and expansion of both this school of thought and Western philosophy and culture in general. Possibility, in the realm of metaphysics, is referred to as "potency" [*dynamis* (δύναμις)], while actuality is called "act" [*energeia* (ενέργεια)]. In this sense, one thing is a possible being, and another is an actual being. Following Heidegger's approach, which in a way escapes the immobility defended by Parmenides, primacy will no longer lie in the act or presence, but in possibility or potentiality, which precedes the act. Everything that exists exists because, at some point, it could exist and not merely because it is a consequent effect of a prior action.

This debate, rooted in Aristotle, had already arisen strongly in medieval philosophy, and more specifically through the work of John Duns Scotus, who supported the thesis of the preeminence of potency, that is, of possibility over act. According to Duns Scotus, the first thing is the non-being or nothingness. Next comes being, which negates non-being; therefore, being is the "non non-being" or the negation of non-being. What Scotus is telling us here is that non-being is pure possibility that becomes actual through the negation of the possibility, which is the actuality.

In light of what has been presented so far, both briefly through Duns Scotus and in greater detail with Heidegger, our focus will not be on the metaphysics of the act, that is, of presence, but on that of potency, thus extending to the realm of all possible beings, and beyond the possible. We are not interested in the real as real, but in the conditions of possibility for the real to manifest as such. What calls us is not the reality in its current state, but the conditions under which this reality has the potential to come into being. We are not interested in effective conditions, but in possible conditions. That is, our study will focus on the realm of what can potentially be realized, not on what has already been realized.

This is where the importance of phenomenology, and of Heidegger's critique lies, as his philosophical approach and critique carve out a path toward a metaphysics not anchored in the presence of the act but open to its potentiality, that is, to the possibility that something could be, even if it is not. Moreover, we are not even concerned with whether it happens; we are only concerned with whether it could happen. Phenomenologically speaking, our interest lies in the conditions of possibility for phenomena to manifest, not in the conditions of their current realization. Our goal will not be to describe phenomena in their static presence or facticity but to open ourselves to their possibility and their genesis beyond their presence.

However, as both Husserl and Heidegger clearly pointed out, possibility is studied, and can only be studied, in actuality, because it is in the manifestation of things that we study their power to manifest, their power to be, just as we can only approach the hidden through the given phenomenon. Otherwise, we would be violating the phenomenological principle of studying what is shown within the limits in which it is shown. The importance of linking Heidegger's critique of the metaphysics of presence and time with phenomenology is that it allows us to understand that the object of study in phenomenology is not the phenomenon as an act, as a factual object that is and shows itself to us here and now in all its presence, but the phenomenon as what it is and what, in turn, can be without being yet, or perhaps never. The phenomenon, although approached from the limits of its manifestation, contains a richness that transcends its presence because every phenomenon is its actuality along with its potentiality to be. One is not only what one is, but also what one is not yet, but can be. One is everything one can be. Our essence is not limited merely to our current state of being, but also encompasses that into which we have the potential to become. Each of us constitutes the totality of all our future possibilities. In this sense, the phenomenon is not what it is, but all that it can be: the effective and measurable, but also, and simultaneously, the hidden and non-effective.

The phenomenon as revelation

Husserl himself makes it clear in many of his texts that his object of interest is not the mere phenomenon as such, qua phenomenon, but rather the phenomenon as a possibility and, therefore, how it can come to be. This was the true Husserlian revolution: shifting the factual phenomenon-object from its centrality as the philosophical object of study to address its condition of possibility, understood as the correlation between how objects present themselves and the ways in which the subject experiences them. The importance of intentionality—a concept we will discuss in greater detail in later chapters—explicitly lies in this point, for what intentionality of consciousness shows us, among other things, is that the phenomenon is, in essence, its condition of possibility as a manifestation in consciousness. That is, the phenomenon does not emerge *ex nihilo* from the ego of consciousness as if it were a product created randomly, but it emerges from its own potentiality as a phenomenon of consciousness. This is an important point that will allow us to synthesize phenomenology with symbolism.

As we suggested in the previous chapter, the appearance of the phenomenon does not follow the regime of cause and effect, but rather that of Heideggerian temporality. Speaking of the phenomenon in terms of temporality inevitably leads us to understand it beyond the metaphysics of presence and, therefore, as a manifestation (*phainómenon*) that is not the effect of a cause, but rather a revelation. If the phenomenon is not merely the effect of a cause, its appearance does not exclude or negate its potentiality, but rather the opposite. That is to say; we can say that the phenomenon reveals itself insofar as it shows or donates itself through what is other than it. Just as the manifest shows the hidden, the foundation is shown by the phenomenon; the invisible is shown by the visible, and the indeterminate by the determinate. In this sense, and as we saw in chapter 2, every phenomenon reveals itself in this way, as a saturated being that integrates the invisible and the visible, the hidden and the manifest, the effective and the potential. In this very sense, and by virtue of all that has been said so far, we can advance the thesis that Being reveals itself through everything and everyone. Although we generally perceive it as a poor phenomenon, Being reveals itself in many ways, but always according to the symbol.

It is from the structure presented in the first four chapters, that is, from the concepts of Being as temporality, the saturated phenomenon, and its revelation as a way of giving itself, that we will later be able to articulate phenomenology as the philosophical field that will allow us to attend to that which exceeds the limits of our understanding, namely, the experience of the sacred. In other words, we will study what is hidden through what is shown and what can be given through what is given, together with what appears. It should be noted that although this study addresses eminently religious themes, such as the question of revelation, the sacred, and faith, our focus will remain within the field of phenomenological philosophy and not of religious discourse.

Bibliography section II

- Heidegger, Martin. *Being and Time*. Translated by John Macquarrie and Edward Robinson. Oxford: Blackwell, 1962.
- Heidegger, Martin. *Introduction to Metaphysics*. Translated by Gregory Fried and Richard Polt. New Haven: Yale University Press, 2000.
- Heidegger, Martin. "The Age of the World Picture." In *The Question Concerning Technology and Other Essays*, translated by William Lovitt, 115–54. New York: Harper & Row, 1977.

Section III
Transcendental phenomenology

CHAPTER 5

FROM SKEPTICISM TO REALIZATION

The fading of Cartesian doubt

It can be asserted that the phenomenology of Edmund Husserl, and thus the phenomenological manifestation of the beings or objects of consciousness, redefines the limits and nature of human experience. This opens a gap in the tradition of Western philosophy. As a result, the fading of Cartesian doubt is triggered, which had allowed modern rationalism to regain philosophical centrality after centuries of scholasticism. We could say that the birth of modern rationalist philosophy occurred at the same time that Descartes proposed the hypothesis of a deceptive being, questioning whether what is perceived as real could, in fact, not be. However, and paradoxically, this question marks the beginning of a shift toward trust in the authenticity of the manifestation of things, urging us to allow their existence without restrictions. For this, obviously, the most strictly phenomenological philosophy must overcome the limitations imposed by Cartesian thought. Let us, however, consider the Cartesian argument for a moment to see in what sense and how phenomenology surpasses Descartes' doubt and opens a new path within Western philosophy.

Descartes presents two main foundations for questioning the reliability of sensible knowledge. The first focuses on the illusions of the senses, arguing that they often deceive us by presenting a distorted reality. The second foundation refers to the experience of dreams, during which one experiences sensations indistinguishable from those of wakefulness, leading us to doubt our senses' ability to discern between reality and fiction. And for this very reason, Descartes writes:

> But I have discovered that they [the senses] sometimes deceive us, and prudence dictates that we should never fully trust those who have deceived us even once.[15]

When someone has clearly deceived us, as could happen in business matters, it would be imprudent and perhaps foolish to trust that person again, rather than remain skeptical about their future actions. Similarly, our senses, which have been shown to mislead us on numerous occasions, invite an attitude of distrust. Since it is a well-established fact that the senses can fail (as mentioned in Chapter I, § 6 of *Principles of Philosophy*), the reliability of "sensible things" is called into question. We cannot be certain that the senses are not constantly deceiving us; at least, we cannot be sure of their infallibility. Therefore, following Descartes' methodological directive to consider as false what does not offer absolute certainty, it is concluded that knowledge derived from the senses must be discarded.

Following Descartes in his *Meditations on First Philosophy I*, it is valid to claim that the senses fail in specific cases, such as seeing a distant tower or observing a tiny particle without instruments. However, they also offer undeniable certainties—for example, that I am here, sitting by the fire, wearing a robe, and holding this paper in my hands.

Nevertheless, could the possibility of doubting evident realities, such as the act of writing at this very moment, not be akin to the illusions of those who lost in their madness, believe themselves to be kings or generals? Descartes responds to this proposition saying:

> But am I not a human being, and therefore in the habit of sleeping at night, when in my dreams I have all the same

---

15. René Descartes, *Meditations on First Philosophy: With Selections from the Objections and Replies*, trans. Michael Moriarty (Oxford: Oxford University Press, 2008), 18.

CHAPTER 5: FROM SKEPTICISM TO REALIZATION

experiences as these madmen do when they are awake—or sometimes even stranger ones?[16]

And he continues reflecting on the experience of dreaming, when at times one finds oneself in a state of wakefulness, writing, just as one could be in reality, when in fact one was sleeping and resting in bed. He says:

> When I think this over more carefully, I see so clearly that waking can never be distinguished from sleep by any conclusive indications that I am stupefied; and this very stupor comes close to persuading me that I am asleep after all.[17]

Crucially, up to this point, we lack a reliable sign that allows us to distinguish with certainty between wakefulness and the oneiric state, as there is no clear way to differentiate between them. From these two arguments, it follows that any knowledge obtained through the senses is subject to doubt.

In light of this, we can argue against Descartes that his methodology obstructs the true revelation of things and suggests that if things do not manifest freely, it is not due to an inherent incapacity within them, but because Descartes himself, through his skepticism, prevents their manifestation. This critique suggests that Descartes attributes the responsibility for this limitation to the senses when, in reality, it is his own predisposition that restricts the genuine perception of reality. In other words, things do not reveal themselves in their beingness due to their possible unreality or lack of truth in their manifestation, but rather because of the predisposition toward distrust in Cartesian discourse.

This "counter-doubt" is based on the phenomenological attitude, which maintains that the appropriate approach is not to doubt but to understand the nature of things as they present themselves, avoiding

---

16. Descartes, *Meditations on First Philosophy*, 19.
17. Ibid.

the assumption that they are not manifesting as they truly are. To understand the nature of what is given in consciousness, we must allow things to present themselves in their own way. As we have already anticipated at certain points in our exposition, and as we will see in more detail later, not everything we perceive always manifests in its true essence, and not everything manifests in the same way. The beings of the physical domain become visible in a tangible manner, while psychic beings express themselves through symbols. Moreover, in the case of the Divine, its presence is known through revelation. It is thus crucial to begin by understanding the specific way in which each entity reveals itself.

Applying absolute skepticism to all of reality, and especially to its manifestation, is ultimately unsustainable. Philosophers may begin their inquiry from universal doubt, but this stance cannot be sustained indefinitely. Eventually, certainty becomes necessary for the inquiry itself to hold any value or meaning. To preserve that value, Cartesian skepticism grants primacy to individual consciousness, or the subject, suggesting that only reason offers incontestable truths. If the senses can deceive, reason emerges as the sole source of indubitable principles. Therefore, instead of allowing things to manifest so we can understand them in their own beingness, Cartesian rationalism grounded in doubt ends up (re)constructing reality under the protection of reason and its own norms.

Under the Cartesian spirit, things are not seen for how they are shown or revealed in consciousness, but rather as they are filtered through the structures of a rationality that shapes them. In response to this, and following this same spirit, we could still pose the question of why we should not also doubt that very reason, its own structures, and by extension, the very capacity to doubt. One who questions everything must be willing to subject even their own skepticism to scrutiny. Ultimately, if we follow this line, we will reach the conclusion that the only thing that resists any doubt is the very subjectivity that doubts.

Thus, and against the Cartesian perspective under which things remain trapped in conceptual schemes imposed by reason, the phenomenological approach suggests that the human being must liberate things from these conceptual schemes to allow them to manifest on their own terms and beingness. In light of this, we can now affirm that the enemy of phenomenology and the symbol is none other than the "evil genius" of Descartes, who establishes suspicion of what is shown, while at the same time instituting the regime of conceptuality as its foundation. More specifically, the evil genius distrusts what appears to be real and concludes that either it lies hidden behind a false appearance or remains entirely veiled. As a result, we can only know what we create in the concept. Because according to Cartesian reasoning, the senses deceive us, and ultimately, the visible will never lead us to the invisible. All I can know as true is what I myself think.

However, and as Rilke states: "While you do not collect what you yourself cast, everything will be just skill and insignificant loot."[18] That is to say, under Cartesian reasoning, reality can never be more than the product of the thinker's skill; as such, it lacks intrinsic value. From this perspective, the evil genius can only be understood as a wound within consciousness. For a consciousness that doubts itself is a wounded or fractured consciousness, expressing a rupture between sensible certainty and the invisible world. This is why the genius is evil, that is, *diabolo*, because it is that which, as the term itself suggests in Latin, separates or divides.

The illusion according to Vedanta

Far from the perspective of Western philosophy, and more specifically its Cartesian dimension, Advaita Vedanta holds precisely that the essence of our being is divine, that is, we are purity, perfection, and eternal freedom. It is not about transforming ourselves into Brahman, but about recognizing that we already are Brahman. Our *ātman*, or true self, is inherently one with Brahman. However, the question arises: if our essence is divine, why do we find it so difficult to perceive it? The answer lies in the Sanskrit concept of *māyā*, which

---

18. Rainer Maria Rilke, "Poem to Nike" (January 1922) (Translated by Walter Kaufmann).

we can translate as "ignorance or illusion." *Māyā* acts as a veil, hiding our true nature and the reality of the world. It is a mystery whose origin and purpose elude us, but at the same time, we know that it dissipates before the knowledge of our intrinsic divinity.

Brahman constitutes the fundamental Truth of our existence; it is in Brahman where we find life, movement, and Being. According to the Upanishads, which are sacred texts of Vedanta, "All this is Brahman."[19] The ever-changing universe is like images from a movie projected on a screen; without the permanent screen of Brahman, the world would have no reality. Our perception of reality, however, is distorted by time, space, and causality. This erroneous vision is worsened by our identification with the body, mind, and ego rather than with the *ātman*, our divine self, triggering a cycle of ignorance and suffering. By identifying with the fleeting aspects of our existence, we fear illness, aging, and death. By clinging to the ego, we experience destructive emotions. However, none of this alters our true essence, the *ātman*.

Śaṅkara, the great 7th-century C.E. master, used the analogy of the rope and the snake to explain *māyā*. One may fear a snake in the dark, but the fear disappears upon discovering it is only a rope. Similarly, the illusion of our mortality and the appearance of the universe dissolve when we recognize that everything is Brahman. Ultimately, we understand that Brahman pervades everything. *Māyā* is like the clouds that obscure the sun; the sun continues to shine, but we cannot see it due to the clouds. Our "clouds"—selfishness, hatred, greed—dissipate through meditation on our true nature and the practice of altruism and discipline, thus revealing our divinity.

19.*Chāndogya Upaniṣad*, 3.14.1

Chapter 6

The return to the Being of things

Husserl: intentional consciousness and the birth of phenomenon

The criticism from which Husserl's phenomenology originates is that, under the guidance of traditional metaphysics, we have gradually come to approach things in light of the concepts that metaphysics itself has created, rather than allowing things to show themselves in their own phenomenality. This conceptual construction, rooted in Cartesianism and a direct result of the evil genius doubt, is so significant that we have gradually stopped creating concepts that allow us to express things as they truly are, ultimately ending up seeking things that fit into the pre-created concepts.

In this sense, traditional philosophy and metaphysics, especially 19th-century Kantianism, which occupied the philosophical centrality of the time, prioritize the concepts we have created a priori, so that things ultimately make sense only when they conform to those concepts. In other words, the metaphysical and philosophical conceptual map is what ends up injecting meaning into the world, regardless of how the world may reveal itself to us through experience. In this context, Husserl's phenomenology embarks on a long journey to return to the things themselves, as Husserl himself proclaims, in order to do justice to them and save them from the conceptualization and meaning that has been imposed upon them.

Heidegger later picks up this criticism in a particularly detailed way, addressing the Greek term *orthótes*, which we can translate as "the correction of representation," through which he refers us to Plato to illustrate how reality, upon presenting itself to us, is later reinterpreted through our ideas. This implies that Truth does not reside in the direct manifestations of reality but in our thought about those manifestations. According to Heidegger, the origin of the notion of subjectivity, characteristic of modernity, can be found in Plato's philosophy. In this philosophical paradigm, human beings come to be conceived as the subject, the foundation of truth, thus situating the essence of Truth in the human subject rather than in the "external" reality that manifests itself. Furthermore, this perspective inaugurates a turn toward interiority, where Truth is understood as something that underlies the human being, and not necessarily in the world as it is presented to us through experience.

Therefore, the accusation by both Husserl and Heidegger is that once the primacy of the concept is established, the thing no longer speaks freely because it can only speak according to the mode and framework of the concept. It is precisely in front of this position, grounded in traditional philosophy and metaphysics, that both propose returning to the things themselves. Husserl suggests returning to the things themselves, and Heidegger to the Being of things. Although each will design a different philosophical response, with divergent procedures and objectives, both will share the notion of allowing the things to speak to us, to penetrate us, to inhabit us.

In Husserl's case, once the things are in our consciousness, we can study them closely as the field of appearance or manifestation of the things. However, the consciousness to which Husserl refers is not a supposed pure consciousness, as if it were an empty box, but a consciousness inhabited by things. To explain this notion, Husserl himself articulates the concept of the "intentionality" of consciousness, with which he postulates that consciousness is always, and by default, directed toward an object. Therefore, speaking of consciousness is inevitably speaking of consciousness-of-something, as a kind of unity whose founding elements—the consciousness and its object—although eminently different from each other, can only be understood in relation to one another. That is why Husserl, in response to Descartes, will say that there is no pure *cogito* but *cogito* with *cogitatum*, just as there is no thought without something to be thought, with what is thought inhabiting consciousness as thought. With this argument, Husserl's phenomenology seeks to liberate the thought from the chains of thinking so that the object can emerge, and with its emergence, the very act of thinking, the act of consciousness, in all its richness. According to Husserl, we can study it as it appears to our philosophical reflection. In this sense, Husserl affirms that phenomenology is the science of consciousness, that is, the study that grants access to an objective and unadulterated understanding of the world as an object of consciousness. We will address this issue in greater depth later.

Husserl's response on the intentionality of consciousness thus involves a revision of the Platonic and Cartesian notions of subject and object. This intentional relation, which is more original than the subject and object themselves, opens up a new field that Husserl will call "intentional consciousness" and sometimes "the subjectivity of the subject." The correlation of consciousness with its intentional object is transformed in such a way that any specific action adapts and changes over time; it is not an isolated or static relationship, but rather one that occurs in an environment endowed with multiple possible actions that could be performed. These options can, at any time, fulfill their function, relegating the original action to a less prominent position. In this framework, each action undergoes a change in itself and also competes with other possibilities, creating a complex dynamism. In this context, the correlation between consciousness and the object is dynamic and transformative. When the thing appears in consciousness, it becomes an intentional object of consciousness. Consciousness imparts the form of consciousness to the thing, which modifies both.

This change or modification, however, should not be understood as a return to the traditional metaphysical positions previously seen, whether from Plato or Descartes. In them, consciousness, like a lighthouse in the middle of the night, fills its objects with light, creating them from nothing with its own pre-established form and meaning. On the contrary, the interaction between the thing and consciousness gives rise to a hybrid entity known as the "phenomenon," which, as we will see, constitutes the basis for the mutual penetration of consciousness by things and vice versa. In this context, we must distinguish between, on one hand, pure consciousness free from any external influence and, on the other, the "pure thing" as a merely theoretical concept since its existence independent of consciousness is unverifiable. In other terms, this means that the human being, for Husserl, experiences things through consciousness, that is, by being conscious of them. As we mentioned earlier, there cannot be consciousness by itself if it is not conscious of something. Similarly, it is not possible to assign objectivity to anything beyond our consciousness of it.

Therefore, this approach leads us to conclude that the theoretical "pure things," what Kant would call the "things in themselves,"[20] as things with their own life and meaning separate from conscious perception, are philosophically indeterminable. From phenomenology, we can only speak of the thing insofar as it is the intentional object of consciousness, that is, as a thing that has manifested or appeared in consciousness, but in its own way.

The correlation between consciousness and the thing in that encounter implies that neither of the two remains identical. If the thing presents itself to us in its own way or in its transformation into a phenomenon, consciousness must also resemble, open itself to the thing qua phenomenon in order to understand it in its own manifestation. This transformation of both consciousness and the thing that occurs in their intentional encounter has also been referred to as "ontological inversion."

Phenomenology as transcendental philosophy

The way in which Husserl outlines this relationship between consciousness and the intentional object in terms of transformation and change, both of the one and the other, has a clear link to Hegel's philosophy, for whom being and thinking are the same. Briefly and simply put, we can say that for Hegel, Being is what he himself calls Spirit, and we could take this as God, while thinking it would be its activity. When Being creates the world, this activity emancipates itself

---

20. Georges Dicker, "Kant's Transcendental Idealism," *in Kant's Theory of Knowledge: An Analytical Introduction* (Oxford: Oxford University Press, 2004), 43.

from Him, because in order to think, God needs to compare Himself, as the "I" can only know itself through the "not-I." Therefore, there is always an *exitus*, or "exit," and a *reditus*, or "return," because from Hegel's logic, thinking is returning to oneself. However, it would be impossible to return without first leaving, getting lost, transcending oneself, which is why in this case, what we would call divine straying is necessary. In this straying of Spirit, being and thinking are distinct because God's thought is lost, and identity is regained in the self-knowledge of Being in itself. It is there where God recovers Himself through thinking.

From Hegel's conception, in the principles of history, God says, "I am" and then asks "what am I?" This question is a necessity, since the "I" alone lacks something or someone with which to compare itself, and therefore does not know that it is not, because there is no other outside of it and no standard against which to measure itself. The answer to the statement "I am" and the question "what am I?" is: "nothing." In response to this, despair arises, and the fullness, or *pléroma*, is broken, and it is this despair that creates the objective universe. This would be the history of the universe with a God estranged or lost in the universe, but who, through the history of philosophy, progresses in His self-knowledge, until the knowledge of God reaches God Himself and recovers His identity. This same progress is what Heidegger will later call the *itinerarium admentideum*, or "the itinerary of the mind toward God," but which Hegel adopts from Plotinus' *pléroma* to make his articulation. In his Introduction to the *Philosophy of Right*, Hegel will say that "what is rational is real, and what is real is rational,"[21] pointing precisely to this meeting of thought and Being.

What has been said here about Hegel and this conception of God and creation clarifies Husserl's "transcendental phenomenology." For Husserl, phenomenology is transcendental because it understands that consciousness, or cognitive potential, does not rest merely in itself. Consciousness is not directed, tensed, or stretched

---

21. G. W. F. Hegel, *Introduction to the Philosophy of History: With Selections from The Philosophy of Right*, trans. and introd. Leo Rauch (Indianapolis: Hackett Publishing Company, 1988), 10 (x).

toward itself but toward the world, that is, "outside" of it. This idea of the intentionality of consciousness is what, later, Sartre will also call "the transcendence of the ego." As we have seen, initially, Husserl asserts that there is no *cogito* without *cogitatum*, or no consciousness without a world to be thought because, otherwise, what would consciousness think? At the same time, he is telling us that "there is no world without consciousness,"[22] as we argued earlier when defining the object as necessarily intentional. This relationship between consciousness and the intentional object implies that consciousness is never primarily consciousness of itself. Although all reflection or meditation signifies a return to itself, every return will first involve a loss, an exit, a straying, as Hegel has well shown. That is, self-consciousness, being aware of oneself, implies a prior consciousness of the world, without which no self-consciousness could exist.

That is why Sartre asserts that, in Husserl's philosophy, the ego is directed toward things, so that there is not a consciousness on one side and a world on the other, as some authors have mistakenly asserted, but rather there is a consciousness-world or consciousness-of-the-world. Sartre himself maintains that I am conscious of myself when I am conscious of the world because I am a being in the world.[23] I cannot be conscious of myself if I am not conscious of the world. There is no Being on one side and a world on the other; but rather consciousness is "thrown" into the world, as Heidegger would say, so it can only be consciousness of the world.

In this context, we must understand the criticism made by phenomenology in general, and Husserl in particular. He criticized what he called "psychologism," which is the position that asserts that human beings can know themselves in their consciousness without having gone through the mediation of the world as a phenomenon of consciousness. For Husserl, psychologism implies that consciousness immerses itself in itself without having been directly influenced

---

22. Quoted in James K. A. Smith, *The Fall of Interpretation: Philosophical Foundations for a Creational Hermeneutic* (Baker Publishing Group, 2012), 94.
23. Jean-Paul Sartre, *Being and Nothingness: An Essay on Phenomenological Ontology*, trans. Hazel E. Barnes (London: Methuen, 1957), 10 (x).

by the "external" world. Psychologism focuses exclusively on the contents of the psyche, ignoring any external influence. In response to this position, Husserl asserts that the world and consciousness are inseparable—as we have shown above with the help of Sartre—so that it becomes unfeasible to investigate the world without considering consciousness, as science tries to do, or to explore consciousness without considering its relationship to the world, as psychology does. Those who know themselves without having known the world engage in intestinal philosophies or philosophies of interiority. They take refuge in interiority, but things do not populate that supposed interiority; things do not penetrate it, and therefore, it is nothing but an introversion, but in no case can it be considered an introspection.

It is from this critique of psychologism that Husserl's phenomenology can be presented as strictly transcendental, because its object of study is not an introspective consciousness that has lost its relationship with the world, but one that is related to it and in whose relationship, it transcends itself by default. Only a consciousness that is capable of observing something, after all, can turn back on itself and observe the observation itself, as Hegel has well exposed. If it cannot observe an object, it will not be able to observe itself. Since it can only see itself, it must go out and transcend itself in order to know itself. In other words, only a consciousness that can look at itself in a mirror can know itself.

CHAPTER 7

THE DESTRUCTION OF THE CONCEPT

Heidegger's critique of classical ontology

As we have seen, the emergence of Husserl's phenomenology—beyond all positivism and psychologism—entails a radical rethinking of the relationship between human beings and the world. It proposes intentional consciousness as the condition of possibility for the object to be given as phenomenon, that is, without presuppositions or conceptualizations. Thus, the object can be known in its own beingness as an object-of-consciousness. However, and now following Martin Heidegger, this approach halts and settles within the limits of epistemology, that is, knowledge, reducing both the existence of the phenomenon and consciousness to objects of knowledge. In this context, Heidegger opens the philosophical investigation to the domain of ontology, that is, of Being, transcending epistemology or knowledge. However, before doing so, Heidegger himself will first unfold a critique of traditional ontology. In *Being and Time*, Heidegger states the following:

> In provisionally characterizing the object which serves as the theme of our investigation (the Being of entities, or the meaning of Being in general), it seems that we have also delineated the method to be employed. The task of ontology is to explain Being itself and to make the Being of entities stand out in full relief. And the method of ontology remains questionable in the highest degree as long as we merely consult

75

those ontologies which have come down to us historically, or other essays of that character.[24]

In his reflection, Heidegger asserts that the subject of ontology lies in the question of Being. However, he criticizes the methodological approach that has predominated in Western thought for such an inquiry, considering it inadequate and deficient. According to him, the path to Being has been wrongly traced. Therefore, he proposes rethinking this fundamental question that has troubled the West, but from a different methodological perspective, one that properly leads us to Being. In this context, Heidegger continues:

> Since the term "ontology" is used in this investigation in a sense which is formally broad, any attempt to clarify the method of ontology by tracing its history is automatically ruled out. When, moreover, we use the term "ontology," we are not talking about some definite philosophical discipline standing in interconnection with the others. Here one does not have to measure up to the tasks of some discipline that has been presented beforehand; on the contrary, only in terms of the objective necessities of definite questions and the kind of treatment which the 'things themselves' require, can one develop such a discipline.[25]

Heidegger argues that ontology is not a discipline in itself; rather, it represents a field of fundamental topics such as Being, nothingness, entity, time, foundation, and essence, which can be approached from various disciplines. In this way, he prevents ontology from being confined to a single disciplinary category and presents it as an amalgamation of deep philosophical questions. In this context, Heidegger adds:

---

24. Martin Heidegger, *Being and Time*, trans. John Macquarrie and Edward Robinson (New York: Harper & Row, 1962), §7.
25. Ibid.

Chapter 7: The destruction of the concept

With the question of the meaning of Being, our investigation comes up against the fundamental question of philosophy. This is one that must be treated *phenomenologically*. Thus our treatise does not subscribe to a 'standpoint' or represent any special 'direction'; for phenomenology is nothing of either sort, nor can it become so as long as it understands itself. The expression 'phenomenology' signifies primarily a *methodological conception*. This expression does not characterize the what of the objects of philosophical research as subject-matter, but rather the *how* of that research. The more genuinely a methodological concept is worked out and the more comprehensively it determines the principles on which a science is to be conducted, all the more primordially is it rooted in the way we come to terms with the things themselves, and the farther is it removed from what we call "technical devices," though there are many such devices even in the theoretical disciplines.[26]

Therefore, according to Heidegger, the method of phenomenology shifts the traditional focus of philosophy, which places the method before experience, and instead prioritizes the direct experience of the "things themselves." Unlike the conventional philosophical attitude, which insists on defining a method before addressing the object of study, phenomenology inverts this order, arguing that it is in the immediate encounter with the "things themselves" where the most appropriate method for understanding them is revealed. It is not prior methodological reflection that illuminates the way toward knowledge of beings, but the direct relationship with it. This perspective was initially introduced by Husserl, but it was Heidegger who brought it to its fullest expression, emphasizing that approaching the "things themselves" must be a process free from methodological interference. Heidegger's stance, then, implies recognizing that we are already in the presence of the being and that it, in turn, resides in us. According to phenomenology, and as we saw in the previous

---
26. Ibid.

chapter, subject and object are not dissociated but are intrinsically interconnected. This implies asserting, both from Husserl's and Heidegger's perspectives, that knowledge is not a journey toward an "other," but an act of reciprocal revelation. In this context, Heidegger states that the method does not lead to being but to a recognition of the inherent union between subject and object.

> Thus the term "phenomenology" expresses a maxim which can be formulated as "To the things themselves!" It is opposed to all free-floating constructions and accidental findings; it is opposed to taking over any conceptions which only seem to have been demonstrated; it is opposed to those pseudo-questions which parade themselves as problems', often for generations at a time. Yet this maxim, one may rejoin, is abundantly self-evident, and it expresses, moreover, the underlying principle of any scientific knowledge whatsoever.[27]

Heidegger asserts that phenomenology transcends the notion of being merely a scientific discipline or a compilation of concepts and procedures, adopting a stance of exclusive attention to the "things themselves." This approach involves stripping the object of study of all the conceptual apparatus previously constructed that obscures the direct perception of things. According to Heidegger, philosophy has tended to construct concepts that ultimately mask the objects of its study. That is, things manifest before us, but philosophy tends to wrap them in concepts that end up concealing their true nature. Therefore, the task of phenomenology is to unravel or unveil these things, stripping them of the conceptual shell that hides them. This is why, according to Heidegger, grounding does not mean adding or superimposing concepts but rather clearing away or extracting elements to reveal what lies at the foundation.

Thus, in *Phenomenological Interpretations of Aristotle*, Heidegger refers to destruction in the following words:

---

27. Ibid.

Chapter 7: The Destruction of the Concept

For the most part, the philosophy of today's situation moves inauthentically (*uneigentlich*) within the Greek conceptuality, and indeed within a conceptuality which has been pervaded by a chain of diverse interpretations (*Interpretationen hindurchgegengen ist*). The basic concepts have lost their primordial functions of expression (*ursprünglichen*), functions which are particularly suited to particularly experienced regions of objects. [...] Thus the phenomenological hermeneutic of facticity sees itself as called upon to loosen up the handed-down and dominating interpretedness in its hidden motives, unexpressed tendencies, and ways of interpreting; and to push forward by way of a dismantling return toward the primordial motive sources of explication; the phenomenological hermeneutic of facticity sees itself called in this way, insofar as it wants to help today's [philosophical] situation along through interpretation toward a radical possibility of appropriation (and this in the manner of a making attentive which first provides concrete categories). The hermeneutic carries out its task only on the path of destruction [*nur auf dem Wege der Destruktion*]. [...] Philosophical research is "historical" knowing in the radical sense of that term. For philosophical research, the destructive confrontation with philosophy's history is not merely an annex for the purposes of illustrating how things were earlier; it is not an occasional review of what others "did" earlier; it is not an opportunity for the projection of entertaining world-historical perspectives. The destruction is rather the authentic path upon which the present must encounter itself in its own basic movements; and it must encounter itself in such a way that through this encounter the continual question springs forth from history to face the present: to what extent is it (the present) itself worried about the appropriations of radical possibilities of basic experiences and about their interpretations? The tendencies toward a radical logic of origins (*eine radikale Ursprunglogik*) and the approaches to ontologies thereby gain a principal critical elucidation. [...] What we do not interpret and express primordially (*ursprünglich*) is what we do not possess in authentic (*eigentlicher*) truthful safekeeping.[28]

Grounding does not consist in adding or applying new concepts but in extracting or removing the superfluous to let the fundamental emerge. It is not about accumulating concepts that ultimately obscure the object, but dismantling or removing the conceptual structures that prevent a clear vision of it. It is only after dismantling or removing the metaphysical tradition and philosophical history that Being can be revealed clearly and distinctly.

The "way of remotion"

In relation to the subject of dismantling the philosophical and metaphysical tradition, Heidegger paid special attention to Saint Thomas Aquinas and his "way of remotion." One of the first statements in *Summa Contra Gentiles* is precisely that "we cannot know what God is, but what He is not," for, as he later adds, "for the knowledge of God, it is necessary to use the way of remotion." He writes:

> Accordingly having proved that there is a first being which we call God, it behaves us to inquire into His nature. Now in treating of the divine essence the principal method to be followed is that of remotion. For the divine essence by its immensity surpasses every form to which our intellect reaches; and thus we cannot apprehend it by knowing what it is. But we have some knowledge thereof by knowing what it is not: and we shall approach all the nearer to the knowledge thereof according as we shall be enabled to remove by our intellect a greater number of things therefrom. For the more completely we see how a thing differs from others, the more perfectly we know it: since each thing has in itself its own being distinct

---

28. Martin Heidegger, *Phenomenological Interpretations with Respect to Aristotle: Indication of the Hermeneutical Situation*, trans. Michael Baur, Magazine Man and World Number 25 (1992): 370–371.

from all other things. Wherefore when we know the definition of a thing, first we place it in a genus, whereby we know in general what it is, and afterwards we add differences, so as to mark its distinction from other things: and thus we arrive at the complete knowledge of a thing's essence.

Since, however, we are unable in treating of the divine essence to take what as a genus, nor can we express its distinction from other things by affirmative differences, we must needs express it by negative differences. Now just as in affirmative differences one restricts another, and brings us the nearer to a complete description of the thing, according as it makes it to differ from more things, so one negative difference is restricted by another that marks a distinction from more things. Thus, if we say that God is not an accident, we thereby distinguish Him from all accidents; then if we add that He is not a body, we shall distinguish Him also from certain substances, and thus in gradation He will be differentiated by suchlike negations from all beside Himself: and then when He is known as distinct from all things, we shall arrive at a proper consideration of Him. It will not, however, be perfect, because we shall not know what He is in Himself.

Wherefore in order to proceed about the knowledge of God by the way of remotion, let us take as principle that which is already made manifest by what we have said (above), namely that God is altogether unchangeable. This is also confirmed by the authority of Holy Writ. For it is said (Malach. iii. 6): I am God (Vulg., the Lord) and I change not; (James i. 17): With Whom there is no change; and (Num. xxiii. 19): God is not as a man . . . that He should be changed.[29]

---

29. Thomas Aquinas, *Summa Contra Gentiles*, trans. English Dominican Fathers, from the latest Leonine edition, Book I, ch. 14 (London: Burns Oates & Washbourne Ltd., 1924), 33–34.

Therefore, Aquinas proposes a strategy of conceptual purification in the study of divine nature, eliminating any finite characteristic attributed to divinity. Human reason, limited in its essence, tends to assign finite attributes to God that stem from our own finite experience. Therefore, any attribute that the human being can assign to God inevitably falls within the domain of the finite, given our inherent finite referential framework. We know, for example, what it means to be finite, but it is impossible for us to conceive of infinity fully. Therefore, we deny finitude when speaking of God. Similarly, our innate familiarity with mortality makes it difficult to conceive of God's immortality. Yet through the technique of progressive negation, we can deny God's mortality and thus advance toward a purer understanding of the Divine, stripping it of imperfections conceivable from a human perspective.

The idea of eliminating our preconceptions about divinity introduces us to the apophatic or negative path, defending the premise that a genuine approach to God requires freeing ourselves from the adjectives and preconceived notions we have assigned to His being. This methodology suggests that our linguistic and conceptual tools are deficient, and even misguided, in capturing the true essence of the Divine, whose nature is of a transcendence and mystery without limits. Within the framework of this path, we are invited to dispense with any image or definition of God as a strategy to initiate a true process of understanding His essence. This should not be understood as a denial of divine existence, but rather as a recognition of the limits of human language and thought when attempting to encompass the entirety of His reality.

This "purification" procedure involves an intellectual as well as a spiritual process of detaching from mistaken or limited ideas about the Divine, thus fostering an immersion into a more intimate and mystical experience with God. The objective sought is to experience God in such a way that logical understanding is transcended, embracing the enigma and the impossibility of defining Divinity. This itinerary toward God, centered on recognizing what "He is not," as Saint Thomas argues, facilitates the development of a more direct bond, less conditioned by the barriers inherent in our human reasoning.

Chapter 7: The Destruction of the Concept

This negative apophatic path of Saint Thomas has its roots in what we could call the "Socratic approach" to philosophy. Although it may seem atypical to us today, this approach was, in fact, a reflection of a current of thought spread among several Greek predecessors, who placed great value on dialogue and personal interaction as a means of inquiring into philosophical issues. Plato, deeply marked by the influence of Socrates, composed almost all of his work in the dialogical format. Socrates, for his part, stands out in the philosophical landscape as the last great itinerant philosopher of Greece, distancing himself from the writing of treatises and considering teaching as a commitment both to spirituality and society. Through his pedagogical methodology based on dialogue, Socrates aimed to guide society toward a deeper and more genuine understanding of the cosmos, inciting a thorough examination of the foundation of our existence.

What is relevant to our discussion is that Socrates emphasized that recognizing our own ignorance is the first step toward acquiring true wisdom, thus laying the foundation for probing into the depths of our being. With an approach to knowledge similar to that of a child, Socrates discarded the accumulated knowledge, the elaborated philosophy, the exceptional intelligence, and the reasoning he had forged over the years in order to approach Truth through debates with his dialectical rivals in the agoras of the polis. Such effort elevated him to the position of the most learned among the Greeks. Nevertheless, he showed notable courage when declaring, "I only know that I know nothing."

With the death of Socrates, Greece metaphorically executed its own end. If it had listened to what Socrates suggested instead of condemning him to death, it would have freed itself from its prejudices. Greece, the cradle of democracy and Western thought and, in particular, the effervescent Athens of the time, as the prime exponent of the political, philosophical, scientific, and even artistic model of the West, would have transcended itself, becoming a society based on the pursuit of discovering Truth.

Philosophically speaking, Socrates' dialogical strategy constitutes one of his most notable traits. This Athenian scholar opposed the relativism that dominated his era, promoted by many sophists who stripped the concepts of "good" and "evil" of any absolute value, treating them as mere social constructions. Socrates took a critical stance against moral skepticism for its logical incoherence. However, he does not propose a detailed alternative moral system in the texts that mention him, especially in those of Plato.

In general terms, we can define Socratic dialectics as a method divided into two crucial segments, the *parts destruyens* and the *parts construyens*, which belong to the "Socratic irony." *Parts destruyens*, in Latin "the negative part of criticizing opinions," focuses on dismantling prejudices, the false sense of knowledge, and assumptions of complete understanding. According to Socrates, believing with certainty that one possesses knowledge before beginning the inquiry into Truth represents a considerable barrier to acquiring authentic knowledge. Only one who openly recognizes their ignorance and limited understanding of reality, freeing themselves from preexisting notions suggesting some degree of knowledge, can genuinely approach understanding. This first "ironic" stage of the Socratic method develops through the formulation of carefully structured questions, with which Socrates guided his interlocutors toward this understanding without proposing categorical statements. Through this questioning technique, he broke down his counterpart's assumptions, causing bewilderment among those who considered themselves wise and exposing their fallacies. For example, we read in Xenophon's Symposium:

> Critobulus. "In faith, my opinion is that beauty is to be found quite as well in a horse or an ox or in any number of inanimate things. I know, at any rate, that a shield may be beautiful, or a sword, or a spear."
> Socrates. "How can it be that all these things are beautiful when they are entirely dissimilar?"
> "Why, they are beautiful and fine," answered Critobulus, "if they are well made for the respective functions for which we obtain them, or if they are naturally well constituted to serve our needs."

Chapter 7: The Destruction of the Concept

Socrates. "Do you know the reason why we need eyes?"
Critobulus. "Obviously to see with."
Socrates. "In that case, it would appear without further ado that my eyes are finer ones than yours."
Critobulus. "How so?"
Socrates. "Because, while yours see only straight ahead, mine, by bulging out as they do, see also to the sides."
Critobulus. "Do you mean to say that a crab is better equipped visually than any other creature?"
Socrates. "Absolutely; for its eyes are also better set to insure strength."
Critobulus. "Well, let that pass; but whose nose is finer, yours or mine?"
Critobulus. "Mine, I consider, granting that Providence made us noses to smell with. For your nostrils look down toward the ground, but mine are wide open and turned outward so that I can catch scents from all about."
Critobulus. "But how do you make a snub nose handsomer than a straight one?"
Socrates. "For the reason that it does not put a barricade between the eyes but allows them unobstructed vision of whatever they desire to see; whereas a high nose, as if in despite, has walled the eyes off one from the other."
"As for the mouth," said Critobulus, "I concede that point. For if it is created for the purpose of biting off food, you could bite off a far bigger mouthful than I could. And don't you think that your kiss is also the more tender because you have thick lips?"
Socrates. "According to your argument, it would seem that I have a mouth more ugly even than an ass's. But do you not reckon it a proof of my superior beauty that the River Nymphs, goddesses as they are, bear as their offspring the Seilenoi, who resemble me more closely than they do you?"[30]

---

30. Xenophon, *Symposium (Banquet)* IV.58–61, in *Xenophon: Memorabilia, Oeconomicus, Symposium, Apology*, trans. O. J. Todd, Loeb Classical Library (Cambridge, MA: Harvard University Press, 1923; repr. 1997), 599–603.

Therefore, irony is employed to reveal that, in fact, what one considers to know or understand does not always coincide with true knowledge.

This negative or apophatic way, known both in philosophical and religious spheres, traces its origins through various intellectual and spiritual lineages, spanning from Greek philosophy to the foundational teachings of Christianity, Islam, and Judaism. Within the Vedantic tradition, for example, this methodology is expressed under the concept of *neti-neti*, a Sanskrit expression that translates as "neither this nor that," as we see in the following quote:

अथात आदेशः—नेति नेति, न ह्येतस्मादिति नेत्यन्यत्परमस्ति; अथ नामधेयम्—सत्यस्य सत्यमिति ।

athāta ādeśaḥ—neti neti, na hy etasmād iti nety anyat param asti;
atha nāmadheyaṁ satyasya satyam iti.

[...] Now, therefore, the instruction is *neti-neti* or "not this, not this." There is no instruction more excellent than *neti*, or "not this"; it is called the Truth of truths. [...]

(*Bṛhad-āraṇyaka Upanishad*, 2.3.6b)

This expression is prominently integrated into *jñana-yoga*, serving as a vehicle for self-realization. Its essence lies in the use of the mind to deny and detach from all forms and designations, facilitating the distinction between the phenomenal world, which is limited and relative, and the eternal and unchanging perfection of absolute reality. The practice of *neti-neti* leads to the understanding that any entity or concept that the mind can conceive does not correspond to Brahman, the ultimate reality. In this way, the practice progressively guides toward the revelation of this fundamental truth.

It is within this apophatic framework that we must understand the birth of Heidegger's critique and, more importantly, his approach. Heidegger's hermeneutic phenomenology seeks to reach Being not by conceptualizing it as an object, but by allowing it to appear as a phenomenon (*phainómenon*) and attending to it in its own way of being and revealing itself. That will be, as we will see, the task of what we can call "Heidegger's phenomenological ontology."

BIBLIOGRAPHY SECTION III

- Aquinas, Thomas. *Summa Contra Gentiles.* Translated by English Dominican Fathers, from the latest Leonine edition. Book I, chapter 14. London: Burns Oates & Washbourne Ltd., 1924.
- Descartes, René. *Meditations on First Philosophy: With Selections from the Objections and Replies.* Translated by Michael Moriarty. Oxford: Oxford University Press, 2008.
- Dicker, Georges. *Kant's Theory of Knowledge: An Analytical Introduction.* Oxford: Oxford University Press, 2004.
- Dogan, Sevgi. *Marx and Hegel on the Dialectic of the Individual and the Social.* Lanham, MD: Lexington Books, 2018.
- Hegel, G. W. F. *Introduction to the Philosophy of History: With Selections from The Philosophy of Right.* Translated and with an introduction by Leo Rauch. Indianapolis: Hackett Publishing Company, 1988.
- Heidegger, Martin. "Phenomenological Interpretations with Respect to Aristotle: Indication of the Hermeneutical Situation." Translated by Michael Baur. Man and World 25 (1992): 355–93.
- McGushin, Edward F. *Foucault's Askesis: An Introduction to the Philosophical Life.* Evanston, IL: Northwestern University Press, 2007.
- Sartre, Jean-Paul. *Being and Nothingness: An Essay on Phenomenological Ontology.* Translated by Hazel E. Barnes. London: Methuen, 1957.
- Sartre, Jean-Paul. *Jean-Paul Sartre: Basic Writings.* Edited by Stephen Priest. London: Routledge, 2001.
- Xenophon. *Memorabilia,* Oeconomicus, *Symposium, Apology.* Translated by E. C. Marchant and O. J. Todd. Loeb Classical Library. Cambridge, MA: Harvard University Press, 1923. Reprint, 1997.

SECTION IV

PHENOMENOLOGY OF THE MANIFEST AND THE HIDDEN

CHAPTER 8

PHENOMENOLOGY
OF THE UNMANIFESTED

Martin Heidegger: ontology as phenomenology of Being

As we will see below, Heidegger's ontological vision alters how Husserl had conceptualized and founded the study of phenomenology. However, this revision is not a mere philosophical whim but the result of a profound, philological and philosophical study. In his study of the term, Heidegger reminds us that, after an initial use of the word by Erik Wolff, prior to the Kantian philosophical era, phenomenology comes to mean the "science of phenomena." Heidegger writes:

> This expression [phenomeno-logy] has two components: "phenomenon" and "logos." Both of these go back to terms from the Greek: φαινόμενον and λόγος. Taken superficially, the term "phenomenology" is formed like "theology," "biology," "sociology"—names which may be translated as "science of God," "science of life," "science of society." This would make phenomenology the science of phenomena. We shall set forth the preliminary conception of phenomenology by characterizing what one has in mind in the term's two components, 'phenomenon' and 'logos', and by establishing the meaning of the name in which these are put together.[31]

---

31. Martin Heidegger, *Being and Time*, trans. John Macquarrie and Edward Robinson (New York: Harper & Row, 1962), §7.

Section IV: Phenomenology of the Manifest and the Hidden

Heidegger continues:

> The Greek expression φαινόμενον (*phainómenon*), to which the term 'phenomenon' goes back, is derived from the verb φαίνεσθαι (*phainesthai*), which signifies "to show itself." Thus φαινόμενον (*phainómenon*) means that which shows itself, the manifest [*das, was sich zeigt, das Sichzeigende, das Offenbare*]. φαίνεσθαι (*phainesthai*) itself is a middle-voiced form which comes from φαίνω (*phainō*) — to bring to the light of day, to put in the light. φαίνω (*phainō*) comes from the stem φα-(*pha-*), like φῶς (*phōs*), the light, that which is bright — in other words, that wherein something can become manifest, visible in itself. Thus we must keep in mind that the expression 'phenomenon' signifies that which shows itself in itself, the manifest. Accordingly the φαινόμενα (*phainomena*) or 'phenomena' are the totality of what lies in the light of day or can be brought to the light — what the Greeks sometimes identified simply with τὰ ὄντα (*ta onta*) (entities).[32]

In other words, phenomenology will be the study of that which becomes evident, visible in itself, but as an objectual reality that comes to light, rather than remaining hidden. The phenomenon, therefore, is a phenomenon insofar as it shows itself. Moreover, as we have just seen, and according to Heidegger himself, the term in plural refers to "the totality of what is or can be brought to light" (the beings). And Heidegger continues:

> Now an entity can show itself from itself [*von ihm selbst her*] in many ways, depending in each case on the kind of access we have to it. Indeed it is even possible for an entity to show itself as something which in itself it is *not*. When it shows itself in this way, it 'looks like something or other' ["*sieht*"... "*so aus wie...*"]. This kind of showing-itself is what we call "seeming" [*Scheinen*].

---

32. Ibid.

Thus in Greek too the expression φαινόμενον ("phenomenon") signifies that which looks like something, that which is 'semblant', 'semblance' [*das "Scheinbare," der "Schein"*].

φαινόμενον ἀγαθόν (*phainómenon agathon*) means something good which looks like, but 'in actuality' is not, what it gives itself out to be.

If we are to have any further understanding of the concept of phenomenon, everything depends on our seeing how what is designated in the first signification of φαινόμενον ('phenomenon' as that which shows itself) and what is designated in the second ('phenomenon' as semblance) are structurally interconnected.

Only when the meaning of something is such that it makes a pretension of showing itself—that is, of being a phenomenon—*can* it show itself *as* something which it is *not*; only then *can* it 'merely look like so-and-so'.[33]

Heidegger's argument in this paragraph is that the self-revelation of a being, which chooses to show itself solely of its own initiative, presents an inherent complexity. On the one hand, if the being in question declares "I am a being and choose to reveal myself," an intrinsic dilemma immediately arises, for if its existence is limited to a mere act of manifestation, the being itself is not truly unfolding its complete essence. To effect an authentic self-revelation, the being will need to transcend mere exposure of itself. However, this process involves an alternating rhythm of concealment and revelation in which the being is exposed in its true nature. That is, to genuinely reveal itself, the being must show its enigmatic nature. If it limits itself to merely showing itself and nothing more, it will not truly be unveiling its enigmatic nature. This is similar to the notion of a God who constantly explained His Being and essence; if that were the

---

33. Ibid.

case, He would not be manifesting His mysterious or transcendent nature and, instead, would be in a state of constant presencing. Heidegger explains to us in these passages that every being has an unmanifested aspect, an unfathomable mystery that escapes any presencing. The being, therefore, exhibits a manifested facet, which is temporary and even illusory, and another unmanifested, which is eternal. For this reason, Heidegger himself insists that a being that shows itself only superficially, creating the illusion of reality, is not revealing itself in its authenticity.

> When φαινόμενον (*phainómenon*) signifies 'semblance', the primordial signification (the phenomenon as the manifest) is already included as that upon which the second signification is founded. We shall allot the term 'phenomenon' to this positive and primordial signification of φαινόμενον (*phainómenon*), and distinguish "phenomenon" from "semblance," which is the privative modification of "phenomenon" as thus defined. But what both these terms express has proximally nothing at all to do with what is called an "appearance," or still less a "mere appearance."[34]

In this context, the notion of appearance is not limited to mere visual manifestation, so it should not be understood simply as the act of becoming visible. A phenomenon is not something that merely appears, but rather manifests itself in a way that transcends superficial obviousness. One cannot consider as a phenomenon something that shows itself as clear and distinct, for upon achieving that clarity, it would cease to be a phenomenon in the strict sense of the term. The unmanifested cannot be exhibited as it is, for by doing so, it would lose its unmanifested character. To establish a relationship with the unmanifested aspect of being requires more than just sight: a clue, an impression, a sign that guides us toward that hidden dimension. That is why Heidegger will say:

---

34. Ibid.

> This is what one is talking about when one speaks of the "symptoms of a disease" (*Krankheitserscheinungen*). Here one has in mind certain occurrences in the body which show themselves and which, in showing themselves as thus showing themselves, "indicate" (*indizieren*) something which does not show itself.[35]

The symptoms that Heidegger refers to in the paragraph we have just quoted act as signs of hidden phenomena. In the detailed study of symptoms, we face a scenario where these act as heralds of subterranean realities. Take, for example, the case of abdominal pain. This phenomenon, in a superficial inspection, may be interpreted as a passing physical discomfort. However, under a more rigorous examination, framed in the intersection of medicine and philosophy, it reveals itself as a significant indicator: a messenger of a latent pathology, elusive to direct observation. This type of pain, beyond its apparent triviality, rises as a portal to a deeper understanding of an underlying ailment. The pain is not, in itself, the illness, but rather a manifestation, a projection of a phenomenon inaccessible to perception and touch.

Symptoms, in this perspective, challenge our ordinary understanding of reality, positioning themselves on the border between the known and the unknown. In the medical field, diagnosis becomes a hermeneutic exercise, where each symptom is interpreted as a key clue guiding the practitioner in identifying the underlying disease. Thus, stomach pain is not merely an alert indicator, but an invitation to explore and decipher the hidden layers of our physiology.

This concept, however, transcends the field of medicine and becomes a principle applicable across various disciplines, from psychology to philosophy. Symptoms, in all their forms, urge us to transcend the surface, to investigate the deeper layers of existence to unravel answers to the mysteries that present themselves to us. They teach us that reality is a complex web where the manifest and the

---

35. Ibid.

latent, the visible and the invisible, are intrinsically interconnected. That is why Heidegger himself, as we advanced above, writes:

> The emergence [*Auftreten*] of such occurrences, their showing-themselves, goes together with the Being-present-at-hand of disturbances which do not show themselves.[36]

Being constitutes the very essence of the being which, in order to manifest itself as a distinct entity, requires a transformation, a process of ontification. Within the framework of Christian theology, this is illustrated with the concept that the Father incarnates in the Son to reveal Himself. However, and as happens with Being and the being, it is crucial to distinguish here between the Father and the Son, avoiding the simplification of considering them identical. Father and Son are not identical, just as Being should not be confused with the being. They are essentially different, and it is that difference which allows one to show itself (in its Being) in the other. Being appears, always and inevitably, through a process of ontification. And although Being is the essence of the being, that which truly is can only be so when it shows itself as a phenomenon when it shows itself in the being. In this sense, Being shows itself, and at the same time remains hidden, in the being.

Being-in-the-world or transcendence in immanence

This relationship that Heidegger outlines when describing the perception and understanding of the Being of the surrounding beings in the world follows in some ways the approach of Husserlian phenomenology we introduced earlier, under whose perspective the idea of cognitive isolation from the world would simply be absurd. According to Husserl himself, human existence is intrinsically intertwined with its environment; we are beings immersed in the world through intentional consciousness in which objects are revealed. Similarly, but now without using the term "consciousness,"

---

36. Ibid.

under Heidegger's conception, human beings are inextricably linked to their environment as a being-in-the-world. This union should not be understood as a posterior union, as if the human being (*Dasein*) and the world preexist both filled with meaning independently of one another and then encounter each other. Heidegger's approach is made even clearer in the thought of José Ortega y Gasset, who formulated the famous phrase: "I am I and my circumstance, and if I do not save it, I do not save myself."

Moreover, Heidegger understands this being-in-the-world that defines us as human beings as an existence impregnated by the universe in which, as Sartre will later explain in his work *The Transcendence of the Ego*, the human being is in a constant and free process of transcending itself. This notion of transcendence will be vital to more precisely understand that the human being's relationship with the world is an active process devoid of fixed essence, since its fundamental nature resides in surpassing its own limits toward what is "external" to it. That externality, however, should not be understood as completely alien, but rather as an immanent transcendence of the human being in relation to the world. That is why, in his work *Existential Phenomenology*, W. Luypen emphasizes that in the search for our authentic nature, no effort to go beyond ourselves can be made, for transcendence always occurs in immanence. The essence of nature is not limited to the existence of trees, flowers, plants, and birds; rather, we ourselves are an integral part of nature. The path to a deep understanding of nature leads us to immersion in the innermost part of our being. The recognition of our true natural essence can occur at the core of our existence.

Speaking of recognition, however, does not mean reducing this relationship with the innermost Being to its mere knowledge as if it were just another object in the world. This attentiveness to Being—as Heidegger also calls it on several occasions—should be understood here as experiencing our own authenticity through adopting an attitude of relaxation that allows our true nature to reveal itself effortlessly, in its beingness. That is why Heidegger emphasizes the urgent obligation of each individual to care (*Sorge*) for their Being, implying that it is not enough to understand oneself, but it is essential to recognize, accept, and take decisive actions regarding the context in which one lives. This reflection highlights the inseparable connection, but at the same time, it is based on transcendence between the individual and their environment, pointing out that personal salvation is intrinsically linked to the ability to transform the circumstances surrounding us positively. Or as Heraclitus put it: "I investigated myself," (fr. B101)[37] and "all people have a claim to self-knowledge and sound thinking" (fr. B116).[38]

---

37. Heraclitus, *Fragments: A Text and Translation with a Commentary*, trans. and comm. T. M. Robinson, Phoenix Presocratics 2 (Toronto: University of Toronto Press, 1987), 61 (frag. 101 = DK B101).

38. Ibid., 67 (frag. 116 = DK B116).

CHAPTER 9

CRITICISMS OF TRANSCENDENTAL PHILOSOPHY

Transcendental phenomenology, which we have addressed so far, has not been exempt from criticism. On the one hand, it has been reproached for being a form of idealism or essentialism that overlooks history, leading to its consideration as a late manifestation of the metaphysics of subjectivity. This critical view is based on the perception that phenomenology, especially that of Husserl, is founded on an ego around which everything else revolves as if it were a lighthouse that turns and fills the world with light—and meaning—at will. Viewed from this perspective, it has been accused of being a solipsistic and worldless egology which, as a result of the *epoché*, or "phenomenological reduction," is ultimately capable only of emphasizing the transparency of the ego. At the same time, it minimizes aspects such as the opacity of the unconscious and the possibility of error within consciousness itself. Finally, and as a consequence of these points, this very critique that accuses Husserl's phenomenology of being a kind of Neo-Cartesianism has opened a gap in the theory of intersubjectivity, raising doubts about its validity.

There is, however, a common misunderstanding about phenomenology that leads to considering it a study of a solipsistic consciousness disconnected from the world when, in reality, its approach is precisely the opposite. As we briefly mentioned earlier, Husserl's *epoché* is not a denial of the existence of the world rooted in Cartesian doubt—as has been stated on various occasions—but a suspension of judgment regarding that existence, since for Husserl, the existence of the world is indisputable, as will later be demonstrated through his concept of the *Lebenswelt* (lifeworld). This suspension of judgment does not seek to isolate the subject from the world, but rather aims to abstain from presupposing that the world has (or does not have) an objective reality loaded with meaning (whatever that may be) prior to our experience of the world. Therefore, Cartesian doubt and Husserl's *epoché* cannot, and should not, be confused.

Idealism, and more specifically Cartesianism, contemplates the existence of a pure consciousness without a world. Phenomenology, by contrast, focuses on examining the interaction between human cognitive capacity and our world as the fundamental structure through which it accesses the meaning of our existence. The phenomenological *epoché* does not doubt nor deny the existence of the world to which the ego belongs and in which the ego "co"-lives with other egos. In stark contrast to Cartesian skepticism, Husserl seeks to allow the world to inhabit us so that we can investigate it. The term "consciousness" comes from the Latin words *con* (with) and *scientia* (knowledge). *Epoché* is becoming "con-scientious" of the world that resides with us; it is not a denial or exclusion of the external world but an approach to metaphysical matters from a perspective that neither starts from outside the world nor without it.

Another criticism leveled against phenomenology is that it is merely an apology for consciousness in opposition to Freud's notion of the unconscious mind. However, the studies of Husserl himself (especially his writings on the internal time of consciousness) shake such criticisms by introducing terms like the in-conscious or the pre-phenomenological flow of consciousness, which he recognizes as prior to everything. Therefore, it precedes the very language of the ego and all active consciousness, and which we must recognize as "the ineffable." Moreover, these phenomenological studies on the deepest dimension of consciousness open the door for psychoanalysis itself to become a form of phenomenology, capable of inquiring into the most intimate experiences of consciousness, or into its very formation.

At times, using Nietzsche, Kierkegaard, or Freud as a spearhead, phenomenology has been accused of forgetting, or even denying, irrationality, passion, or love, and of focusing solely on the rational dimension of the human being. This contradicts the later writings of Husserl and the works of other phenomenologists to which we will pay attention in the upcoming chapters, which include precisely aspects of the human condition that transcend the limits of reason and even language, while raising and reopening the debate of whether phenomenology itself really manages to free itself from the limitations inherent in traditional modern philosophy.

By the late 20th century and early 21st century, criticisms of transcendental phenomenology have resurfaced, linking it (again) to Cartesian philosophy and, more specifically, rooting it in the concept of the *cogito*, that is, the "I think." These criticisms have questioned the self-satisfaction of the Cartesian *cogito* and the anthropocentrism it culminates in. Using Darwin, and his theory of the evolution of species, phenomenology is reminded that the human being, the subject, in the form of "I" or consciousness, may no longer be any ultimate foundation. From theories close to Freud's psychoanalysis, this view has been expanded, showing how the unconscious beats deep within our rationality. This critical approach is already reflected in the duality of the Apollonian and Dionysian in Nietzsche's philosophy, merging reason and passion. The Romantics also saw reason as inseparable from emotion.

This perspective reemerges powerfully in the structuralist theories led by Foucault. According to him, the subject is no longer an "I" or intimate transcendental consciousness but is a subject anchored in networks of power and history. In *History of Madness in the Classical Age*, Foucault explores how this rational subject, the pillar of modernity, faces new interpretations that question the humanism centered on the human being.[39] Under this optic, phenomenology is once again accused of being nothing more than a new metaphysics of presence that fails in its attempts to analyze temporality adequately. It is also said to be a self-centered philosophy, autonomous and self-contained, which ignores and minimizes any need for genuine transcendence, and as such, could be decentralized and superfluous. It has also been criticized for being a philosophy of identity, focused on autonomy, which, through its focus on objective and constitutive intentionality,

---

39. Michel Foucault, *History of Madness*, ed. Jean Khalfa, trans. Jonathan Murphy and Jean Khalfa (London: Routledge, 2006), part 1, chap. II.

seeks to control and suppress any difference or otherness. The phenomenological approach to identity has also been perceived as the conception of an autonomous and self-sufficient individual, closed off from diversity, reluctant to embrace different voices, perspectives, or alternative ways of life. Moreover, from a political perspective, it has been argued that phenomenology formulates the notion of a homogeneous humanity, deprived of the freedom to adopt divergent modes of existence. In short, the accusation is that transcendental phenomenology avoids fundamental issues like heteronomy and other critical aspects related to human understanding and ends up locking itself in an epistemological space with Cartesian and anthropomorphic roots based on a notion of the modern, self-centered subject.

In response to its stance, its critics have advocated for the need to move toward a more plural and democratic conception of existence, where individual consciousness does not occupy the central place. They also argue that the core of our reflection should be alterity, a commitment to the radical diversity of the other, emphasizing the importance of plurality and difference. In this sense, they direct a political critique toward phenomenology, questioning its approach to the concept of consciousness.

However, this perception is mistaken. Phenomenology emphasizes precisely the interaction between human beings and the world as the fundamental structure of its study. In *The origin of geometry*, Husserl himself analyzes this interaction and the intergenerational connection between humans, like waves of the sea, emerging and merging into one another, or like rivers converging in the ocean.[40]

Consciousness and the world, initially distant from other philosophical perceptions, reappear and merge in the discipline of phenomenology. In fact, and as we have shown earlier, Husserl does not restrict his analysis to isolated consciousness but always understands it in dialogue with the environment. This dialogue gains strength in Heidegger's work through *Dasein*, that is, being-

---

40. Jacques Derrida, *Edmund Husserl's "Origin of Geometry": An Introduction*, trans. John P. Leavey Jr. (Lincoln: University of Nebraska Press, 1989).

in-the-world as a starting point. Bridging the gaps and differences and respecting the critiques that Heidegger himself will direct at Husserl, it must be clear that they agree on the coexistence of the human being and the world, integrated into experience, whether in the form of intentional consciousness or *Dasein*. This co-existence should not, and cannot, be understood as a mere expression of the metaphysics of presence. Husserl himself argues in his work *Phenomenology of immanent consciousness of time* that consciousness is temporality and a flow of lived experiences, manifesting in the now: in what is yet to be and in what has already been. This temporal dimension emphasizes how the self-experiences and perceives the world in terms of temporality, and never outside of it.

The intentional consciousness of the world is protension, consciousness of the future, as an "advent," while also being retention, or consciousness of the past, generating simultaneous containment, or tension, between the future and the past. It is thus "where" and "how" consciousness is constituted. It is in light of this Husserlian conception of temporality that penetrates and allows the understanding of consciousness that Heidegger will later define Being as a "a future which makes present in the process of having been." In his work *Being and Time*, he will say that time exists, but as the time of consciousness or even as consciousness itself, and not outside of it. This intrinsically temporal character of consciousness and experience allows phenomenology to address the phenomenon in terms of both the manifest and the hidden in a single stroke. The criticisms and misunderstandings that have been directed, in our opinion unjustly, against phenomenology have thus been definitively clarified.

CHAPTER 10

THE MYSTERY OF GIVENNESS

To trace the origins of phenomenology, it is necessary to return to the teachings of Franz Brentano, which were later deepened and renewed by Husserl and Heidegger, respectively. In addition to being Husserl's professor, Franz Brentano was Sigmund Freud's thesis advisor. Therefore, he exerted an important influence on nothing less than the phenomenology inaugurated by Husserl, Freud's psychoanalysis, and Heidegger's hermeneutic phenomenology. His main texts, which can be regarded as the origin of phenomenology, are the essay *Down with Prejudices!* and the book *On the Several Senses of Being in Aristotle*, a work so influential that it inspired Heidegger to study philosophy.

One of Brentano's fundamental concepts is the intentionality of consciousness, a term that indicates that consciousness is directed toward things at the same time that things are directed toward consciousness. This kind of reciprocity, if we want to call it that, reveals to us the impossibility of studying things apart from consciousness or studying consciousness apart from things. Anyone who wishes to know consciousness or things cannot do so separately, as both are intimately intertwined or connected. Based on this structure proposed by Brentano, phenomenology will later become the study of our experiences of things and the ways in which things show themselves or present themselves to our consciousness.

Edmund Husserl's phenomenology concretely arises from these precepts developed by Brentano. In his work titled *The Idea of Phenomenology*, published in 1907, he agrees with him in affirming—against Kant—that pure things do not exist, for every perceived object resides in the mind or the individual consciousness of the perceiver. The presence or absence of an observer thus becomes a critical factor in determining the objective existence of any entity. The lack of a direct witness or interaction with an object leaves its state of being in a limbo of uncertainty, without being able to assert its presence in the realm of reality with certainty. For an object to be integrated into what we consider real, it must transcend the barrier of the invisible to break into a realm that is perceptible to a subject. That is, the essence of what we perceive as real and tangible is inextricably tied to our ability to experience it through the senses. This sensory connection between the subject and the object is what grounds our understanding of reality in the first place. Without the senses, the object would remain in our consciousness as a possibility, more than as a certainty. Therefore, in the broad spectrum of human experience, a phenomenon acquires meaning and is considered part of our reality only when it is inscribed within our conscious perception, thus making palpable what was in potential.

However, in order to reach this justified assertion, Husserl had to introduce a methodology to explain the meaning of the human being. This investigative procedure takes the form of philosophical self-reflection. From this, the researcher pauses and reflects on how they themselves relate to the world, to what is not them, to the other. Aware that presuppositions always taint all research, phenomenology establishes that each step must be freed from a priori concepts, that is, from prejudices developed independently of our experience.

As we have already advanced, Husserl refers to this freeing with the Greek term *epoché*, or "phenomenological reduction," which consists of suspending everything that, at first glance, we take for granted. It is important to clarify that this suspension is momentary and, therefore, does not equate to denying or doubting the existence of that which we set aside, as we will analyze in greater detail later. Thus, if the object of phenomenology is the experience and its meaning, our first reflective glance will place in parentheses what might seem obvious: the objective reality of what we perceive.

By focusing our gaze on consciousness itself, the first thing we "see" is that we are conscious of something, but we cannot presuppose that the perceived has an objective reality or a meaning independent of our consciousness. In other words, what the *epoché* establishes first, and this is perhaps the first great discovery of Husserl's phenomenology, is that we cannot study the world as if it were outside of consciousness, nor can we study consciousness as if it could be isolated from the world. For, as Husserl argues, when we reflect and focus our attention on consciousness, we realize that we cannot think about our consciousness without it being conscious of something.

All acts of consciousness, whether acts of thought, dreams, memories, or fantasies, are revealed to us as acts of something, without which they could not be objects of our reflection. Every act, therefore, whatever it may be, is always tied to something through an elemental relation that Husserl calls "intentionality." However, intentionality should not be understood as if it were an intention or desire of consciousness that springs from itself, generating its objects in its own image and likeness. On the contrary, intentionality describes a relation in which consciousness maintains, above all, a relation to an object, with this object being an intentional object of consciousness and not an object to which we can yet assign any objective reality.

For example, one could dream of a unicorn and describe that dream as an act of consciousness that is inexorably linked to an object, regardless of its possible real existence. Whether or not the unicorn has an objective existence, the unicorn dream has "taken place," and that is how we describe it. Based on this first exposition of the *epoché*, we can affirm that, for Husserl, studying things in our consciousness or cognitive potential, and not outside of it, allows us to know both consciousness and things as we know them. The study of experience, for Husserl, is based on the study of intentional consciousness, which is understood as the field of experience in which the objects of the world acquire meaning, regardless of whether their objective reality is possible or impossible.

Phenomenological reduction, then, could be understood as a methodological strategy that allows us to escape both possible prejudices and the "natural attitude," as Husserl himself calls it. This attitude is defined by a naive trust in the reality of what presents itself to consciousness, without recognizing any mystery. That is, it is assuming that the objective reality of the object, of nature in the case of the sciences, presents itself to consciousness as it truly is, with its own meaning, regardless of the cognitive and perceptive abilities of consciousness, without raising doubts or questions.

Furthermore, the natural attitude engages in a constant task of gathering judgments, managing contradictory relations, and organizing a complex structure of tools, which Marion will later call "paradoxes." This is done to make decisions in conflictive situations and to construct the foundation of science. Surprisingly, this process presents itself as if it were transparent and clear, containing no shadows or inaccessible aspects. However, the natural attitude conceals the flaws and weaknesses that underlie the entire structure, giving us an impression of solidity where there may not be any. For the natural attitude of consciousness is to be oriented toward things not with suspicion, but with trust and, as Husserl repeats on several occasions, with naivety.

The *epoché*, therefore, is the phenomenological response to the natural attitude. Now that we have more tools at our disposal, it is worth reiterating that *epoché* is not equivalent to the skeptical attitude characteristic of modernity. Suspending prejudice does not mean doubting the appearance of things or assuming that their true essence can only be understood through individual reasoning. The skeptical position argues that it is reason itself that establishes the nature of what surrounds us, rather than allowing things to reveal their true Being. In contrast to this approach, phenomenology, through the *epoché*, advocates for a suspension of this skepticism, urging us to set aside our preconceptions to welcome the essence of things as they present themselves to us.

Phenomenology, as a way of understanding philosophy, invites us to remain open to the influence of objects, to be permeable to their essence. Only through unconditional receptivity can we articulate lived experience. In contrast, holding onto an attitude of distrust and skepticism blocks our capacity to be genuinely affected by our environment. By softening these prejudices and allowing ourselves to be shaped by our experiences, we enable a true encounter with the real, which only then can be faithfully described. Thus, the authentic reality of things shall present itself to consciousness in the fullness of its Being.

In this context, the practice of the *epoché* leads us to total receptivity, which was called "meditation" both by Husserl and Heidegger at different stages. As we will explain later, meditation is a state we access once we have freed ourselves from prejudices. In this meditative state, the phenomenologist allows themselves to be surprised by the phenomenon. When the events experienced in meditation perfectly align with our expectations, there is a high probability that they are manifestations of our mind or fantasy. However, when what is experienced surprises us and breaks in, emerging without ties to our anticipations and projections, then we can have confidence in its authenticity. This detachment from our projections and openness to the unexpected ensures that what we experience is rooted in the reality of consciousness, of experience itself, beyond the shadows of imagination. Maintaining a skeptical and controlling attitude hinders the full manifestation of phenomena in our consciousness. If we doubt the existence and veracity of phenomena, we replace them with the conceptual constructs of reason. The *epoché*, on the other hand, represents an act of surrender that involves the deliberate suspension of critical judgment regarding the reality of the objective world.

The essence of phenomenology is to have trust in the givenness of things, without assuming a natural attitude that involves accepting that things, prior to their givenness, already contained their own rational meaning that we simply have to unravel and understand. Despite our inability to perceive them in their entirety, things reveal themselves to consciousness in their authentic essence as intentional objects of consciousness. This statement should not surprise us, for what it simply highlights is that every intentional object is given temporally, gradually, manifesting certain dimensions while simultaneously hiding itself. The object of knowledge is never an object that appears and is given fully formed, but quite the opposite. In other words, we only know an object to the extent that it reveals itself to us as a mystery that eludes our cognitive and perceptual capacities.

Therefore, we can affirm that phenomenology, thanks to the *epoché*, has unveiled its first object of study, which we have described as a structure formed by the correlation between consciousness and the intentional object, but which, at the same time, hides the existence of a mystery that resides deep within our own capacity to know. This mystery is not superficial or easy to discard, but instead is rooted deeply in the very essence of knowledge itself. For Husserl, knowledge appears as a mystery: we know that we know because we are aware of an object or experience. However, we do not know why that object is made known to us, that is, why we perceive it, dream about it, or remember it. Likewise, I can conceive of myself as a cognizing being, endowed with a conceptual framework for understanding, and I can do so because I have the capacity to objectify myself within the scope of my own study. Therefore, when we stop and reflect phenomenologically on this intentional correlation of consciousness with the object, and attempt to understand it, we find that we are confronted with an unexpected enigma. Rather than being something clear and defined, knowledge presents itself to us as full of nuances and complexities, challenging our expectations and inviting us to explore further.

CHAPTER 11

INTENTIONALITY AND KNOWLEDGE

The *epoché* and the enigma of transcendence

The inclination toward philosophical thought is intrinsically linked to mystery. It arises when it is no longer possible to avoid reflecting upon this enigmatic dimension of Being. It is essential to recognize that progress in understanding cannot occur without first defining the conditions that make it possible. For the present development, we will rely on some quotes carefully selected by Hernán G. Inverso in his article, *From the mystery of transcendence to the wonder of givenness: the enigma in The Idea of Phenomenology by Husserl* (Universitas Philosophica 71, 2018), which are particularly relevant to illuminate our analysis.

In order to shed light on the nature of mystery, this chapter will outline the general foundations of Husserl's phenomenological investigation. Within it, we already find the early traces of what will later become Jean-Luc Marion's "saturated phenomenon," which we briefly introduced in previous chapters.

Husserl himself introduces the characterization of the philosophical disposition, which is influenced by curiosity in the face of an enigmatic circumstance, with the premise that:

Die dem natürlichen Denken selbstverständliche Gegebenheit der Erkenntnisobjekte in der Erkenntnis wird zum Rätsel.

Section IV: Phenomenology of the Manifest and the Hidden

The unproblematic manner in which the object of cognition is given to natural thought to be cognized now becomes an enigma.[41]

The givenness progresses until it reaches a universal character, in such a way that all forms of certainty or trust are completely neutralized. And it continues explaining:

Denn objektive Triftigkeit der Erkenntnis überhaupt ist nach Sinn und Möglichkeit rätselhaft und dann auch zweifelhaft geworden, und exakte Erkenntnis wird dabei nicht minder rätselhaft als nicht exakte, wissenschaftliche nicht minder als vorwissenschaftliche.

For cognition's reaching its object has become enigmatic and dubious as far as its meaning and possibility are concerned, and exact cognition becomes thereby no less enigmatic than inexact, scientific knowledge no less than the pre-scientific.[42]

Husserl is telling us in these quotes that, in essence, every discovery constitutes a revelation. The scientist, who presupposes having mastery over the phenomena they study, often does not recognize that both the emergence and the understanding of these phenomena are, in themselves, acts of givenness and revelation that occur within the paradigm of the intentionality of consciousness. That is to say, no one who understands the matter could fail to be amazed in front of mathematical, physical, chemical, or any other kind of knowledge because behind every perception and every form of knowledge, there always lies the mystery of not knowing why that knowledge is given. We only know that it is given, and although my consciousness intends an object, I am unaware of the enigma of the givenness itself. This enigma grows and entirely

---

41. Edmund Husserl, *The Idea of Phenomenology*, trans. William P. Alston and George Nakhnikian, with an introduction by George Nakhnikian (The Hague: Martinus Nijhoff, 1973), Lecture I, 15.
42. Ibid., 20.

envelops knowledge, affecting the ability to understand and describe objects correctly and their intrinsic possibility, influencing each of their aspects.

This position of Husserl regarding the enigma of givenness should be understood as a response to the figure of Descartes, who, even without being constantly named, continues to appear in the background of a modern philosophical tradition whose convictions extend into the 18th century. In Husserl, unlike in Descartes, there is a sense of estrangement by which consciousness feels that the world is thrown at it. When it asks why, an insurmountable abyss opens up. Consciousness wonders why there are things there and what those things are—in other words, why can I know them? And who is the one who is knowing them?

These questions are part of Husserl's central approach, where he presents the strategy of "assigning the index of questionability [...] to the entire world" (*die ganze Welt ... die sich mit dem Index der Fraglichkeit zu verstehen*[43]), which he himself defines as the factor that leads toward an understanding that is completely free of doubt or ambiguity. Let us now examine this issue in more detail.

We can use suspicion as a means to access certainty. The ability to doubt one's own doubt radically differs from the naive openness toward the unknown. This critical stance, far from being blind acceptance, represents a deliberate search for understanding beyond the initial Cartesian skepticism. The process resembles what is known as the *analogia fidei*, or analogy of faith, a hermeneutical concept within the Reformed tradition. According to this principle, since it is considered that all the Scriptures form a coherent whole free from fundamental contradictions, any interpretation of a specific passage must be examined in the context of the entirety of biblical teachings. Essentially, we place our trust in the fact that the manifestation of any phenomenon reveals itself as it is in its presentation. The notion of mystery manifests particularly in two situations that we can use as illustrations. In the first, Husserl

---

43. Edmund Husserl, *Die Idee der Phänomenologie: Fünf Vorlesungen*, ed. Walter Biemel, Husserliana II (Den Haag: Martinus Nijhoff, 1950), 29. Translation mine.

examines the very viability of understanding when the question becomes absolute, in such a way that:

und ist der Erkenntnistheorie alle Erkenntnis ein Rätsel, so auch die erste, mit der sie selbst beginnt.

If all cognition must be a riddle to the epistemologist, so must any initial cognition with which epistemology itself begins be a riddle.[44]

What Husserl fails to explain is how it is possible for us to know anything; that is, why is it possible to know things? Unlike Cartesian doubt, as we have seen earlier, the *epoché* eliminates even the very ability to acquire knowledge. Whereas for Descartes, the question of how knowledge of the world is possible comes before knowing the world, in Husserl, the same question comes after because, from the phenomenological perspective, it is precisely because I know and am conscious of the world that I ask how it is possible to know it. Husserl's position does not differ greatly from Kant's in that both focus on analyzing the necessary prior conditions for the emergence of knowledge. Kant carefully examines the tools of understanding without applying them in practice. Although he delves into the bases that make knowledge possible, he refrains from addressing the objects of knowledge themselves. He focuses on clarifying the requirements for the cognition of phenomena, never venturing into a specific discussion of the phenomena themselves. In a way, and like Husserl, he assumes the trust that the world is donated to us, and it is from this givenness that the questions that are later addressed arise.

This evokes the Megarian paradoxes found in the fragments of *Meno*, 90a. Through these, it is shown that any effort aimed at knowledge leads to a standstill.

---

44. Edmund Husserl, *The Idea of Phenomenology*, trans. William P. Alston and George Nakhnikian, with an introduction by George Nakhnikian (The Hague: Martinus Nijhoff, 1973), Lecture II, 26.

Chapter 11: Intentionality and Knowledge

Meno — [i] And how will you search, Socrates, for what you absolutely do not know what it is? Indeed, [ii] which of the things you do not know will you set out to search for? [iii] And if you actually find it, how will you know that this is the one you did not know?[45]

To understand this quote more deeply, it will be necessary to analyze Socrates' version of the Paradox:

Socrates — I understand what you mean, Meno. Do you see the eristic argument you are introducing? That it is not possible for a person to search either for what they know or for what they do not know? Indeed, [1] they cannot search for what they know, because they already know it, and there is no need for such a search; [2] but they cannot search for what they do not know either, because they do not know what it is they should search for.[46]

The one who seeks to know cannot know. If we seek to know something we already know, it would be a lie that we are searching for it, while if we do not know it, we cannot search for it because we would not know what we are looking for. The one who seeks does not find, and the one who finds is because they were not really searching. This passage from *Meno* is already, in itself, a response to the Cartesian position, since it questions how Descartes could doubt the existence of a world external to the *cogito* if it was not already given beforehand. In other words, although Husserl affirms in his *Cartesian Meditations* that he follows Descartes' philosophical spirit (which, in certain aspects, cannot be denied at all), it is precisely because he follows this critical spirit that he must doubt the Cartesian doubt itself. He must put it in parentheses, since it detects the prejudice of doubting the existence of the world that is given to us and of which we are conscious, and without which we could not

---

45. Plato, *Meno*, in *Platonis Opera*, ed. John Burnet (Oxford: Oxford University Press, 1903), 80d5 – 8.
46. Ibid., 80e1 – 5.

even formulate the doubt itself. For as Husserl himself asserts in *Ideas I*, doubting the existence of the world of which I am permanently conscious would be to fall into the most absurd skepticism.

In this sense, the *epoché* is a correction of Cartesian doubt, since phenomenology does not "suspend" the existence of objective reality but rather suspends any judgment about it. In the same text, Husserl clarifies that even if that world were an illusion or even a hallucination, or if it were given to us in a way different from what we presume, the *epoché* in no case assumes a negative position regarding the existence of the world that is given to us. We suspend any thesis about the world, both the doubt about its existence and the affirmation of its objective reality. The Cartesian doubt, by which Descartes ends up simply accepting the *ego cogito* as an undoubtable, necessary reality completely separate from the world, implies that his approach merely replicates the traditional subject-object structure. Modern science is based on this structure and asserts that the world is an object with its own objective reality that pre-exists the mind. Descartes argues that the ego *cogito* pre-exists the world and that all meaning in the world can be deduced from it. As a consequence, instead of offering us a transcendental subjectivity, as Husserl does, Descartes ends up simply affirming a transcendental realism. All that Descartes has achieved with his method of doubt is to invert the order of a subject-object structure in which, in any case, the meaning of both the subject and the object is only the product of a deduction.

This first critique of Descartes helps to clarify the purpose of the *epoché* in relation to knowledge and the mystery it contains. First of all, then, it is a matter of attending, without prejudice, to the relationship between consciousness and its objects, but without affirming or denying the preexistence of one over the other, or vice versa. This leads phenomenology to address, without prejudice, the matter of transcendence, that is, how we can explain that the world is given in consciousness and that this is always consciousness-of-the-world. Husserl understands the issue of transcendence and immanence as an enigma when he asserts:

Chapter 11: Intentionality and Knowledge

sie ist das Rätsel, das der natürlichen Erkenntnis in den Weg tritt und den Antrieb für die neuen Forschungen bildet.

It is the riddle that stands in the path of cognition of the natural sort and is the incentive for new investigations.[47]

Accepting without doubt that the world is donated to consciousness is not a prejudice. On the contrary, the *epoché* frees us from all presuppositions concerning the relationship between consciousness and the world. We observe that the world, as transcendent to consciousness, appears a posteriori, since, unlike Descartes, we cannot deduce it from consciousness itself. In other words, it is a givenness, and therefore does not necessarily have to be given. The fact that the world is donated to consciousness is a marvel, precisely because it could have not been given. Therefore, by default, it is a relationship in which neither party is reducible to the other. This is why Husserl affirms that the world is necessarily transcendent to consciousness, and not merely a product of it.

es darf danach Transzendentes nicht als vergegeben benützt werden.

Nothing transcendent must be used as a presupposition.[48]

Therefore, the mysterious question that Husserl attempts to resolve is how it is possible for something that is "outside" of consciousness at one moment, that is, transcendent to it, to then be "inside."

das Wie ist rätselhaft, während das Dass absolut sicher ist.

But it is only the how that is puzzling, whereas the that is absolutely certain .[49]

---

47. Edmund Husserl, *The Idea of Phenomenology*, trans. William P. Alston and George Nakhnikian, with an introduction by George Nakhnikian (The Hague: Martinus Nijhoff, 1973), Lecture II, 28.
48. Ibid., Lecture II, 29.
49. Ibid., Lecture II, 29.

SECTION IV: PHENOMENOLOGY OF THE MANIFEST AND THE HIDDEN

The exposition of the enigmatic problem of transcendence, as a way of approaching the mystery of knowledge, leads Husserl to admit, as we have seen, the existence of knowledge as a fundamental premise and that which emerges after the *epoché* as a fundamental reality. That is to say, we ask ourselves why there is consciousness (of something) and how it is that (this something) is given, but we ask ourselves because it is undeniable that there is consciousness (of something). The consciousness of something, the relationship of consciousness with a world that transcends it and that is given to it, is prior to all Cartesian doubt and the transcendental ego that formulates it.

Husserl argues this first result of the *epoché* through the question of "being conscious of consciousness (of something)." If we ask whether we are conscious of consciousness and answer no, we are already acknowledging a certain consciousness: we are conscious of "not being conscious" of consciousness. That is to say, even the negative response will attest to the "givenness" of consciousness as an object of our reflection. In the process of grasping the enigmatic nature of certain subjects, a question arises: how can we make use of immanent data, and how can we access objects that lie beyond our immediate perception, thereby establishing a connection between them and the act of knowing? I am conscious of the tree, but I do not perceive consciousness itself as such; I know the tree, but I do not know the knowing itself of the tree. We cannot be conscious of consciousness by itself. All consciousness can only be given to us as the object of our reflective consciousness of consciousness when it is consciousness-of-something. The relationship of the tree to consciousness, in terms of the transcendent, must not—and cannot—be confused with a position of pure exteriority to consciousness.

Through intentionality, Husserl will explain the relationship of transcendence between the object and consciousness, a relationship that is neither objective exteriority nor mere deduction. Intentionality allows us to elucidate and determine both the access of consciousness to these objects and the unique relationship between the real aspects and those that are a construction of consciousness. Things are given, shown, they want to be known, because the being does not decline, it shows itself and wants to be known. We could even say it with

Heraclitus: "How can one hide from that which never sets?"[50] Nature loves to hide, but by showing itself, not by setting or declining. Let us recall for a moment Pythagoras, when he asserts in the "harmony of the spheres" that, since we arrive in the world, these sounds are always present, never cease, and therefore it is impossible to differentiate them from silence, for we are born with them. In that sense, we could speak of the knowledge of consciousness that goes unnoticed. Intentionality, in this context, refers to the process through which a singular connection is established, linking real elements with the intentional aspects of human consciousness, explaining that knowledge occurs because consciousness per se tends toward things, and these, in turn, tend toward consciousness.

Let us pay attention to the term that Husserl uses. The word *intentionality* comes from the Latin *intentio*, which in turn derives from *tendere*, meaning "to tend," in the sense of having a tendency toward something or someone. In this context, we can say that two fundamental elements converge: the givenness of the thing, which refers to the way it appears to consciousness, and the intentionality of the same consciousness, characterized by its tendency to not refer to itself but to what is not itself. In that sense, consciousness as such would be a constant projection beyond itself, toward the world. Its very nature would seem to be one of remaining inherently open and in connection with its surroundings. This kind of interaction between consciousness and the world gives rise to an intersection of perspectives that would later, especially in the field of hermeneutics, come to be known as a fusion of horizons. The intentionality of consciousness, on the one hand, and the givenness of the object, on the other, constitute the phenomenon: that which constitutes the realm of direct experience of consciousness.

As we have said, this transcendence of the intentional object should not be confused with any type of objective exteriority. As Husserl himself warns, it is a transcendence that is, paradoxically, immanent to consciousness, for the object must dwell immanently

---

50. Heraclitus, in John Burnet, *Early Greek Philosophy*, 4th ed. (London: A. & C. Black, 1920), 135 (frag. B16= DK 22B16).

in consciousness so that consciousness itself can become the object of our reflection. As we saw earlier, we can think of the tree, but we cannot think on its own of the act of consciousness of thinking about the tree. To think about the act of consciousness through which we think of the tree, we must think of it as thought-of-the-tree. That is to say, according to Husserl, the object of consciousness is transcendent to consciousness because it is neither a piece of it nor deduced from it, yet at the same time, it is immanent to it. In other words, that which appears after the *epoché* is a phenomenon constituted by the immanent transcendence of the intentional object of consciousness.

Thus, when we carry out a phenomenological exploration of the transcendent, the phenomenological procedure under no circumstances admits considering the objective reality of that transcendent object. We only turn our attention to the domain of thoughts, reflections, and any other acts of consciousness. These belong, as we have also seen earlier, to a sphere that "it is free from the riddle of transcendence" (*ist vom rätsel der Transzendenz frei*)[51]. Even if transcendental objects exist, we do not know them in their transcendence, but in the immanence of consciousness. In other words, there may be things that transcend my consciousness, but when I know them, I do not know them outside of it, but as things-in-consciousness, that is, as transcendent but in the immanence of consciousness. It is impossible for us to consider as real what transcends the threshold of consciousness, for we could not attend to the act that thinks, feels, or dreams of that object foreign to consciousness. This allows us to affirm that we cannot consider the existence of anything outside of consciousness and that, therefore, there is nothing other than consciousness. That is why phenomenology is, as it was sometimes called in the beginning, "the science of consciousness." This leads us to affirm that, for Husserl, Being, or that which is, is consciousness. That is, the revelation of the intentional object of consciousness is not just another characteristic,

---

51. Edmund Husserl, *The Idea of Phenomenology*, trans. William P. Alston and George Nakhnikian, with an introduction by George Nakhnikian (The Hague: Martinus Nijhoff, 1973), Lecture III, 33.

trait, or function of the object, but is its very and only being. For this reason, and as Marion later explained, it is "the revelation revealing itself" because, outside of revelation, there is nothing, not even the intentional object as such.

This phenomenological approach, therefore, not only calls into question the method of Cartesian doubt and the transcendental realism to which it condemns us, but it also questions the Kantian noumenon and, therefore, the foundations of Kantian epistemology. Kant defines the phenomenon of knowledge as the appearance of the "thing in itself" (noumenon), whose existence precedes the realm of the cognitive capacities of the subject. But for phenomenology, there is nothing outside of the phenomenon, that is, the appearance, the revelation itself, the intentional object. Phenomenology suspends all judgment about the possibility or impossibility of what Kant calls the "thing in itself," that is, an object with its own objective reality, outside of consciousness. If the *epoché* is important, it is because it precisely unveils the phenomenon in all its phenomenality, in all its being, as appearing, as revelation. For Husserl, the phenomenon is not a trait or mode of being of an object, say, pure and original, as in the Kantian phenomenon, but it is its own showing, and it is in that showing that the experience occurs. There is no object and phenomenon separately; rather, the object is a phenomenon inasmuch as it is given or revealed in consciousness as an intentional object.

Therefore, in a certain sense, phenomenon and experience are two terms that go hand in hand. To be considered as such, a phenomenon must manifest itself in the intuitive perception of the subject, which implies that the existence of a phenomenon is conditioned by its appearance in this intuition. In the absence of this manifestation, the phenomenon lacks existence, which would, in turn, imply that the act of consciousness in which it manifests would also lack existence because, as we have seen, only the act correlated with an object can be the object of reflection and understanding. Here, we are wielding, following Husserl but also Marion, what we can call "the simultaneity or concomitance" that defines the relationship between givenness and intentionality. On one hand, the givenness describes the process through which the object presents itself to consciousness, while, on the other, intentionality characterizes the mode of being of consciousness, always stretched, open to what is not itself and transcends it. That is to say, the act of appearance of the object in consciousness and the orientation of consciousness toward the object occur interdependently, highlighting a reciprocal interaction where each influences and defines the other. This dual dimension reflects a continuous dialogue between consciousness and its object, emphasizing the interactive nature of perception and knowledge. If an object, supposedly external to our mind, does not integrate into the sphere of consciousness, it will remain out of the reach of our knowledge. Thus, from the perspective of phenomenology, the cognition of any object necessarily implies its assimilation into our consciousness, understanding this assimilation as transcendence in immanence.

Perception and intentionality in Aristotle

The position of phenomenology regarding intentionality has its origins in Aristotle, who held that the beginning of human knowledge lies in sensory perception. He proposed that all learning starts from the interaction with the environment through the senses. Through this sensory interaction, the human being comes into contact with the realities of the world, although this initial, eminently sensory, and ephemeral knowledge does not exhaust the depth of knowledge. He identifies different strata or degrees in the spectrum of knowledge, starting with sensible knowledge, which is direct and transitory, fading with the sensation that originates it and which is characteristic of less complex beings. In more advanced organisms, this sensory knowledge, combined with memory and imagination, evolves into more enduring forms of knowing. In humans, this process is enriched and leads to the formation of experience, the result of memory. Although this experience does not reveal the ultimate causes of objects, it does allow for the affirmation of their existence, opening the way to the knowledge of the particular.

Chapter 11: Intentionality and Knowledge

However, for Aristotle, the pinnacle of knowledge is not reached until theoretical or contemplative knowledge, which represents the highest aspiration toward wisdom. This supreme level of knowledge is achieved through the intellect, which is capable of understanding substances through their causes and principles, thus understanding their unity, identity, and general nature. The Stagirite differentiates humans from other living beings by their capacity for thought, elevating knowledge as a distinctive human virtue. Thus, since the sensible world is the stage of our existence, sensation is posited as the foundation of knowledge. This stage, in which all fundamental experience occurs, consists of matter and form. Matter constitutes the primordial essence from which knowledge arises, while form defines the essence of things. Unlike sensory perception, which captures the individual and requires the physical presence of the object, human thought reaches the essence, capturing the universal within the particular.

Thus, Aristotle emphasizes that the reality of substances is first apprehended sensorially, and then, through mental representation, integrates both the material and sensory aspects and the formal aspects of the substance. The form, inherent in the substance, reveals that the sensible world—the world we see, perceive, and experience—constitutes our only reality, composed of the individual substances we know, each one an amalgam of matter and form. For Aristotle, knowledge arises from the incorporation of the object within the subject, in the quality of the object. This process means that, in knowing something, the subject is transformed to some extent into the object of its knowledge, since the essence or form of the object is internalized in the subject. This internalization changes the subject and makes it more similar to the known object. As the subject acquires knowledge of the object, it becomes more like it, given that the form of the object becomes part of its being. This theme is called "the first intentional," and expresses the presence of the object in the subject. The second intentional is the concept, but that is another matter.

Section IV: Phenomenology of the Manifest and the Hidden

This same internalization of the object in the subject and the subsequent resemblance of the subject to the object is clearly elucidated in Talmudic thought, as we can see next:

הִנֵּה, כָּל שֵׂכֶל כְּשֶׁמַּשְׂכִּיל וּמַשִּׂיג בְּשִׂכְלוֹ אֵיזֶה מֻשְׂכָּל, הֲרֵי הַשֵּׂכֶל תּוֹפֵס אֶת הַמֻּשְׂכָּל וּמַקִּיפוֹ בְּשִׂכְלוֹ, וְהַמֻּשְׂכָּל נִתְפָּס וּמֻקָּף וּמְלֻבָּשׁ בְּתוֹךְ הַשֵּׂכֶל שֶׁהִשִּׂיגוֹ וְהִשְׂכִּילוֹ. וְגַם הַשֵּׂכֶל מְלֻבָּשׁ בַּמֻּשְׂכָּל בְּשָׁעָה שֶׁמַּשִּׂיגוֹ וְתוֹפְסוֹ בְּשִׂכְלוֹ. דֶּרֶךְ מָשָׁל: כְּשֶׁאָדָם מֵבִין וּמַשִּׂיג אֵיזוֹ הֲלָכָה בַּמִּשְׁנָה אוֹ בַּגְּמָרָא לַאֲשׁוּרָהּ עַל בּוּרְיָהּ הֲרֵי שִׂכְלוֹ תּוֹפֵס וּמַקִּיף אוֹתָהּ, וְגַם שִׂכְלוֹ מְלֻבָּשׁ בָּהּ בְּאוֹתָהּ שָׁעָה. וְהִנֵּה, הֲלָכָה זוֹ, הִיא חָכְמָתוֹ וּרְצוֹנוֹ שֶׁל הַקָּדוֹשׁ־בָּרוּךְ־הוּא, שֶׁעָלָה בִּרְצוֹנוֹ, שֶׁכְּשֶׁיִּטְעוֹן רְאוּבֵן כָּךְ וְכָךְ דֶּרֶךְ מָשָׁל וְשִׁמְעוֹן כָּךְ וְכָךְ – יִהְיֶה הַפְּסָק בֵּינֵיהֶם כָּךְ וְכָךְ. וְאַף אִם לֹא הָיָה וְלֹא יִהְיֶה הַדָּבָר הַזֶּה לְעוֹלָם, לָבוֹא לְמִשְׁפָּט עַל טְעָנוֹת וּתְבִיעוֹת אֵלּוּ, מִכָּל מָקוֹם, מֵאַחַר שֶׁכָּךְ עָלָה בִּרְצוֹנוֹ וְחָכְמָתוֹ שֶׁל הַקָּדוֹשׁ־בָּרוּךְ־הוּא, שֶׁאִם יִטְעֹן זֶה כָּךְ וְזֶה כָּךְ, יִהְיֶה הַפְּסָק כָּךְ, הֲרֵי כְּשֶׁאָדָם יוֹדֵעַ וּמַשִּׂיג בְּשִׂכְלוֹ פְּסַק זֶה כַּהֲלָכָה הָעֲרוּכָה בְּמִשְׁנָה אוֹ גְמָרָא אוֹ פּוֹסְקִים, הֲרֵי זֶה מַשִּׂיג וְתוֹפֵס וּמַקִּיף בְּשִׂכְלוֹ רְצוֹנוֹ וְחָכְמָתוֹ שֶׁל הַקָּדוֹשׁ־בָּרוּךְ־הוּא, דְּלֵית מַחֲשָׁבָה תְּפִיסָא בֵּיהּ וְלֹא בִּרְצוֹנוֹ וְחָכְמָתוֹ, כִּי אִם בְּהִתְלַבְּשׁוּתָם בַּהֲלָכוֹת הָעֲרוּכוֹת לְפָנֵינוּ, וְגַם שִׂכְלוֹ מְלֻבָּשׁ בָּהֶם.

(רבי שניאור זלמן מלאדי, ספר התניא, ליקוטי אמרים, פרק ה')

Now, when an intellect conceives and comprehends a concept with its intellectual faculties, this intellect grasps the concept and encompasses it. This concept is [in turn] grasped, enveloped, and enclothed within that intellect which conceived and comprehended it. The mind, for its part, is also clothed in the concept at the time it comprehends and grasps it with the intellect. For example, when a person understands and comprehends, fully and clearly, any *halachah* in the *Mishnah* or *Gemara*, his intellect grasps and encompasses it and, at the same time, is clothed in it. Consequently, as the particular *halachah* is the wisdom and will of God, for it was His will that when, for example, Reuben pleads in one way and Simeon in another, the verdict as between them shall be thus and thus; and even should such a litigation never have occurred, nor would it ever present itself for judgment in connection with such disputes and claims, nevertheless, since it has been the will and wisdom of the Holy One, blessed is

Chapter 11: Intentionality and Knowledge

He, that in the event of a person pleading this way and the other [litigant] pleading that way, the verdict shall be such and such—therefore, when a person knows and comprehends with his intellect such a verdict in accordance with the law as it is set out in the *Mishnah*, *Gemara*, or *Poskim* (codes), he has thus comprehended, grasped, and encompassed with his intellect the will and wisdom of the Holy One, blessed is He, Whom no thought can grasp, nor His will and wisdom, except when they are clothed in the laws that have been set out for us. [Simultaneously] the intellect is also clothed in them [the divine will and wisdom].

(Rabbi Shneur Zalman of Liadi, *Tanya*, "*Likkutei Amarim*," chapter 5)

Setting aside the differences between Talmudic philosophy, Aristotle, and Husserl, this notion of the internalization of the object in the subject and the corresponding resemblance of the subject to the object helps us understand the phenomenon. As defined by phenomenology, the phenomenon refers to the interaction between the world of consciousness and the consciousness of the world, showing that things, when known, dwell within us, even though they are not a piece of our consciousness.

CHAPTER 12

PERCEPTION AND INTUITION ACCORDING TO HUSSERL

On transcendence in immanence

Often, our expectations do not align with the reality of events that unfold in our daily lives. This discrepancy causes us frustration. For example, we buy a lottery ticket hoping that it will be the winning one, but the inevitable disappointment arises when our number does not win. This phenomenon illustrates a universal human tendency: the propensity to feel deceived when results do not match our hopes or desires. Expectation, fueled by our own longings and perceptions of what is just or deserved, collides with the wall of objective reality, thus triggering feelings of frustration and discontent. One strategy to mitigate experiences of frustration is to manage our expectations and recognize the unpredictable nature of life.

The experience of frustration seems to be rooted in a view that the act of consciousness, in this case, longing, maintains a very specific relationship with the desired object. This relationship corresponds to a structure that, particularly in the Western world, has been internalized and considered valid and unquestionable. It is based on understanding human beings as subjects who interact with objects in a cause-and-effect model. This chapter, following the line of inquiry opened in the pages preceding it, offers a revision of this structure. To do so, we will delve again into the notion of intentionality in consciousness and immanent transcendence, and we will do so based on the concepts of sensible intuition and categorial intuition as proposed by Husserl.

Section IV: Phenomenology of the Manifest and the Hidden

In *Shōbōgenzō Bukkojoji* (*Going Beyond Buddha*), Dōgen wrote:

> The vast sky does not hinder the white clouds from flying. These are Shitou's words. The vast sky does not hinder the vast sky. Just as the vast sky does not hinder the vast sky from flying, white clouds do not hinder white clouds. White clouds fly with no hindrance. White clouds' flying does not hinder the vast sky's flying. Not hindering others is not hindering self. It is not that self and others need or have no hindrance. None of these requires no-hindrance or remains in no-hindrance. This is the no-hindrance brought out in the phrase The vast sky does not hinder the white clouds from flying. [52]

At dawn, the sky adorns itself with clouds of pure white that, as the sun rises and the day unfolds, dissolve beyond our visual reach. We are filled with curiosity about their origin, their process of transformation, and their eventual disintegration. The white cloud emerges before us as an enigma: its initial manifestation, its fading, and its intrinsic essence. This cloud, in its fundamental nature, is free from any bond, floating without a determined beginning or end. However, its existence is palpable. Every entity possesses this ephemeral and mystical quality, devoid of an obvious primordial origin. The white clouds move without following a fixed path, devoid of a clear goal or purpose to fulfill, immune to disappointment, as the absence of expectations precludes the emergence of frustration.

The experience of life, when circumscribed to defined goals, invariably leads to disenchantment. Those whose thoughts are directed toward specific ends find themselves in a state of tension and discontent, as this contradicts the inherently indeterminate nature of the universe. The attempt to impose a personal will in the face of the immensity of the whole translates into a conflict destined

---

52. Dōgen, *Shōbōgenzō Bukkojoji, Going Beyond Buddha*, trans. Kazuaki Tanahashi and Mel Weitsman (n.p.: n.d.), 5.

for defeat; no matter how intense, human effort proves insufficient against the magnitude of the Absolute.

The white cloud, allowing itself to be carried by the wind, offers no resistance. Being free from the pursuit of dominion is precisely what makes it ethereal and invincible and allows it to dissolve into the whole. A similar idea, though expressed differently, already shines through in the book of Matthew in the New Testament, where we read:

> Then Jesus said to his disciples: "If anyone would come after me, let him deny himself and take up his cross and follow me. For whoever would save his life will lose it, but whoever loses his life for my sake will find it. For what will it profit a man if he gains the whole world and forfeits his soul? Or what shall a man give in return for his soul?
>
> (Matthew, 16:24–26)

The inevitability of defeat awaits one who insists on reaching a specific purpose, as such insistence directly opposes the essential character of what it means to exist. In this way, the white cloud stands as an emblem of the infinity of possibilities, welcoming the totality of what exists without distinction. This is the essence of meditative practice, which is not defined as a path in the traditional sense but rather as a wandering without a precise destination, a progression-free from all pretension. It is essential to recognize that the inclination toward defining purposes and goals is an intrinsic characteristic of the human psyche. Therefore, the idea of living without a determined end seems incomprehensible at first, as it is in the search for and accomplishment of goals that the mind finds sustenance.

The paradox arises, however, when one questions the ultimate purpose of practices like meditation without realizing that, at its core, meditation represents a state of mental vacuity, a total immersion in the present, devoid of any orientation, in which the simple act of being becomes the final goal. Existence acknowledges a single space, here, and a single moment, now. When extended beyond these temporal and spatial parameters, our purposes initiate a projection process toward the future based on what has already been lived in the past. Let us imagine a white cloud in the sky, freed from the chains of time and objectives, floating in the present as a part of an eternal continuum.

Human consciousness is in a constant search for meaning, goals, and purposes, whether of a worldly or spiritual nature. As the importance of the material diminishes, its search for utility shifts toward the spiritual. The mind attempts to fill its existential void with some form of meaning. Buddha's teaching reveals to us that true spirituality lies in the liberation of consciousness from any end, thus implicating the overcoming of the mind itself, transforming into an entity without thoughts. This analogy of the white cloud illustrates the understanding of life as an incessant flow, without a predetermined form, challenging any conception of a static and permanent identity. The essence of existence is change and transformation, a constant dynamism that opposes the crystallization of specific identities and forms.

Already in the realm of Western philosophy, Heidegger proposes a reinterpretation of the fundamental nature of metaphysics, challenging the notion that this discipline is limited to the exploration of abstract and universal concepts. In his view, metaphysics delves into the study of matters that essentially affect our existence and are crucial to our life. Heidegger argues that the true domain of metaphysics lies in addressing those questions that directly affect the essence of the human being, engaging in an inquiry into the meaning of Being, the constitution of reality, and how we interact with our environment. His approach suggests a philosophical practice that surpasses merely theoretical speculation, orienting toward an exploration of those elements that significantly shape our life experience.

Both Heidegger and Nietzsche can be interpreted as critics of the metaphysical tradition, arguing against the tendency to detach the essence of Being from the immediacy of lived experience. Nietzsche vehemently criticizes what he calls "Platonism," for its tendency to value a world of ideal forms above the perceivable reality. He asserts that this approach leads to alienation of the individual from their own existence and lived experiences. This rejection targets the notion of a truth that lies outside the individual, implicit in external structures such as sacred texts, belief systems, religions, or academic methodologies. He argues that these structures are opposed to the idea of an intrinsic truth, which is reached after an introspective journey to the core of one's being.

These two perspectives on the search for Truth find parallels in the theological realm, specifically in the conceptions known as the via *exterioris* and the via *interioris*. The former advocates for the search for the Divine in the exterior, possibly in the heavenly realm or in tangible religious manifestations, a view that Saint Thomas Aquinas vigorously defended. In contrast, the via *interioris*, promoted by Saint Augustine of Hippo, holds that true understanding of God is found by exploring the depths of the human soul. This dichotomy between the externalization and internalization of the search for Truth illustrates a fundamental tension in human experience, even within the same religious confession. While Truth is conceived as something that resides within us, it is also presented as something that transcends us.

Nietzsche and Heidegger's critiques of metaphysics are directed along this same line. They question the foundations of our traditional conceptions of Truth. They also invite a reconsideration of how we relate to our environment, our beliefs, and ultimately, to ourselves. This dialogue between introspection and transcendence reflects the complexity of the human search for meaning in a world that constantly challenges us to reconcile the internal with the external, the immanent with the transcendent. In reality, the inside and outside are illusory. When the walls of the room fall, the boundaries between inside and outside disappear. Just like the relationship between the ocean and the wave, the ocean is both inside and outside and is the wave simultaneously.

This reconceptualization demands philosophical reflection that transcends the traditional confines of metaphysical abstraction, focusing attention on discerning the principles that underlie our daily reality. Heidegger's perspective emphasizes the importance of engaging with problems that have a tangible impact on our existence, thus promoting a deeper and more applied understanding of metaphysics, focused on the more intimate and significant dimensions of human experience.

Sensible, eidetic, and categorial intuitions

This relationship between interiority and exteriority, namely, between the immanent and the transcendent, plays a fundamental role in phenomenology, even if the issue is not directly thematized. Husserl, who addresses this issue in particular, initially proposed that the intentional objects of consciousness are endowed with an *eidos*, or "essence," a fundamental notion originally inspired by Platonic ideas. According to Plato, every singular object ultimately refers to universal ideas. Likewise, Edmund Husserl postulates that there is a fundamental essence inherent in each phenomenon. This implies that every experience or phenomenological manifestation reveals certain elements of reality, which Husserl identifies as noema.

The concept of noema refers to the meaning or specific content of an experience as perceived by consciousness. Complementary to the noema, noesis refers to the cognitive dynamics or the act of consciousness by which the phenomenon is grasped. Thus, Husserl understood the interaction between noesis and noema as the essential structure in which reality acquires its meaning. In this structure, the noema is that aspect, essence, or idea of the real that becomes present in consciousness when it pays attention, observes, or reflects on a phenomenon. Every event or phenomenological manifestation, therefore, reveals an aspect of the Being of the object, which we refer to as essence or noema and which, as such, represents the dimension of reality apprehended by our conscious perception.

This cognitive structure is important in Husserl's phenomenology, who holds that specific objects are revealed to consciousness along with essences and through them. Above all, this means that the physical perception of an object, in the first instance, only determines the perception of an "something," still lacking identity.

CHAPTER 12: PERCEPTION AND INTUITION ACCORDING TO HUSSERL

Therefore, whether it is a tree or a row of trees, perception only offers us something indeterminate. In this sense, for Husserl, perception equates to the act of consciousness that is capable of extracting a singular thing from a context. However, this is not the extraction or perception of a crude corporeality (*körper*) of the perceived. Rather, it is a perception that is always accompanied and linked by imagination, through which what we perceive is not the ontic dimension (*körper*) of an object but what we might call its living corporeality, what Husserl called *leib*, namely, the living dimension that beats within the onticity of the object.

The importance of imagination in Husserl's work lies in the fact that it allows him to present a notion of perception that is not confined within the limits of empirical reality. If that were the case, phenomenology would end up reduced to a mere expression of neo-realism, for it would have to accept that empirical reality precedes the knowledge and understanding of it, a stance that directly conflicts with Husserl's phenomenology. By linking perception with imagination, he considers the object of perception as an intentional object whose "existence" does not depend on an assumed objective reality of it, but on its appearance in consciousness, whether it is a horse or a unicorn. In other words, what perception presents to consciousness is the object in all its potentiality and not in its mere actuality. At the same time, it should be clarified that, by itself, perception does not embody any meaning, although it does equate to the foundations or the bases upon which consciousness will confer meaning to the object. That is to say, while perception alone does not provide us with a fully meaningful object, nothing could have any meaning without perception.

Husserl introduces the topics of intuition and essences in this field of perception. He begins by referring to the intuition of essences, or eidetic intuition, as the act through which we perceive the essences that allow the perceived object—or that which is presented to consciousness as a "something"—to appear to us as what it is. For example, in that "something" indeterminate that perception offers us, one does not simply see a red square box, but the essences "box," "square," and "red," just as one does not see a

135

figure with three faces but the triangle as an idea. Husserl states that what we first perceive intelligibly are the essences through which that concrete and particular object is given to us. In our example, it is given to us as "a red square box" in which one stores certain objects. This eidetic intuition designates the ability to see the essences that determine the perceived thing in its potentiality, but now in greater determination, that is, as a thing actualized: "that red square box." However, the perceived object does not contain just one essence, but several: "box," "square," "red," and so on. Husserl poses a fundamental question: How do we manage to intuit different essences in combination with each other? This question is philosophically important, because without this other ability, we would only see essences separately and would never fully see a single "red square box."

At this point, Husserl introduces what he himself calls "categorical intuition." He defines it as the act that conceives the laws or formal categories through which, ultimately, we can see the object in its fullness of meaning. To explain this point, Husserl differentiates between "material essences," which depend on sensible perception, and their formal categories, which are "empty essences" incapable of being represented through the senses or imagination. The "empty essences" are essences in the sense of laws that articulate and connect the "material essences" to each other. For example, the essence "color" must always be accompanied by the essence "material thing," since it would be impossible to perceive "color" without "extension." In this sense, categories are formal laws that pulse within the internal dimension of material essences. Husserl also calls categories "basic concepts of pure logic" and mentions some of them, such as property, unity, identity, plurality, number, totality, part, and so on.

Husserl argues that eidetic intuition and categorical intuition occur simultaneously and one within the other, and it is only in this combination that objects can be given to our consciousness with full meaning. Once we have perceived an object, that is, we have extracted it from a context and singularized it, intuition is the combination of acts that allows the object to appear in consciousness as an object with meaning. That is, the object did not have a fully formed meaning before it became the object of our consciousness, just as it is not consciousness that injects meaning into the object as such. On the contrary, the object is given to the capacities of the subject who perceives and thinks it. Therefore, every object perception involves the capturing of the material and categorical essences that form the meaning of that reality we perceive, since, if we did not perceive these essences, we would not perceive the object as what it is.

This approach provoked criticism of Husserl and his phenomenology, with some accusing it of being a variation of Plato's philosophy of ideas. In response to such criticism, Husserl clarified his position in the second edition of the *Logical Investigations*. In it, he denied the independent existence of ideal entities, a stance that he considered philosophically outdated, and stated that things do not exist autonomously, but rather have value in and for consciousness. Dialoguing with the "truths in themselves" of Bolzano and reinterpreting the Platonic doctrine according to Lotze, his perspective became aligned with the theory of values: Being is not, but has value. Lotze argued that Being, in itself, does not exist, but acquires relevance through the consciousness that conceives it, becoming a truth relative to it. In a sense, this position deprives Being of independent existence, that is, transcendent in relation to the consciousness that conceives it, relegating it to being a concept valued by and for consciousness.

In this sense, consciousness values the objects it finds within itself, since it is impossible for it to generate something *ex nihilo* outside of itself. In other words, the world is not a construct created randomly by consciousness. Trying to conceive and describe something entirely unknown is a futile exercise because, if we conceive it, it already forms part of our consciousness. Unlike the abstract ideality of universals, Husserl argues that ideas possess no qualities outside of consciousness. Hence, intelligibility occurs solely within the bounds of sensible perception, which he regards as the domain of true reality.

Sensible intuition, enriched by the categorial intuition, allows entities to disclose themselves in consciousness, thereby forming an authentic and concrete experience. This cognitive mechanism enables a deep and precise understanding of the primordial truths that shape our environment. The phenomenological perspective highlights human beings' intrinsic faculty to identify, through an unmediated intuition, the essential foundations that structure and give meaning to the multiplicity of phenomena that surround them. This approach emphasizes a shift toward a deeper and more authentic appreciation of reality. It privileges direct access to essence over the indiscriminate accumulation of empirical data and emphasizes the importance of an elevated perception for the philosophical understanding of existence.

For instance, let us say we perceive a book. Our sensible intuition is activated: visually, we identify its red color, and through touch, we perceive its hard cover, thus transcending mere sensory attributes to recognize the object as a whole. While we perceive the book through the senses, its essence unfolds beyond these perceptions, inviting the intervention of eidetic intuition, which grasps its deeper concept. Finally, categorial intuition extends beyond the tangible and the episodic toward the recognition of universal and eternal properties, which constitute the fundamental being of entities.

Sensible intuition allows us to discern details such as color, taste, shape, smell, and texture, while eidetic intuition captures the intrinsic essence of objects. Eidetic and categorical intuitions teach us that understanding objectively implies a profound interpretation that integrates our personal perceptions, surpassing mere physical observation to achieve a holistic understanding of reality.

The intentionality as original openness to the world

The matter of perception and the intuition of essences, both material and categorical, must always be understood in coordination with intentionality. At the beginning of the fourth lesson in *The Idea of Phenomenology – Five Lectures* Husserl states:

> *Die Erkenntniserleibnisse, das gehört zu ihrem Wesen, haben eine intentio.*

Chapter 12: Perception and Intuition according to Husserl

> Cognitive mental processes (and this belongs to their essence) have an *intentio*.[53]

This implies that our experiences not only denote and generate something, but also focus beforehand on an object. This object, whether physically present or not, retains a nature distinct and separate from the experience itself, as we pointed out earlier. In such a way that:

> *das Gegenständliche kann erscheinen, kann im Erscheinen eine gewisse Gegebenheit haben, während es gleichwohl weder real im Erkenntnisphänomen ist, noch auch sonst als cogitatio ist.*

> And what is objective can appear, can have a certain kind of givenness in appearance, even though it is at the same time neither genuinely (*reell*) within the cognitive phenomenon, nor does it exist in any other way as a *cogitatio*.[54]

In our consciousness, objects like trees or houses, present in our perception, are not defined as mere thoughts, but as entities whose existence transcends our cognition, being known beyond mere conscious perception. When we state that "this book does not exist," we transform its existence into a mental concept. This process illustrates that a book is not simply an emotion or thought; it is a perception, even if it does not translate into a tangible entity. The same could be said of every act of consciousness, since, as we have previously outlined, according to Husserl, perception is intertwined with imagination.

In the sphere of consciousness, the non-existence of an object, such as a unicorn or a winged horse, does not imply its absolute absence, but rather underscores the nature of our perception and cognition, where what is perceived is not always a direct component of our conscious reality. It is contradictory to assert the non-existence

---

53. Edmund Husserl, *The Idea of Phenomenology*, trans. William P. Alston and George Nakhnikian, with an introduction by George Nakhnikian (The Hague: Martinus Nijhoff, 1973), Lecture IV, 43.
54. Ibid.

of an object, because at the moment its absence is stated, it is granted a kind of reality in the realm of thought that turns it into an intentional object of consciousness. The moment an "object" appears in consciousness as mentioned or as an intentional object, both sensible and categorical intuitions come into play to confirm or frustrate our expectations. For example, I could mention a unicorn until perception and intuition confirm or deny it. But even if they deny it, the unicorn will still be an object of my imagination, which is another act of consciousness, and will retain its intentional existence in my consciousness. The same could be said of memories. In other words, the mere act of reflecting on or speaking about the non-existence of an object incorporates it into our consciousness and assigns it a mode of being in the world of thought. The non-existence of something does not eliminate its existence in the realm of thought. This generates a fascinating philosophical paradox about what it means to exist and how our perception shapes the reality of objects.

The notions of sensible and categorical intuition actively contribute to grounding both intentionality and the immanent transcendence with which Husserl himself defines the nature of the intentional object of consciousness. Moreover, intuition emphasizes the intricate relationship between the concepts of being and non-being, proposing that the essence of an object can transcend its physical presence to nest in the abstract realms of thought and discourse. This approach invites us to consider how conceptual and linguistic dimensions complement and expand our understanding of existence, beyond the merely observable. In other words, the existence of an object does not depend solely on our consciousness, since, as we have previously indicated, consciousness and the object are distinct entities, though necessarily interdependent. The key to this paradox, as we have called it, lies in the following distinction: when we declare the non-existence of a book, we transform it into a conceptual entity. However, in the sphere of non-conscious perception, a book becomes an indefinable entity, known only through our internal perception. This reality highlights that the perception and knowledge of objects transcend the simple categories of physical or mental existence. A book is not only part of consciousness, but it is more accurately perceived as a sensory impression, distinct from a concrete thought. Beyond our conscious perception, the existence of the book sinks into the realm of the indefinite, and we know it internally only as a perception. Therefore, this entity is neither exclusively defined by consciousness nor by its physical materiality, but resides in a perceptual space, being both part of our consciousness and something beyond it.

In light of all that has been said so far, we can affirm that, from Husserl's phenomenology, life reveals itself as perception perceiving itself, highlighting the autonomy of intentionality in consciousness, which is not based on external representations. The characterization of an object as non-constitutive implies its independence from the external world. This phenomenon is due to the intrinsic nature of intentionality in our consciousness, which does not operate through simple external representations, but maintains its self-determination. From this philosophical angle, the inquiry of knowledge encompasses both the immanent aspects that are part of our consciousness and those that relate to our deeper intentions and purposes. The term "intention," therefore, transcends the simple idea of harboring a specific desire or longing. It refers to the dynamic by which consciousness projects itself toward external objects, that is, those that are not consciousness, but which are objects inasmuch as they are given in its intentionality and acquire their own meaning.

As we also outlined earlier, the term "intention," originating from the verb *tendere*, implies an action of extending or directing oneself toward something that is beyond. Therefore, when speaking of the capacity of consciousness to "intend," we highlight its natural inclination to establish a connection with the environment. This principle indicates that consciousness is not characterized by its inactivity or isolation, but by its open and expansive nature, as well as its active orientation outward. Therefore, intentionality emerges as an essential attribute of consciousness, demonstrating its permanent connection with the environment through this projective impulse. This perspective emphasizes that consciousness, far from being an isolated entity, is invariably focused on interaction with the world that surrounds it, highlighting its constant openness and search for connection and relationship with what is not itself. This perspective highlights the uniqueness of intentionality, a fundamental attribute of our consciousness that stands on its own, without depending on external representations. This suggests that consciousness directs itself independently toward objects, without the essence of these influencing its orientation, but whose meaning is only perceived when given as intentional objects of consciousness.

Therefore, the intentionality we speak of is not merely related to individual desires or choices, but reveals itself as an intrinsic quality of consciousness that enables it per se to project itself outward. It does not project occasionally, as if the result of a choice or randomness, but permanently and without being conditioned by the particular properties of the objects to which it is focused. Husserl's intentionality and intuition demonstrate that intentional consciousness precedes any desire because, in order to desire, consciousness (intentional) must already be open to the world, to what is not it, to what transcends it, but always within the parameters of intentionality (what is immanent to it). At times, in the realm of knowledge, we delve both into the intrinsic elements that constitute our perception and into the underlying intentions behind these, thus unraveling the complex relationship between perception and tangible reality. In phenomenology, the perception of an object transcends mere consciousness or the intention directed toward it, detaching from both the mere objective existence and the intentional projections of consciousness. Consciousness is not a static entity but is defined by dynamic aspects such as perception and attention that keep it originally open to the world, transcending the notion of mere cogitation. And so, Husserl affirms:

> Reason itself and its [object,] "that which is," become more and more enigmatic—reason as giving, of itself, meaning to the existing world and, correlatively, the world as existing through reason— until finally the consciously recognized world-problem of the deepest essential interrelation between reason and what is in general, the enigma of all enigmas (*Rätsel aller Rätsel*), has to become the actual theme of inquiry.[55]

---

55. Edmund Husserl, *The Crisis of European Sciences and Transcendental Phenomenology*, trans. David Carr (Evanston, IL: Northwestern University Press, 1970), 13.

CHAPTER 13

PURE SELF-GIVENNESS

Phenomenon, givenness, and understanding

Husserl extended the scope of phenomenology beyond the mere act of thought (or *cogitatio*, to use Cartesian terminology), encompassing what we know with the expression "pure self-givenness." This represents a dimension that deepens understanding, thus transcending simple reflection into a more holistic and profound perception. As we anticipated in the early sections of this study, Husserl, and especially Jean-Luc Marion, explain that a phenomenon reveals itself because, intrinsically and ultimately, it is given to our perception. In this regard, Husserl also affirms that the "absolute givenness of something ultimate" represents its highest expression, free from any mediation. This leads him to argue that denying self-givenness would mean falling into the Cartesian illusion that our perception is deceptive, which in turn would lead us to skepticism. If we doubted self-givenness, we would end up assuming that all reality is preceded by an ego that knows everything. Finally, this Cartesian line of thought, which dismisses self-givenness, leads to a circle of contradictions that even challenges the very meaning of experience itself, which ends up being little more than a whim of a transcendental ego from which everything emanates.

The phenomenological approach, however, transcends the identification of an object in consciousness and focuses on how that object "gives itself" to consciousness, thus revealing the true essence of its presence and perception. From a phenomenological perspective, the focus is not merely on a transcendental ego from which everything derives, nor on the object itself, but on how this object "gives itself" to consciousness, that is, how it "is born" as an object of our consciousness. What is perceived in consciousness is not generated *ex nihilo* by an individual consciousness or an isolated "I." Therefore, it is not our subjective creation but rather corresponds to a givenness from pure and universal consciousness to our perception. It is "but when you're suddenly the catcher of a ball thrown by an eternal partner"[56] as Rilke once said.

In other words, what we experience and perceive is not merely a product of our thought or ego, but rather a manifestation of a broader and encompassing consciousness. This phenomenon transcends the realm of individual mental thought, revealing a profound interaction between the universal and the personal. Pure self-givenness entails a total revelation, as Husserl himself states when he affirms that:

> [...] *in dem Sinn, in dem es gemeint ist, auch gegeben ist und selbstgegeben im strengsten Sinn* [...].

> [...] actual self-givenness in the strictest sense and not another sort of givenness [...].[57]

Phenomenology, thus, guarantees the unalterable purity of revelation, ensuring that the truth of our perceptions remains authentic, without distortions caused by mediations or conceptual alterations. We find ourselves facing an unequivocal and pure reality, revealed to our consciousness without the intervention or filter of reason, and presenting itself in its most authentic and direct form. This statement does not deny reason at all, but simply does not allow for the overflow of its functions, since we understand it as the receiver of reality and not its creator. That is, reason embraces the universe as it presents itself, trying to understand it and endowing it with meaning according to its faculties, but without intervening in

---

56. Rainer Maria Rilke, "Poem to Nike" (January 1922) (Translated by Walter Kaufmann).

57. Edmund Husserl, *The Idea of Phenomenology*, trans. William P. Alston and George Nakhnikian, with an introduction by George Nakhnikian (The Hague: Martinus Nijhoff, 1973), Lecture III, 39–40.

its creation. Far from being a construction of our mind, the universe is revealed and manifested in it, being received, but not generated by our reason.

Contrary to the precepts of Descartes, which lead to affirming that the thing exists because I know it, rather than I know it because it exists, Husserl and phenomenology, in general, understand that the thing is given in consciousness and is projected. We are not the creators of the objective universe we perceive, but rather, it is projected or given through us. We are not creators of the cosmos we observe, but rather receivers of its projection or givenness. At the same time, Husserl warns of the risk of grounding abstract and intuitive methods in absolute experiences, as this could lead to incorporating unverified elements, and for this reason, he states that:

Schauende Erkenntnis ist die Vernunft, die sich vorstzt, den Verstand eben zur Vernunft zu bringen.

"Seeing" cognition (intuitive knowledge) is that form of reason which sets itself the task of converting the understanding into reason.[58]

This quote reflects that intuitive knowledge is the reason that attempts to elevate understanding. Knowledge is not approached through abstraction, in which the subject extracts elements from the object. This method entails risks, since it is often difficult to distinguish between what is generated by our own consciousness and what actually emanates from the object. Everything emanates from the intentional object as a givenness. We do not generate knowledge; it is the fruit of what is presented to us. Human perception is not shaped by objective reality but by how it reveals itself in our consciousness. In fact, the human being does not perceive what is as it is, but as it appears, shows, or gives itself in consciousness. This difference is important, and we will address it in the following sections and chapters.

---

58. Ibid., Lecture IV, 50.

So far, we have shown how phenomenology has explained the notions of intentional object, transcendence in immanence, and givenness, with which it defines the term "phenomenon" and its relationship with the consciousness in which it is given. The next step can only be to address knowledge and the way in which it is produced. We have already seen that the terms "sensitive intuition" and "categorical intuition" play a fundamental role here. The previously mentioned quote clarifies that, according to Husserl, reason does not create understanding; rather, reason is given within understanding. That is, intuitive knowledge is not generated by reason as if the former were a tool of the latter, but rather, reason resides in understanding. By grounding understanding in both sensitive and categorical intuition, Husserl asserts that it is not an act caused by us but a process that emerges as a result of the givenness of the phenomenon. Our understanding of things does not come from the spontaneity of an isolated ego that understands the world through a reason that produces and generates its products *ex nihilo*. Therefore, we are not causal agents of our own understanding. Instead, we find ourselves immersed in an ongoing process of understanding. This perspective suggests a technical passivity in the act of understanding, where knowledge emerges independently of our will or conscious effort.

Although we will expand on these aspects later, what has been said so far allows us to assert that both understanding and the reason that structures it from within can only take place in the domain of the phenomenon as a givenness and never outside of it. Consciousness is merely receptive to the occurrence that penetrates it. Everything is revealed, offered, donated. Personal consciousness is the receptacle of influences that come toward it, but that do not originate in it. There is nothing that it can conceive by itself. It is here that reason and understanding make sense.

Tone and listening: beyond vision

Understanding and reason operate within the rich and broad domain of givenness. Phenomenology has insisted on exploring and describing the giving of phenomena in great detail because it is where and how all comprehension occurs. Marion, in particular, explores the phenomenon as givenness in its wide variety of modalities, especially the phenomena that he himself calls "poor" and "saturated," which we have already briefly introduced. These modalities, if we can call them that, exemplify the range of expressions of givenness, from minimally informative manifestations to those with great significant richness. Such diversity underscores the richness and depth of phenomenological processes and their multiple manifestations.

The duration of tone illustrates the integration of the temporal into the phenomenon, evidencing its subtle presence "and yet it is constituted within the phenomenon," as Husserl explained.[59] This concept emphasizes how certain temporal aspects, though not immediately perceptible, are integrated and reveal their presence within the phenomenon under study. While this temporal dimension may not be evident at first glance, it remains an integral component of our object of study. When observing something, we do not always perceive the influence of time right away; however, upon closer examination, we become aware that time, in fact, plays a significant role in the unfolding of events. In the field of acoustics, tone—intrinsically linked to frequency—organizes sound along a scale from high to low, thus delineating its sonic structure. The nature of musical tone illustrates how temporal aspects, although not directly evident in a phenomenon, are effectively integrated and manifested in its essence.

A musical tone, despite not being time per se, unveils and communicates the essence of time through its singular expression. Its sound is a reflection and expression of time. Without being time, it reveals time to us. However, since this revelation is audible, it must be perceived in the form of listening. As Pythagoras reveals to us, understanding the phenomenon in its givenness is listening to it; it is hearing its temporality in whose givenness knowledge occurs.

Similarly, Pythagoras held that to know Being, one must find the tone of the universe. He also said that the essence of the universe

---

59. Ibid, Lecture V, 53.

resided in harmony and number.[60] On the one hand, number represents the visual, geometric, and astronomical characteristics of cosmic beings, similar to a vast stage. Harmony, on the other hand, evokes the sounds of tuned instruments, transforming the cosmos into a grand symphony. This teaching invites us to observe the sky and attend to the silent melody of the celestial spheres, for the sky is number and harmony at once. Like music, it is audible only to those who, like Pythagoras, know how to appreciate silence. He perceived even the harmony of the entire universe: the one that encompasses the universal harmony of the spheres and the stars that orbit within them, a harmony that our human limitations usually do not allow us to grasp. According to Pythagorean thought, there were ten spheres, and the "theory of the harmony of the spheres" stands as the quintessence of perfection. It articulates the vision that the cosmos is majestically coordinated through mathematical and musical proportions. These relationships, once integrated into the cosmic order, suggest that celestial bodies create harmonic sounds through their movement. When these sounds merge, an ethereal and uninterrupted melody is formed, known as "The Music of the Spheres."

Pythagoras may have found inspiration in mythological accounts, as shown in Homer's hymn to Ares, in which the stars are described as an ensemble of divine voices. This interest in numerical and musical elements, so dear to the rituals practiced by followers of Orphic philosophy, deeply resonates with this postulate. In this way, Pythagoras achieves a fusion that imbues this framework with both a mystical and scientific character, promoting an elevation and rationalization of the understanding of the cosmos under this singular optic. The Neoplatonic philosopher from Syria, Iamblichus, who lived between the 3rd and 4th centuries CE, relates:

> Pythagoras, however, did not procure for himself a thing of this kind through instruments or the voice, but employing a certain ineffable divinity, and which it is difficult to

---

60. Arthur Fairbanks, *The First Philosophers of Greece* (London: Kegan Paul, Trench, Trübner & Co., 1898), chap. 9, "Pythagoras and the Pythagoreans," 137.

apprehend, he extended his ears, and fixed his intellect in the sublime symphonies of the world, he alone hearing and understanding, as it appears, the universal harmony and consonance of the spheres, and the stars that are moved through them, and which produce a fuller and more intense melody than any thing effected by mortal sounds.[61]

Western modernity has insisted on "locking" knowledge or understanding into the sense of sight. The musical tone, as addressed by Pythagoras and more recently by Jean-Luc Marion, allows us to begin "devisualizing" both perception and givenness, as well as knowledge or understanding itself. The givenness, and therefore the phenomenon as such, cannot be reduced to the structures of vision, either physical or intellectual. Therefore, attending to the phenomenon in its givenness in consciousness requires allowing its revelation in its own way of being. While Husserl contributed, to some extent, to strengthening this visualizing notion of understanding through the concepts of perception and intuition, Marion strives to open it beyond vision, whether physical or mental. This important step taken by Marion refocuses on the givenness of the phenomenon, opening the door to interpreting the givenness in terms of revelation.

---

61. Iamblichus, *Life of Pythagoras, or Pythagoric Life*, trans. Thomas Taylor (London: J. M. Watkins, 1818), chap. 15, 32–33.

BIBLIOGRAPHY SECTION IV

- Burnet, John. *Early Greek Philosophy*. 3rd ed. London: A. & C. Black, 1920.
- Derrida, Jacques. *Edmund Husserl's "Origin of Geometry": An Introduction*. Translated by John P. Leavey Jr. Lincoln: University of Nebraska Press, 1989.
- Dōgen. *Shōbōgenzō Bukkojoji (Going Beyond Buddha)*. Translated by Kazuaki Tanahashi and Mel Weitsman.
- Fairbanks, Arthur. *The First Philosophers of Greece: An Edition and Translation of the Remaining Fragments of the Pre-Sokratic Philosophers*. London: Kegan Paul, Trench, Trübner & Co., 1898.
- Floridi, Luciano. *Scepticism and the Foundation of Epistemology: A Study in the Metalogical Fallacies*. Leiden: Brill, 1996.
- Foucault, Michel. *History of Madness*. Edited by Jean Khalfa. Translated by Jonathan Murphy and Jean Khalfa. London: Routledge, 2006.
- *Heraclitus. Fragments: A Text and Translation with a Commentary*. Translated and with commentary by T. M. Robinson. Phoenix Presocratics 2. Toronto: University of Toronto Press, 1987.
- Heidegger, Martin. *Being and Time*. Translated by John Macquarrie and Edward Robinson. London: S.C.M. Press, 1962.
- Husserl, Edmund. *The Crisis of European Sciences and Transcendental Phenomenology*. Translated by David Carr. Evanston, IL: Northwestern University Press, 1970.
- Husserl, Edmund. *The Idea of Phenomenology*. Translated by William P. Alston and George Nakhnikian. Introduction by George Nakhnikian. The Hague: Martinus Nijhoff, 1973.

- Husserl, Edmund. *The Nexus of Phenomena: Intentionality, Perception, and Temporality.* Vol. 3. Edited by Donn Welton, Gina Zavota, and Rudolf Bernet. London: Routledge, 2005.
- Iamblichus. *Life of Pythagoras.* Translated by Thomas Taylor. London, 1818.
- King, Magda. *A Guide to Heidegger's Being and Time.* Edited by John Llewellyn. Albany: State University of New York Press, 2001.
- Kirk, G. S., J. E. Raven, and M. Schofield. *The Presocratic Philosophers: A Critical History with a Selection of Texts.* 2nd ed. Cambridge: Cambridge University Press, 1984.
- Marion, Jean-Luc. *Being Given: Toward a Phenomenology of Givenness.* Translated by Jeffrey L. Kosky. Stanford, CA: Stanford University Press, 2002.
- Pythagoras. *Fragments and Commentary.* Edited and translated by Arthur Fairbanks. n.d. Accessed August 8, 2025.

Section V
Phenomenology of Revelation

CHAPTER 14

THE HISTORY OF THE RELIGIOUS REVELATION

The importance of revelation in Semitic religions

Before addressing the topic of revelation from the phenomenological perspective, both from Heidegger's and Marion's viewpoints, we will analyze the influence that revelation has had on religion. The historical and conceptual trajectory of "revelation" is characterized by its rich complexity and variability, highlighting how it has been reinterpreted throughout different eras, beliefs, and philosophical systems. In the ancient era, revelation, deeply rooted in the mythology of ancient civilizations, manifested through divine communications that delivered wisdom, norms, or direction to the people, often mediated through visions, dreams, interpretations of natural signs, or consultations with oracles. In the vast landscape of Semitic religions, which include Judaism, Christianity, and Islam, a complex history of divine revelations intertwines spiritual narratives, doctrinal teachings, and devotional practices focused on the interaction between divinity and humanity. These traditions, deeply rooted in the Middle East, share a fundamental belief in a single God who manifests to humanity to guide, correct, and redeem.

Jewish revelation is mainly articulated through the Torah, composed of the five books attributed to Moses, and viewed as the direct communication of God to Moses and the Hebrew people on Mount Sinai, an event traditionally dated to the 13th century BCE. The Torah is the foundation of the Tanakh, or "Old Testament," expanded with the voices of prophets (*Nevi'im*) and other texts (*Ketuvim*) that document successive revelations. The prophets, figures such as Abraham, Moses, Isaiah, and Jeremiah, among others, are seen as the intermediaries of the divine word revealed to Israel. As intermediaries, these prophets serve as bearers of commandments, laws, and prophetic visions intended for the Jewish people and the world.

Kabbalah, written in Hebrew as קבלה, translated as "tradition, vessel, reception, or correspondence," constitutes an esoteric system of thought and a discipline deeply rooted in the traditions of the Essenes and Hasidic Judaism. Within the context of Rabbinic Judaism, a traditional practitioner of Kabbalah is known as a *mekubal* (מקובל). This path focuses on deciphering the hidden and profound meanings of the Sinaitic revelation, the Torah. Kabbalah thus presents itself as an interpretive bridge to understand the divine connection between "The Infinite" (*ein sof* - אין סוף) and the finite universe.

Christianity, for its part, posits that in Jesus Christ, the ultimate revelation of God is incarnated, with Jesus acting not only as the messenger but as the very message of salvation. The Gospels, written in the early centuries of the Common Era, recount his ministry, death, and resurrection as the fulfillment of Jewish scriptures and the definitive expression of divine love. The apostolic letters, particularly those of Paul and the Apocalypse, provide a deeper understanding of Christian revelation, offering guidance for emerging communities and perspectives on the end of times.

For Islam, revelation culminates with the Qur'an, delivered to Muhammad by the angel Gabriel, marking Allah's final and complete communication to humans. Revealed in the 7th century CE, the Qur'an is the heart of the Muslim faith, consolidating teachings, legal precepts, and ethical principles. Complementing the Qur'an, the actions and sayings of Muhammad (*Hadiths*) and his model of life (*Sunna*) serve as guides to implement the divine will in daily existence, interpreting, and living according to the Qur'anic revelations. Sufism, often characterized as Islamic mysticism, represents the esoteric and mystical facet of Islam. Throughout history, Sufis have commonly formed part of various orders or *ṭuruq*, which are groups centered around a distinguished spiritual master, known as *wali*. This spiritual leader possesses an uninterrupted chain

CHAPTER 14: THE HISTORY OF THE RELIGIOUS REVELATION

of teachings extending back to the prophet Muhammad. Sufi orders gather in spiritual sessions (*majalis*) within dedicated spaces such as *zawiyas*, *khanqahs*, or *tekkes*, with the goal of attaining *ihsan*, meaning "perfection in devotion." This concept is summarized in a Hadith that says: "*Ihsan* is to worship Allah as if you see Him; and if you do not see Him, He certainly sees you." Sufis elevate Muhammad to the status of *al-Insān al-Kāmil*, the perfect human being who embodies moral divinity, and consider him their supreme guide and spiritual leader. The traditions and teachings of nearly all Sufi orders derive from Muhammad through Ali, his cousin and son-in-law. However, the *Naqshbandi* order constitutes a notable exception, as its teachings trace back to Muhammad through Abu Bakr, his companion and father-in-law. Sufism does not contradict Islam but deepens its spiritual and mystical dimensions, seeking a more intimate and personal connection with the Divine.

These Semitic religious currents have shaped revelation as a persistent conversation between the Divine and the human, in which God reveals Himself, forging a bond with His creation and unveiling His design for it. Despite the various theological and doctrinal interpretations, revelation stands as the foundation of understanding as a dynamic relationship between the divinity and humanity, pointing the way toward understanding the sacred, moral values, and the ultimate destiny of Being.

The issue of revelation, however, is not confined solely to the purely religious realm, but also penetrates both philosophy and theology, and therefore culture and Western thought throughout its history and development. This penetration, moreover, is not equivalent to its inclusion as just another topic, but rather must be understood as a factor that has contributed to shaping the structures of the very concept of thought, and even of reason.

Both the Middle Ages and the Renaissance were periods of fervent discussion about the essence of revelation, debating how the divinity communicates with humanity and the role of revelation in relation to human reason. During the Enlightenment and modernity, a critical revision of the concept questioned traditionally accepted revelations, privileging the role of reason and subjective experience.

Despite this, thinkers like Kant explored morality and the interaction between revelation, faith, and rationality. In liberal and dialogical theology, figures like Karl Barth and Paul Tillich offer readings of revelation focused on the existential and personal, overcoming literal textual interpretations. Subsequently, in philosophy linked to phenomenology, thinkers like Derrida and Marion have expanded the idea of revelation through concepts like givenness and event, thus transcending the traditional boundaries within which it had been thought and understood until then.

In the context of globalization and the interreligious dialogue of the current era, the very globalized world and the exchange between diverse spiritual beliefs have enriched the understanding of revelation, opening it to more inclusive and diverse interpretations and covering practices and worldviews beyond the Abrahamic scope. This evolution of the concept of revelation from its roots to contemporary times illustrates a movement that leads us from strict interpretations toward more symbolic and personal visions, reflecting a wide spectrum of human interactions with the Divine and the transcendental.

Revelation beyond the West

However, the historical trajectory of the concept of "revelation" is not limited to the foundations of what we now understand as the West. In Eastern traditions, the issue of revelation is intertwined with a diverse mosaic of sacred scriptures, devotional practices, and philosophies that have left an indelible mark on the civilizations and religions of Asia. This principle, essential for understanding how divine or esoteric knowledge is transmitted to human beings, shows notable variability across different spiritual currents, yet maintains the common denominator of uniting the individual with the supremely transcendent.

Within the Vedic framework, dating back to approximately 1500 BCE, we encounter the Vedas, texts of an *apauruṣeya* nature, meaning "of non-human origin." It is recognized that these writings were divinely revealed to the *ṛṣis*, or "seers," who, immersed in deep meditation, received these truths directly from the divinity. The evolution of this revelation continues in the Upanishads, texts that internalize this spiritual knowledge, shedding light on the essential union between the *ātman* (the individual self) and Brahman (the supreme reality). Unlike other spiritual currents that identify a concrete historical originator, *Sanātana-dharma* emerges as a notable exception, characterized as *apauruṣeya*, suggesting that its genesis is not attributable to human creation but is perceived as a revealed tradition.

In the context of identifying precursors or key figures in establishing Vedic culture, the *ṛṣis* occupy a primary place. These scholars and sanctified individuals were the receivers of eternal truths, responsible for codifying these revelations into what we now recognize as the Vedas, thus being the custodians of ancient knowledge.

The term *ṛṣi*, which extends throughout antiquity to the present day, originates from the Sanskrit root *ṛṣ*, interpreted as "to advance quickly," which led the Sanskrit scholar Taranatha Tarkavachaspati to define the *ṛṣi* as one who, through knowledge, surpasses the limitations of the material world (*ṛṣati jñānena saṃsāra-pāram*).

However, the most widespread meaning associates the *ṛṣi* with the verb *dṛś*, or "to see," designating them as "seers," capable of perceiving beyond what is evident to the ordinary eye. The *ṛṣis*, enlightened by divinity, were appointed to reveal Vedic wisdom to humanity. However, it is important to note that their deep perception did not necessarily respond to supernatural powers of foresight or interdimensional communication, although some *ṛṣis* indeed possessed such abilities. Rather, it was a vision that corresponded to authentic religious beings, beings of meditation. The *ṛṣis* functioned as conductors, channeling the intuitive illuminations bestowed upon them to the human collective. The truths contained in the Vedas manifest as direct revelations, distinguishing Hinduism from other religions that are based on the teachings of specific divine emissaries. These revealed scriptures stand by themselves as sources of authority, conceived as eternal scriptures that constitute the supreme knowledge of the transcendent.

According to tradition, Lord Brahma, the creator, was the one who transmitted this sacred wisdom to the *ṛṣis*, who in turn spread it among humans. As beings of elevated spiritual realization, the ancestral seers were perfectly aligned with Brahman. They stood as enlightened masters who established a religious and philosophical framework that was both sublime and integral, the source from which the founders of other spiritual doctrines drank. In this sense, the Vedic seers, along with the biblical prophets, remind us of the poets to whom Heidegger refers in his response to the question, "What are poets for?" when he argues:

> Poets are the mortals who, singing earnestly of the wine-god, sense the trace of the fugitive gods, stay on the gods' tracks, and so trace for their kindred mortals the way toward the turning. The ether, however, in which alone the gods are gods, is their godhead. The element of this ether, that within which even the godhead itself is still present, is the holy. The element of the ether for the coming of the fugitive gods, the holy, is the track of the fugitive gods. But who has the power to sense, to trace such a track? Traces are often inconspicuous, and are always the legacy of a directive that is barely divined. To be a poet in a destitute time means: to attend, singing, to the trace of the fugitive gods. This is why the poet in the time of the world's night utters the holy. This is why, in Holderlin's language, the world's night is the holy night.[62]

In this way, the Vedic revelation represents the human being's awakening toward full awareness of oneself and the surrounding universe, not as a transmission from others but as the progressive unfolding of reality in human consciousness.

In the realm of Buddhist religion, while Siddhartha Gautama, the historical Buddha of the 6th century BCE, is recognized as

---

62. Martin Heidegger, *Poetry, Language, Thought*, trans. Albert Hofstadter (New York: Harper & Row, 1971), 92.

its initiator, Buddhism as a religion understands its doctrines as revelations about the essence of suffering, desire, and the path to enlightenment. Fundamental Buddhist principles, such as the Four Noble Truths and the Noble Eightfold Path, are presented as revealed guides to attain nirvana, liberation from the cycle of birth and suffering (*saṃsāra*).

Jainism, contemporaneous with Buddhism, associates its teachings and practices with the revelations granted to the Tirthankaras, enlightened beings who have attained total perception (*Kevala Jñāna*). Mahavira, the last of these Tirthankaras, is seen as the founder of contemporary Jainism, whose doctrines are interpreted as revelations of immutable truths about the cosmos, karma, and the path to liberation.

When analyzing Taoism, we find the figure of Laozi, its founder in the 6th century BCE. Taoism centers its revelation in the *Dao De Jing*, a work that presents the *Dao* (the Way) as the omnipresent and transcendent principle. Although the direct authorship of Laozi is debated, the *Dao De Jing* is valued as the revelation of a way of life in harmony with the *Dao* and virtue (*De*). Unlike the founders of mystical movements, Confucius did not proclaim to receive divine teachings. However, his doctrines, compiled in the *Analects* by his followers, have been foundational for the moral, social, and political ethos of vast Asian communities. Confucianism, focusing more on applied ethics than mysticism, emphasizes the relevance of divine order and behavioral harmony.

Sikhism, initiated by Guru Nanak in the 15th century CE and continued by nine other Gurus, views the *Guru Granth Sahib*, its sacred scripture, as a perpetual and definitive revelation. The compositions and teachings contained in this text are considered direct expressions of God (Waheguru), transmitted through the Gurus.

From its singular perspective, each tradition contributes to the understanding of revelation, showing the rich diversity and depth of spiritual quests in the East. From the direct transmission of sacred teachings to the internal realization of spiritual and moral truths, revelation in the East encompasses a vast spectrum of expressions of the Divine and the transcendental in human experience.

Section V: Phenomenology of Revelation

On the other hand, the history of "revelation" within shamanism unfolds over countless generations, permeating a diversity of cultures and spiritual practices carried out globally by shamans. Unlike Semitic religions, and also different from Eastern traditions, which base revelation on scriptures and prophets, shamanism emphasizes direct and experiential interaction between the shaman, nature, and spiritual realms.

This ancient spiritual practice, dating back to the Upper Paleolithic, around 40,000 years ago, does not emerge from the vision of a single founder but rather arises autonomously in different regions, from Siberia to the Americas, through Africa, Asia, and Oceania. Regardless of geographic location, however, at the heart of shamanism lies the immediate experience of the shaman with the spiritual realm. Through rituals that include the use of drums, dances, fasting, or psychoactive substances, the shaman enters altered states of consciousness, allowing them to interact with spirits, ancestors, or deities to gain guidance, healing, or prophetic visions.

Serving as a bridge between the spiritual and earthly worlds, the shaman is a receiver of revelations useful for healing, divination, resolving community disputes, or spiritually leading their people. This intercession is grounded in a bond of mutual respect and reciprocity with spiritual entities and the forces of nature. The word *shaman* has its roots in the Tungusic term *šamán*, emblematic of millennia of Siberian shamanic practice, where revelations often revolve around healing, climate influence, and hunting practices.

In the Americas, shamanism places particular emphasis on spiritual connection with plants, animals, and elements, essential for maintaining community and environmental balance and harmony. In Africa, shamans confront illnesses and bad omens through revelations, while in Oceania, they integrate into the tribal fabric, playing a key role in maintaining social and spiritual unity. Today, the resurgence of interest in shamanism in the Western world reflects a search for spiritual alternatives, healing, and reconnection with the natural environment. This highlights the relevance of personal revelation in the pursuit of self-knowledge and spiritual growth. In this sense, shamanic revelation stands out for its experiential depth, the importance of the relationship with the essentially natural and spiritual. Its resilient adaptability through the ages showcases the rich diversity and depth of global indigenous and shamanic spiritual practices.

Although it seems obvious that the Semitic concept of revelation has had a significant influence on the structuring of Western notions of thought and rationality, we should not dismiss the importance that the notion of revelation from both Eastern traditions and shamanism has had over the centuries in shaping thought and its possibilities, both outside and within Western culture.

All of this shows us that revelation is not merely a religious or philosophical theme, but a key to understanding. Through it, both religion and philosophy engage with the relationship between the human being and Being, the finite and the infinite. In this way, the possibility is opened to reflect on what it truly means to be human in the face of the Absolute that transcends us.

CHAPTER 15

REVELATION IN WESTERN PHILOSOPHY ACCORDING TO SAINT AUGUSTINE

The revelation in Christian philosophy: from Plato to Saint Augustine

In the field of study of Western philosophy, we find the conception of revelation already in Plato's *Epinomis*, a text that attributes the origin of poetic inspiration to a divine intervention. Plato portrays the poet not as a mere mortal, but as a receiver of divine ecstasy, blessed by the muses with the gift of creativity. However, this divine gift is not dispensed lightly; it requires as a prerequisite a spirit endowed with delicacy and purity. Under such conditions, the one favored by the muses is elevated to the status of a true poet, whose work becomes an authentic reflection of poetry. In this framework, Socrates maintains that the merit in poetry does not arise from human skill but is granted by divinity. It is solely through this celestial gift that one may aspire to create works of true value. Then, he emphatically proclaims:

> Third comes the kind of madness that is possession by the Muses, which takes a tender virgin soul and awakens it to a Bacchic frenzy of songs and poetry that glorifies the achievements of the past and teaches them to future generations. If anyone comes to the gates of poetry and expects to become an adequate poet by acquiring expert knowledge of the subject without the Muses' madness, he

will fail, and his self-controlled verses will be eclipsed by the poetry of men who have been driven out of their minds. [63]

The essential madness or mania that drives poetic creation comes exclusively from the muses. The poet who receives such a gift surpasses by far both the individual who is possessed but lacks the muses' favor and the one who, devoid of their assistance, attempts to venture into the poetic art by his own good fortune. It is only the poet touched by the muses who truly manages to transcend the illusion of the everyday and enter into what is known as wakefulness, which would be the state in which the poet receives divine inspiration. Upon verifying this, it is revealed that:

[...] madness (mania) from a god is finer than self-control of human origin [...].[64]

Centuries later, following Plotinus, Saint Augustine reinterprets, adapts, and Christianizes the concept of Plato's ideas. Following the itinerary of Augustinian citations compiled by Juan Pegueroles in his article "Formation or Illumination in the Metaphysics of Saint Augustine," we will explore revelation within Christian philosophy. According to Augustine, the conduct of the Divine is grounded in logic. Before beginning any creation, God reflects on the end He pursues, which means that, before initiating the creative act, He already holds a clear "idea" of what He aspires to accomplish. This is why Saint Augustine writes:

Quis audeat dicere Deum irrationabiliter omnia condidisse? Quod si recte dici vel credi non potest, restat ut omnia ratione sint condita. Nec eadem ratione homo qua equus: hoc enim absurdum est existimare. Singula igitur propriis sunt creata rationibus.

---

63. Plato, *Complete Works*, ed. John M. Cooper, trans. Alexander Nehamas and Paul Woodruff (Indianapolis: Hackett Publishing, 1997), 245a; 523.
64. Ibid., 244d; 523.

CHAPTER 15: REVELATION IN WESTERN PHILOSOPHY ACCORDING TO SAINT AUGUSTINE

> Who would dare to say that God has created all things without a rational plan? But if one cannot rightly say or believe this, it remains that all things are created on a rational plan, and man not by the same rational plan as horse, for it is absurd to think this. Therefore individual things are created in accord with reasons unique to them.[65]

And in virtue of the above, he proceeds to define these *rationes* or *ideae* as follows:

> *Sunt ideae principales formae quaedam vel rationes rerum stabiles atque incommutabiles, quae ipsae formatae non sunt, ac per hoc aeternae ac semper eodem modo sese habentes, quae in divina intelligentia continentur.*

> The ideas are certain original and principal forms of things, i.e., reasons, fixed and unchangeable, which are not themselves formed and, being thus eternal and existing always in the same state, are contained in the Divine Intelligence.[66]

Therefore, divine creation is governed by a pre-established scheme, following specific fundamental patterns or concepts that, far from being external to the divinity, reside within its being, integrated into its eternal and unalterable essence. To place such archetypes outside the Supreme Being would imply a contradiction, suggesting a form of dependence on that which is absolute and independent by nature. Consequently, these universal principles are within the very nature of God, fused with His eternal substance that does not admit change. As Saint Augustine himself writes:

> *Has autem rationes ubi arbitrandum est esse, nisi in ipsa mente Creatoris? Non enim extra se quidquam positum intuebatur, ut secundum id constitueret quod constituebat: nam hoc opinari sacrilegum est. Quod*

---
65. St. Augustine, *Eighty-Three Different Questions* (*De diversis quaestionibus* LXXXIII), trans. David L. Mosher (Washington, D.C.: Catholic University of America Press, 1982), 81.
66. Ibid., 80.

si hae rerum omnium creandarum creatarumve rationes in divina mente continentur, neque in divina mente quidquam nisi aeternum atque incommutabile potest esse; atque has rerum rationes principales appellat ideas Plato: non solum sunt ideae, sed ipsae verae sunt, quia aeternae sunt, et eiusmodi atque incommutabiles manent; quarum participatione fit ut sit quidquid est quoquomodo est.

As for these reasons, they must be thought to exist nowhere but in the very mind of the Creator. For it would be sacrilegious to suppose that he was looking at something placed outside himself when he created in accord with it what he did create. But if these reasons of all things to be created or [already] created are contained in the Divine Mind, and if there can be in the Divine Mind nothing except what is eternal and unchangeable, and if these original and principal reasons are what Plato terms ideas, then not only are they ideas, but they are themselves true because they are eternal and because they remain ever the same and un changeable. It is by participation in these that whatever is exists in whatever manner it does exist.[67]

And, in a brief and rigorous deduction, he continues with regard to this notion of the idea:

Neque ea faceret nisi ea nosset, nec nosset nisi videret, nec videret nisi haberet, nec haberet ea quae nondum facta erant nisi quemadmodum est ipse non factus.

He would not make them unless He knew them, nor would He know them unless He saw them, nor would He see them unless He had them, nor would He have them, those that were not yet made, unless as He Himself is not made.[68]

---

67. Ibid., 82.
68. St. Augustine, *De Genesi ad litteram imperfectus liber (The Literal Interpretation of Genesis: Unfinished Book)*, V.16.34, PL 34:333; trans. Isabella Image, rev. ed. (2020), 24–25.

Chapter 15: Revelation in Western Philosophy according to Saint Augustine

Plato initially situated platonic ideas in an abstract realm. In his reinterpretation, Plotinus had already relocated the Platonic ideas within the Intelligence or *Nous*. However, Saint Augustine introduced a crucial distinction in the relationship between the Word and the Father, considering them as equals in essence and not hierarchically arranged. Saint Augustine thus states that the ideas reside in the Word, suggesting a deep integration of the ideal principles within the very structure of the divinity, without inferring any subordination within the Trinity.

> *Quia unum Verbum Dei est, per quod facta sunt omnia, quod est incommutabilis veritas, ibi principaliter atque incommutabiliter sunt omnia simul; non solum quae nunc sunt in hac universa creatura, verum etiam quae fuerunt et quae futura sun.*

> Because therefore the Word of God is One, by which all things were made, which is the unchangeable truth, all things are simultaneously therein, potentially and unchangeably; not only those things which are now in this whole creation, but also those which have been and those which shall be.[69]

In the sixth book of the same work, Saint Augustine expounds a complementary idea, emphasizing that God the Father conceives a single Idea, which is the Word. This Word is identified with wisdom, which is in turn conceived as the divine art of the Father. This approach underscores that, in the divine essence, the principle of knowledge and creation unite in a singular entity: the Word. The Word embodies the entirety of the divine thought and acts as the means through which the Father expresses His will and creative power:

> *Verbum perfectum, cui non desit aliquid, et ars quaedam omnipotentis atque sapientis Dei, plena omnium rationum viventium atque incommutabilium; et omnes unum in ea, sicut ipsa unum de uno cum quo unum.*

---

69. St. Augustine, *On the Trinity*, trans. Arthur West Haddan, in Nicene and Post-Nicene Fathers, First Series, vol. 3, ed. Philip Schaff (Buffalo, NY: Christian Literature Publishing Co., 1887), Book IV, chap. 1, §3.

As though a perfect Word, John 1:1 to which nothing is wanting, and a certain skill of the omnipotent and wise God, full of all living, unchangeable sciences, and all one in it, as itself is one from one, with whom it is one.[70]

In parallel to the redefinition of the Platonic Idea, Augustine of Hippo also articulates with conviction the premise that materiality constitutes the foundation of all beings capable of experiencing transformations. This argument is based on the premise that any observable alteration in the characteristics of an entity necessarily presupposes the presence of an unchanging base or substrate that facilitates and supports such a process of change. In the Book XII of his emblematic *Confessions*, the thinker highlights the fundamental role of a permanent support in the phenomenon of the transition of states or forms that characterizes beings in the cosmos. This stance reinforces Augustine's view of matter, understood as the primordial element that makes possible both the existence of variety and the ability to adapt and transform within the fabric of material reality. This analysis demonstrates the sharpness of Augustine in ontology and metaphysics. It evidences his ability to weave reflections of great depth, characterized by clear and accessible language, albeit imbued with the complexity inherent in the topics addressed. The elucidation of these principles reveals, therefore, an effort to understand the changing nature of the physical world, placing matter as the central axis in the discussion of permanence and transition within the realm of the existent.

> *Et intendi in ipsa corpora eorumque mutabilitatem altius inspexi, qua desinunt esse quod fuerant et incipiunt esse quod non erant, eumdemque transitum de forma in formam per informe quiddam fieri suspicatus sum, non per omnino nihil... Mutabilitas enim rerum mutabilium ipsa capax est formarum omnium in quas mutantur res mutabiles.*

---

70. Ibid., Book VI, chap. 10, §11 (PL 42:931).

Chapter 15: Revelation in Western Philosophy according to Saint Augustine

... and I applied myself to the bodies themselves, and looked more deeply into their mutability, by which they cease to be what they had been, and begin to be what they were not; and this same transit from form unto form I have looked upon to be through some formless condition, not through a very nothing... For the mutability of mutable things is itself capable of all those forms into which mutable things are changed.[71]

The diversity of objects such as guitars, tables, or chairs, all derived from wood, exemplifies the multiplicity of forms that a single material can adopt, thus evidencing wood as the constant support underlying these formal variations. However, Augustine's understanding of the ontological status of this primordial matter, described as a *quiddam informe* (something formless), presents certain ambiguities. From a Platonic perspective, which values entities based on their forms—associated with goodness and unity—what lacks form approaches non-existence. Nonetheless, Augustine recognizes that, despite its apparent lack of form, this matter must enclose some form of reality, however minimal it may be. In Book XII of his *Confessions*, he delves into this paradox, exploring the essential nature of matter as something that, while seeming to lack form and, therefore, Being, in reality possesses a concrete existence, albeit in its most elemental state. This reflection points to Augustine's attempt to reconcile the apparent contradiction between the lack of form and the necessity of a material base that ultimately sustains the variability of forms in the physical world. Thus, he challenges the traditional understanding of matter in the context of Platonic metaphysics.

Si dici posset nihil aliquid et est non est, hoc eam dicerem; et tamen iam utcumque erat, ut species caperet istas visibiles et compositas.

---

71. St. Augustine, *Confessions*, trans. J. G. Pilkington, in Nicene and Post-Nicene Fathers, First Series, vol. 1, ed. Philip Schaff (Buffalo, NY: Christian Literature Publishing Co., 1886), Book XII, chap. 6, §6 (PL 32:828).

Could it be said, Nothing were something, and That which is, is not, I would say that this were it; and yet in some manner was it already, since it could receive these visible and compound shapes.[72]

Therefore, the essence of matter resides in its primal state, lacking its own form until divine ideas shape it. It is these divine conceptions that impress structure upon matter. Augustine of Hippo deduces, from this premise, that matter, in its natural state, is equivalent to nothingness due to its lack of form; however, it possesses the intrinsic capacity to be formed, which makes it potentiality. This duality reveals the nature of matter as an entity awaiting actualization, a substrate ready to receive form and meaning through the intervention of an external ordering principle, in this case, the ideas emanating from the Divine. In the words of Saint Augustine:

Ipse (materiam) informem ac formabilem instituit.

He (God) established matter as formless and formable.[73]

The capacity to be endowed with form resides in the matter itself, though it has not yet constituted that form. Such matter, like form, has been created by divinity. Thus, Saint Augustine, distancing himself from the postulates of his Neoplatonic predecessors, refutes the idea that matter is eternal and uncreated, existing alongside God. This Christian thinker emphasizes the conception that both the material essence and the formal essence originate from a divine creative act. He contrasts with the Neoplatonic notion that attributes to matter a state of co-eternity with the Divine. He highlights an epistemological and theological rupture with his predecessors. He proclaims the primacy of a single creative principle, responsible for the totality of the existent,

---

72. Ibid., XII.6.6.
73. Augustine, *The Literal Meaning of Genesis*, trans. John Hammond Taylor, S.J., Ancient Christian Writers 41–42 (New York: Newman Press, 1982), VIII.20.39. Translation mine.

including matter, which is presented not as an autonomous and pre-existing entity, but as the product of divine will and action. Saint Augustine states:

> *Nullo modo credendum est illam ipsam materiam de qua factus est mundus, quamvis informem, quamvis invisam, quocumque modo esset, per se ipsam esse potuisse, tamquem coaeternam et coaevam Deo. Sed quemlibet modum suum quem habebat ut quoquomodo esset et distinctarum rerum formas posset accipere, non habebat nisi ab omnipotente Deo, cuius beneficio est res non solum quaecumque formata, sed etiam quaecumque formabilis. Inter formatum autem et formabile hoc interest, quod formatum iam accepit formam, formabile autem potest accipere. Sed qui praestat rebus formam, ipse praestat etiam posse formari.*

Yet we are under no manner of necessity to believe that this very material of which the universe was made, although it might be without form, although it might be unseen, whatever might be the mode of its subsistence, could possibly have subsisted of itself, as if it were co-eternal and co-eval with God. But whatsoever that mode was which it possessed to the effect of subsisting in some manner, whatever that manner might be, and of being capable of taking on the forms of distinct things, this it did not possess except by the hand of Almighty God, by whose goodness it is that everything exists, — not only every object which is already formed, but also every object which is formable. This, moreover, is the difference between the formed and the formable, that the formed has already taken on form, while the formable is capable of taking the same. But the same Being who imparts form to objects, also imparts the capability of being formed.[74]

---

74. St. Augustine, *On Faith and the Creed*, chap. 2, "Of God and His Exclusive Eternity," in Nicene and Post-Nicene Fathers, first ser., vol. 3, ed. Philip Schaff, trans. J. H. S. Burleigh (Buffalo, NY: Christian Literature Publishing Co., 1887).

SECTION V: PHENOMENOLOGY OF REVELATION

The enigma of Divine illumination

Let us now examine why this discussion about form and matter plays a fundamental role in the debate about revelation. Saint Augustine's conception of divine illumination of the human intellect in its quest for Truth is, essentially, an extension of the broader idea we have just shown about how the Supreme Being illuminates or gives form to the existence of all entities. This notion holds that the act of illumination transcends the purely human realm and extends to the entire cosmos, impacting each entity according to its particular nature. The enigma of illumination has a profound metaphysical dimension. It is not limited exclusively to human beings, but encompasses the totality of entities, assigning each one a specific role according to its essence. This approach emphasizes the role of God not only as a creator but also as the universal illuminator, whose light is metaphorically responsible for granting form, meaning, and direction to reality as a whole. Augustine, therefore, elevates this theory beyond the confines of mere human cognition. It positions it as a guiding principle that permeates the entirety of creation, thus revealing a principle of order and knowledge that is applied in a differentiated yet coherent manner across the spectrum of existence. It is by virtue of this that Saint Augustine can affirm:

illuminatio nostra, participatio Verbi est

For our enlightening is the partaking of the Word.[75]

That is, God imprints upon the spirit the rules of wisdom, just as He imprints upon bodies the spatial and temporal numbers. Saint Augustine himself asserts:

---

75. St. Augustine, *On the Trinity*, book 4, chap. 2, sec. 2, in Nicene and Post-Nicene Fathers, first ser., vol. 3, ed. Philip Schaff, trans. Arthur West Haddan (Buffalo, NY: Christian Literature Publishing Co., 1887).

Chapter 15: Revelation in Western Philosophy according to Saint Augustine

Dedit numeros omnibus rebus etiam infimis et in fine rerum locatis; et corpora enim omnia quamvis in rebus extrema sint habent numeros suos. Sapere autem non dedit corporibus, neque animis omnibus, sed tantum rationalibus, tamquam in eis sibi sedero locaverit, de qua disponat omnia illa etiam infima quibus numeros dedit.

Wisdom has given numbers to all things, even the lowest and those ranked least of all; all bodily things, though they are below everything else, possess these numbers. But it has not given the power to be wise to bodily things, nor to all souls, but only to rational souls. It is as if it has made its dwelling among them, so that from there it may set in order all those things, even the lowest, to which it has given numbers.[76]

Illumination, understood as formation—specifically, the givenness of form to matter—gains importance as Saint Augustine develops this topic and his philosophy in general. One of his early steps in this direction was to establish a fundamental differentiation between two types of illumination or formation, applied respectively to bodies and spirits. In the case of physical bodies, the divine action manifests through the imposition of numbers (which we could call "physical principles"), which, in their most rigorous interpretation, symbolize inevitability and determinism. In other words, material entities act under the yoke of unavoidable laws. On the other hand, in spiritual entities, the divine influence manifests in a bifurcated manner. This approach suggests that, while the material world is governed by a predetermined and necessary structure that dictates its behavior and evolution, spirits experience a form of divine influence that is more complex and multifaceted. He distinguishes between the nature of the material and the spiritual, and emphasizes the existence of a divine order

---

76. St. Augustine, *The Problem of Free Choice* (De libero arbitrio), trans. Dom Mark Pontifex, Ancient Christian Writers: The Works of the Fathers in Translation, no. 22 (Westminster, MD: The Newman Press; London: Longmans, Green and Co., 1955), book 2, chap. 11, sec. 31.

that adapts and applies differently depending on the essence of the beings it affects. That is, as he explains in *De libero arbitrio*, or *On Free Will*, there are certain rules of numbers (*regulae numerorum*) and certain rules of wisdom (*regulae sapientiae*). Let us examine the difference between both and their implication in the topic we are dealing with here, which is revelation.

The *regulae numerorum*, or "logical numbers," constitute the prior knowledge stored in memory about the fundamental notions and initial principles of science. Saint Augustine illustrates how the concept of unity is established as an innate, a priori notion. In this way, he emphasizes that, through divine illumination, all human beings inherently possess the idea of unity. This approach underscores the presence of universal truths pre-printed in the human intellect, thus revealing a direct link between divine illumination and intuitive access to essential concepts that underpin understanding and scientific reasoning, without the need for prior learning or experience. Saint Augustine writes:

> *Unum quisquis verissime cogitat, profecto invenit corporis sensus non posse sentiri. Quidquid enim tali sensu attingitur, iam non unum, sed multa esse convincitur; corpus est enim et ideo habet innumerabiles partes … Cum enim quaero unum in corpore, et me non invenire non dubito, novi utique quid ibi quaeram, et quid ibi non inveniam etnon posse inveniri, vel potius omnino ibi non esse. Ubi ergo novi quod non est corpus unum, quid sit unum novi: unum enim si non nossem, multa in corpore numerare non possem.*

> But if you have a true notion of 'one,' you certainly find that it cannot be perceived by the bodily senses. Whatever is the object of a bodily sense is proved to be many, and not one, because it is a bodily thing and so has countless parts. [...] I look for 'one' in a bodily thing, and undoubtedly do not find it. I know indeed what I am looking for, and what I do not find there; and I know that it cannot be found, or rather, that it is not there at all. While I know that a bodily thing

is not one, I know what 'one' is. If I did not know 'one,' I could not count 'many' in a bodily thing. [77]

The capacity of the rational being to comprehend the numbers embedded in the universe and, therefore, attain deep knowledge (*scientia*) of phenomena, is due to the presence of logical numbers, pre-imprinted in the memory by divine action. This initial imprint of the idea of numbers by God makes it possible for humans to perform acts of measurement and quantification of the world around them.

Similarly, the *regulae sapientiae*, or "ethical numbers," represent the prior knowledge of the fundamental notions and basic principles of wisdom (*sapientia*), likewise stored in memory. This set of preexisting ethical principles guides the human being in understanding and applying moral values and ethical decisions, thus grounding the ability to discern and act in accordance with a universally recognized moral order. Saint Augustine, performing a true transcendental reduction, shows that we know and love a priori the Truth and the good:

> *Ut constat nos beatos esse velle ita nos constat velle esse sapientes, quia nemo sine sapientia beatus est. Nemo enim beatus est nisi summo bono, quod in ea veritate quam sapientiam vocamus, cernitur et tenetur. Sicut ergo antequam beati simus, mentibus tamen nostris impressa est notio beatitatis; per hanc enim scimus fidenterque et sine ulla dubitatione dicimus beatos nos esse velle; ita etiam priusquam sapientes simus, sapientiae notionem in mente habemus impressam, per quam unusquisque nostrum si interrogetur velitne esse sapiens, sine ulla caligine dubitationis se velle respondet.*

Therefore, just as we agree that we wish to be happy, so we agree that we wish to be wise, for no one is happy without wisdom. No one is happy without the supreme good, which is distinguished and grasped in that truth which we call

---

77. St. Augustine, *The Problem of Free Choice (De libero arbitrio)*, trans. Dom Mark Pontifex, Ancient Christian Writers: The Works of the Fathers in Translation, no. 22 (Westminster, MD: The Newman Press; London: Longmans, Green and Co., 1955), book 2, chap. 8, sec. 22.

wisdom. So, as, before we are happy, the idea of happiness is nevertheless impressed on our minds—for through this idea we know and say confidently and without any doubt that we wish to be happy—so too, before we are wise, we have the idea of wisdom impressed on the mind. It is through this idea that each of us, if asked whether he wishes to be wise, replies without any shadow of doubt that he does so wish.[78]

The *regulae sapientiae*, or "ethical numbers," serve as guides for human moral conduct, though they do not predetermine it absolutely. These principles enable the individual to recognize the need for the inferior to be subordinated to the superior, for equals to correspond to one another, and for each to be given what is due to them. Through numbers, divine illumination enables the human being to progressively understand reality. Thus, they discover unity in the essence of Being, while identifying duality in creation. Between the concept of one and two, there lies the same proportional relation as between two and four, just as the proportion between five and ten is replicated between twenty and forty. This proportional harmony reveals to the human being the nature of justice and, through its order, uncovers beauty; similarly, its logical coherence unveils the Truth. In this way, the individual deduces all these concepts from the divine numerical illumination imprinted in their human consciousness.

Therefore, at the heart of Saint Augustine's philosophical reflection lies the theory of illumination. It is a central axis that intertwines his explorations of Being and knowledge, and sheds light on essential questions about what entities are and how we come to know them. This positioning is reinforced in his work *De Magistro*, written in 381 in Tagaste, where he founded the first African monastery. The work unpacks this examination through an intellectual and dialogical path that moves from the realm of the external to the internal, and from the earthly to the elevated, outlining an ontological structure that owes much to Plato's dualism. The work is organized around two

---

78. Ibid., Book II, chapter 9, sec 26.

main thematic axes. It begins by exploring the connection between language and reality, then delves into the doctrine of illumination, understood as the immediate access to the essences of things. *De Magistro* is notable for its content and its method, presenting a philosophical dialogue between Augustine and his son Adeodatus, in which it is assumed that the ideas expressed faithfully reflect Augustinian thought. The structure of *De Magistro* traces a cognitive progression from the analysis of signs and symbols to the capture of reality itself, culminating in the revelation of internal truths or pure essences. This journey reveals a bipartite ontological framework, distinguishing between the visible and the invisible, the material and the spiritual, a division that reflects the impact of Platonic philosophy on Augustine's conception of the world.

According to Saint Augustine, the acquisition of knowledge by the human being transcends mere effort, being, in reality, a grace granted by the Divine. Knowledge that humans achieve regarding divinity is not the result of reasoning or their own intellectual speculation. It comes from a celestial inspiration revealed as an illumination granted by the Divine. Saint Augustine's argument is important because it strengthens the foundations of how Christianity conceptualizes and understands revelation, and the role it plays not only in the realms of knowledge and epistemology but also in the field of religion and the relationship between human beings and God.

CHAPTER 16

REVELATION ACCORDING TO SCHELLING: A PATH TOWARD THE DIVINE

Revelation as the foundation of knowledge

In the 19th century, the German philosopher Friedrich Schelling expanded the concept of revelation beyond the traditional boundaries of Christian revelation, which Saint Augustine had largely delineated. He proposed the notion that revelation is found in everything. This perspective emphasizes the omnipresence of revelation, suggesting that every aspect of reality may be viewed as a manifestation of the Divine. Every phenomenon and experience is an unfolding of the Absolute. Therefore, Schelling speaks of "the universality of revelation" in a way that echoes Marion's approach. For Schelling, revelation is not limited to sacred texts or dogmatic truths but extends to the entirety of existence, where every element reveals something of the underlying mystery of Being. This understanding emphasizes a worldview in which the Divine continuously manifests through the created, inviting constant philosophical reflection and discovery. In his famous letter titled *Philosophy of Revelation*, Schelling writes:

> I now want to correct another possible misunderstanding. Those who hear the word "revelation" might think only of the act by which divinity becomes the cause or author of representations in some individual human consciences. The theologians who consider the content of Christian revelation to be true not in itself, but only because it has been given by God Himself to those through whom it

was announced, must necessarily attribute a very special weight to this act. Now, I do not want to deny that in the *Philosophy of Revelation* there may be a moment in which the possibility or impossibility of revelation must also be investigated, even in this sense, but this question will always be, in the *Philosophy of Revelation*, only a subordinate issue; and if it receives an answer in general, it will do so as a consequence of inquiries that go beyond this specific question. The *Philosophy of Revelation* does not refer to the merely formal aspect of a divine act, which would in any case only be a particular act, but refers to the universal nature of revelation, especially its content and the great universal connection in which this content is only conceivable.[79]

Revelation differs from metaphysics, which studies the primordial principle (*arché*), and from mythology, which recounts narratives. Acting in a symbolic manner, revelation unravels myths. According to Schelling, when confronted with myths, we encounter a distinct type of history, one that is not common or sequential in time, but kairological. That is, it focuses on the opportune, decisive moment, prior to creation itself, since nothing existed before it. This pre-existing reality is introduced or integrated into the phenomena of the world, implying that it was already present, albeit in a ciphered or hidden form, and finally manifests in consciousness. Schelling anticipates an idea that Marion will later develop by arguing that revelation occupies a place within philosophy. However, Schelling maintains that, in order to comprehend revelation fully, it will be necessary to adopt a renewed philosophical approach:

---

79. Friedrich Wilhelm Joseph Schelling, *Philosophy of Revelation*. Lecture VII: Reason and Revelation, trans. the author from Juan Cruz Cruz's Spanish edition (Filosofía de la revelación. Libro I: Introducción o Fundamentación de la filosofía positiva [Pamplona: Cuadernos de Anuario Filosófico, Serie Universitaria n. 51, 1998]), §16, "Two Concepts of Revelation: the Authentic and the Historical." Translation mine.

> The content of revelation is, first of all, a historical content, but not a common or temporally historical one; it is a content that manifests itself at a certain time, that is, it is inserted into the phenomena of the world. But, by its very nature, it was present and prepared, although not yet manifested and hidden, 'before the creation of the world,' before the foundation of the world was laid. Therefore, its origin, its proper understanding, traces back to the supramundane. It is such a content that in the *Philosophy of Revelation* must become the content of philosophy. If this is truly taken seriously, that is, if this content must become, in all its truth and specificity, the content of philosophy, then you already realize that a philosophy capable of receiving this content in such a way must be made completely differently from the philosophy that has dominated most circles until today. Now, this matter of the *Philosophy of Revelation* is truly being taken seriously.[80]

In this passage, Schelling argues that revelation must be incorporated into the realm of philosophy precisely because, traditionally, it has been placed primarily and exclusively within theology. Moreover, his position emphasizes the need to overcome the conventional division between philosophy and theology, recognizing that revelation, although deeply rooted in theological discourse, contains truths and dimensions that philosophy can and must explore. Furthermore, Schelling believes that by integrating revelation into its discourse, philosophy enriches itself and opens up to a deeper understanding of reality, transcending the limits of purely speculative reason. This proposal seeks to establish a fruitful dialogue between faith and reason, where revelation acts as a bridge that connects and enriches both spheres of human knowledge.

> As a fundamental principle, it must be affirmed (and it has already been affirmed) that this union of philosophy and revelation should not occur at the expense of philosophy

---

80. Ibid.

or revelation, that neither of them should lose anything at any time, nor should suffer violence. If, for example, we were to understand revelation in an inappropriate sense, as if every unexpected broadening of human consciousness or unforeseen illuminations in the realm of science could be called revelations of the spirit of this science, then it would indeed be very easy to accept a revelation in this sense, but in no case would it be appropriate to philosophy.[81]

According to Schelling, the importance of revelation lies in the fact that this illumination coming from Being expands human consciousness, opening horizons toward deeper dimensions of understanding and perception. Thus, the spirit acts as a catalyst that broadens the limits of consciousness, revealing new enigmas and mysteries for each field of knowledge. Thus, human understanding is enriched, and appreciation for the complexity of the universe is deepened. Schelling urges us to search for truths beyond the apparent. For this reason, he writes:

> Similarly, if only universal or rational knowledge were admitted as the content of revelation (and this is what is primarily at stake, for with the content, its mode of proceeding is also understood), and to resolve the particular and concrete truths of revelation into those universals, it were necessary to resort to the distinction between content and form or covering (*Einkleidung*), then, again, it would not be worth the effort to deal with revelation. If revelation only contained what is already in reason, it would have no interest at all. Its specific interest can only consist precisely in that it contains something that surpasses reason, something more than reason contains. We will indicate later how that something beyond reason is thinkable, moreover, how in many cases it is actually thought.[82]

---

81. Ibid
82. Ibid.

CHAPTER 16: REVELATION ACCORDING TO SCHELLING: A PATH TOWARD THE DIVINE

Thus, according to Schelling, the concept of revelation transcends the mere exposition of universal truths, also encompassing specific aspects of individual reality. Revelation allows humanity to connect with great truths that affect us all, such as immortality and reincarnation. However, it can also refer to concrete and personal situations, such as the attraction to studying with a particular classmate. Revelation acquires its meaning and value precisely in the context of those truths we cannot access through the exercise of reason alone. Revelation would be unnecessary if we could access these realities through our rational faculties. Without it, transcendental truths would remain hidden or inaccessible to human understanding. In the words of Schelling himself:

> Everything that can only be known through experience is something that goes beyond reason; and, moreover, in universal human history and even in the actions of some excellent individuals, something emerges that cannot be comprehended by mere reason.[83]

Thus, everything that can be known through human experience transcends the limits of pure reason. Even the knowledge we acquire through introspection or direct experience constitutes a form of revelation, as it is something that is unveiled or manifested before us. As we have seen in earlier chapters, Husserl, in this context, argues that things present themselves to consciousness, not merely as objects of rational analysis, but as phenomena that reveal themselves through intuition and direct perception. This phenomenological approach emphasizes how reality reveals itself to the consciousness. It highlights the active role of perception and experience in the process of knowledge, beyond reason. And this is maintained by Schelling when he asserts:

---

83. Ibid.

A rational man is not yet, by the mere fact of being rational, a hero in the world history. It would not be worth dealing with revelation if it were not something special, if it did not contain something beyond what we already have without it. Perhaps I should not express from the outset that I reject the methods that others often use for their own interests. Thus, some may already feel repelled or at least reluctant to the investigation. However, I hope not to be judged by mere prejudices or by provisional expressions. Whoever wishes to listen to me, let them listen until the end. It could happen that they then find something entirely different from what they might have expected to find from their previous perspective, perhaps restricted, something against which the usual objections, so common today in many circles, against anything beyond reason, do not apply. I want to note, however, the following. Let us assume that revelation is a reality (*Realität*) and that it is truly something factual (*Faktisches*). And this we must presuppose, since if the factual in it were only a universal covering, then common knowledge would suffice to comprehend it. (But precisely to recognize this, that revelation is something factual, really, other historical mediations and other foundations are undoubtedly necessary, beyond those which revelation has had up until now). Well then, if the revelation is such, it must be justifiable—if it is justifiable at all—only through a higher historical connection—that is, one that is more elevated and even goes beyond the revelation itself and Christianity as a special phenomenon—in something different from what is normally in view.[84]

Revelation makes religion possible

According to Schelling, the phenomenon of revelation transcends both deduction and abstract reasoning, as well as sensory perception.

---

84. Ibid.

It stands as a fact in its own right. If human knowledge were limited exclusively to what could be discerned through reason, concepts such as gods and the sacred would have no presence in the world, since these elements escape reason's ability to apprehend them on its own. The mere existence of discourse about the sacred and God acts as testimony, not necessarily of God's existence in empirical terms, but of the presence of revelation. This argument underscores the importance of revelation as a channel through which we access knowledge and realities that go beyond the realm of the tangible and rationally comprehensible, thus highlighting the limitation of human reason in the face of the depth and breadth of total reality. In this sense, revelation opens a new avenue of "knowing" that adheres neither to the principles of classical rationalism nor to the tenets of empiricism.

As we read, Schelling affirms that "It would not be worth dealing with revelation if it were not something special, if it did not contain something beyond what we already have without it."[85] The absence of revelation would imply the non-existence of religion, as its teachings transcend ordinary human understanding. This argument holds that religion is not merely a construct of the mind, since the mind cannot generate or invent what is completely foreign to its experience or prior reasoning. The essence of the religious, with its notions of divinity, the sacred, and the transcendent, suggests a source of knowledge and truth that goes beyond what human beings can discover on their own.

Although revelation surpasses empiricism and rationalism, especially Cartesian rationalism, it should not be considered a reduction to "imagination." Schelling himself argues that revelation also transcends mere imaginative faculty to become an authentic fact. This perspective emphasizes that the human capacity to engage in discourse about the sacred, the gods, and the very existence of religion intrinsically depends on the presence of revelation. If revelation were not a reality, humans would live detached from the notion of religion and the profound questions

---

85. Ibid.

about the Divine and transcendence that have shaped their history and spiritual development.

Revelation is not just a spiritual or religious phenomenon; it can also be examined in a scientific light, as it provides empirical evidence of its impact on cognition and human culture. Schelling's argument, then, holds particular significance because it sheds light on a new "reality of knowing" that transcends both reason and the senses. It explains how and why religion is possible and clears certain paths that would later be traversed by the phenomenologies of Husserl, Heidegger, and Marion, among others.

CHAPTER 17

REVELATION ACCORDING TO RENÉ DESCARTES

The revelation in innate ideas

Until now, we have discussed revelation from the field of philosophy and have related it, primarily and with few exceptions, to mythology, symbolism, and religion. Moreover, to a certain extent, we have even differentiated revelation, especially when understood phenomenologically, from all logical-rational thought. To put it concisely, we have aligned revelation with the givenness of the phenomenon and the Being that presents itself in consciousness in its *haecceity*, and, in general terms, we have partially set aside the question of revelation in the field of rationalism. However, in his famous work *Meditations on First Philosophy*, specifically in the Third Meditation, Descartes introduces the topic of revelation in relation to the "giving" of the ideas of infinity and perfection, and asks how these ideas have reached me as the thinking thing that I am.

In this context, Descartes makes an important distinction between adventitious, fictitious, and innate ideas. As we will see later in a more contextualized manner, adventitious ideas are those that we obtain through our interactions and experiences in the world. For instance, we are not born with an understanding of public figures like Lionel Messi. That is, these are the ideas, including sensations, images, and concepts, that emerge as a direct result of our interaction with the environment through sensory perception. These ideas can be exposed through perceptual experiences. In this sense, they constitute the basis of empirical knowledge, acquired through contact with the objects and events of the physical world. Adventitious ideas provide us with the raw material on which we reflect, analyze, and construct more abstract concepts to understand the world.

On the other hand, Descartes defines factitious ideas as those that are the product of our imagination, such as the idea of a green flying cat. They arise from the exercise of the creative power of our imagination and not from the observation of reality. When we imagine an animal with the body of a dog and the head of a dragon, we create a factitious idea—that is, a concept that does not directly correspond to any observed external reality. It results from manipulating known elements to create something new and original. This process reveals how the human mind transcends the limits of the senses and accesses infinite possibilities through imagination. In sum, factitious ideas are the mental combination, alteration, or expansion of other previously acquired ideas, whether through adventitious ideas or innate ideas, which we shall explore next.

Thirdly, the French philosopher defines innate ideas as those pieces of knowledge or concepts that we possess from birth and, therefore, do not derive from external experience or from the invention of our mind. Descartes sees in these ideas evidence of knowledge prior to sensory experience, suggesting an innate capacity of the human mind to access certain fundamental principles. At this point, he introduces the idea of God as infinity and perfection, to which he attributes the notion of form in act, not in potency, since—as he himself holds—it is perfection that could not be more perfect; it is the infinite that can no longer be more infinite. This idea of God does not come from the senses, nor is it rationally deduced from the ideas I have of myself. Perfection, which is the act, cannot be derived from imperfection, that is, from potency.

Although these ideas are indeed innate, as they do not proceed from the senses nor are they products of imagination, they cannot be considered innate "in me" and understood in the same way we understand the idea I have of myself, as a thinking being. Being the case, Descartes argues that these innate ideas must have been "placed in me," which already emphasizes that what Descartes is particularly interested in is how the idea of God, of infinity, and of perfection appears in me, if these cannot be deduced from anything that is in me, as a finite and imperfect being that I am. If the idea of God did not come from beyond reason and the senses, we would have to accept that I have deduced it from myself, which would not be philosophically possible, as we have just indicated.

These ideas of the existence of God, that is, of infinitude and perfection, or the concepts of thought and extension, which Descartes himself understands as form in act, are fundamental to the functioning of human thought and provide the basis upon which all subsequent knowledge is built, whether rational or empirical. Let us now directly read Descartes' original text in his work *Meditations on First Philosophy*, Third Meditation titled "On God; that He exists."

> **I will now shut my eyes, stop up my ears, and withdraw all my senses. I will also blot out from my thoughts all images of corporeal things, or rather, since the latter is hardly possible, I will regard these images as empty, false and worthless. And as I converse with myself alone and look more deeply into myself, I will attempt to render myself gradually better known and more familiar to myself. I am a thing that thinks, that is to say, a thing that doubts, affirms, denies, understands a few things, is ignorant of many things, wills, refrains from willing, and also imagines and senses. For as I observed earlier, even though these things that I sense or imagine may perhaps be nothing at all outside me, nevertheless I am certain that these modes of thinking, which are cases of what I call sensing and imagining, insofar as they are merely modes of thinking, do exist within me. In these few words, I have reviewed everything I truly know, or at least what so far I have noticed that I know. Now I will ponder more carefully to see whether perhaps there may be other things belonging to me that up until now I have failed to notice. I am certain that I**

am a thinking thing. But do I not therefore also know what is required for me to be certain of anything?[86]

Thus, Descartes begins by saying that he is sure he is a thinking being and asks whether, in order to be sure of something, it is necessary to think.

Surely in this first instance of knowledge, there is nothing but a certain clear and distinct perception of what I affirm. Yet this would hardly be enough to render me certain of the truth of a thing, if it could ever happen that something that I perceived so clearly and distinctly were false. And thus I now seem able to posit as a general rule that everything I very clearly and distinctly perceive is true. Be that as it may, I have previously admitted many things as wholly certain and evident that nevertheless I later discovered to be doubtful. What sort of things were these? Why, the earth, the sky, the stars, and all the other things I perceived by means of the senses. But what was it about these things that I clearly perceived? Surely the fact that the ideas or thoughts of these things were hovering before my mind. But even now I do not deny that these ideas are in me. Yet there was something else I used to affirm, which, owing to my habitual tendency to believe it, I used to think was something I clearly perceived, even though I actually did not perceive it at all: namely, that certain things existed outside me, things from which those ideas proceeded and which those ideas completely resembled. But on this point I was mistaken; or rather, if my judgment was a true one, it was not the result of the force of my perception. But what about

---

86. René Descartes, *Discourse on Method and Meditations on First Philosophy*, 4th ed., trans. Donald A. Cress (Indianapolis: Hackett, 1998), Meditation Three: Concerning God, That He Exists, 69–81.

Chapter 17: Revelation according to René Descartes

> when I considered something very simple and easy in the areas of arithmetic or geometry, for example that two plus three make five, and the like? Did I not intuit them at least clearly enough so as to affirm them as true? To be sure, I did decide later on that I must doubt these things, but that was only because it occurred to me that some God could perhaps have given me a nature such that I might be deceived even about matters that seemed most evident.[87]

It is at this point that Descartes refers to what he himself calls the "evil genius":

> But whenever this preconceived opinion about the supreme power of God occurs to me, I cannot help admitting that, were he to wish it, it would be easy for him to cause me to err even in those matters that I think I intuit as clearly as possible with the eyes of the mind. On the other hand, whenever I turn my attention to those very things that I think I perceive with such great clarity, I am so completely persuaded by them that I spontaneously blurt out these words: "let anyone who can do so deceive me; so long as I think that I am something, he will never bring it about that I am nothing. Nor will he one day make it true that I never existed, for it is true now that I do exist. Nor will he even bring it about that perhaps two plus three might equal more or less than five, or similar items in which I recognize an obvious contradiction." And certainly, because I have no reason for thinking that there is a God who is a deceiver (and of course I do not yet sufficiently know whether there even is a God), the basis for doubting, depending as it does merely on the

---

87. Ibid.

above hypothesis, is very tenuous and, so to speak, metaphysical. But in order to remove even this basis for doubt, I should at the first opportunity inquire whether there is a God, and, if there is, whether or not he can be a deceiver. For if I am ignorant of this, it appears I am never capable of being completely certain about anything else. However, at this stage good order seems to demand that I first group all my thoughts into certain classes, and ask in which of them truth or falsity properly resides.

Some of these thoughts are like images of things; to these alone does the word "idea" properly apply, as when I think of a man, or a chimera, or the sky, or an angel, or God. Again there are other thoughts that take different forms: for example, when I will, or fear, or affirm, or deny, there is always some thing that I grasp as the subject of my thought, yet I embrace in my thought something more than the likeness of that thing. Some of these thoughts are called volitions or affects, while others are called judgments.

Now as far as ideas are concerned, if they are considered alone and in their own right, without being referred to something else, they cannot, properly speaking, be false. For whether it is a she-goat or a chimera that I am imagining, it is no less true that I imagine the one than the other. Moreover, we need not fear that there is falsity in the will itself or in the affects, for although I can choose evil things or even things that are utterly non-existent, I cannot conclude from this that it is untrue that I do choose these things. Thus there remain only judgments in which I must take care not to be mistaken. Now the principal and most frequent error to be found in judgments consists in the fact that I judge that the

> **ideas which are in me are similar to or in conformity with certain things outside me.**[88]

From the final steps of his argument, Descartes asserts that the ideas that are in him are not like the things that are outside of him.

> **Obviously, if I were to consider these ideas merely as certain modes of my thought, and were not to refer them to anything else, they could hardly give me any subject matter for error. Among these ideas, some appear to me to be innate, some adventitious, and some produced by me.**[89]

From this point onward, and as we introduced at the beginning of this chapter, Descartes divides ideas into adventitious, fictitious, and innate.

> **For I understand what a thing is, what truth is, what thought is, and I appear to have derived this exclusively from my very own nature. But say I am now hearing a noise, or looking at the sun, or feeling the fire; up until now I judged that these things proceeded from certain things outside me, and finally, that sirens, hippogriffs, and the like are made by me. Or perhaps I can even think of all these ideas as being adventitious, or as being innate, or as fabrications, for I have not yet clearly ascertained their true origin. But here I must inquire particularly into those ideas that I believe to be derived from things existing outside me. Just what reason do I have for believing that these ideas resemble those things? Well, I do seem to have been so taught by nature. Moreover, I do know from experience that these**

---

88. Ibid.
89. Ibid.

ideas do not depend upon my will, nor consequently upon myself, for I often notice them even against my will. Now, for example, whether or not I will it, I feel heat. It is for this reason that I believe this feeling or idea of heat comes to me from something other than myself, namely from the heat of the fire by which I am sitting.

Nothing is more obvious than the judgment that this thing is sending its likeness rather than something else into me. I will now see whether these reasons are powerful enough. When I say here "I have been so taught by nature," all I have in mind is that I am driven by a spontaneous impulse to believe this, and not that some light of nature is showing me that it is true. These are two very different things. For whatever is shown me by this light of nature, for example, that from the fact that I doubt, it follows that I am, and the like, cannot in any way be doubtful. This is owing to the fact that there can be no other faculty that I can trust as much as this light and which could teach that these things are not true. But as far as natural impulses are concerned, in the past I have often judged myself to have been driven by them to make the poorer choice when it was a question of choosing a good; and I fail to see why I should place any greater faith in them than in other matters. Again, although these ideas do not depend upon my will, it does not follow that they necessarily proceed from things existing outside me. For just as these impulses about which I spoke just now seem to be different from my will, even though they are in me, so too perhaps there is also in me some other faculty, one not yet sufficiently known to me, which produces these ideas, just as it has always seemed up to now that ideas are formed in me without any help from external things when I am asleep. And finally, even if these ideas did proceed from things other than myself, it does not therefore follow that they must resemble those things. Indeed it seems I have frequently noticed a vast difference in many respects. For example, I find within myself two distinct ideas of the sun. One idea is drawn, as it were, from the senses. Now it is this idea which, of all those that I take to be derived from outside me, is most in need of examination. By means of this idea the sun appears to me to be quite small. But there is another idea, one derived from astronomical reasoning, that is, it is elicited from certain notions that are innate in me, or else is fashioned by me in some other way. Through this idea the sun is shown to be several times larger than the earth. Both ideas surely cannot resemble the same sun existing outside me; and reason convinces me that the idea that seems to have emanated from the sun itself from so close is the very one that least resembles the sun. All these points demonstrate sufficiently that up to this point it was not a well-founded judgment but only a blind impulse that formed the basis of my belief that things existing outside me send ideas or images of themselves to me through the sense organs or by some other means.

But still another way occurs to me for inquiring whether some of the things of which there are ideas in me do exist outside me: insofar as these ideas are merely modes of thought, I see no inequality among them; they all seem to proceed from me in the same manner. But insofar as one idea represents one thing and another idea another thing, it is obvious that they do differ very greatly from one another.

SECTION V: PHENOMENOLOGY OF REVELATION

> Unquestionably, those ideas that display substances to me are something more and, if I may say so, contain within themselves more objective reality than those which represent only modes or accidents. Again, the idea that enables me to understand a supreme deity, eternal, infinite, omniscient, omnipotent, and creator of all things other than himself, clearly has more objective reality within it than do those ideas through which finite substances are displayed. Now it is indeed evident by the light of nature that there must be at least as much [reality] in the efficient and total cause as there is in the effect of that same cause. For whence, I ask, could an effect get its reality, if not from its cause?[90]

That is, for Descartes, God would be the truly real, whose effect would be the "thinking I."

> And how could the cause give that reality to the effect, unless it also possessed that reality? Hence it follows that something cannot come into being out of nothing, and also that what is more perfect (that is, what contains in itself more reality) cannot come into being from what is less perfect. But this is manifestly true not merely for those effects whose reality is actual or formal, but also for ideas in which only objective reality is considered. For example, not only can a stone which did not exist previously not now begin to exist unless it is produced by something in which there is, either formally or eminently, everything that is in the stone; nor heat be introduced into a subject which was not already hot unless it is done by something that is of at least as perfect an order as heat—and

---

90. Ibid.

the same for the rest—but it is also true that there can be in me no idea of heat, or of a stone, unless it is placed in me by some cause that has at least as much reality as I conceive to be in the heat or in the stone. For although this cause conveys none of its actual or formal reality to my idea, it should not be thought for that reason that it must be less real. Rather, the very nature of an idea is such that of itself it needs no formal reality other than what it borrows from my thought, of which it is a mode. But that a particular idea contains this as opposed to that objective reality is surely owing to some cause in which there is at least as much formal reality as there is objective reality contained in the idea. For if we assume that something is found in the idea that was not in its cause, then the idea gets that something from nothing. Yet as imperfect a mode of being as this is by which a thing exists in the intellect objectively through an idea, nevertheless it is plainly not nothing; hence it cannot get its being from nothing. Moreover, even though the reality that I am considering in my ideas is merely objective reality, I ought not on that account to suspect that there is no need for the same reality to be formally in the causes of these ideas, but that it suffices for it to be in them objectively. For just as the objective mode of being belongs to ideas by their very nature, so the formal mode of being belongs to the causes of ideas, at least to the first and preeminent ones, by their very nature. And although one idea can perhaps issue from another, nevertheless no infinite regress is permitted here; eventually some first idea must be reached whose cause is a sort of archetype that contains formally all the reality that is in the idea merely objectively. Thus it is clear to me by the light of nature that the ideas that are in me are like images that can easily fail to match the perfection of the things from which they have been drawn, but which can contain nothing greater or more perfect. And the longer and more attentively I examine all these points, the more clearly and distinctly I know they are true. But what am I ultimately to conclude? If the objective reality of any of my ideas is found to be so great that I am certain that the same reality was not in me, either formally or eminently, and that therefore I myself cannot be the cause of the idea, then it necessarily follows that I am not alone in the world, but that something else, which is the cause of this idea, also exists. But if no such idea is found in me, I will have no argument whatsoever to make me certain of the existence of anything other than myself, for I have conscientiously reviewed all these arguments, and so far I have been unable to find any other. Among my ideas, in addition to the one that displays me to myself (about which there can be no difficulty at this point), are others that represent God, corporeal and inanimate things, angels, animals, and finally other men like myself. As to the ideas that display other men, or animals, or angels, I easily understand that they could be fashioned from the ideas that I have of myself, of corporeal things, and of God—even if no men (except myself), no animals, and no angels existed in the world.[91]

In this context, Descartes asserts that the entirety of existence is framed within my own thoughts, which constitute the genuine reality. This assertion posits that the entire cosmos is nothing but a projection of my cognitive sphere, placing ideas of my own as the fundamental elements of what is real. These ideas are in me because I was born with them. I was not born with the idea of a dog, but I learned it in

---

91. Ibid.

the world. However, I am born with ideas like soul, consciousness, or God. In light of this, Descartes wonders how I could have been born with such ideas, and from this point onward, the philosopher himself opens the door to the matter of revelation.

> As to the ideas of corporeal things, there is nothing in them that is so great that it seems incapable of having originated from me. For if I investigate them thoroughly and examine each one individually in the way I examined the idea of wax yesterday, I notice that there are only a very few things in them that I perceive clearly and distinctly: namely, size, or extension in length, breadth, and depth; shape, which arises from the limits of this extension; position, which various things possessing shape have in relation to one another; and motion, or alteration in position. To these can be added substance, duration, and number. But as for the remaining items, such as light and colors, sounds, odors, tastes, heat and cold and other tactile qualities, I think of these only in a very confused and obscure manner, to the extent that I do not even know whether they are true or false, that is, whether the ideas I have of them are ideas of things or ideas of non-things. For although a short time ago I noted that falsity properly so called (or "formal" falsity) is to be found only in judgments, nevertheless there is another kind of falsity (called "material" falsity) which is found in ideas whenever they represent a non-thing as if it were a thing. For example, the ideas I have of heat and cold fall so far short of being clear and distinct that I cannot tell from them whether cold is merely the privation of heat or whether heat is the privation of cold, or whether both are real qualities, or whether neither is. And because ideas can only be, as it were, of things, if it is true that cold is merely the absence of heat, then

an idea that represents cold to me as something real and positive will not inappropriately be called false. The same holds for other similar ideas. Assuredly I need not assign to these ideas an author distinct from myself. For if they were false, that is, if they were to represent non things, I know by the light of nature that they proceed from nothing; that is, they are in me for no other reason than that something is lacking in my nature, and that my nature is not entirely perfect. If, on the other hand, these ideas are true, then because they exhibit so little reality to me that I cannot distinguish it from a non-thing, I see no reason why they cannot get their being from me. As for what is clear and distinct in the ideas of corporeal things, it appears I could have borrowed some of these from the idea of myself: namely, substance, duration, number, and whatever else there may be of this type. For instance, I think that a stone is a substance, that is to say, a thing that is suitable for existing in itself; and likewise I think that I too am a substance. Despite the fact that I conceive myself to be a thinking thing and not an extended thing, whereas I conceive of a stone as an extended thing and not a thinking thing, and hence there is the greatest diversity between these two concepts, nevertheless they seem to agree with one another when considered under the rubric of substance. Further more, I perceive that I now exist and recall that I have previously existed for some time. And I have various thoughts and know how many of them there are. It is in doing these things that I acquire the ideas of duration and number, which I can then apply to other things. However, none of the other components out of which the ideas of corporeal things are fashioned (namely extension, shape, position, and motion) are contained in me formally, since I am merely a thinking thing. But since these are only certain modes of a substance, whereas I am a substance, it seems possible that they are contained in me eminently. Thus there remains only the idea of God. I must consider whether there is anything in this idea that could not have originated from me. I understand by the name "God" a certain substance that is infinite, independent, supremely intelligent and supremely powerful, and that created me along with everything else that exists—if anything else exists. Indeed all these are such that, the more carefully I focus my attention on them, the less possible it seems they could have arisen from myself alone. Thus, from what has been said, I must conclude that God necessarily exists. For although the idea of substance is in me by virtue of the fact that I am a substance, that fact is not sufficient to explain my having the idea of an infinite substance, since I am finite, unless this idea proceeded from some substance which really was infinite. Nor should I think that I do not perceive the infinite by means of a true idea, but only through a negation of the finite, just as I perceive rest and darkness by means of a negation of motion and light. On the contrary, I clearly understand that there is more reality in an infinite substance than there is in a finite one. Thus the perception of the infinite is somehow prior in me to the perception of the finite, that is, my perception of God is prior to my perception of myself.[92]

Divine revelation as immanent transcendence

Although the notions of both divinity and humanity are upheld as authentic, that of divinity holds greater truth due to its infinite

---

92. Ibid.

nature, in contrast to the finitude that characterizes human being. This distinction is grounded in the attribute of infinitude of divinity, which elevates its level of certainty, perfection, and truth above any finite conception. Thus, the idea of divinity stands as the axis around which all other notions are integrated and understood. This integration occurs because the ideas of finite nature find their resolution in the infinite idea, that is, in divinity. The latter is not a product of the human mind, but is directly conferred upon us by divinity through revelation, marking a divine origin of our understanding of the infinite.

> **For how would I understand that I doubt and that I desire, that is, that I lack something and that I am not wholly perfect, unless there were some idea in me of a more perfect being, by comparison with which I might recognize my defects? Nor can it be said that this idea of God is perhaps materially false and thus can originate from nothing, as I remarked just now about the ideas of heat and cold, and the like. On the contrary, because it is the most clear and distinct and because it contains more objective reality than any other idea, no idea is in and of itself truer and has less of a basis for being suspected of falsehood. I maintain that this idea of a being that is supremely perfect and infinite is true in the highest degree. For although I could perhaps pretend that such a being does not exist, nevertheless I could not pretend that the idea of such a being discloses to me nothing real, as was the case with the idea of cold which I referred to earlier. It is indeed an idea that is utterly clear and distinct; for whatever I clearly and distinctly perceive to be real and true and to involve some perfection is wholly contained in that idea. It is no objection that I do not comprehend the infinite or that there are countless other things in God that I can in no way either comprehend or perhaps even**

touch with my thought. For the nature of the infinite is such that it is not comprehended by a being such as I, who am finite. And it is sufficient that I understand this very point and judge that all those things that I clearly perceive and that I know to contain some perfection—and perhaps even countless other things of which I am ignorant—are in God either formally or eminently. The result is that, of all the ideas that are in me, the idea that I have of God is the most true, the most clear and distinct. But perhaps I am something greater than I myself understand. Perhaps all these perfections that I am attributing to God are somehow in me potentially, although they do no yet assert themselves and are not yet actualized. For I now observe that my knowledge is gradually being increased, and I see nothing standing in the way of its being increased more and more to infinity. Moreover, I see no reason why, with my knowledge thus increased, I could not acquire all the remaining perfections of God. And, finally, if the potential for these perfections is in me already, I see no reason why this potential would not suffice to produce the idea of these perfections. Yet none of these things can be the case. First, while it is true that my knowledge is gradually being increased and that there are many things in me potentially that are not yet actual, nevertheless, none of these pertains to the idea of God, in which there is nothing whatever that is potential. Indeed this gradual increase is itself a most certain proof of imperfection. Moreover, although my knowledge may always increase more and more, nevertheless I understand that this knowledge will never by this means be actually infinite, because it will never reach a point where it is incapable of greater increase. On the contrary, I judge God to be actually infinite, so that nothing can be added to his perfection. Finally, I perceive that the objective being of an idea cannot be produced by a merely potential being (which, strictly speaking, is nothing), but only by an actual or formal being. Indeed there is nothing in all these things that is not manifest by the light of nature to one who is conscientious and attentive. But when I am less attentive, and the images of sensible things blind the mind's eye, I do not so easily recall why the idea of a being more perfect than me necessarily proceeds from a being that really is more perfect. This being the case, it is appropriate to ask further whether I myself who have this idea could exist, if such a being did not exist. From what source, then, do I derive my existence? Why, from myself, or from my parents, or from whatever other things there are that are less perfect than God. For nothing more perfect than God, or even as perfect as God, can be thought or imagined. But if I got my being from myself, I would not doubt, nor would I desire, nor would I lack anything at all. For I would have given myself all the perfections of which I have some idea; in so doing, I myself would be God! I must not think that the things I lack could perhaps be more difficult to acquire than the ones I have now. On the contrary, it is obvious that it would have been much more difficult for me (that is, a thing or substance that thinks) to emerge out of nothing than it would be to acquire the knowledge of many things about which I am ignorant (these items of knowledge being merely accidents of that substance). Certainly, if I got this greater thing from myself, I would not have denied myself at least those things that can be had more easily. Nor would I have denied myself any of those other things that I perceive to be contained in the idea of God, for surely none of them seem to me more difficult to bring about. But if any of them were more difficult to bring about, they would certainly also seem more difficult to me, even if the remaining ones that I possess I got from myself, since it would be on account of them that I would experience that my power is limited. Nor am I avoiding the force of these arguments, if I suppose that perhaps I have always existed as I do now, as if it then followed that no author of my existence need be sought. For because the entire span of one's life can be divided into countless parts, each one wholly independent of the rest, it does not follow from the fact that I existed a short time ago that I must exist now, unless some cause, as it were, creates me all over again at this moment, that is to say, which preserves me. For it is obvious to one who pays close attention to the nature of time that plainly the same force and action are needed to preserve anything at each individual moment that it lasts as would be required to create that same thing anew, were it not yet in existence. Thus conservation differs from creation solely by virtue of a distinction of reason; this too is one of those things that are manifest by the light of nature. Therefore I must now ask myself whether I possess some power by which I can bring it about that I myself, who now exist, will also exist a little later on. For since I am nothing but a thinking thing—or at least since I am now dealing simply and precisely with that part of me which is a thinking thing—if such a power were in me, then I would certainly be aware of it. But I observe that there is no such power; and from this very fact I know most clearly that I depend upon some being other than myself. But perhaps this being is not God, and I have been produced either by my parents or by some other causes less perfect than God. On the contrary, as I said before, it is obvious that there must be at least as much in the cause as there is in the effect. Thus, regardless of what it is that eventually is assigned as my cause, because I am a thinking thing and have within me a certain idea of God, it must be granted that what caused me is also a thinking thing and it too has an idea of all the perfections which I attribute to God. And I can again inquire of this cause whether it got its existence from itself or from another cause. For if it got its existence from itself, it is evident from what has been said that it is itself God, because, having the power of existing in and of itself, it unquestionably also has the power of actually possessing all the perfections of which it has in itself an idea—that is, all the perfections that I conceive to be in God. However, if it got its existence from another cause, I will once again inquire in similar fashion about this other cause: whether it got its existence from itself or from another cause, until finally I arrive at the ultimate cause, which will be God. For it is apparent enough that there can be no infinite regress here, especially since I am not dealing here merely with the cause that once produced me, but also and most especially with the cause that preserves me at the present time.

Nor can one fancy that perhaps several partial causes have concurred in bringing me into being, and that I have taken the ideas of the various perfections I attribute to God from a variety of causes, so that all of these perfections are found somewhere in the universe, but not all joined together in a single being—God. On the contrary, the unity, the simplicity, that is, the inseparability of all those features that are in God is one of the chief perfections that I understand to be in him. Certainly the idea of the unity of all his perfections could not have been placed in me by any cause from which I did not also get the ideas of the other perfections; for neither could some cause have made me understand them joined together and inseparable from one another, unless it also caused me to recognize what they were.

Finally, as to my parents, even if everything that I ever believed about them were true, still it is certainly not they who preserve me; nor is it they who in any way brought me into being, insofar as I am a thinking thing. Rather, they merely placed certain dispositions in the matter which I judged to contain me, that is, a mind, which now is the only thing I take myself to be. And thus there can be no difficulty here concerning my parents. Indeed I have no choice but to conclude that the mere fact of my existing and of there being in me an idea of a most perfect being, that is, God, demonstrates most evidently that God too exists. All that remains for me is to ask how I received this idea of God. For I did not draw it from the senses; it never came upon me unexpectedly, as is usually the case with the ideas of sensible things when these things present themselves (or seem to present themselves) to the external sense organs. Nor was it made by me, for I plainly can neither subtract anything from it nor add anything to it. Thus the only option remaining is that this idea is innate in me, just as the idea of myself is innate in me. To be sure, it is not astonishing that in creating me, God should have endowed me with this idea, so that it would be like the mark of the craftsman impressed upon his work, although this mark need not be something distinct from the work itself. But the mere fact that God created me makes it highly plausible that I have somehow been made in his image and likeness, and that I perceive this likeness, in which the idea of God is contained, by means of the same faculty by which I perceive myself. That is, when I turn the mind's eye toward myself, I understand not only that I am something incomplete and dependent upon another, something aspiring indefinitely for greater and greater or better things, but also that the being on whom I depend has in himself all those greater things—not merely indefinitely and potentially, but infinitely and actually, and thus that he is God. The whole force of the argument rests on the fact that I recognize that it would be impossible for me to exist, being of such a nature as I am (namely, having in me the idea of God), unless God did in fact exist. God, I say, that same being the idea of whom is in me: a being having all those perfections that I cannot comprehend, but can somehow touch with my thought, and a being subject to no defects whatever. From these considerations it is quite obvious that he cannot be a deceiver, for it is manifest by the light of nature that all fraud and deception depend on some defect. But before examining this idea more closely and at the same time inquiring into other truths that can be gathered from it, at this point I want to spend some time contemplating this God, to ponder his attributes and, so far as the eye of my darkened mind can take me, to gaze upon, to admire, and to adore the beauty of this immense light. For just as we believe by faith that the greatest felicity of the next life consists solely in this contemplation of the divine majesty, so too we now experience that from the same contemplation, although it is much less perfect, the greatest pleasure of which we are capable in this life can be perceived.[93]

---

93. Ibid.

Chapter 17: Revelation according to René Descartes

Summarizing what we have previously advanced, the ideas that penetrate our consciousness are considered adventitious, fictitious, and innate. Those called adventitious come to us from the outside, like the notion of "dog"; fictitious ideas are created by our mind, like "green dog"; and innate ideas are intrinsic to our being from birth.

This conception of "dog" requires the prior existence in our mind of the concept of "world," since a dog inhabits it and forms part of our environment. Recognizing that both adventitious and fictitious ideas acquire meaning insofar as the innate idea of "world" preexists in our consciousness is essential. The notion of "world" does not derive from any specific experience that a human being may have, establishing that no one can completely perceive the world. According to Descartes, the lack of experiential confirmation that the world is an external acquisition—contrasted with its undeniable presence within us—points to its innate origin.

Similarly, the conception of God, since it cannot be confirmed by external experiences, but is present in our mind, is also classified as an innate idea. This reasoning extends to the idea of the soul; since we possess the notion of the soul without a direct experiential correlate, it is concluded to be an innate idea. Thus, if we consider that each psychic phenomenon is framed in the concept of the soul, and if the concept of the soul is itself an emanation of the Divine, it is possible to argue that all psychic phenomena, in some way, are reflections of the divine projection.

If the understanding of the dog depends solely on the concept of the world, and this world emanates from God, then it follows that all our worldly perceptions have their origin in the Divine. This is because the notion of the world, implanted by God in us, is the prism through which all elements of the world make sense. Ideas enter our consciousness from external entities However, these entities only have meaning through the ideas of the world, the soul, and God, which implies that these three fundamental concepts are the core where all other ideas converge. Since these conceptual pillars are not mental fabrications of our own but revelations to our individual mind, it is concluded that the origin of all our ideas is, in the final analysis, divine.

Section V: Phenomenology of Revelation

Despite the prevailing confusion, Descartes clarifies that at the core of his philosophy, there is not merely a human being reflecting, but rather the divine revelation. The human capacity to think derives from the presence of divine concepts revealed in the mind. At the heart and center of the issue is not a human thinking, but God revealing Himself. This leads us to affirm that the aim of this meditation is to argue for the existence of God.

The fragment from the *Meditations* that we have just read and commented on thus presents us with the idea of infinity and perfection, of God, which Descartes himself understands as pure form or form in act, and not in potency, and which would come to contain all idealities. These idealities allow us, later, to perceive, interact with, and understand the world in which we live and ourselves as beings who think and see that world. However, this idea is not given to us like the rest of the ideas and things; that is, neither by the imagination of reason nor by the senses, since being the idea in act, and not in potency, it cannot be derived from me.

The analogy of "taking a lion out of an empty hat" explains the impossibility that we, limited and faulty creatures, could conceive on our own the idea of something completely perfect and unlimited. This limitation suggests that the concept of perfection surpasses our own constraints and must come from a source or principle that is intrinsically perfect. Descartes considers that this understanding of divinity, or specifically of God, is integrated into our essence from the beginning of our being. Perfection does not seem to be a construction of our thought but a reality preexisting in our consciousness, indicating a natural inclination toward the Divine or toward the infinitely perfect. Since that idea of infinity and perfection is the pure form in act, it is prior to me. But this "innate" idea of God is not innate like the idea I have of myself. Therefore, it must have been "placed in me," that is, it must have been revealed to me. This is an important point, as it allows us to see that Descartes is especially careful not to apply here the same correlations that he previously applied between "I think" and the world or between "I" and the senses, nor even deductive reason.

God is not deducible, perceptible, or thinkable like any other thing or idea. On the contrary, Descartes suggests that God reveals Himself in me, and it is in this revelation that subjects can then perceive and understand the world in which they live. To put it in phenomenological terms, the final lines of the Third Meditation seem to suggest that the idea of God—the pure form—is a transcendence within immanence that "dwells" (is innate) in my consciousness insofar as it "gives itself," "reveals itself," in that very consciousness (it transcends me). Revelation, therefore, as a mode of givenness or phenomenon, must be understood philosophically in terms of an immanent transcendence.

CHAPTER 18

THE IMPORTANCE OF DIVINE REVELATION ACCORDING TO KIERKEGAARD

Kierkegaard's Denmark

The early decades of the 19th century represent Denmark's Golden Age. It was a period of remarkable cultural flourishing amidst the economic hardships that followed the Napoleonic Wars. Despite the financial challenges the nation faced, this era is distinguished by its extraordinary contributions and developments in the arts, literature, and, significantly, theology. Painters, writers, philosophers, and theologians explored new ideas and forms of expression, contributing to a rich cultural legacy. We can see how challenges often serve as catalysts for creativity and deepen the search for meaning and beauty.

In the theological sphere, the period was marked by intense debates and reflections on faith, morality, and the individual's relationship with the Divine. It was heavily influenced by the rise of Romanticism, which emphasized the importance of emotion and subjectivity in contrast to the reason of the Enlightenment. The visions that emerged from this era continue to shape contemporary thought on faith, ethics, and human existence.

The period was also characterized by a renewed interest in Danish national identity, partly in response to the political and territorial pressures facing Denmark. This interest was reflected in a flourishing of the arts aimed at capturing and defining what was essentially Danish—both in terms of natural landscapes and human character. The dominant theological outlook maintained a rationalist orientation, though there was a conscious effort by the Church, under the guidance of bishops such as N. E. Balle and Frederik Münter, to affirm the intrinsically supernatural nature of

Christian revelation. The Danish Church sought to strike a balance that would embrace the divine nature of revelation without rejecting human reason as a tool for its interpretation. The insistence that the Bible, despite its supernatural origin, did not contradict human reason, was an effort to preserve a space in which faith and intellect could coexist without conflict. This approach sought to strike a balance between extremes: it avoided a deistic theology devoid of mystery and rejected the anti-rationalist fervor of certain revivalist movements that were emerging in reaction to intellectual coldness.

However, this mediating position of the Danish Church generated distrust among the supporters of the awakening movements, or evangelical revivalism, who viewed with skepticism any attempt to subject divine revelation and the interpretation of Scriptures to the rational scrutiny of professional theologians. For these groups, such an approach threatened to institutionalize biblical exegesis and, therefore, the definition of orthodoxy, moving it away from the personal and direct religious experience with God that they defended as the ideal. This complex scenario reflects the rich and tense religious dynamics of the time. In an effort to define the nature of faith and religious practice in a rapidly changing world, there was a striving to balance tradition and innovation, ecclesiastical authority and individual spiritual experience.

In this period of transition, some theologians advocated for an interpretation of the Bible that would harmonize with scientific knowledge and rational understanding of the world. According to this perspective, since God is the creator of the natural order, it is inconceivable that divine revelation would contain statements that contravene this order established by God himself. Therefore, they argued that the miraculous events described in the Scriptures should be understood as metaphors or allegories, not as literal descriptions of historical events. For example, the biblical statement that Jesus walked on water would be interpreted as a symbolic teaching, focusing on the spiritual or moral meaning that this story could have, rather than on its physical feasibility according to natural laws. This hermeneutical approach reflects an attempt to adapt the Christian message to the sensibilities and knowledge of an era increasingly

CHAPTER 18: THE IMPORTANCE OF DIVINE REVELATION ACCORDING TO KIERKEGAARD

influenced by science and reason. By doing so, these theologians sought to preserve the relevance and authority of the Scriptures in a society that valued logical coherence and empirical evidence, promoting a faith that could be both profoundly spiritual and intellectually satisfying. However, this stance also generated debates and controversies, both with biblical literalists and with those who defended a more mystical experience of faith.

Henrik Nicolai Clausen firmly argued that it is both possible and necessary to approach divine revelation with the instrument of human reason. By advocating for this approach, Clausen aligned with a broader current within Protestantism, which appreciates and promotes the autonomy of the individual in their search for understanding and personal connection with the Divine, relying on a solid intellectual foundation. Such a perspective proclaims the inherent harmony between faith and reason and fervently advocates for the believer's active participation in the process of theological interpretation. It highlights the incalculable value of human reason as an essential key for exploring and apprehending the essence of divine revelation.

As previously mentioned, the effort to harmonize supernatural revelation with theological rationalism provoked negative responses and, at times, hostility. On the one hand, the Catholic position maintained that the authorized interpretation of the Bible fell exclusively to the Pope and bishops. Clausen, in contrast, argued that this task belonged solely to professional theologians. Moreover, there was a third group that defended the idea that every believer has the capacity and the right to interpret the Scriptures for themselves. This panorama reflects the diversity of opinions regarding access to and understanding of sacred texts, highlighting a field of tension between institutional authority, specialized knowledge, and personal religious experience.

Figures such as Søren Kierkegaard, one of Denmark's most influential philosophers and theologians of the time, played a crucial role in this cultural renaissance. With his profound inquiry into existence, faith, divine revelation, and individuality, he challenged the complacency of the established Church and promoted a more personal and committed understanding of religiosity. The writings of Søren Kierkegaard must be situated within this broader philosophical-theological debate.

The influence of Adler's case on Kierkegaard

Adolph Peter Adler (1812–1869) was a Danish theologian and a classmate of Kierkegaard at Copenhagen's most prestigious private school, the School of Civic Virtue (*Borgerdydskolen*), from 1823 to 1827. Adler studied philosophy and theology at the University of Copenhagen and became a fervent and prominent representative of the Danish Young Hegelians. In 1841, he was appointed a Lutheran pastor, combining both vocations. The following year, he claimed to have experienced a divine revelation. He asserted that Jesus Christ dictated messages to him, which he published in the book *Various Sermons* (*Nogle Prædikener*). In 1845, Bishop Mynster determined that Adler was mentally unfit for the ministry and formally removed him from the Church.

Using Adler's experience as an illustrative example, Kierkegaard reflects on religious authority, divine revelation, and the spiritual crisis of modern Christianity. He argued that the underlying problem is confusion about what revelation truly is. This case reflects the state of misunderstanding that had given rise to religiosity within the Christianity of his time, particularly in a society that considered itself Christian but had, according to him, lost all sense of what a divine revelation genuinely entails.

Kierkegaard addressed this in a book titled *The Book on Adler*, a fascinating case study at the intersection of theology, philosophy, and religious psychology. The title might suggest that the central focus is Adler's experience. However, we gain a broader perspective on his intentions from the title he originally gave the manuscript drafts before publication: *The Religious Confusion of the Present Age, Illustrated by Magister Adler as a Phenomenon*. His analysis does not focus on the legitimacy of Adler's revelation, but rather probes how faith, authority, and revelation intertwine in both individual and collective religious experience. In his words: "[…] as with regard to

Chapter 18: The Importance of Divine Revelation According to Kierkegaard

a letter from heaven, if you will imagine such a thing, precisely the most important point is the fact that it has fallen from heaven, not always so much what is in it."[94] If a revelation truly occurs, what is transcendent is the act of revelation itself—not the content disclosed nor the recipient's identity; what matters is the sheer fact that a revelation was experienced.

In an age characterized by rationalism and common sense, such as the Enlightenment era in which Adler lived, any claim to revelation by an exceptional figure is expected—or rather demanded—to conform to prevailing rational standards, that is, to be comprehensible to reason. Yet Kierkegaard maintains that if we consider revelation as a real event, this fact in itself endows the recipient of that revelation with divine authority, regardless of the message it contains.

The figure of the exceptional individual receives divine authority precisely because the revelation—assuming it to be real—is understood as emanating directly from God. However, the manifestation of such divine authority, particularly in someone holding a public office like Adler, becomes a challenge and even a scandal to an age governed by rationalism and pragmatism. Kierkegaard notes that when a member of organized religion claims direct communication with the Divine, it provokes skepticism and mistrust among modern mentalities.

Nonetheless, for the orthodoxy of the Danish Church, the notion of supernatural divine authority posed no real dilemma. Clausen, in fact, advocated the need for a rational theology—one that remained autonomous from ecclesiastical authority—to clarify Christianity's authentic principles. Even so, this rational exploration was to be limited strictly to the Truth revealed supernaturally through Scripture. Mynster, who led the case against Adler, opposed the conciliatory ideas of Hegelianism, insisting that the dichotomy between the rational and the supernatural formed the very basis of Christianity, and that the Church must prioritize the revealed Scriptures over human understanding. Kierkegaard criticizes the Church's reaction,

---

94. Søren Kierkegaard, *Fear and Trembling; The Book on Adler*, trans. Walter Lowrie, intro. George Steiner (New York: Everyman's Library, Alfred A. Knopf, 1994), 131.

implying that the outcome of the Adler case reflects an institutional inability to understand and adequately handle the complexities of faith and revelation in the modern context.

The idea that a member of the organized Church might proclaim divine illumination arouses suspicion, given that institutionalized religion tends to fossilize the image of God and relies on the premise that no one else can establish direct contact with the Divine. When someone claims to have received a revelation, they implicitly suggest that others might likewise have such experiences, which undermines the necessity of a religious institution as the mediator between God and the faithful. The organized Church thus critically depends on its role as an exclusive intermediary. Kierkegaard, like Adler, understood that the true reason behind the trial was not merely some unorthodox declarations, but the supposed reality of the revelation and the consequent divine authority granted to a clergyman ordained within the Church of Denmark.

The Lutheran Church, as the state's official institution, faced a significant challenge in the possibility that someone might claim to have direct communication with the Divine. Should the populace come to understand that divine revelation is accessible to any individual, the ecclesiastical monopoly over the interpretation and mediation of the sacred would be called into question.

Within the institution of the Papacy lies the tacit acceptance that the Vicar of Christ on Earth maintains divine communication; the idea is so ingrained that proclaiming it explicitly might seem redundant. The implicit expectation is that those chosen for leadership roles within organized religion are, by definition, in dialogue with the Divine. Ironically, if the Supreme Pontiff were to declare he was receiving direct messages from God, such a statement could jeopardize his position within the Vatican. This scenario underscores the tension between institutionalized perceptions of holiness and the authenticity of personal spiritual experience.

For Kierkegaard, the Adler case exposes the prevailing confusion about revelation—a dimension that defies comprehension by natural reason, and ultimately confronts Christianity with what he describes as the paradox that the eternal has been incarnated in time. This is

Chapter 18: The Importance of Divine Revelation According to Kierkegaard

so because it represents a contradiction that resists rational scrutiny, both in past and present times, and which can only be accepted through faith or confronted through scandal. For Kierkegaard, Christianity presents itself as a paradox precisely because at its core is the figure of Christ, who, being God and creator of the universe according to Christian doctrine, suffers at the hands of one of his own creatures—Pontius Pilate.

Kierkegaard urges us to recognize that the heart of Christianity lies in its ability to endure as a perennial paradox, a truth that defies conventional logic and is sustained through faith and divine revelation as the pillars of all experience. From this standpoint, the Danish philosopher criticizes modern theology for its tendency to overly rationalize the mysteries of faith. He suggests instead that we should remain open to the wondrous and the supernatural, embracing the depth of the Divine as it reveals itself to us, without reducing it to the narrow confines of rational explanation.

According to Kierkegaard, the importance of faith for Christianity lies in the fact that it transforms the believer into a contemporary of Christ, allowing access to a knowledge of Christ equal to that of his immediate disciples. Transported mentally back to the time of Christ, it is possible to experience the dawn of Christianity. This raises the question: if we had been there, would we have accepted his teachings immediately, or would they have provoked resistance or skepticism?

Although the official Church claims to understand and embrace the complexities and contradictions inherent in Christianity, Kierkegaard criticizes this stance for failing to empathize truly with the historical and experiential perspective of those times. In fact, he argues that contemporary interpretation, filtered through centuries of theology and doctrinal debate, dilutes the intensity and revolutionary nature of early faith, turning it into something more palatable and less unsettling.

This concept is vividly illustrated in the episode of Adler—a bureaucrat committed to persuading the public that the age of divine communication had ended—, while simultaneously claiming to be the recipient of divine messages, resulting in his dismissal. This act of dismissal embodies the paradox at its fullest: it challenges the conventional expectation that divinity should communicate with transgressors and not with moralists, as was the case with the Pharisees in Jesus' time. Adler represents the moralists, to whom—against all expectations—the divine word is revealed, exposing the irony of a divinity that, from a bureaucratic standpoint, had been neutralized by theology.

In this context, Adler's episode is met with skepticism and critical scrutiny by the Church, which prefers to question his sanity rather than consider the possibility of a genuine supernatural phenomenon. Adler's hesitation under scrutiny does not discredit him; rather, it reveals a failure within the ecclesiastical community to receive and value such experiences properly. A genuine revelation should not require justification or defense, as Kierkegaard demonstrates through the case of Abraham.

Kierkegaard's knight of faith

Kierkegaard argues that institutionalized religion has sought to rationalize faith, forgetting that faith, by its very nature, transcends the need for explanation. The Old Testament (Genesis, 22) shows that when Abraham hears God's command to sacrifice his son Isaac, he does not stop to demand explanations but sets off with Isaac toward the land of Moriah. As Kierkegaard reminds us in his book *Fear and Trembling*, Abraham remains silent because his act of faith is inexplicable and inexpressible. His faith transcends all rational explanation and cannot be conveyed.

The actions of heroes in tragic epics may be comprehensible, no matter how appalling, as when Agamemnon sacrifices his daughter Iphigenia for the greater good. But Abraham seeks neither to save his people, nor to defend the good of his community, nor appease any God's wrath. On the contrary, Abraham's faith operates in the realm of the absurd and arises solely by virtue of divine revelation. The father of Isaac establishes a relationship with God not based on communication, ethics, or even his own individual freedom, but on an intimate and infinite faith. This is why Kierkegaard calls him the "knight of faith."

Therefore, Abraham's absolute faith is paradoxical and, as such, neither demands nor requires any rational explanation. It is a faith that transcends all rationality, all ethics or morality, and indeed, all epistemological criteria—yet it inaugurates within every human being a dimension that opens them to the Divine, to the Absolute. As Kierkegaard compellingly argues, the more improbable this faith is, the greater its capacity to enrich Christian life.

The believer's adherence is not due to the rationality or logic of the beliefs—and in many cases, not even to their ethical character. The story of Abraham shows precisely that faith transcends all logic and becomes the very foundation of all subsequent reason and ethics. Kierkegaard seems to suggest that, without a radical openness to the Absolute and the Infinite, there would be no rational or ethical discourse at all.

This chapter on Kierkegaard has highlighted two main points. The first is that divine revelation opens the conditions of possibility for faith. This faith, like Abraham's, transcends language, reason, and even ethics, reshaping the notion of what might be called religious experience—and by extension, all human experience beyond the dictates of reason. But at the same time, the chapter shows that this debate on revelation and faith should not be confined to theology. These are foundational matters at the religious, philosophical, and sociopolitical levels. To some extent, they help define a society, the credibility of its official religious institutions, and its cultural paradigms.

Kierkegaard's criticism of the structures and practices of organized religion lies in the fact that it has conceptualized the very foundations on which religion is based: faith and revelation. As a result, religion has lost the most intimate dimension: human beings' relation with the absolute and inexplicable.

CHAPTER 19

Phenomenological Foundations of the Revelation of the Sacred

Understanding according to phenomenology

As we saw when presenting various authors and topics of phenomenology, this philosophical movement studies how we comprehend and come to know entities or objects. In a certain way, it seeks to understand how knowledge is possible, investigating its progressive formation as we interact with the object of knowledge. Knowledge is conceived as a process in which the concept gradually takes shape in the mind of the knowing subject. Beginning with perception, the object becomes increasingly intelligible until it assumes a complete form. In this sense, it is analogous to assembling a puzzle: initially, we perceive scattered pieces, but as we connect them, the whole image is revealed to us. This procedure also sheds light on how our perception of things is linked to tangible reality. It is not exclusively about our reflections on an object, but about how these thoughts are associated with concrete elements in the world. In essence, phenomenology helps us understand how our ideas and perceptions intertwine and shape what we consider real.

Guided by Husserl, phenomenology proposes that the intentionality of consciousness intertwines with the object as it is given in experience, constituting the phenomenon in which knowledge crystallizes. His "phenomenological reduction" constitutes the fusion of the subject and the object into a single, more primordial reality: the phenomenon. Without taking anything for granted, it explores the dynamic interaction between consciousness and its objects of attention. Reality cannot be taken as containing meaning prior to our experience of it, nor can it be reduced to a mere mental construct. This approach, founded on the fusion of intentionality and givenness, illustrates that knowledge does not arise in a vacuum but is forged and validated within the context of lived experience. Therefore, for phenomenology, experience becomes the central axis of all understanding.

Later, Heidegger will characterize this same concept with the term *Dasein* (being-there), with which he intends to emphasize the essence of a human being whose main trait is being-there-in-the-world. This fundamental dialogue that reflects *Dasein* as an underlying experience highlights the importance of personal lived experience as a means to access a deeper understanding of our existence and our interaction with the world. Despite the differences between Husserl and Heidegger, to which we will pay special attention later, it must be acknowledged that both perspectives, though arising from different angles, converge on the idea that lived experience is central to the understanding of Being.

In its attempt to define experience, phenomenological study must explain how an object becomes an "object of knowledge." That is, how any object is given or appears in the first instance in our consciousness, turning into an object of our attention, differentiated from other objects. For example, we look at a wall and see a painting. In order to see the painting, something must happen that allows us to focus on the painting as an individualized object distinct from the rest of the wall. That is, initially, and before it can be considered an object, "that something" must be given or appear (*phainómenon*) in our consciousness as something different. The phenomenological reduction involves suspending our judgment about the object, stripping it of all its attributes, and even its name as "object," and allowing it to show itself in its simplest originality. The result is that we gain access to the most original moment of the "object," that is, to its own individualized appearance in consciousness. In other words, the phenomenological reduction brackets everything we "presuppose" about the object in order to reach its purest state: the phenomenon. Thus, the phenomenon presents itself as a givenness, appearing or disclosing itself in consciousness of its own accord.

For his part, Heidegger conceives of Truth as a givenness in his turn toward the question, or *kehre*, about the essence of Truth (rather than the truth of essence). That is, what is, is what is given, what appears, what is unveiled, manifested, or revealed. Truth, thus, is in a certain way an apocalypse; it is *alétheia*, the act of unveiling or discovering what was hidden. However, it is not the entity (the empirical object, the painting we mentioned above) that reveals Being, but rather Being itself that reveals or uncovers itself in the entity. In Heideggerian philosophy, this process is detached from any conceptual framework through the invocation of the sacred, understood as that which escapes the reach of technique and conceptual thought.

For his part, Jean-Luc Marion argues that any phenomenon, whether considered sacred, supernatural, or natural, constitutes a revelation. Each phenomenon that emerges in consciousness does so as an act of givenness, marking what could be called an expanded revelation or an expanded *aletheology*. In this way, Marion extends Heidegger's notion of truth beyond ontology, applying it to all phenomena of consciousness. This suggests that knowledge ultimately rests on revelation.

From phenomenological givenness to the revelation of the sacred

Up to this point, we have addressed "external" perception—that is, how the object comes to be regarded as such. What follows is a fascinating notion: the emergence of the object, as a phenomenon, is not the result of observation, but rather the object itself unfolds, offering a profound knowledge of its nature. That is to say, the perceived object, in order to be perceived, offers itself fully, beyond the influence of the observer.

This clarifies that the intentionality of consciousness is not a productive engine that creates objects, as some critics of phenomenology have suggested, but rather the attention, the openness, of the subject's consciousness to the phenomenon that appears according to its own rules. This illustrates precisely the independence of the object in its act of offering itself. Therefore, its essence as a phenomenon of consciousness becomes manifest without the need for mediation by the observing subject. As Husserl explains:

> [...] the givenness of the different forms of imagination and memory, as well as the givenness of perceptions and other sorts of representations which unify themselves synthetically in many ways in fitting associations. Of course there is also logical givenness, the givenness of universals, of predicates, of states of affairs, etc.; also the givenness of something absurd, of something contradictory, of something which does not exist.[95]

In this sense, givenness, being non-mediated, could be understood as if it were the dream of Viṣṇu, or the divine dream, which projects a dreamlike reality. Husserl uses the notion of *Gegebenheit* (which we can translate from German as "immediate fact or datum") to describe the phenomenon, implying that the phenomenon is given directly and immediately to consciousness, revealing itself without dependence on or need for reasoning or any kind of conceptualization. Therefore, this revelation would be an inherent quality both in people with rudimentary thought and in infants, marking a fundamental feature of human experience that precedes and surpasses the limits of formal instruction and academic learning. This clarifies that the reality of what appears or is given in consciousness immediately and directly is not a mere construct of that same consciousness, and thus, the phenomenon transcends the interiority of the subject.

That is, without transcendence, there would be no givenness, for the object would already be inside, meaning, it would already

---

95. Edmund Husserl, *The Idea of Phenomenology*, trans. William P. Alston and George Nakhnikian, introduction by George Nakhnikian, 5th impression (The Hague: Martinus Nijhoff, 1973), 59 (Fifth Lecture; Hua II, 74).

CHAPTER 19: PHENOMENOLOGICAL FOUNDATIONS OF THE REVELATION OF THE SACRED

be conceived prior to the experience. However, the givenness of the phenomenon is inherent to consciousness, as if it were a fundamental feature of it. Therefore, the transcendence of givenness is only possible in the immanence of consciousness. Thus, as we mentioned earlier, phenomenology, especially in Husserl, conceives of the transcendence of the object within the parameters of the immanence of consciousness and experience. At the same time, it necessarily understands immanence as transcendent to consciousness. This paradoxical situation will define the framework of phenomenology.

It is important to remember that what is revealed or given in consciousness, that is, the phenomenon, should not yet be understood as an object of knowledge. The appearance of the phenomenon in consciousness brings to light the existence of something, still not conceptualized. That is, as the revelation of itself in consciousness, the phenomenon is not reducible to knowledge on the epistemological plane. Heidegger is clear about this when he identifies "the immediately indeterminate" as that which, presenting itself to consciousness as "something," nevertheless remains unknown, though undeniably existent. This conceptualization underscores an essential aspect of our perception: the ability to recognize the existence of something in consciousness, even when its concrete identity or essence remains indefinite. This phenomenon illustrates how certain entities can be present in our understanding, yet remain in a state of indeterminacy. What Heidegger wishes to express here is that the deeper dimension of experience does not occur in the realm of knowledge but of existence. In other words, ontology precedes epistemology.

There is an aspect that can be revisited concerning the phenomenological reduction, as carried out in the texts of Husserl and, indirectly, in those of Heidegger. As we stated earlier, the reduction suspends the objective reality of the object and the subject in order to access a more original dimension of experience. This suspension has sometimes been described in terms of the suspension of the transcendent and transcendental approaches. At the same time, we have spoken of the phenomenon resulting from the reduction in terms of transcendence or immanent transcendence. The apparent contradiction is resolved by understanding that what we bracket is exteriority—that is, the belief in an objective reality with its own meaning. In other words, a reality that would exist beyond consciousness and, therefore, independently of our experience of it. Husserl, nor Heidegger, dismiss transcendence, except when it is understood in terms of absolute exteriority. The reduction provides us with precisely an immanent transcendence, or even a transcendental immanence, with which Husserl can explain especially the relationship between intentional consciousness and the phenomena as givenness or revelation, without falling into a relationship of dependency or cause-effect.

This reduction of transcendence qua absolute exteriority applies in two directions. On the one hand, the reduction suspends what we can call vertical transcendence, which refers to what exists as objective reality beyond the world of our experience. On the other hand, we suspend horizontal transcendence or exteriority, concerning everything within the dimension of the subject, of consciousness, that could be conceived as prior to the experience of the phenomenon. This includes an ego, a creative subject, or any other figure understood as the creator of meaning independently of the world that is lived and experienced in phenomenological consciousness.

It is important to clarify that, just as we find a phenomenological reduction in Husserl, we encounter a phenomenological expansion in Marion. The phenomenological reduction involves the exclusion or omission of the transcendent understood as absolute exteriority. This concept of transcendence refers to the objective reality that exceeds us and transcends our immediate and tangible experience. According to Husserl, concepts like the "I," the soul, and God are not isolated entities, but coexist and integrate within the individuality of consciousness. As he himself states:

> *das Ich und Welt und Gott und die mathematischen Mannigfaltigkeiten und was immer für wissenschaftliche Objektivitäten dahingestellt bleiben*

I, the world, and God, as well as the mathematical multiplicities and scientific objectivities, remain undecided.[96]

Therefore, and similarly to Descartes, "I," "world," and "God" do not present themselves as independent entities in individual consciousness, but coexist harmoniously within the domain of personal consciousness. Understanding does not emerge from the active effort of the knower, but from the total and absolute givenness of the object or the known thing, fully revealing itself to consciousness. What is known, including the "I" as a transcendent phenomenon, is given to individual consciousness. For this reason, and unlike Descartes, Husserl takes a further step and discards everything, including the "I" and individual consciousness, by applying his phenomenological reduction. The subject is suspended in order to access a transcendental and pre-egoic subjectivity of experience. This practice ultimately discards the transcendent exterior and unveils a field of the a priori in total self-givenness.

In the phenomenological reduction, subject and object take root together, forming an integral relationship that culminates in an inextricable unity: the phenomenon. The object becomes part of the phenomenon by merging with the subject or cognition. That is, object and phenomenon are not two words that describe the same thing, but rather the object emerges in the phenomenon as it is revealed to the subject. Phenomenology unveils the way in which the object, in its essence and transcendence, is progressively and systematically configured. This process highlights the evolutionary development in the constitution of the object, thereby emphasizing the essential connection between perception and tangible reality.

Heidegger's philosophy also offers a phenomenon, which is called *Dasein* in this case. A common mistake among contemporary philosophers is to misinterpret *Dasein* as the human being itself when, in reality, it represents the interaction of the human being with Being. This principle goes beyond mere individual identification,

---

96. Ibid., Introduction, "B. The Second Step in the Phenomenological Consideration" (Hua II, 9, §3).

focusing on the vital relationship between the person and the essence of Being. Understanding *Dasein* properly means recognizing that it is not just human existence per se, but the dynamic and continuous process of human encounter with Being, a fundamental aspect in exploring our existential reality.

As Heidegger himself explains in *Being and Time*, within the context of our lived experiences, we encounter situations that range from interactions with inauthentic aspects of Being to moments of connection with authentic Being. These diverse experiences, which range from the trivial to the meaningful, emphasize the constant presence of Being in each of them. Regardless of the degree of authenticity in our experiences, our immediate relation to Being remains constant. Being is decisive in the formation of our understanding and perception of the world.

This line of thought leads to the reflection on what is known as "problems of givenness" or "problems of the constitution of all types of objectualities in knowledge" (*der Konstitution von Gegenständlichkeiten jeder Art in der Erkenntnis*). Our primary interest lies not in the existence of God outside of my mind, but—as already occurs in Descartes—in the process by which the notion of God has manifested in our consciousness. However, this approach is less about an external validation of divinity and more about an introspection on how transcendent ideas develop and persist within the realm of individual consciousness. Similarly, the central enigma is not the external existence of the universe, but the process by which objective reality is integrated and perceived within our consciousness. The inquiry into whether the universe exists apart from our consciousness is a metaphysical question, a perspective that is not the subject of study in this analysis.

The exploration we undertake in the field of phenomenology can be defined as an eidetic science dedicated to detailing and describing the experiences of consciousness after undergoing a transcendental reduction. This eidetic approach examines the idea of the thing immersed in consciousness, opening a search that transcends the tangible to immerse in the realm of the fundamental and the experienced. Within this framework of transcendental consciousness, we dare to contribute a new concept of Being to Western philosophy: Being is to be captured by consciousness. Our attention moves away from the object itself and the thought about it to our own direct experience of the thing. The intentionality of consciousness and the givenness of the object unite in the experience or phenomenon, where authentic knowledge is configured and revealed, this being the only scenario where genuine knowledge manifests and is acquired.

As we have seen in detail in this chapter, in the phenomenological discipline, the orientation of consciousness toward the object constitutes its intentionality, while the manifestation of the object before consciousness is its givenness; both dynamics merge in the phenomenological experience, the authentic realm where knowledge crystallizes. We can illustrate this dual dynamic through an example. Let us imagine we examine an object of our everyday experience, say, a book. Normally, we would consider only the book itself. However, our personal interaction with the book is vital from a phenomenological perspective. Our experience consists of two dynamics. The first is the "intentionality of consciousness," which involves the orientation of our mind toward the book. The second is the "givenness of the object," which is the way the book presents itself to our mind. Both merge in our experience, through which we grasp the true nature of the book, and this understanding is what we can define as real and true knowledge.

Nevertheless, in the realm of lived experience, the limited intertwines with the unlimited, giving rise to an exceptional interaction between the knowing being and the known being (the book in our previous example). In ordinary circumstances, both retain their fundamental distinction, even as they are intricately connected through perception and lived experience. Such a conjunction does not erase the boundaries that separate them but rather fuses them within the phenomenological process, ensuring the preservation of their identities even amidst their union. Thus, the experience of the limited facilitates an interrelation in which, despite a transient fusion, the knowing being and the known being mutually acknowledge each other in their singularity.

The lived experience of the unlimited, or of the sacred, inaugurates a profoundly different dimension of experience. In this framework, the sacred surpasses the spectrum of the limited experience of the knowing being. In these moments, the knowing being yields its independence before the vastness of the sacred. According to Marion, the experience of the sacred is a saturated phenomenon, a lived experience that overwhelms our capacities for perception and thought.

In such an experience, what predominates is the manifestation of a "pure experience" in which the differentiation between the cognizing being and the known being ceases to be pertinent. This state of pure experience can be understood as a moment of absolute communion or integration with the whole, where individual consciousness integrates with the object of its reflection or veneration, overcoming the barriers of limited existence. This lived experience is typical of moments of intense spirituality or mysticism. In them, the Divine or sacred is revealed so strikingly that the conventional structures of experience are surpassed. They generate a state of consciousness where the usual categories of analysis and understanding become obsolete, and only what is, as it is, remains.

Bibliography section V

- Descartes, René. *Discourse on Method and Meditations on First Philosophy*. Translated by Donald A. Cress. 4th ed. Indianapolis: Hackett, 1998.
- Heidegger, Martin. *Poetry, Language, Thought*. Translated by Albert Hofstadter. New York: Harper & Row, 1971.
- Husserl, Edmund. *Collected Works*, vol. 2. Translated by F. Kersten. Dordrecht: Kluwer Academic Publishers, 1990.
- Husserl, Edmund. *The Idea of Phenomenology*. Translated by William P. Alston and George Nakhnikian. Introduction by George Nakhnikian. 5th impression. The Hague: Martinus Nijhoff, 1973.
- Kierkegaard, Søren. *Fear and Trembling; The Book on Adler*. Translated by Walter Lowrie. Introduction by George Steiner. New York: Everyman's Library, Alfred A. Knopf, 1994.
- McGrath, Sean J. The Philosophical Foundations of the Late Schelling: The Turn to the Positive. Edinburgh: Edinburgh University Press, 2021.
- Plato. *Complete Works*. Edited by John M. Cooper. Translated by Alexander Nehamas and Paul Woodruff. Indianapolis: Hackett Publishing, 1997.
- Schelling, Friedrich Wilhelm Joseph. *Philosophy of Revelation*. Lecture VII: Reason and Revelation. Translated from Juan Cruz Cruz's Spanish edition. Pamplona: Cuadernos de Anuario Filosófico, Serie Universitaria n. 51, 1998.
- St. Augustine. *Confessions*. Translated by J. G. Pilkington. In Nicene and Post-Nicene Fathers, First Series, vol. 1, edited by Philip Schaff. Buffalo, NY: Christian Literature Publishing Co., 1886.

- St. Augustine. *De Genesi ad litteram imperfectus liber* (*The Literal Interpretation of Genesis: Unfinished Book*). Translated by Isabella Image. CPL 2681, rev. ed., 2020.
- St. Augustine. *De libero arbitrio*. Translated by Dom Mark Pontifex. London: Longmans, Green and Co., 1955.
- St. Augustine. *Eighty-Three Different Questions* (De diversis quaestionibus LXXXIII). Translated by David L. Mosher. Washington, DC: Catholic University of America Press, 1982.
- St. Augustine. *On Faith and the Creed*. In Nicene and Post-Nicene Fathers, First Series, vol. 3, edited by Philip Schaff. Translated by J. H. S. Burleigh. Buffalo, NY: Christian Literature Publishing Co., 1887.
- St. Augustine. *On the Trinity*. Translated by Arthur West Haddan. In Logos Virtual Library, edited by Darren L. Slider, 1999–2008. Book IV, Chapter 20.
- St. Augustine. *The Literal Meaning of Genesis*. Translated by John Hammond Taylor, S.J. 2 vols. Ancient Christian Writers 41–42. New York: Newman Press, 1982.
- Williams, Christi. *The Concept of Eternity in Kierkegaard's Philosophical Anthropology*. Durham, UK: Ethics International Press, 2024.

Section VI

From phenomenology to ontology

CHAPTER 20

THE PHENOMENOLOGICAL EXPLORATION OF CONSCIOUSNESS

The phenomenon and consciousness according to Husserl

Throughout the previous chapters, we have seen how phenomenology delves into two essential questions. On the one hand, and what we might call the "critical level," it addresses the process of acquiring knowledge, that is, how perception presents the object in such a way that it can acquire meaning in our consciousness of it and be understood. At the same time, but now at a "metacritical level," phenomenology also questions our ability to discern the feasibility of knowledge itself. The fundamental matter, therefore, is not only how knowledge is possible, but also whether we can know the possibility of such knowledge. In order to address this dual question, phenomenology focuses on the conditions that allow something to give itself in consciousness, focusing on deciphering the capacities of our cognitive potential.

Phenomenology delves into our capacity to understand the viability of these experiences. As a result of the phenomenological reduction, it describes an "intrinsic or immanent givenness of consciousness," which configures an area immune to doubts or uncertainties. Thus, it provides an unshakable solidity, rooted in a direct understanding that overcomes the need to seek external explanations. As we have also seen at various points in this book, the understanding of the world and of existence does not transcend the limits of our consciousness, but rather is anchored in its depths, providing a singular interpretation of reality, just as it is experienced. Consequently, our attention is focused solely on the givenness intrinsic to consciousness. Unlike the Western philosophical tradition, phenomenology holds that subject and object neither oppose nor precede one another; they mutually transcend and belong to one another at the same time. This approach provides us with a solid foundation for understanding the world and our relationship with it, insofar as it is internalized and revealed within our consciousness—that is, exclusively in the experience.

Immanuel Kant's epistemological philosophy investigates our capacity to experience the object through the senses and the categories (formal concepts), as well as the way in which these experiences contribute to our knowledge of reality. He holds that there is a noumenal world and a phenomenal version of it, though he does not consider them as two separate realities or parallel worlds. He distinguishes the noumenon from the way it appears in consciousness through the senses and understanding—that is, the phenomenon. For phenomenology, to affirm the existence of such a noumenal reality would be to succumb to prejudice. Unlike Kant, phenomenology maintains that this world of experience cannot be regarded as a version of a more real or objective one that lies beyond our capacities of understanding. Rather, it offers precisely a reinterpretation of reality, but without any gaps between the world and its givenness to consciousness. The human being does not live merely a version or modality of reality. On the contrary, reality is what is lived—there is no other, no purer or more objective reality.

That is to say, from the standpoint of phenomenology, the phenomenon is its own givenness and revelation in consciousness. There is no phenomenon that is subsequently given to consciousness, as if such givenness were merely a possibility or an attribute of the phenomenon. Accepting this view would mean returning to those philosophical approaches that simply assume the existence of an objective reality prior to its understanding by consciousness or endowed with meaning prior to experience. According to these, the external world as a totally transcendent object can only remain hidden from our understanding. We could only perceive this pure world in the way it manifests in the sphere of our consciousness. The understanding of the world as a transcendent being would elude us because our understanding is limited to deciphering the way entities are projected into our consciousness, without access to their intrinsic essence. Ultimately, these approaches based on a separation between reality and its givenness sketch the notion of a human being confined or trapped in their conscious perception and ignorant of the possibility of knowing the true nature of the observed, reducing them to having only a superficial and prejudiced view of reality. Consequently, under this approach, we would not have the right to conclude that we perceive a tree, but that we perceive something whose real essence escapes our understanding, limiting us to a mere superficial perception of reality. This critique of phenomenology toward Kantian philosophy, and by extension, to the conceptual frameworks from which modern sciences stem, extends also, and especially, to the discipline of psychology.

According to Husserl, the laws of empirical psychology were insufficient to provide clarity, as explained in both his text *The Idea of Phenomenology* and in the writings of his course *Fundamental Problems of Phenomenology*. On the contrary, he defended the idea that what was crucial was exploring consciousness itself, its forms, meanings, and the ways it expresses or generates. Phenomenology studies pure or universal consciousness, which makes it a fully transcendental discipline. Despite its similarities with empirical psychology, there are many differences because it reduces consciousness to a set of neural laws from which human behavior and the subsequent existence of the world as an extension of empirical consciousness are explained. Empirical psychology asserts that the world is a mere representation of consciousness, leading us to abandon questioning the external and how such exteriority is given in our consciousness. It limits us to investigating reality as if it were only internal contents of our conscious perception. Under this lens of psychology, the human being reorients their gaze toward the depths of their interior, abandoning the mistaken conception of an objectual diversity, as they see the external as an extension of their interior. In other words, the world is nothing more than a construct that beats in the mind of consciousness or, if we prefer, a mirror of our interior. Psychology, in its attempt to bridge the gap between reality and representation, between noumenon and phenomenon, errs by annihilating transcendence and reducing it to a modality of mere immanence.

As a result of all this, phenomenology shows us that applying empirical methods to explore an objectual world beyond our perception is futile. Such an approach distances us from the true nature of our inquiry, which is none other than the meticulous examination of our own interior. Instead of unraveling the mysteries of an external world that arises in our consciousness, empirical psychology navigates the intricate labyrinths of our psyche. It seeks for answers that lie in the depths of our consciousness as if they were creations *ex nihilo* of the same. Therefore, and under the lens of this empirical psychology, the possibility of knowing something beyond consciousness is an illusion, as even when referring to the external, we reaffirm its existence within the realm of our consciousness, as if it were only part of it, belonged to it, or was a construct of the same.

Contrary to the empirical conception of the psyche, phenomenological reduction reveals that the world is neither wholly transcendent to consciousness nor radically immanent as a part of it. The world acquires its meaning through being lived—not before, nor after. Thus, the object is transcendent (because it is not a fragment of consciousness) yet remains within the immanence of consciousness (as it does not exist independently of it). This perspective dissolves the traditional boundaries between subject and object, opening onto a deeper and more intricate field of experience.

Heidegger's philosophy, taking a step further and somewhat distancing himself from certain Husserlian precepts, he transforms consciousness and its thoughts (*cogitationes*) into *Dasein*, that is, a human being who, before being consciousness, already is being-in-the-world. Heidegger's turn, and his question about Being, holds the conception that the world and *Dasein* are given, as we would say, in the same stroke, and neither precedes the other. In fact, their meaning is only possible in that relationship of experience that underlies everything else. This position has received several criticisms from different philosophical positions as well as from other disciplines. Although we will not address all of them, we will attempt to respond to the accusation of solipsism, an attack often directed at both Husserl and

Heidegger's thought. The work of both is precisely characterized by a notion that we propose to call the intrasubjective subject, contrary to the prevailing perception in certain fields—especially psychology—that each person manages a private sphere of consciousness, distinct and separate from others. Without going into excessive detail on the matter, this intrasubjectivity would defend the idea that all human beings are intrinsically connected by a universal consciousness, a shared network that transcends individual barriers.

The deepest truth reveals that individuality is only a facet, an aspect of a vast shared consciousness that encompasses us all, and this includes human beings from the past, present, and future. However, this universal consciousness should not be understood as an umbrella or a matrix to which all consciences are connected, but rather, to put it in Heidegger's own terminology, *Dasein* is *mitsein*. That is, being-in-the-world is equivalent to being-with-others-in-the-world. Being-with is not an additional attribute but part of the essence of being-in-the-world. The Other, therefore, is not something purely external to me with which I never fully coincide, but is an integral part of my experience of the world. Being-in-the-world is living-the-world-with-others, without whom the world itself could neither be lived as it is lived nor have the meaning it has.

Heidegger's response to this problem clarifies that any study of the most intimate experience that defines us as human beings, whether under the name of consciousness (Husserl) or *Dasein* (Heidegger), is a purely transcendental and not empirical approach. Therefore, there is no possibility of confusing Husserl and Marion's phenomenologies, or Heidegger's hermeneutical philosophy, with psychological introspection that simply ends with a transcendental ego living in isolation and solitude. Far from any egoic introspection and isolated individuality, transcendental phenomenology guides us toward a deeper perception of universal consciousness, considered the foundation of all existence. This approach leads us to a more complete and holistic understanding of reality, seeing universal consciousness as the underlying foundation of all being and existence. Let us now examine this issue in greater detail.

The transcendental ego, the Other, and universal consciousness

Husserl points out that his phenomenological approach is neither pioneering nor innovative. Intellectuals such as Carl Stumpf and Theodor Lipps, inspired by Brentano, had already attempted to address the problems we have outlined. However, in an era dominated by Kantian philosophy—and more specifically by what is now known as Neo-Kantianism—their work was poorly received and dismissed as dogmatic. This hindered progress in the study of immanence beyond the prevailing academic frameworks of the time.

Husserl's initial diagnosis and critique arise, in part, from his reading of the very origin of philosophy. The fundamental question of how human beings acquire knowledge was first posed by the Sophists. This inquiry led Plato and Aristotle to explore the validity and legitimacy of knowledge, responding from a critical perspective to the approach the Sophists had taken toward the Pre-Socratics. In addressing the challenges presented by the Sophists, Plato and Aristotle laid the foundations for what Husserl would later seek to structure as a scientific discipline. He addressed these issues in his lecture titled *Introduction to Philosophy* (*Einleitung in die Philosophie*), delivered in the winter of 1922–23, which originated from four lectures given in London in 1922 under the title *Phenomenological Method and Phenomenological Philosophy*. In his dissertation, he established a new paradigm for approaching epistemology, through a rigorous phenomenological methodology capable of fulfilling its original purpose.

Heidegger's diagnosis is ostensibly different, as his reading is not merely epistemological, but ontological. Unlike Husserl's view, which focuses on reformulating philosophy into a phenomenology that serves as *prima philosophia* in order to respond to epistemological concerns, Heidegger identifies the root of the foundational problem in a confusion between Being and beings, which he attributes to Plato, and which results in the gradual corruption of what has sometimes been called a certain initial purity. From Heidegger's point of view, the Greek beginnings of philosophy represent the drive to know the Truth, that which truly is. However, the parameters under which Plato inaugurates philosophy as a discipline represent a transformation of the concept of *alétheia*. Although commonly translated as "truth," the Greek term carries an original notion that transcends the simple correspondence between words and facts, and refers to a process of unveiling, revelation, or manifestation of what is. This process is not, however, just another activity, such as philosophy as a discipline might be, but rather, according to Heidegger, it is a fundamental characteristic of our existence. To exist, then, is to show oneself open to Being. Instead of "seeing" the Truth, and reducing Truth to the exact and static correspondence between word and thing, Heidegger defends the need to immerse ourselves again in human experience to explore how Being is "revealed" or "unconcealed" in our existence. That is, in the face of the Platonic confusion and the subsequent sophistic skepticism that emerges from this same confusion (as Husserl also denounces in *Erste Philosophie* or *First Philosophy*), Heidegger proposes a phenomenological ontology that, in a sense, allows a return to the pre-Platonic origins, where the pre-Socratic ontological sages, in contrast to Plato's philosophy, did not engage in rigorous analysis of how the world could be known, but rather immersed themselves directly in the experience of its unifying foundation.

Heraclitus and Parmenides, far from focusing on the theoretical speculation of the inherent possibilities of Being, centered on the direct and profound understanding of its nature. Their work was not an exercise in hypothetical conjectures, but rather a path to the true understanding of the fundamental reality of Being. Therefore, the phenomenological ontology that Heidegger proposes would not study the conditions of possibility for accessing Being, as philosophy from Plato to Kant has done, but would simply seek to access Being. As Heidegger himself explains in his *Letter on Humanism* it is about returning to an attitude (*ethos*) of remaining "open to Being."

In this context, both Husserl and Heidegger develop their notion of universal consciousness. In one of his texts, Husserl writes:

SECTION VI: FROM PHENOMENOLOGY TO ONTOLOGY

Also ich gewinne als der philosophisch Meditierende neben der individuellen apodiktischen Evidenz des ego cogito, die hinsichtlich der Möglichkeit tatsachenwissenschaftlicher Erforschung fraglich bleibt, das unendliche Reich komkreter Wesensanschauungen und komkret geschöpfter unmittelbarer Wesensgesetze für alle idealen möglichkeiten eines Ich und eines cogito überhaupt.

As one who philosophically meditates, I have thus gained, for all the ideal possibilities of an ego and of any *cogito* in general, the infinite realm of concrete intuitions and concretely created immediate laws of essence, in addition to the individual apodictic evidence of the ego *cogito*, which remains uncertain with respect to the possibility of scientific investigation of facts.[97]

The reflection that Husserl carries out, which we have partially described in previous chapters, involves discerning all the possibilities of an "I" and a *cogito* in a broad sense. The "I" is individual consciousness or *cogito*, while *cogitatio* must be understood as consciousness at the universal level. Philosophical meditation consists of understanding how individual and general consciousness converge, relating to each other through ideal possibilities. Let's explore this issue more closely.

Husserl refers to what he himself calls "the infinite realm of concrete intuitions and concretely created immediate laws of essence," obtained when universal consciousness imparts its influence on individual consciousness. This means that, for Husserl, philosophically meditating consists of allowing individual consciousness to be infiltrated or impregnated by general consciousness. When the individual consciousness receives the influence of the universal consciousness, the ego *cogito* or "I think" emerges, dedicating its thought to the investigation and analysis of consciousness and phenomena. Thus, rather than asserting that everything emerges from an ego *cogito*

---

97. Edmund Husserl, *Einleitung in die Logik und Erkenntnistheorie*. Vorlesungen 1906/07, ed. Ullrich Melle, Husserliana XXXV (Dordrecht: Kluwer Academic Publishers, 2002), 328–29. Translation mine.

that transcends and precedes everything, as if it were a lighthouse whose light illuminates reality in the night from nothing, for Husserl, the ego *cogito* that investigates, reflects, and thinks about the world is the result of the influence exerted by *cogitatio*. The elements of knowledge that reside within individual consciousness are, in truth, seeds planted by a broader universal consciousness. In a way, we are referring to Descartes' innate ideas mentioned earlier. These ideas are both innate and not innate, for we have already seen how Descartes himself argues that they "must have been placed in me." They dwell within us and enable us to undertake a deeper inquiry.

To conceive of this relationship between individual and universal consciousness in terms of a distinction between "inside" and "outside" inevitably leads us to a mere relative duality that simply does not correspond to Husserlian thought, and perhaps not even to Cartesian thought. In fact, the phenomenological approach dissolves the dualism that opposes the adverbs inside and outside. It discerns an underlying field of transcendence within immanence, in which certain structures of interiority and exteriority simply vanish. Profound questions such as *aieka* or "where are you?" in Hebrew, and the *ātma-vicāra advaita* "Who am I?," are examples of inquiries that descend into personal consciousness from ultimate consciousness. Those who receive fundamental questions like these can consider themselves privileged. However, it is not fair to blame those who have not been graced with such questions.

This "transcendental ego," a philosophical term primarily associated with Immanuel Kant and expanded by Edmund Husserl in his work *Cartesian Meditations*, denotes the essence of consciousness that grounds all our experiences and thoughts. Essentially, it represents the facet of the mind responsible for unifying and giving meaning to our varied experiences. That is why Kant calls it the "transcendental unity of perception" or even, simply, the "I think," and defines it as that which accompanies all my representations. That is to say, for my acts of consciousness, and by which are meant all and any of my perceptions, memories, dreams, imaginings, and so on, to be "mine" acts, something must "weave" them together as they take place, or else they would be isolated acts, unrelated to each other, and thus, I would not recognize them as "mine." In other words, if my life is in some way the result of all "my" acts of thought, desire, memory, fantasy, and so on, all of them interconnected or even intertwined, it is because the "I think" thinks them as these acts take place. That is, every time I think, dream, or remember the world, I think of myself doing it.

Therefore, it is important to differentiate this transcendental ego from the common personal "I" or the "I" of empirical psychology. The transcendental ego functions more as an essential and pure "I" that constitutes the root of our ability to understand and perceive the environment.

Kant and Husserl understand the concept of the "I" or transcendental ego in different ways. While Kant says that the transcendental ego creates essences, Husserl maintains that it does not create them but intuits them. For Kant, the "I" is essential for cohesive self-consciousness, synthesizing sensations into mental categories, although in itself, this "I" is not directly accessible, being an underlying condition of knowledge and not an object of it. On the other hand, Husserl defines the "transcendental ego" as the "I" in its purest state, obtained through the mental distancing from the world, a process known as "phenomenological *epoché*." As we have already seen, the *epoché* entails suspending or setting aside all our automatic beliefs and assumptions about the world, those we take for granted as self-evident or natural. This step leads us to a deeper state of reflection that, when applied, reveals a renewed perspective, where our perceptions and experiences are perceived with greater authenticity and solidity. In this newly discovered space, both science and philosophy—as well as we ourselves, as subjects of knowledge—find a more solid and evident foundation. This foundation is free from the distortions caused by our pre-existing notions, which Husserl, and later Gadamer, referred to as "prejudices." Heidegger referred to these prejudices as "ontological pre-understanding" or as "middle-range understandings of the pre-ontological." On the one hand, the *epoché* reveals to us the domain of the intentional object as the givenness of the phenomenon; on the other, it discloses that the transcendental ego does not dwell in an ivory tower from which it constructs the world. Rather, it underlies all subjective activity, outlining an "environment" in which this ego intrinsically coexists with other transcendental egos. As Husserl himself reminds us in his *Cartesian Meditations*, these other transcendental egos are not copies or projections of mine, but other transcendental egos that I recognize as such and with which I am intertwined. This shows us, above all, that the transcendental ego, in its quality as bodily consciousness, does not exist in isolation. On the contrary, it is linked with other beings, forming part of a transcendental network. In this complex web of unique entities, called monads or particles, a coherent and meaningful universe is built, specifically adapted to this intricate configuration. The self-reflection expressed by *epoché* leads me to recognize myself as a transcendental ego that is always and inevitably co-present [*Mitgegenwärt*] with other transcendental egos. In other words, I appear to myself, in my absolute purity, as a transcendental ego incarnate, in whose primordial level of existence I am with other transcendental egos. That is, the other egos are not yet objects of my thought, fantasy, dreams, or memories, but are, in a sense, part of my "I" at the deepest level, or what we previously called "a universal or general consciousness." The most intimate "I" is nothing but an ego that is singular and plural at once.

This unified egoic reality, which is more original and profound than any empirical individuality, presents us, in a sense, with a transcendental communion. Speaking in these terms means speaking of a universal consciousness that belongs to the sphere of the One, in which unity and difference are not mere opposites. The other "transcendental egos" that emerge in association with my "transcendental ego" are, nonetheless, "other" egos, for otherwise, they would be reducible to me or to a projection of myself. Therefore, they must be distinct from me but, at the same time, an integral part of my own "transcendental ego." What this shows is that neither Husserl's phenomenology nor Heidegger's ontology fall into any solipsism. Quite the contrary, they help dissolve the very conditions of possibility for any form of solipsism or empirical psychologism.

SECTION VI: FROM PHENOMENOLOGY TO ONTOLOGY

The temporal dimension of universal consciousness

The topic of the transcendental ego opens the door to the issue of time. Although we will address this in more depth later, in this section, we will outline the notion of phenomenological time that emerges alongside universal consciousness, whether we understand it in the manner of Husserl or with Heidegger's *mitsein*. At the level of this transcendental reality, time does not conform to a notion of quantifiable temporality, nor is it linear. Although time is perceived as temporeity by the empirical entity, at the level of Being, that is, of what lies latent in all existence, time expresses itself as temporality, as Heidegger reminds us. This temporality is not the measurable or calculable time that orders our everyday life, but rather time temporizing itself, emerging in the form of Being; or, as Husserl would put it, in the form of transcendental consciousness at its deepest level of intimacy or spirituality. Expressed in another way, it is time understood as the mystical time of the opportune moment or the timely event, a concept illustrated in Christianity with the arrival of Jesus Christ on Earth, described as *Kairós*. Unlike the time associated with the entity, which is characterized by its sequence of before and after and its ability to be measured, the time of Being is kairological, for it exists outside these linear and quantifiable dimensions.

Kairós is an ancient Greek notion that translates to "appropriate moment" or "opportunity," contrasting with *chrónos*, which refers to chronological and sequential time that emphasizes duration. While *chrónos* is linear and quantitative, *kairós* is qualitative and timeless, marking decisive instances that transcend the conventional measure of time. The New Testament uses the notion of *kairós* and related terms 86 times to denote a divinely ordered concept of time for certain actions, as seen in passages like Matthew 8:29, Luke 19:44, and Acts 24:25. This concept is central to understanding timely events such as the Day of Judgment, highlighted in the parable of the wheat and the tares in Matthew 13:30, where Jesus uses *kairós* to point to the eschatological moment of the harvest. *Kairós* also appears in contexts where the predetermined time for significant events is defined, such as the birth of John the Baptist (Luke 1:20) and critical moments predicted by Jesus regarding the judgment on Israel (Luke 19:44). Moreover, it is imperative to capture these divine opportunities, as Jesus urges in his first sermon (Mark 1:15), where he declares the nearness of the kingdom of God and the necessity for repentance and faith. The biblical narrative warns against neglecting these opportunities, as illustrated in the interaction between Paul and the governor Felix in Acts 24:25. Felix, by postponing his decision to follow the gospel, personifies the rejection of the present *kairós*. This episode underscores the urgency and fleeting nature of *kairós*, which Paul emphasizes by saying, "now is the day of salvation" (2 Corinthians 6:2), referring to the brief window for redemption.

In addition to its biblical use, *kairós* encompasses a rich temporal philosophy. It represents a "culminating moment," as well as the confluence of circumstances that demand an immediate and appropriate response. If, in Western culture, *chrónos* has often been associated with the mythological figure who governs ordered and predictable time, *kairós* symbolizes that other, special time—intangible and laden with meaning—that bursts forth with transformative forces. This is the time of revelation, of critical decisions, and of divine action that interrupts the continuity of *chrónos*. The importance of *kairós* is that it invites us to reconsider our perception and experience of time. It exhorts us to be alert to those unique moments which, although ephemeral, offer the possibility of a transcendental change and a profound encounter with the Divine. *Kairós* redefines time, not as a sequence of events, but as moments of truth where life acquires new meaning and direction. In this framework, each *kairós* moment is an invitation to live fully, capturing the essence of existence in its highest expression.

The problem of this *kairological* time of Being, or the transcendental ego, raises important issues, and in turn, significant problems. For this reason, Kant avoids any debate or description of the "I think," as it would have to refer to yet another "act," even more intimate, that synthesizes all the acts of the "I think." This would inevitably lead him into an *ad infinitum* regress, ultimately leading to absurdity. In contrast to Kant, Husserl introduces an innovative element in this regard. In his *Lectures on the Internal Consciousness of*

Time, he presents the issue of double intentionality. As we have seen, Husserl describes every act of consciousness as an intentional act through which we think, remember, dream, or imagine objects of different natures. However, for our consciousness to be defined as a flow, such acts must be synthesized and integrated with each other. To achieve this, Husserl speaks of a second intentionality, which he calls "horizontal intentionality," and which he defines as a self-immediate perception integrated into the same act, unlike an act of consciousness ("horizontal transversal"). That is to say, a tacit self-consciousness, a self-affectivity, as Michel Henry would later call it, inherent in every act of consciousness, from which consciousness, as a flow, temporizes itself and emerges as such in the form of a transcendental ego interpenetrated by other egos with which it lives the world in plurality.

Thus, unlike Kant, the self-temporalization and formation of consciousness are not given solely by acts but by acts and by a self-consciousness that is not an act in itself but is embedded in every act of consciousness. With this second intentionality, Husserl argues precisely that time is what organizes consciousness and, therefore, all our experiences. Unlike measurable and calculable time, and even more so the time of natural sciences, which appears converted into a graph where everything else is inscribed, time, as Husserl understands it, is immanent to consciousness, or as Heidegger would say, time is Being.

To understand time as immanent to consciousness implies saying that, for both Husserl and Heidegger, time is interior to universal consciousness, not just to that of an individual empirical consciousness. Each individual perception, or *cogito*, encapsulates a wide spectrum of potential experiences, implying its development in a context of varied expectations, a horizon of multiple projections, and networks of possible connections. All of them are governed by an immanent normativity that allows for their synthesis. Nonetheless, this synthesis consists in the integration of all my acts, which includes both my current and potential projections. These acts are not individual in nature, but rather constitute the integration of experiences projected from universal consciousness into the individual one. In other words, "horizontal" intentionality is what allows the transformation of the indeterminate of universal consciousness into something tangible and immediate that beats in every experience of each individual consciousness through a total givenness. Every concrete act implies a universal givenness that gives meaning to all those concrete acts. Even a phenomenological self-reflection, in the form of *epoché*, will be a concrete act, and if it has the ability to reveal this universal consciousness, it is because, as an act, it inherently carries within itself that other immediate intentional self-perception that accompanies all acts.

Therefore, the synthesis of all the acts of consciousness leads us to the issue of the self-temporalization of consciousness itself, which equals our capacity to perceive the universal in the individual and plural at the same time, which allows us to weave our life of experiences. These experiences, with which we shape our life, though personal, are experiences that spring from a dimension of universal consciousness in which my transcendental ego is permanently intertwined and open to other transcendental egos. Husserl's phenomenological investigation has made it clear that all experiences descend from a final transcendental consciousness, which beats permanently in our particular experiences. This consciousness palpitates in each experience, appearing tacitly as if it were a backdrop. In other words, it would be as if all our lived moments carried within them the imprint or engraving of universal consciousness, without which particular lived experiences would paradoxically not be our particular lived experiences.

This idea of a givenness, which implies that universal consciousness deposits its content in the personal, was already explored by Averroes with his thesis of the "separated understanding." According to Averroes, the separated understanding is constituted by both the agent understanding and the passive one. One is active and generates knowledge, and the other is passive and receives or understands that knowledge. These understandings are the same for all humanity and are not specific to each person. Furthermore, Averroes believes that knowledge is a process in which these two understandings combine. When a person achieves complete knowledge, in some way, they lose their individuality and join a sort of soul or understanding common to all, which he calls "monopsychism." This means that our individual soul must be understood as an integral part of a great universal soul shared by all. Universal consciousness not only influences but also shapes individual consciousness through projections or influences that create horizons through which selected experiences can be given by general consciousness. Contrary to what might be assumed, the issue at hand does not originally stem from Averroes, but directly from Aristotle's reflections in his work *Peri Psyche*. Averroes, in his interpretive work, offers a particular exegesis of Aristotelian ideas.

In a later development, Saint Thomas Aquinas introduces a refined distinction, arguing that what is conceived as a separated understanding is not situated externally to the individual; rather, it is distanced from the materiality inherent in the human condition without being detached from it. Averroes, on the other hand, holds a divergent view, asserting that such understanding is indeed segregated from the human being. This controversy remained resolved in favor of the Thomistic interpretation until the 20th century, when Enrico Berti, after a meticulous study of Aristotelian works, claimed Averroes' view to be the most faithful interpretation of Aristotle's texts. This interpretive shift reopens the debate on the nature of understanding and its relationship with Being, inviting a deep reconsideration of the premises that have guided philosophical thought for centuries.

CHAPTER 21

HEIDEGGER'S ONTOLOGICAL TURN

Observation as the first approach to consciousness

In the present chapter, we will examine how Heidegger redirects Husserl's research, shifting from the dimension of consciousness and the transcendental ego to the matter of the unveiling of Being and *Dasein*. In doing so, Heidegger proposes overcoming the epistemology to which Husserl confines phenomenology and establishing ontology instead. In this Heideggerian turn, the question of consciousness and knowledge takes on a new dimension, focusing on Being. Heidegger suggests that it is not epistemology that describes us as human beings, that is, the ability to know and understand, but our ontological reality. It is the fact that we are in the world with others and that we "think" Being without reducing it to an object of our knowledge. In the following pages, we will break down what Heidegger means by this other thinking (*denken*) that underlies and defines our existence before we can define ourselves as knowing beings, with intentional consciousness and open to the givenness of the phenomena that are revealed to us.

Heidegger's philosophy focuses, from the very beginning, on the topic of Being. Heidegger writes:

Wenn das Seiende in mannigfacher Bedeutung gesagt wird, welches ist dann die leitende Grundbedeutung? Was heisst Sein?

Section VI: From Phenomenology to Ontology

> If the being is said in many meanings, what will then be the fundamental and guiding meaning? What does it mean to be?[98]

In his work *Phenomenological Interpretations of Aristotle*, Heidegger takes up the thread from Aristotle and Brentano to embark on a rigorous exploration of the meaning of existence through the understanding of beings. To do this, he merges phenomenology, with its emphasis on the appearance (*phainómenon*) of things before us, with the Greek conception of *alétheia* (the act of unveiling). For the Greeks, the act of discovering the Truth involves drawing back the veil of reality to contemplate that which truly "is" in its pure state. Also for Heidegger, *alétheia* is to unveil the essence of Truth. In this way, he seeks to integrate the attention to immediate lived experiences with the Greek notion that Truth consists in the uncovering of reality.

At the same time, this link between the phenomenon and its givenness and revelation constitutes a central aspect of phenomenology, which, in turn, marks a point of connection between the phenomenological manifestation and the philosophical understanding of Being. The "thing itself" involves the direct experience of the thing in itself, or the direct lived experience of reality. To speak of the phenomenon in terms of its givenness leads us to a fundamental question about the origin of our experiences, the very essence and the being of beings in their manifestation, that is, their appearance. The key question is the nature of this emergence or the character of this becoming. For Heidegger, this analysis is a phenomenological evolution of his early inspiration from Brentano, marking a central point in his work and reflecting the transformation of his philosophical inquiry from his youth.

His approach to these ideas was gradual during his early courses at Freiburg and Marburg. A crucial point in his trajectory was the publication of *Being and Time* in 1926, required by the academic authorities as a prerequisite for his appointment as the successor

---

98. Heidegger, Martin. *Zur Sache des Denkens* [What Is Called Thinking?]. Tübingen: Max Niemeyer Verlag, 1969. Translation mine.

to N. Hartmann, following the initial rejection by the Ministry in Berlin due to the lack of publications in the past decade. The urgency to compile the works culminated in the submission of preliminary drafts, which were deemed insufficient for the academic appointment. Nevertheless, the Faculty persisted, and approval was finally granted. The work begins by highlighting the publication in honor of the seventieth anniversary of Husserl in 1928, continues with the study of the spread of his doctrines, conducted a decade later, and concludes by evaluating the enduring influence of phenomenology, as presented in *Zur Sache des Denkens*, where we read:

> *Die Zeit der phänomenologischen Philosophie scheint vorbei zu sein. Sie gilt schon als etwas Vergangenes, das nur noch historisch neben anderen Richtungen der Philosophie verzeichnet wird. Allein die Phänomenologie ist in ihrem Eigensten keine Richtung. Sie ist zu Zeiten sich wandelnde und nur dadurch bleibende Möglichkeit des Denkens, dem Anspruch des zu Denkenden zu entsprechen. Wird die Phänomenologie so erfahren und behalten, dann kann sie als Titel verschwinden zugunsten der Sache des Denkens, deren Offenbarkeit ein Geheimnis bleibt.*

The time of phenomenological philosophy seems to be over. It is already considered something of the past; something recorded only historically alongside other directions in philosophy. However, in its most intimate essence, phenomenology is not a direction, but the changing possibility of thinking that reappears, varied, and thus remains the permanent possibility of thought, in order to correspond to the demand of what must be thought. When phenomenology is experienced and retained in this way, it can then disappear as a title in favor of the matter of thinking, whose openness remains a mystery.[99]

---

99. Martin Heidegger, "Mein Weg in die Phänomenologie," in *Zur Sache des Denkens*, Gesamtausgabe Band 14 (Frankfurt am Main: Vittorio Klostermann, 2007), 101. Translation mine.

Section VI: From Phenomenology to Ontology

Years later, in 1963, phenomenology was regarded as a completed project, which does not imply it lacked development; in fact, by that time, multiple expansions of its approach had already manifested. Despite this, and while desiring to maintain the "spirit" of phenomenology, much like Husserl did with Descartes, Heidegger now proposes a philosophical evolution, or even a phenomenological one in spirit, that gradually distances him from Husserl's phenomenology and the parameters within which it had always developed.

Heidegger identifies a series of arguments that unveil this gradual departure, beginning from within the limits of phenomenology, but ending beyond them. First and foremost, Heidegger sought to revitalize the practical aspect of philosophy as a fundamental aspect in discovering an understanding of the world and existence that is stripped of the distortions inherent in a merely theoretical orientation. In other words, Heidegger pursues, albeit unsuccessfully, a phenomenological solution that comprehends our relationship with the world as practical, not theoretical. Human beings do not engage with the world by interrogating the void about their existence, as if they could abstract themselves from it, but rather by inquiring into its functioning, utility, and purpose, that is, asking what it is for. The approach that our connection with the cosmos is practical rather than theoretical already establishes a clear differentiation between his phenomenological approach and that of Husserl. Furthermore, this new approach by Heidegger is already, in itself, a first critique of Husserl's *epoché*, which he considers an abstract theoretical exercise, as he believes one cannot practice the *epoché* and disconnect from the world in which one lives and with which one constantly interacts.

According to Heidegger, in order to truly know objects, it is not enough to think or theorize about them; rather, it is necessary to interact with things, with which we cannot stop interacting. If we wish to grasp and discern the true essence of objects or what things are, we must carefully observe each activity and action. Therefore, from a Heideggerian perspective, it is important to emphasize that the act of thinking and that of observing follow opposing paths. The difference lies in that thought, understood as the act through which we know objects, is projected outward, while observation focuses inward. Thinking enables us to understand the other, the thing that is not me, and is therefore foreign to me, while observing provides a way to know our own Being.

However, we must not confuse the act of intellectual reflection with this idea of observing. Reflection is an act that mirrors the structure of the act of thought in order to objectify the interior on which it focuses. On the other hand, observation represents a condition of inaction and, as such, does not constitute an action per se, but rather a state of union with oneself, a way of dwelling in our essential Being.

The practice of observation is employed in various meditative techniques, such as the tea ceremony, ikebana, martial arts, the fulfillment of the *mitzvot*, Hatha Yoga, or Tai Chi. These practices, carried out with an attentive and conscious focus, are known as active meditation. Through observation, it is possible to apprehend the essence of what is observed. What is observed, therefore, manifests itself before the observer, while the observer extends something of themselves toward the observed. By interacting with the observed, we register its form, color, and aroma, and attention returns to the observer, providing an understanding of its nature without turning it into a completed object of our knowledge.

Western philosophical tradition has mostly understood "knowledge" based on the "active" capabilities of the intellect. Following Heidegger, we propose to ground the origin of human knowledge in the "passive" faculty of observation. This faculty of observation involves three elements: the observed, the observer, and the relationship between both, that is, the process of observing, with the latter serving as the bridge connecting what traditional philosophy has called subject and object.

Thinking arises from a subject's desire to aim at something specific, but observation attends to the observed from passivity. The thinking subject, active and knowing, casts its net over the world to name it and attribute concepts and categories to it.

Phenomenology holds that the world is inherently in consciousness. Therefore, any introspective exploration of consciousness does not imply a detachment from the external world, but a reaffirmation of its presence. Consciousness is not a closed or isolated realm; it is the place where the totality of the world unfolds. Thus, by directing attention toward it, the external reality is not evaded, but accessed more directly and essentially. In this sense, one who delves into the knowledge of consciousness simultaneously gains knowledge of the world, as this, as it appears to us, is nothing but a manifestation within consciousness itself. Phenomenology, therefore, reveals that introspection is also a path toward understanding the world, since both consciousness and the world are inseparable in their existence and mutual constitution.

In observation, the subject fades before the passivity of the observation, which orbits around the object more than the observer. In that sense, the agent of observation only emerges when we redirect this observation upon the observer. At this moment, observation offers us the possibility to understand both the world and ourselves. Unlike thinking, which is an act of the subject that is freely oriented and directed toward an object, observation precedes both the observer and the observed.

This new way of understanding the relationship of the knowing agent with surrounding objects opens a dimension of existence that is not reducible to that of a subject who knows or desires, and in which the observer that arises from observation is neither the object nor the subject of any knowing. Observation, understood as passivity, allows us to define ourselves more as witnesses than as active subjects. In this sense, we can say that there is, and we are, observation itself, that is, consciousness in a pure state, in which neither free subjects nor thinkable objects have yet appeared. In other words, observation would be the original passivity from which an active consciousness will later emerge—one capable of thinking objects and the world in which it pulses. The importance of this first approach, with its clear Heideggerian cut, is that it already determines that prior to the activity that defines subjective consciousness, the human being emerges in a presubjective observation that makes them a witness of Being, of what is, of what there is. This state of observation is, and here lies its importance, preepistemological.

Observation and its link to language and Being

The word *phenomenon* originates in the Greek verb *phaíno*, which translates as "to bring to light," and includes *phôs*, meaning "light." Since observation is Retroprogressive, we not only know the phenomena as they present themselves before the light, but we also recognize the light of pure consciousness as our authentic reality. The passivity of observation does not replace the activity of the act of thought, but rather underlies it permanently. This principle is the foundation for studying the very essence of an object. However, this study does not consist of a direct analysis of the "object-phenomenon" itself. Far from it, Heidegger turns to Aristotle, specifically to his study on visual perception, where he proposes that "that of which there is sight, then, is visible" (*De Anima*, II.7)[100], which Heidegger translates as: "What is perceivable in seeing is the visible,"[101] as an example of which we can put that what is seen in the light is color. Although invisible in itself, *clarity* is ultimately what allows us to see things, and it is what Heidegger will call in *Einführung in die Phänomenologische Forschung (Introduction to Phenomenological Research)*, "a manner of presence of."[102] Therefore, the importance in perception lies, in the ability to make an object visible. We do not perceive or observe visibility as we see the object that this visibility makes visible, but it is what allows us to see it, and that is the essence of phenomenology. We do not observe visibility as another object, but thanks to it, we can observe; likewise, we do not see the phenomenon directly, but it allows us to discern the object.

This leads us to affirm, therefore, that the human being cannot perceive the phenomenon directly, but instead experiences it, and lives it, tacitly, in the same way that one experiences clarity each time one sees an object. For, although light can illuminate

---

100. Aristotle, *De Anima: Books II and III*, with Passages from Book I, trans. D. W. Hamlyn, with a report on recent work and a revised bibliography by Christopher Shields (Oxford: Clarendon Press, 1968; rev. ed., 1993), 418a26.
101. Martin Heidegger, *Introduction to Phenomenological Research*, trans. Daniel O. Dahlstrom (Bloomington: Indiana University Press, 2005), §1, 4.
102. Ibid., §1, 5.

everything and everyone, it cannot illuminate itself as if it were another object. If light could turn upon itself, we would have to concede that there must be yet another light that would allow such a turning of light upon itself, which would ultimately lead us back to *ad infinitum* (an infinite regression) and, therefore, to absurdity. Similarly, knowingness or consciousness, although it understands an objective experience, cannot be apprehended objectively in the same way that such an objective experience is understood. In other words, the way we see an object cannot be the same as the way we "see" seeing, the phenomenon, in which the object becomes visible.

For this reason, both from the epistemological phenomenology of Husserl and from the ontological phenomenology of Heidegger, the question of that almost non-objectifiable dimension has been emphasized, such as the immanent time of consciousness, or observation, or now the issue of Aristotelian visibility. These underlie and accompany all our experiences and acts of consciousness, giving shape and making it possible to speak of our consciousness or vital experience in terms of a flow, our flow. Observation, light, and immanent time are given to us; they manifest tacitly within each act and experience, but their givenness is not the result of any mediation, idea, thought, or subjective will.

This very difference between the object of vision and light is perfectly captured in Heidegger's work through what he himself called "the ontological difference." That is, the difference between the entity and Being, and therefore, in the ways in which both must or can be given. Precisely in this context, both Husserl and Heidegger recognize the limits of phenomenology, the "impossibility" of describing what allows us to describe everything else. At this point, Heidegger introduces the topic of the Aristotelian logos in terms of voice or *phoné semantiké*, to distinguish it from mere sound. This elucidation is essential, as it links language with a specific form of Being, grounded in its deep association with *phantasía*. Logos, beyond being a concept or sound, stands as language and its meaning, facilitating the revelation of all entities to human perception. As Heidegger himself will say, language is the home of

Being, which is equivalent to saying that Being becomes meaning through language.

Language constitutes the realm in which Being manifests, reveals, and acquires meaning, transforming it into something comprehensible and accessible. This process of manifestation and meaning highlights the primordial importance of language as the vehicle through which the essence of all things becomes intelligible and integrated into our understanding of the world. By articulating thoughts, emotions, and concepts, language acts as a bridge between the abstract and the concrete. It becomes the space where Being finds expression and, consequently, translates into a meaningful entity within human reality. Therefore, language is not merely a tool for naming the things we interact with in our daily lives, but it is the texture—so to speak—in which objects are shown to us as such in an intelligible manner. Being, however, is not a mere object of language, but is tacitly revealed in all our relationships with the world and its objects. Heidegger asserts:

> Only because language is the home of the essence of the human being can historical humankind and human beings not be at home in their language, so that for them language becomes a mere container for their sundry preoccupations.[103]

Human beings can acquire knowledge of various languages. Nevertheless, when they use a language that is not native to them, they find themselves, metaphorically, dwelling in a home that is not their own. The essence of human existence is intrinsically linked to the particular language they speak, since it constitutes the framework within which Being unfolds and experiences reality. This premise is evident in the observation that those who adopt a language different from their own may experience a sense of displacement, as if inhabiting a space that does not fully belong to them. In its deepest function, language facilitates communication and shapes perception

---

103. Martin Heidegger, "Letter on Humanism," in *Pathmarks*, ed. William McNeill, trans. Frank A. Capuzzi (Cambridge University Press, 1998), 274.

and thought. Ultimately, it gives form to the individual's identity. Therefore, immersion in a language that is not one's own may limit a person's ability to express themselves and develop fully, thus suggesting the vital importance of finding resonance and grounding in the native tongue. The language understood as one's own is the framework, the home, in which passive consciousness, the observation prior to personal and subjective identity, relates to Being.

Heidegger delves deeper into this matter by linking language, logos, with *phantasia*, which manifests as an image, born from language or words, revealing its nature as intimately connected with verbal expression. What this means is that our reflections and mental images are intrinsically shaped by language. That is, language is not the tool that explains images a posteriori, but it is the way in which they take shape and are shown. Speaking of images, however, means speaking of thought, for thinking of an object means imagining it, forming it as an image, through language. For this reason, in *Introduction to Phenomenological Research*, Heidegger presents language as the essence of the human being, recognizing the presumption of meaning inherent in all its expressions. Language is, therefore, crucial in the understanding of our human essence, because everything we articulate is imbued with underlying meanings.

Since language is the home of Being or the essence of humans, Heidegger considers language to be intrinsically linked to two other essential terms: *logos apophantikós*, or "manifestation," and *aletheúein*, or 'unveiling'. *Logos apophantikós* is the manifestation, the un-concealing, or the decoding of Being in the entity. If, following Heidegger, we understand Being as hidden or encrypted, *alétheia* would then mean decoding it. *Logos apophantikós* would be the revelation of reality as it is, while *aletheúein* would involve a search for the hidden truth, similar to deciphering an enigmatic code.

Regarding *logos apophantikós* (affirmative logos), Heidegger suggests that it is associated with *aletheúein* (giving beings as unconcealed), and its opposite is *pseúdesthai* (to conceal). *Pseúdesthai* refers to the egoic experience of considering oneself a separate, independent, and individual being, that is, a subject already formed, after the passivity of observation that dwells in language through which the possibility of all meaning emerges. In turn, *logos apophantikós* is what Vedanta calls *jīvan-mukti*, or "liberated in life," or the "awakened" of Buddhism who is aware of one's oceanic aspect. This helps us see that the issue of observation, understood as "dwelling in language," implies speaking of a state of wakefulness in which Being emerges as the condition of possibility for all meaning.

In *Introduction to Phenomenological Research*, Heidegger points out that the philosophical tradition, beginning with the Greeks, has identified *ousía*—derived from the feminine participle *ousa* of the verb *einai* (to be)—with presence (*parousía*), understood as the manner in which a being appears as being-there. This identification reduced the meaning of Being to its concrete presence, which Heidegger critically summarizes with the formula *ousía estin parousía* ("Being is presence"). In contrast to this conception, the phenomenological approach seeks a comprehension of Being not merely as what is present, but in terms of its capacity to show and disclose itself. Heidegger criticizes the metaphysics of presence, arguing that, in reality, the phenomenon is not Being but the showing of Being. This turn occurs, above all, in *Phenomenological Interpretations of Aristotle*. Heidegger says that Being is not, but rather that Being gives itself, and giving itself is showing itself; therefore, presence is not Being, but rather a result of the showing of Being. The phenomenon is thus understood as the manner in which Being reveals or hides itself.

Phenomenology focuses on the introspective nature of the Being of *Dasein* and its propensity for self-interrogation. The act of manifesting involves the act of emerging from concealment, which presupposes that the very existence of Being has been relegated to oblivion. Truth is a process of "un-forgetting" or *alétheia*. Emerging from oblivion implies revealing itself through a process that deciphers what was previously encrypted. The responsibility for deciphering was historically attributed to the subject. However, here it is understood that Being becomes self-evident without external intervention. This self-manifestation can be considered phenomenological insofar as Being offers itself as givenness, a gift to understanding.

In this context, phenomenology becomes the study of how Being unfolds and manifests in a latent way in all our acts of knowledge, perceptions, or even dreams, in all our experiences, marking a transcendental event in the understanding of reality. Thus, Heidegger's argument does not negate Husserlian phenomenology, but seeks to explain its condition of possibility, both with the issue of observation we have suggested in this section, and with the notions of Being, phenomenon, and logos we have exposed in this chapter. The step taken by Heidegger has ontologized the issue of phenomenology, relegating the epistemological dimension of the human being to a secondary place.

CHAPTER 22

THE OBJECT OF PHENOMENOLOGY: FROM HUSSERL TO HEIDEGGER

The divergence between Husserl and Heidegger

Throughout the last two chapters, we have exposed the object of study of phenomenology and how it can describe it. Following Husserl, we have talked about the immanent time of consciousness as the articulator or synthesizer of the experiences of a transcendental ego. This ego, far from being isolated, remains linked to other transcendental egos. Together, they form a common magma where each human being then develops their personal experiences. We have then linked this auto-temporalization to the issue of observation, which we have defined from a Heideggerian perspective as a passive state that precedes both the subject and the object of all experience, accompanying all acts of consciousness. In this way, phenomenology, guided by Husserl and Heidegger, has delved into the depths of consciousness, going beyond the limits and parameters of acts. In other words, the phenomenology of Husserl, in its proper sense, does not stop at the acts of consciousness, but rather penetrates them to reach their passive origins, prior to any conceptualization of subject and object.

We have also seen that, despite Husserl's efforts to redefine the boundaries of consciousness and its phenomenological study, in Heidegger's view, his conception never quite severs the umbilical cord that connects it to knowledge in its traditional epistemological meaning. From this perspective, we have also seen how Heidegger's phenomenology bursts into Husserl's parameters and overflows its limits in order to reach the origins of all existence and meaningfulness. To achieve this, we have paid attention to the "Aristotelian light," that is, the clarity that reveals everything but cannot reveal itself as such, and—following Heidegger—we have linked it to the topic of Being and language.

In the present chapter, we will connect the divergences we have seen in both authors with their respective concepts of phenomenology and philosophy, in general, to better understand their projects, the reasons for their differences, and the impact this has on the exploration of the meaning of the human being.

In *Ideas I* and his *Cartesian Meditations*, Husserl presents phenomenology not only as a discipline but as a meticulous and detailed science dedicated to the study of transcendental consciousness in its purest and most essential state. This definition places consciousness at the epicenter of research, making it the object of study of this new rigorous science called phenomenology. To explain how and why consciousness assumes this central role, Heidegger revisits the Aristotelian view of perception. Although Aristotle did not formulate a specific concept of consciousness as such, for the Stagirite, the act of seeing constitutes an autonomous entity, a perception that later reappears in the writings of countless philosophers under the notion of *noesis*. It is not until the appearance of Husserl's *Logical Investigations* that the notion of consciousness acquires a much richer and more concrete meaning. The *Logical Investigations* focused on bringing objects closer to consciousness, employing a direct and fundamental method based on the principle of "going directly to the things themselves,"[104] that is, to reality as such.

In response to the neokantian philosophy of the time, Husserl developed a theoretical analysis in which the idea of meaning plays a fundamental and defining role. Here, meaning is not limited to singular acts of signification, but rather encompasses an ideal unity that encapsulates all possibilities, acting as a representative type for

---

104. Martin Heidegger, *Introduction to Phenomenological Research*, trans. Daniel O. Dahlstrom (Bloomington: Indiana University Press, 2005), §4, 37–38.

all individuals. Meaning, a notion that serves as the unifying link of everything, arises because it is precisely there that the thing manifests itself. In other words, the phenomenon manifests itself where meanings spring forth. In this sense, Husserl's phenomenology could also be understood as a study of the origin of the meaning of both things and consciousness. From a Husserlian perspective, one could even suggest that meaning, where the phenomenon itself emerges, is what makes all perception and understanding possible. Although Heidegger also conceives of language as the dwelling place of Being(-in-the-world), his project advocates for an understanding of consciousness in terms of the nature of its being. In this, he stands in contrast to Husserl's theoretical approach, whose limitations he clearly points out.

While Husserl opts for an inquiry aimed at refounding the sciences upon a phenomenological philosophy understood as *prima philosophia*, Heidegger focuses on uncovering unnoticed or overlooked aspects; he calls this "what has been truly neglected,"[105] proceeding in such a way that it is not disturbed or "in any way disrupted in its neglect"(*nicht in ihrem Versäumnis gestört wird*).[106] Heidegger moves away from traditional paths, focusing on uncovering aspects that have been ignored or overlooked in analysis. He is not interested in following philosophical conventions but in illuminating what has been disregarded or excluded from attention and critical reflection. In this sense, Heidegger's main concern is precisely, and as we have already indicated, the practical relationship with the world that traditional philosophy has undervalued.

Heidegger's perspective holds that the world should not be reduced to being the object of theoretical reflection, but should be understood as lived experience. In his view, questioning the reality or unreality of the world is pointless. The essence lies in discerning how to optimize our existence amid the world as it unveils itself to us. For him, at first, the world is not given to us as an enigma to be intellectually deciphered, but as a stage in which we act

---

105. Ibid., §50, 213–218.
106. Ibid., §50, 217–218.

and become directly involved. This alone suggests a practical and existential approach to life and our surroundings. The important part of this proposal is that, unlike Husserl, who undertakes a purely theoretical procedure that disregards human involvement in their world, Heidegger starts from the relationship of Being with the world, that is, from *Dasein*.

By replacing consciousness with being-in-the-world (*Dasein*) as the main object of his investigation, Heidegger also transforms the notion of "intentionality." In philosophy, intentionality is traditionally considered as the orientation of every act of thought or noetic activity. Although Husserl's notion of intentionality surpasses the traditional notion of *intentio*, Heidegger chooses to redefine it within a broader context, linking it to concern. He argues that it cannot be confined to the parameters of acts of consciousness but should be rethought and taken as the compass that orients our understanding toward the complexity of the world.

At the same time, Heidegger presents a significant rethinking of the necessary conditions for givenness. While Husserl privileges the path of pure consciousness in his analysis, Heidegger veers toward an alternative route that allows him to incorporate the individual into tangible reality. Thus, he contrasts with the abstract theorization of intentional connection, which could lead to conceptual misunderstandings. Heidegger conceptualizes what he calls the "phenomenology of the factual path" as the lived experience and materialization of the tangible existence that surrounds us. This method approaches our existence not as a mere series of abstract speculations, but as a sequence of immediate and vivid experiences, anchored in the particular and daily context of each individual. Consequently, factual phenomenology aims to reveal the deep meaning of existence, achieved through full immersion in personal experience, focusing on its uniqueness, urgency, and utility.

From this perspective, Heidegger calls us to a thorough investigation of our existential condition from an internal position, giving special relevance to the specific expressions of being-in-the-world and promoting genuine and committed participation with our own existence and the surrounding environment. This approach aspires to cultivate a deeper and more authentic relationship with life, through careful and reflective attention to the dynamics that shape our daily existence.

This difference between both authors stems from the topic of *epoché*, as its implementation, according to Heidegger, redraws or even perverts our relationship with the world, which, after this suspension, becomes of a merely theoretical nature. Thus, while Husserl applies the *epoché* to focus on pure consciousness, Heidegger repositions the subject in the mundane, which is the only place where Being can be given. Heidegger's criticisms of Husserl are not directly attributable, considering that the notions allegedly neglected by Husserl are implicit in his original concepts. This is more evident in Husserl's later works, where these concepts were already implicit from the outset. Husserl's *epoché*, far from limiting and *de-worlding* experience, as Heidegger suspected, expands it, seeking an unprejudiced access to the world, preserving its authenticity from the very beginning. That is why Husserl himself asserts that constitution is a crucial process, revealing the constituted, where "I" and "not I" are inseparable and irreplaceable components. Husserl develops a notion of consciousness that gravitates both in the "I" and the "not I," and therefore, not everything is reducible to a transcendental ego, as some of his critics have claimed. Despite all of this, Husserl remains Cartesian in the way he parametrizes research and formulates his questions.

In contrast to Husserl, Heidegger integrates theory and practice, holding that reality resides exclusively in the practical and considers theory as an external contemplation of the authentic practical world from which it can never and should never be separated. This divergence, however, arises from two different conceptions of philosophy. If, on the one hand, we can say that Husserl inherits an eminently Platonic conception, Heidegger clearly follows the line of Aristotle. This leads Husserl to analyze the practical world through a theoretical optic, thus establishing a clear distinction between the practical and theoretical spheres. Plato, in his philosophical perspective, conceives that the existence of individual material things is understood through the contemplation of universal ideas, housed in an ideal dimension. This conceptualization establishes a clear divide between the realm of ideas, immaterial and eternal, and the domain of physical entities, tangible, temporal, and changing. Aristotle, in contrast, integrates the concept of ideas within the physical things themselves, considering them as the form of matter. Just as Aristotle simplifies Platonic dualism, Heidegger reinterprets Husserl's theory in practical terms, merging abstract concepts into the tangible reality of the world.

Let us briefly reflect on the philosophical interconnections between Plato and Aristotle, as well as between Husserl and Heidegger, to illustrate the unique dialectic these authors maintain in the evolution of philosophical thought. In their reflections, both connections and divergences intersect, forming a complex and sophisticated web of thought that reflects subtlety and intellectual depth. In the first case, Aristotle's methodology is seen as a refinement of Platonic theories. In his search for structural efficiency, Aristotle opts to simplify the structure of the system, ensuring its accessibility and clarity, without relinquishing explanatory depth and solid grounding in the legitimation of knowledge. Moving into a contemporary era, characterized by Husserl and Heidegger, we find parallels with the theories of the former pair, reflecting philosophical continuities through time. Within this intellectual panorama, these philosophers delve into a phenomenology, which, though not the dominant current, aspires to provide a comprehensive approach and a solid foundation for general understanding. In this philosophical domain, Heidegger's work reveals itself as an effort dedicated to refining and clarifying Husserl's postulates, aiming for greater accuracy and clarity.

The interpretations of the Husserl-Heidegger relationship go beyond mere assumptions or unfounded conjectures, as they are grounded in the statements of the philosophers themselves. In fact, Heidegger dedicates his work *Being and Time* to Husserl, only later to remove this dedication. In particular, we can refer to the letter Heidegger wrote to Karl Jaspers on May 26, 1926, where he discusses some of these topics. The correspondence they maintained for years has been documented in the work of the same name, edited by W. Biemel and H. Saner (2003, 67), offering an intimate view of Heidegger's reflections on his journey in phenomenology. Furthermore, his comments in *My Path in Phenomenology* reflect a similar sentiment. These texts deepen our understanding of the interaction between these thinkers, shedding light on how they endeavored to improve and reevaluate each other's theories, aiming for a more precise and less equivocal perception of the world. The clarity sought by Heidegger aims to discard interpretive multiplicity, turning phenomenology from an abstract theory into an exercise that demands detailed observation of the tangible world.

In the interactions between both Aristotle and Plato, as well as Husserl and Heidegger, we see an effort to purify and clarify, without distorting the essence and depth of the original ideas. These parallels highlight the constancy and evolution of philosophical thought through time. Husserl proposes a duality between two spheres, one of a theoretical nature and the other focused on practical aspects. In some way, he replicates Plato's structure, who distinguishes between the realm of ideas and tangible reality. Unlike Plato and Husserl, Aristotle strongly argues that reality is composed of a singular world populated by concrete entities. The way in which Aristotle condenses multiplicity parallels the simplification that Heidegger carries out in his studies on Husserl, following a similar process of conceptual reduction. The explanation of the practical world through the theoretical prism entails a conceptual bifurcation of the world, effectively dividing it into two distinct spheres in this sense, which allows us to suggest that Aristotle and Heidegger applied Ockham's razor because, as the Irish philosopher would argue, it is not good to divide entities unnecessarily.

This differentiation we have established should not be understood as a mere curiosity, but as the root of two different conceptions of phenomenology and its main pillars. Therefore, Heidegger's approach to these issues leads us, in a way, to distance ourselves from the Husserlian phenomenon. We acquire knowledge about objects through the process of interacting directly with them, thereby establishing a relationship that underpins our understanding. Contrary to traditional conceptualization, our understanding of the world does not emerge from abstract categories but from the direct and tangible interaction with objects, with the very essence and true nature of the objects being revealed precisely through our relationship with them.

These two views can be translated, while acknowledging the distances, into a scenario where two people, let us call them Viṣṇu Dāsa and Kṛṣṇa Dāsa, seek to understand me, directing their efforts toward a deep understanding and knowledge of my individuality. Viṣṇu Dāsa would say that Prabhuji is an individual substance of rational, animal, and political nature, defining me as a rational individual essence, embodying both animal rationality and political nature. Kṛṣṇa Dāsa, on the other hand, would conceptualize me as a sensitive being, deeply attracted to music and friendship, a painter and writer. It is clear that Kṛṣṇa Dāsa's understanding of me is deeper, thanks to the direct and meaningful connection we share. It is viable to establish a correlation between Husserl and Viṣṇu Dāsa, as well as between Heidegger and Kṛṣṇa Dāsa, thus reflecting the similarities in their approaches and visions.

Meditative introspection

From Heidegger's perspective, therefore, our understanding of an object deepens through direct interaction rather than through its mere conceptualization. Specifically, Heidegger argues that concepts and abstract categories are insufficient, and that it is essential to focus on the relationship we maintain with objects in our daily lives, at the most pragmatic level. Within this relationship, objects unveil themselves and deliver their true essence. By adopting this stance, where objects are no longer withdrawn, instead of distancing ourselves from the world toward Being, we approach being-in-the-world, engaging in a relationship from which we can never escape, no matter how much we employ an *epoché*.

Personally, I do not support evasion as a doctrine. I have never suggested retreating from adverse or uncomfortable circumstances. It is imperative to face each context with full awareness, whether in business or in sacred places. And whether we are in the midst of a crowd or in the solitude of our room, with friends or with adversaries, in the family circle or in front of strangers; with human beings or with animals. In the face of every challenge that arises, it is essential to learn to operate from a place of compassion and meditation, for confronting these various experiences and situations contributes to our development and maturation. Avoiding any context will only result in a lost opportunity for growth. It is essential to experience life in all its complexity, living in the world, being-in-the-world—as Heidegger would say—but without belonging to it and without being just another piece of it. As human beings, we must aspire to be like the lotus flower, which, although submerged in water, remains untouched by it. Only in this way can we attain knowledge of supreme consciousness, which translates into freedom, into perpetual joy, into a blessing. Ignoring this truth is to disregard the purpose of existence completely. In fact, the path to personal growth is not designed for the fearful, but for those whose courage predisposes them to embrace life with all its uncertainties.

In line with the position we have just expressed, Heidegger proposes that ignoring the world is equivalent to ignoring Being, and we would add that evading the world is, likewise, evading Being. This expansion of the argument further emphasizes the intrinsic connection between individual existence and the universal context in which it unfolds. Such a stance suggests that both ignorance and evasion of the environment in which we live constitute a renunciation of our own Being, since Being and the world are inextricably linked. As we have said on several occasions, Being is being-in-the-world, and the hyphens should be used to indicate the inseparability of the terms and their realities. Therefore, a full understanding of Being demands a conscious commitment to the world, rejecting any form of evasion, abstraction, or denial of the reality that surrounds us.

However, while it is possible to flee from reality by abstracting ourselves from it, there is also the possibility of fleeing toward reality, through the practice of observation, or meditation, as we can also call it. While we will return to this issue later and in more detail, we can state that meditation, or the meditative attitude, does not constitute an evasion of reality, but rather an immersion in it. This is because the most authentic essence in us is Being, and to the extent that we distance ourselves from Being, we also distance ourselves from reality itself. Meditation acts as a bridge that leads us to a deeper and more genuine connection with both Being and the reality that surrounds and permeates us, revealing that the true approach to the real involves an introspective return to our existential core.

This introspection must be distinguished from introversion in that the former involves a detailed examination of our inner world and a conscious analysis of our thoughts as well as emotions. In contrast, introversion describes the predisposition to turn attention inward, without necessarily involving deep analysis. The introverted person is turned or oriented toward their inner self. However, genuine introspection occurs in connection with the external environment, suggesting that true self-understanding emerges from interaction with the world around us. Barriers and obstacles are not found in the world. I direct my reflection toward ascetics and monks of various beliefs, arguing that renunciation of the world is nothing but a manifestation of fear and a tendency toward evasion. Such abdication does not demonstrate a true spiritual understanding, but rather evidence of their fears. For the individual who operates in a state of full consciousness, no element can cause disturbance or discomfort. This is because, within the framework of a conscious life, an attitude of acceptance is adopted toward everything, including adversities. Therefore, fleeing from worldly responsibilities and challenges is groundless. What Heidegger's philosophy shows us is, precisely, that all genuine introspection is always a turning toward Being to allow it to reveal itself to us. In turn, however, this turning toward Being is always a turning that can only take place in the world, living its complexities and even its contradictions. The unveiling of Being, its revelation, must be understood in our relationship with the world, and never outside of it.

Heidegger's "squaring"

Carrying out genuine introspection, without Cartesian doubts or Husserlian *epoché*, will allow us to understand our reality in its maximum complexity, without breaking it down or isolating it, only

Chapter 22: The object of phenomenology: from Husserl to Heidegger

to have later reconstruct and rediscover it. In this context, Heidegger introduces the notion of "squaring," a concept that represents a comprehensive approach to examining the multiple aspects that constitute our reality, encompassing both manifest and hidden elements. This paradigm unfolds through four fundamental domains that inaugurate a historical journey marked by acts of revelation and concealment. These domains are (1) the earth, (2) the sky, (3) the divine sphere, and (4) the mortal condition. These dimensions intersect, offering us essential clues about the essence and ultimate purpose of our existence.

Within this structure, Heidegger conducts and develops a philosophical exploration that leads him to understand the square that reveals itself when considering the question of Being as an inquiry into our historical trajectory. Thus, the earth is apprehended both as a foundation and a craftsman, which supports and simultaneously builds, in addition to being seen as a homeland. The crucial aspects of the earth include its role in Truth as that which is veiled and its interpretation as an expression of fate. In contrast, the sky is presented as the forger of cycles and the reference for the ordering of the earth, defined as the expansive domain of the spirit, revealed in the contemplation of technique as the essence of Truth and as a way to disclose the world. The sky, therefore, symbolizes what is revealed, the presence, in contrast to the earth, thus functioning as another manifestation of fate.

Divinities and mortals, on the other hand, represent the other vertices of the square. The divinities act as heralds of the Divine, whose signs give historical character to the people. The manifestation of the Divine through these signs is of particular interest to Heidegger, as upon it rests the historical existence of nations, interpreted as an unexpected revelation of fate. The mortals, on the other hand, are those who can understand death as such. What distinguishes the human being is not the projection of possibilities, but the recognition of the possibilities presented to them. Mortal thought is inherently hidden, and only through divine signs can this confinement be transcended. Another essential element for mortals, according to Heidegger, is their dwelling on the earth, constituting the fourth manifestation of fate. Thus, squaring is interpreted as a reflection on Truth as the destiny of thought. The analysis concludes this section by summarizing squaring as a network of absences and presences, offering a comprehensive view of how these elements interact within Heideggerian thought to shape our understanding of existence.

This approach, to which for various reasons we can only make a brief reference here, resembles the process of unraveling a complex enigma, where each component provides vital clues. Through this perspective, Heidegger invites us to contemplate our existence from a point of view that recognizes the importance of reflecting on the interaction between these elements, which allows us to approach a deeper and more nuanced understanding of the meaning that underlies our life and our final destiny. In this context, squaring becomes a way to explore the depth of our Being, encouraging us to consider how the visible and invisible manifestations of reality combine to shape our understanding of the world and ourselves.

The stages of phenomenology

The two previous chapters have allowed us to see how Heidegger, emerging from the bosom of phenomenological philosophy, gradually distances himself from Husserl's project to the point of questioning his methodology and approach. Moreover, we could even say that he will eventually see Husserl's approach as still too Cartesian, and therefore, incapable of overcoming certain limitations that Descartes had imposed on the tradition of Western philosophy. For some, this departure will even place Heidegger on the margins of phenomenology itself. However, for others, the tacit criticism of Heidegger, and the steps he takes as a result, will make him the true phenomenologist who does not take anything for granted and even considers certain aspects of Husserl's philosophy as prejudices that Husserl himself failed to see and isolate, to put in parentheses, as he perhaps should have done.

That said, we must keep in mind that phenomenology is a complex philosophical current, which we could even call heterodox, encompassing a wide diversity of approaches that reject, support, influence, and transcend one another. In this sense, phenomenology is not a hermetic and linear developmental movement. It is open, alive, and in constant development in various directions. In addition to Husserl's and Heidegger's philosophical approaches, we must include others of great importance, such as those of Levinas, Sartre, Marion, Henry, Janicaud, and many others, who have drawn and redrawn an entire series of problems and ways of addressing them.

Husserl's work already exhibits a remarkable ambivalence regarding his relationship with other philosophers. On the one hand, some of his writings describe an extensive phenomenological community, incorporating several philosophers with whom he collaborated at different stages. On the other hand, there are works that reveal a more restrictive point of view, in which Husserl seems to identify Heidegger as his only true disciple, even though his reading of *Being and Time* later caused him profound disillusionment. The close relationship between Husserl and Heidegger in Freiburg caused discomfort and rejection among others who considered themselves Husserl's followers, such as Eugene Fink, for example. Furthermore, at certain moments, perhaps marked by despair or the need for philosophical affirmation, Husserl proclaims himself the only true phenomenologist. Nevertheless, the ambivalence in Husserl's phenomenology is not limited to his relationship with other thinkers but even boils within the philosophy of the author himself. This should come as no surprise to anyone.

In fact, every philosopher experiences different evolutionary stages in their thought, with varied approaches to address different problems. In the case of Husserl, three significant phases can be identified. Initially, Husserl is described as grounded in naturalism, focusing on natural phenomena and rejecting any transcendence or openness to the religious; this is the Husserl of immanence, the naturalist. Later, a second phase emerges in Husserl's work, more open to transcendence and spiritual, symbolic, and religious issues. Finally, Husserl, in what could be called a third phase, addresses cultural, social, and political issues more directly, for different reasons. The interpretation and adoption of his philosophy varies considerably depending on individual preferences and approaches.

Section VI: From Phenomenology to Ontology

Those who prioritize a naturalized philosophy identify with the first Husserl, prior to his transcendental orientation. Others, inclined toward the exploration of consciousness and a more radical base, are drawn to his second period, although it is important to recognize that much of his work in Freiburg is linked to this approach. As for those who seek to understand phenomenology in terms of intersubjective and cultural interconnections, they identify more with the attributes of his final stage, personally marked by the marginalization he suffered during the rise of Nazism in Germany. Although it is relevant to mention that elements of this last phase appear in earlier works, complicating this structure, this division is useful for maintaining Husserl as a central figure in the organization of phenomenology as a whole.

Phenomenology itself, as we mentioned earlier, is a current marked by its plurality and by the way each author has related philosophically to Husserl's work in particular, but also to Heidegger's. In this context, five key periods have been identified within the study of phenomenology, which respond, to a greater or lesser extent, to both the different stages of Husserl's philosophy and the emergence of Heideggerian discourse. The first period, known as the foundational stage, is associated with realistic phenomenology. This initial stage focuses on understanding how consciousness captures physical phenomena, laying the foundations for phenomenology as a rigorous and detailed science. Constitutive phenomenology, which becomes the second trend, emerges from Husserl's ideas in *Ideas I*, characterized by the use of transcendental reduction and the approach to issues related to corporeality and aspects of cultural and natural sciences. In this phase, Husserl proposes a foundation for phenomenology that transcends physical phenomena also to encompass cultural ones, seeking to expand the reach of phenomenology as a method applicable to all philosophical fields.

Existential phenomenology, emerging as the third trend, develops in the late 1920s and gained importance in France until the late 1950s, focusing on practical and cultural aspects. This third phase is mainly oriented toward the issue of existence and develops through topics such as the meaning of life and the human being in the world. One of its main exponents was W. Luypen, whose *Existential Phenomenology* focuses on examining human existential conflicts from a phenomenological perspective. It includes contributions from Sartre and Heidegger, particularly his work *Being and Time*, with which he inaugurated what would later be called existential phenomenology, focused on the finite essence of *Dasein*. Thus, we could say that this third stage is characterized both by Heidegger's existential philosophy and by the divergence of his thought, as would be the case with Emmanuel Levinas and his phenomenology of the Other.

The fourth stage, aligned with the later Husserl, leans more decisively toward spiritual topics, while also drawing upon Heidegger's philosophy, which became especially influential from the 1960s onward, promoted by major figures such as H. Gadamer and P. Ricoeur. This phase focuses on issues related to technology and history, including the phenomenology of technique, metaphysics, Being, and human history—topics explored by Gadamer and Ricoeur, both disciples of Heidegger. These four phases are essential to the philosophical evolution and extend beyond the life and work of Husserl himself.

CHAPTER 23

THE "THEOLOGICAL TURN" IN PHENOMENOLOGY

In the previous chapter, we detailed four stages within the phenomenological movement. However, we can delimit a fifth phase, which has generated a broad debate within phenomenology due to its object of study and which is of special interest to the research we are conducting. The French philosopher Dominique Janicaud coined this new stage as the "theological turn," which, subsequently, has sparked further debate both within and outside phenomenology. Although there are numerous authors who could be considered part of this latest phase, if we wish to call it that, we will focus on Jean-Luc Marion and Michel Henry.

As we will see in the following paragraphs, the works of these two authors specifically address issues that are innovative yet, at the same time, not entirely new to phenomenology. Although criticized for allegedly introducing religious aspects into philosophy, these authors have simply pushed phenomenological principles, already present in Husserl and later in Heidegger, to their maximum expression. Ideas such as givenness, manifestation, and openness are not theological concepts artificially inserted into phenomenology, but strictly phenomenological aspects already addressed by Husserl himself. At the same time, we must also note that the phenomenology of Marion and Henry, as well as that of Levinas, to name another example, has indeed pushed these concepts and principles to their own limits. In this specific case, Marion has carried the idea of givenness to what he calls the saturation of the phenomenon, that is, beyond the limits of consciousness. In this way, it has surpassed the parameters within which phenomenology had traditionally approached the topic of the givenness of the phenomenon, and has thus brought about a rupture in the notion of consciousness as outlined by Husserl and those who followed him.

Classical phenomenology, as we have seen so far in this study, has focused on exploring those phenomena that present themselves to consciousness and that, by their nature, can be verified by any individual in their daily experience. Examples of this include the red box we mentioned or others such as the appearance of the sun and stars, the human fear of death, the difficulty of fully experiencing love, and the fear of loneliness. These are aspects of existence that most people can recognize and confirm based on their own experience of the world.

However, phenomenology faces greater challenges when it addresses more abstract levels of experience or those less accessible to direct perception. This is the case of the presence of the Divine manifested through the word, a dimension to which we have already paid attention as the object of our study. This includes phenomena that are not immediately evident or verifiable by common experience and are, precisely, those that philosophers such as Jean-Luc Marion and Michel Henry investigate. Both thinkers delve into the complexity of experiences that transcend the limits of what is directly accessible to all, exploring how the Divine, for instance, manifests itself in human experience in a way that challenges conventional verification. This approach marks an expansion of the phenomenological field of study toward aspects of reality and experience that require a philosophical approach that goes beyond the mere acknowledgment of phenomena evident to the collective consciousness. Moreover, by opening up to the study of new phenomena, phenomenology also opens itself to those who have attained a state of awakening or enlightenment, distinguishing itself by not depending on faith in its traditional sense, but on the recognition of the possibility of revelation.

In this sense, spiritual figures such as Moses, Jesus, Muhammad, Buddha, Lao Tzu, Mahavira, and the Edmor Ha Zaken could find in this *extra-muros* phenomenology a field in which their experiences could be the object of phenomenological study. Such *extra-muros* phenomenology would focus on the conscious analysis of the revelations these spiritual luminaries have lived, recognizing these events as phenomena worthy of study. Thus, the proposal emphasizes the universality of certain spiritual experiences and their eligibility to be examined through the lens of consciousness and direct experience, beyond the specific faith doctrines of each tradition. This does not mean that Marion and Henry are importing new religious or theological categories into phenomenology. In fact, what they are doing is exploring the latest and deepest possibilities of phenomenology. On the other hand, it is irrefutable that the topic of God has been a central axis in Western philosophy since its origins with Plato and Aristotle. Talking about God does not necessarily entail a religious approach in the traditional sense, which implies that it is perfectly viable to address topics such as revelation and divine inspiration from a philosophical perspective.

We will approach this fifth stage of phenomenology guided by Hernán Inverso's lucid exposition in *La fenomenología de lo inaparente* (*The Phenomenology of the Unapparent*). This stage has sometimes been called the "theological turn," which can be imprecise and even misleading. If such a theological turn existed, figures not only like Marion and Henry, but also Levinas, Chrétien, Ricoeur, and Derrida would be its representatives. This is because there is no orthodoxy in phenomenology; its history is the history of its variants. Each phenomenologist, according to the problems they have identified and the limits they have encountered, has sought to redefine it in order to reopen it to the phenomenon and its givenness. They have confronted the most essential questions concerning the meaning of human existence. What is indisputable is the richness of approaches that reflect the dynamism of this field. Since its inception, phenomenology has been characterized by its continuous evolution, even under Husserl's guidance, a process that still persists and is likely the reason why phenomenology, as a philosophical approach, remains alive and relevant.

This integrative reading of the limits of phenomenology and its phenomena also has important detractors, whose criticisms and arguments allow us to understand better the significance of this new turn in the realm of phenomenology. Dominique Janicaud's work *The Theological Turn of French Phenomenology* (1991) is a clear example of this. In this book, Janicaud initiated an extensive debate warning about the tendency of French phenomenology toward theology. Through formal criticism of Levinas, Marion, Chrétien, and Henry, Janicaud disapproves of the inclusion of divine concepts in philosophy. Since then, the idea of this so-called "theological turn" has grown, posing challenges in defining the exact point at which this change or turn occurs. Nevertheless, the reception of this category demonstrates a concern that has been addressed through controversy. The existence of a turn suggests the presence of a heterodoxy, a deviation. To discuss a deviation also implies determining what the correct path would be. The intersection of philosophy and theology, an issue dating back to the origins of both disciplines, has found a significant point in this debate.

This is not a completely new idea, as Jean Hering already pointed out in his 1925 work *Phenomenologie et Philosophie Religieuse* (Phenomenology and Religious Philosophy), highlighting the risks of combining both perspectives. For Hering, the risk lies in the possibility that both phenomenology and philosophy, as well as the philosophy of religion, might be reduced to an *eidos*. That *eidos* could then serve to justify the supremacy of a particular institution within history. That is, a set of theories that validate the authenticity of a particular religious tradition, which then uses this to elevate itself above the others. Shortly after the publication of Hering's text in 1925, Heidegger presented a lecture in 1927 titled *Phenomenology and Theology*, adding a new dimension to the debate. This talk, delivered in March of that year in Tübingen, and then in February of the following year in Marburg, would not be published in print until 1969. In it, Heidegger asserted:

> [...] Faith, as a specific possibility of existence, is in its innermost core the mortal enemy of the form of existence that is an essential part of philosophy [...]. Faith is so absolutely the mortal enemy that philosophy does not even begin to

want in any way to do battle with it. [...] Accordingly, there is no such thing as a Christian philosophy; that is an absolute "square circle." On the other hand, there is likewise no such thing as a neo-Kantian, or axiological, or phenomenological theology, just as there is no phenomenological mathematics. Phenomenology is always only the name for the procedure of ontology, a procedure that essentially distinguishes itself from that of all other, positive sciences.[107]

This quote reveals two things: 1) that Heidegger reduces all phenomenological inquiry to the limits of ontology and Being, and 2) that, nevertheless, he rejected any procedure based on faith and religion as methodology and, thus, claims to remain faithful to phenomenology as an ontological procedure.

However, as an objection to Heidegger's position, as Levinas and Marion, among others, will insist later, it must be said that phenomenology establishes itself as a methodology, a philosophical procedure, applicable to an unlimited spectrum of questions related to experience. It goes beyond epistemology, but also beyond ontology. The distinction between topics susceptible to phenomenological analysis and those that are not is nonexistent within the spectrum of experience. This procedure, comparable to the use of lenses that allow us to enjoy a film, contemplate a landscape, or immerse ourselves in reading a magazine, is not confined to a specific domain of inquiry. Therefore, any issue arising from human experience can be the subject of phenomenological study. Thus, it would be erroneous to consider phenomenology as limited to the exploration of ontology, for its scope transcends any domain of interest, facilitating a profound understanding of experiences and phenomena in their manifestation to consciousness. The versatility of this conceptual tool underscores its intrinsic value in philosophical exploration, allowing a detailed and nuanced approach to the vast array of topics that make up the fabric of our reality. In order to delve deeper into this

---

107. Martin Heidegger, "Phenomenology and Theology," in *Pathmarks*, ed. William McNeill, (Cambridge University Press, 1998), 53.

topic, it is recommended to read *Wegmarken* or "*Route Marks*," and in particular the letter of March 11, 1964, which relates theology to non-objectivating thought.

It should be noted, however, that opening phenomenology to issues such as faith as an object of investigation does not mean that phenomenology must proceed through acts of faith. On the contrary, to access the interiority of faith as a dimension of experience and describe it phenomenologically, this faith, like any other phenomenon, must be treated with the utmost scrupulousness. In this sense, and as an object of study, the ethos of faith can be defined as diametrically opposed to that of philosophy. Unlike the philosopher, the believer assumes they already possess what they seek, turning their quest into a farce, an illusion, or a simulacrum. They pretend to search, while in reality, they believe they already have what they declare to seek. In contrast, philosophy embarks on a genuine inquiry. If one has a book in hand, it is illogical to claim they are searching for it. The believer believes they know, but it is only an illusion. This illusion prevents true inquiry, for seeking something one believes to have already found is nonsensical. Doubt will always be preferable to belief. Belief offers certainties, but it diminishes exploration. Doubt, on the contrary, broadens horizons.

The acceptance of faith as a phenomenological object of study beyond the limits of epistemology and ontology does not mean that the investigation should be reduced to a religious procedure and, therefore, should not cease to be as rigorous as it has been with any other phenomenon. Janicaud continued to view the problem of including the Divine or the sacred within phenomenology. According to him, this "theological turn" marks, above all, a deviation from the foundations of phenomenology, as the description of phenomena is gradually relegated to the background in favor of the essence of the phenomenal. This disagreement manifests in the collision of this trend with Husserl's perspective, as detailed in *Ideas I*, 58, a text frequently cited to connect Husserl with an aversion to theological topics. This rejection is particularly evident in his treatment of the reduction, where he characterizes:

CHAPTER 23: THE "THEOLOGICAL TURN" IN PHENOMENOLOGY

> We encounter yet another transcendency which is not given, like the pure Ego, immediately in union with reduced consciousness but becomes cognized in a highly mediated fashion, a transcendency standing, as it were, in polar contrast to the transcendency pertaining to the world. We mean the transcendency pertaining to God.[108]

Building on this comment by Husserl, along with others of a similar nature, Janicaud argues that in our understanding of the world and the Divine, we identify two types of transcendence: horizontal and vertical. Horizontal transcendence refers to the world, something we perceive directly. On the other hand, vertical transcendence refers to God, that is, to a reality we know indirectly through introspection and consciousness. This duality implies that while we have an immediate perception of the world, our understanding of the Divine is mediated and reflective, occurring through the process of revelation. Thus, the mundane presents itself before our sight, accessible and observable, while the sphere of the Divine resides at a higher level that transcends our everyday experience. This bifurcated approach highlights how transcendence manifests in different realms of human existence. Despite the differentiation suggested by Heidegger's work in 1927, Janicaud identifies the origin of this divergence, which will later be followed by Marion, Henry, and others, in a remarkable statement within the Zähringen Seminar in 1973. In this context, while analyzing the prologue of Parmenides' poem and its connection with fragment 6, Heidegger refers to a concept he calls "tautological thinking" and asserts:

> Thus understood, phenomenology is a path that leads away to come before..., and it lets that before which it is

---

108. Edmund Husserl, *Ideas Pertaining to a Pure Phenomenology and to a Phenomenological Philosophy*, First Book: General Introduction to a Pure Phenomenology, trans. Fred Kersten, in Collected Works, vol. 2 (The Hague: Martinus Nijhoff Publishers, 1982), §58, 133–34.

led show itself. This phenomenology is a phenomenology of the inapparent.[109]

This assertion, with which Heidegger introduces the topic of the non-apparent, has its origins in his work *My Path in Phenomenology*, written a decade earlier, in which Heidegger had emphasized the phenomenological principles in his method. This path represented a profound re-evaluation of Husserl's phenomenology, oriented toward exploring existence and advancing toward a phenomenological understanding of the intangible. Janicaud, however, shows reservations about this approach to the point of claiming that Heidegger's later philosophy "has no relation whatsoever with Husserl's endeavor of constitution,"[110] which may entail the risk of "overlooking the phenomena" (*phainómena*) in favor of what does not appear. In this light, Janicaud himself already shows a clear deviation between Heidegger's work and traditional phenomenology. However, this deviation is not at all clear, clean, or concise, as while Heidegger presents the possibility of attending to the non-apparent and intangible. He simultaneously criticized the issue of faith as a way of proceeding and never rejected the phenomenology of the manifest or transcendental. Therefore, rather than a deviation, Heidegger's philosophy represents an initial expansion, whose phenomenological approach admits not only the manifest and apparent but also the intangible and non-apparent. This was demonstrated in his analysis of Parmenides' poem, placing Heidegger within the orbit of Janicaud's "theological turn." Although some critics saw him as an atheistic materialist, Heidegger later focused on topics such as the "pathos of listening," paying attention to the voice of Being, which already separates him both from atheistic materialism and from traditional or merely epistemological phenomenology.

---

109. Martin Heidegger, "Seminar in Zähringen 1973," in *Four Seminars*, trans. Andrew J. Mitchell and François Raffoul. (Indiana University Press, 2003), 80.
110. Dominique Janicaud, *Heidegger in France*, trans. David Pettigrew and François Raffoul (Bloomington: Indiana University Press, 2015), 30. Translation mine.

CHAPTER 23: THE "THEOLOGICAL TURN" IN PHENOMENOLOGY

Heidegger does not abandon manifest phenomena as objects of ontological phenomenology. However, Janicaud maintains that, paradoxically, he ultimately distances himself from phenomenology itself by opening up to the inapparent: that which appears, but not in a strictly phenomenological manner. Based on this argument, Janicaud points out as an error the fact of classifying certain philosophies within the realm of phenomenology when, in his opinion, they are no longer so. This position, which, as we have seen, is called the "theological turn," denotes the tendency to shift phenomenology toward theological reflections, contemplating and integrating the Divine and the sacred, to the point of transforming the discipline into theology. In this sense, Heidegger's work stands out as an exemplary case in Janicaud's analysis, foretelling a current that would influence future thinkers.

Janicaud argues that the "theological turn" in phenomenology originates precisely in the shift, or *kehre*, that occurs in Heidegger's thought, without which it would not have emerged. As a consequence of all this, Janicaud criticizes philosophers like Marion and Henry, among others, accusing them of masking theology as phenomenology, and holds that it was Heidegger who explicitly initiated this turn by differentiating the "last God" from the Christian God, which indicates a departure from traditional phenomenology. As an atheist, Janicaud associates phenomenology with the study of consciousness and constitution, and rejects the inclusion of the Divine within it. Furthermore, he argues that figures such as Heidegger, Levinas, and Derrida, when addressing theological issues, lose their philosophical seriousness, since any mention of God in phenomenology leads to mysticism and not to rigorous science.

According to Janicaud, integrating revelation as a perceptible phenomenon violates what he calls "the principle of all principles" of Husserl, that is, "the principle of intuition" as the apprehension of all intentional objects. This becomes evident in contemporary philosophical theories (which he neither considers nor designates as phenomenological), such as Marion's saturated phenomenon, Levinas's infinity of the face, Derrida's gift, Marion's icon, Henry's flesh, Buber's "absolute Thou," and Chrétien's notions of "the impossible" and "the call." For Janicaud, incorporating these elements into phenomenology would turn it into theology and renounce it as phenomenology.

Contrary to Janicaud's position, the argument developed by Jean-Paul Sartre in the preface to *Being and Nothingness* allows us to reach different conclusions. According to Sartre, if existence were confined merely to the apparent manifestations through which it is revealed, then the nature of the intentional phenomenon would not be objective—that is, it would not be "thing-like," or, in Janicaud's terms, it would not be "apparent." The treatment of this phenomenon requires special caution to avoid slipping into idealism. Sartre finds a solution in Heidegger's approach, more specifically in his proposal of preontological understanding. Based on this philosophical perspective, the French philosopher delves into an exhaustive analysis of the structures of the "for-itself," that is, self-consciousness, seeking a meticulous balance and avoiding any bias toward an idealist viewpoint of Being. In Jean-Paul Sartre's philosophy, the concept of "for-itself" refers to the intrinsic faculty of the human being to self-define or assign their own essence. In contrast, the "in-itself" represents what is inherent or that which remains unaltered in the individual. The "for-itself" symbolizes what is acquired or moldable in the human being, what they can form or reconstruct about themselves. The existence of cells in our body, for example, escapes our control and is not subject to our choice; however, aspects such as the place where we decide to live, whether in India or Israel, fall under the domain of our freedom. Thus, the "for-itself" becomes the manifestation of the individual's self-construction.

The human being recognizes entities, but not Being itself. Sartre points out that if phenomenology were limited only to the perceptible, it would be impossible to establish an ontological difference. In that context, Being would not exist or would be inaccessible to us. Therefore, phenomenology cannot be limited to the observable and perceptible alone, since Being, whose transcendence is crucial, is imperceptible. It is vital to safeguard the transcendence of Being. Preontological understanding suggests that all entities and beings are related to Being, and this relationship deserves to be studied as it is manifest. Although Being is imperceptible, one cannot ignore that the relationship with it is part of the manifest. The human being debates about Being, so that even those who deny its existence cannot refute that at least they speak of it. By referring to Being, even when it is denied, one is admitting that the human being maintains a defined relationship with it. Therefore, what Heidegger suggests in preontology is recognizing that, although we deny Being, we are in relation with it and, with that, we are establishing an inherent relationship.

From this perspective, Heidegger's turn concerning phenomenology, the phenomenon, and Being must be understood, as we have outlined with the help of Sartre, as a rejection of Kantian idealism, which interprets Being as a mental construction. According to Heideggerian preontology, in order to understand Being, it is essential for the human being to analyze their own discourse about it. Here arises a fundamental issue: on the one hand, the rupture with a solely immanent phenomenology, and on the other, the birth of concepts that go beyond the merely visible, such as the Other, givenness, and archirevelation. These concepts open the door to a theological perspective, reflected in the problem posed by Ricoeur regarding God's role as a radical subject or fundamental entity.

Chapter 24

The method as a phenomenological criterion

The methodology in the phenomenology of the sacred

The debate surrounding the "theological turn" has another dimension related to the openness of phenomenology to the inapparent, the intangible, in other words, the sacred. The methodological topic is central, as it defines the study's approach and guides the course of the research. Thus, it either allows or does not allow the integration of certain objects as phenomena and, if they are integrated, categorizes them as one type of phenomenon or another. This centrality, or even prominence, of methodology should not surprise anyone. Janicaud himself has used the topic of the nature of the object and methodology itself as a criterion to determine that certain phenomenological investigations are not, in fact, phenomenological. This demonstrates that, de facto, the object is one type of object or another, that is, it is a phenomenon or not, depending on how it is approached and within what methodological parameters.

As for the method itself—what it is and how it is practiced—a broad and complex field of debate has opened up. This has led to a clash of positions that strains both the understanding and application of phenomenology. On the one hand, some researchers and philosophers claim that phenomenology possesses a clear method. Janicaud, for example, maintains that, ultimately, phenomenology is reduced exclusively to a method. For them, everything would be reduced to following a series of steps within a methodological framework, in which case the object of phenomenology ends up being the indirect result of that methodology. At the opposite end are those who reject the possibility of clearly defining the phenomenological method or reducing it to a set of strict, orderly, and invariable steps and procedures. An illustrative case is that of Antonio Zirión, who, after addressing phenomenology in relation to its method, concludes that this connection is an illusion, primarily due to the lack of a coherent interpretation in Husserl and subsequent phenomenologists (1994). It is also pertinent to mention Elizabeth Behnke (2009) and Thomas Nenon (2011), who have expressed similar opinions to those of Zirión, whose main argument focuses on the absence of a concrete and uniform definition of the phenomenological method, an idea that resonates across various sectors of contemporary philosophical thought.

Faced with this dichotomy, we will suggest a middle ground between the two extremes and present our argument. For our part, we hold that the essence of phenomenology rests upon an ontology that incorporates methodological aspects, without becoming confined or restricted by a rigid and invariable method. Thus, we will defend the idea that applying a single universal method to all realities and phenomena presented to us through experience is impossible. Each element, each phenomenon, that is revealed to us brings with it its own methodological approach at the moment of its appearance and way of being, so we consider that there cannot be a single path to understanding all realities.

Each phenomenal reality opens its own path upon manifesting, revealing a specific route. Husserl's phenomenology aimed to allow the phenomenon to present itself in its own way of appearing in order to ultimately describe and understand it in its way of being. If we were to limit the way of attending to it to a rigid and closed procedure, we would also be stifling it, accommodating it to our vision, which would lead to a totally anti-phenomenological attitude. Every phenomenon, as we will see later in this chapter, outlines its particular routes toward understanding because its appearance, its givenness, does not depend on nor is it delimited by the subject or its a priori method, but rather it is the way of being of each phenomenon itself. This reading aligns with the premise that, in the final instance, phenomenology has always been defined by attempting to do justice to reality, rather than violating it, as Husserl himself reminds us in several of his texts.

This debate is important because, in a certain way, it determines the possibility of opening phenomenology to the sacred, to that which appears without appearing, and does so in its own way, autonomously from any methodology one might have designed or prepared beforehand. On the contrary, and following Husserl himself, when addressing different phenomena, we will also address the issues that these open up in our research. But the goal will always be to allow the phenomenal reality, the Being if one prefers to say so, to present itself under its own conditions. Therefore, we must avoid restricting it to unmovable criteria that could lead us to omit rich aspects of experience that might allow us to understand the human being better.

Our position with respect to the method will be of particular importance in relation to the phenomenology of the sacred, that is, to the possibility that phenomenology can address the question of the Divine, of the hidden. Although a universal truth may exist, the methods to discover it vary widely. The approach to the supreme being, whether called Father, Allah, Śiva, Kṛṣṇa, or Devī, is characterized by the diversity of spiritual paths that each deity proposes. Each manifestation of the Divine or phenomenal initially presents its own strategy of approach, as Jesus said: "I am the way." An interpretation rooted in the institutional structures of faith holds that divinity can only be reached through Christ. However, this perspective restrictively emphasizes the term "I," failing to recognize that each being embodies that "I," which constitutes the path to the sacred. The conception that limits the way to Christ seems to forget that we all possess that universal "I" identity that connects us to the Divine. Those who consider Christ to be the only way seem to overlook that the "I" is a universal presence, not exclusive to a particular entity. Therefore, to claim that there is a single definitive method would be a mistake.

Section VI: From Phenomenology to Ontology

The transcendental subjectivity of Husserl

Against Janicaud's position, therefore, our main hypothesis posits that a phenomenology focused on the hidden or on the inapparent is already preconfigured in Husserl's approaches. The phenomenological methodology is crucial precisely because it provides the steps to return to the things themselves. This concept of the phenomenological reduction, or *epoché*, as we have mentioned on various occasions, serves the task of setting aside preconceived beliefs, prejudices, or assumptions about the existence of the world in order to focus on how consciousness perceives and imparts meaning to reality.

The word *reduction* has its roots in the Latin *ducere*, which implies guidance or direction, an idea reflected in the English term *conduct*. This suggests that consciousness acts as a guide in the perception and formation of our reality. The words *reduce* and *reconduct* share the prefix *re-*, which typically implies a return to something or a repetition of it. In our usage of language, to reduce is associated with the idea of "contracting," which indicates a movement toward an origin or essence, a sort of return to the basic or original. Contrary to common belief, to reduce in this context does not mean a diminishment, but rather an intense concentration on what is essential. Within the framework of phenomenology, reduction means putting into parentheses all assumptions related to the object. We can then immerse ourselves in those elements that appear in our consciousness, drawing them out into their manifestation in reality so that they emerge as objects of our attention in an experience neutralized in which the world reappears as primarily given in consciousness. That is, as a world that is both transcendent and immanent to consciousness and, therefore, should not be taken as an entity alien to consciousness but as a unique phenomenon: our experience of objects in consciousness. Husserl himself also calls this "a transcendental subjectivity," which is prior to and underlying any notion of subject or object. In other words, the importance of *epoché* lies in the fact that it gives us access to the fundamental structure of all experience through which we can understand how reality acquires its meaning or is constituted as such.

"Transcendental subjectivity" involves understanding reality in consciousness and consciousness in objects, highlighting a reciprocal interaction. The study of objects, therefore, provides knowledge of consciousness, as both objects and consciousness merge into an experience or lived experience called a "phenomenon." When we say, "the stone appeared to me," we are experiencing consciousness in the stone and the stone in consciousness. We do not perceive the stone or consciousness in isolation, but rather the experience we have of both. The phenomenological approach, therefore, allows us to see and describe how things, as things, are part of our lived experiences, while at the same time, these latter are only possible if they are experiences of something. We can proceed to its study or analysis only once phenomenology has unveiled this primordial structure. This once again emphasizes that the true object of knowledge in phenomenology is, in essence, the lived experience. Our understanding, whether of a tangible object like a stone or an abstract concept like consciousness, is incomplete in itself, as both define each other.

Epoché is the central method of phenomenology. In this domain, the term "method" must be interpreted from its etymological origin, considering that it is composed of *metá*, meaning "through," and *hodós*, meaning "way." That is, method is the "way through which" a profound exploration or investigation is undertaken. However, this is not a single path; rather, it is tailored to the phenomenological nature of the object of inquiry. This is evident in Husserl's own work, where he introduces fundamental, almost normative, principles and criteria that accompany and enrich the *epoché*. Some of these integrate harmoniously with it, while others exceed its bounds, thereby expanding the very horizon of phenomenology—for reasons that we shall examine below. In this same line, but in a different context, the anecdote is told of a disciple inquiring of his master about the reason for the existence of multiple religions. The master replied that, in essence, religions are insufficient in number, arguing that there should be a religion for each individual. The premise was that each person should forge their own spiritual path. The method, therefore, is not a construction of the researcher, but rather a discovery that emerges from the dynamic relationship with the object of study.

Some of these proposals, criteria, or principles that Husserl includes as his research progresses have been interpreted as the foundations of his phenomenological methodology. Far from being clear-cut and having contributed to clarifying the foundations of phenomenological methodology, these proposals have given rise to a wide variety of interpretations, misunderstandings, and even confusion. In the following paragraphs, we will examine some of these aspects in an attempt to clarify the essence of Husserl's approach.

Discovering genetic phenomenology

The advancements in Husserl's own research led him, around 1917, to establish an essential distinction between two phases and methodologies of phenomenology: the static and the genetic. This distinction, which developed and consolidated during the 1920s, represented a significant transformation in the methodological domain of phenomenology itself, as well as in certain other philosophical currents of the time. These two phenomenological approaches are detailed in the second book of his work *Ideas Pertaining to a Pure Phenomenology and to a Phenomenological Philosophy*. While valuable in their contribution, the difference between them is not absolutely clear. On several occasions, Husserl himself argues that these approaches correspond to different dimensions of consciousness, which, as such, coexist and intertwine. We can say that the static approach focuses on the study of the constant, stable, and unchanging forms of perception, such as the idea that the world exists outside, but within the realm of consciousness. In other words, at the static level, phenomenology, after the *epoché*, understands consciousness as a transcendental subjectivity that operates at the level of its intentional acts. That is, every experience occurs in the form of acts of consciousness. However, at this stage of the research, Husserl takes a further step in that direction and presents, in some texts, what he himself called the "transcendental reduction." This second reduction, now termed "transcendental," consists in suspending the acts of consciousness and their intentional structure. This also includes the eidetic objects present in those acts, which were revealed after the first phenomenological reduction. The aim is to understand the origin of these stable structures and to clarify their evolution and development. This approach deciphers the internal structure of transcendental subjectivity and its intentional organization, shedding light on the fundamental architecture that facilitates its existence to evaluate the formal validity of the world. For example, the notion that the whole is greater than the sum of its individual parts is a manifestation of static phenomenology. Similarly, the concept that consciousness always relates to the world is another example of this approach, as this relationship remains uniform.

On the other hand, the genetic approach is oriented toward exploring the origins of the structures that shape our interpretation of the world. This approach seeks to understand how these structures are formed and developed, how the "transcendental subjectivity" is generated, and what this generative process, known as the genesis of its constitution, entails. Genetic phenomenology focuses on the historical trajectory of these phenomena, observing how they emerge and evolve. What stands out most in this second reduction, and in the genetic dimension of consciousness, is that consciousness is not reducible to its intentional acts, contrary to what Husserl initially claimed. This second reduction represents a true revolution. Thanks to it, Husserl's phenomenology broadens its horizons and turns toward questions that he had not explicitly formulated in his early works. From this transcendental reduction, objects of study begin to emerge such as the temporality of consciousness, the pure transcendental ego, and the pre-egoic and pre-linguistic dimension of consciousness. These issues pose challenges and apparent contradictions within the phenomenological field. Husserl himself recognizes this, and for that reason, he seeks to adapt his methodology to these phenomena.

One of the main problems is that what "emerges" after this second reduction does not become explicitly "visible" and, therefore, cannot be described with precision, as Husserl was indeed able to do with the acts of consciousness and their intentional structure. We might even ask ourselves whether what "emerges" after transcendental reduction really appears, given that it is indescribable and indefinable. If it does manifest, in what terms does it do so, and what does this imply for phenomenology and its own methodology? An example would be the unconscious, which Husserl considers to be that zone of pre-egoic consciousness and which, by its very nature, perhaps we should not even name. To name it, we must borrow the language of the static level of consciousness, with its syntactic-grammatical norms, to describe a dimension that challenges and escapes those norms.

In other words, what kind of phenomenon does genetic phenomenology confront? How can this phenomenon "present itself," appear in our reflective consciousness, when it no longer adheres to the same noetic-noematic structures of static consciousness? To answer these questions, Husserl resorts to methods and tools specifically designed for this purpose. A notable example is the concept of "horizontality," often linked to issues that stimulate research in this field of phenomenology. In his work *Formal and Transcendental Logic*, Husserl makes this connection explicit when he states: "In that case, [inquiry into] the 'static' constitution of objects, which relates to an already-'developed' subjectivity, has its counterpart in [an inquiry into] a priori genetic constitution, (a subsequent inquiry,) based on [the results of] the former, which necessarily precedes it."[111] This quotation is especially revealing because genetic consciousness, although "organized" within a flow and therefore describable, has a counterpart. This underlying genetic constitution, a priori to all experience, does not present itself immediately and thus remains beyond the reach of our direct reflexive-perceptual access.

The question is obvious: how can that which neither presents itself nor submits to our vision nonetheless be presented, given, or appear? Therefore, the problem of this articulation is that although the phenomenon does not conform to our perceptual parameters of static phenomenology, the phenomenon is given and revealed

---

111. Edmund Husserl, *Formal and Transcendental Logic*, trans. Dorion Cairns (The Hague: Martinus Nijhoff, 1969), §98, 250.

to our reflective consciousness. The fact that the parameters of static phenomenology are unable to address it does not mean that phenomenology should renounce this phenomenon. On the contrary, this new phenomenal reality requires a special subjective attitude to perceive these elements, for although it lies beyond our immediate comprehension, it constitutes the foundation of all manifestation and must, therefore, be the object of phenomenological investigation. Otherwise, phenomenology would betray one of its principles, for it would have to accept this genetic reality as an a priori that it could not account for, which would turn it into a prejudice. Faced with this dilemma, Husserl's phenomenology does not renounce the genetic dimension of consciousness, that which eludes us. On the contrary, it revises its methodological approach to address the "nature" of what appears without appearing, is given without giving, and reveals itself without revealing. In this way, it becomes a "phenomenology of the hidden."

CHAPTER 25

PHENOMENOLOGY OF THE HIDDEN

Meditation as an opening to the sacred

The debate conducted in the previous chapters has laid the foundations that will allow us to delve into what we can call the "phenomenology of the hidden." At first glance, and as we exposed in the previous chapter, this domain opens the door to apparent complications within the core of phenomenology. It might seem that speaking of a phenomenology of the unapparent, or of what is not shown, is an illogical contrast. The idea of an imperceptible or unapparent phenomenon seems to be an oxymoron in itself, for, by definition, phenomenon implies an appearance, while imperceptible, hidden, or unapparent would indicate precisely the opposite. Can we even speak of an appearance (*phainómenon*) that does not appear, that is, a noumenal phenomenon?

Certain phenomenologists argue that the only way to access manifestation is through the senses. That is, without sensory perception, there can be no phenomenon as such, and therefore, no phenomenology either. In other words, there is only a static phenomenology, in which the object (consciousness) of phenomenological reflection always refers back to the sensory act of perceiving intentional objects. These, in their most elementary form, are first presented to us through the senses. Against this position, the "hidden phenomenon" requires a particular subjective disposition in order to manifest itself as a phenomenon, even if it is not immediately evident.

Heidegger calls this particular subjective disposition "the ontological pre-understanding."[112] Ontological pre-understanding is given in the very fact of the relationship with Being. This understanding becomes obscured when it is theorized and conceptualized. As Marion would underline years later, the phenomenology of the hidden requires passivity both on the mental and emotional plane so that the entity can manifest without the interference of conceptualizations or intellectual activities. This passivity is not mere inactivity, but a release or postponement of all technical and manipulative attitudes toward the phenomenon so that it can present itself in its authenticity.

One way to understand this notion of passivity is through meditation. Although at first glance, it might seem that "meditation" and "ontological pre-understanding" are completely opposite terms, there is a trait in both that brings them closer. When Heidegger speaks of an ontological pre-understanding, he refers to a state of "relationality" with everything that surrounds us, but without conceptualizing it.

What is decisive here is that what surrounds us has not yet appeared as an intentional object of consciousness, but only in its first, discreet appearance. This is not a matter of unconsciousness; it is a matter of an active and silent consciousness, prior to any thematization and still untouched by the sieve of the concept. Ontological pre-understanding constitutes a non-theoretical consciousness at work, though reluctant to define itself. If I say to my neighbor, "I have little time," he immediately grasps the meaning of time without effort. Faced with the question "What is time?," that understanding slips away, failing to crystallize into a stable concept. If I add, "I am American," the verb *to be* is employed without hesitation. We all understand "to be" when saying, "I am Christian," "I am Jewish," "I am atheist," "I am communist," "I am a doctor." That "I am" is grasped at once, orienting conversation, identification, and belonging. Yet when the inquiry turns to "What is being?," everyday clarity

---

112. Martin Heidegger, *Being and Time*, trans. John Macquarrie and Edward Robinson (Blackwell Publishers Ltd, 1962), §43, 69.

grows dim, and the understanding that sustained those statements refuses to settle into a definition.

This mode of being in the world may be called a state of relationality with everything that surrounds us—an openness prior to the filter of conceptualization. If one prefers, it can be described as a pre-theoretical or anti-theoretical relation, grounded in practices and usages before reflection. In this, properly speaking, consists the understanding of Being.

Hence the Heideggerian turn directs thought back toward the source prior to the concept and away from reliance on already elaborated definitions of being. The point of departure no longer lies in finished conceptual schemes; it lies in that shared understanding prior to theory, which guides our dealings with the world. This is not a renunciation of thinking; rather, it compels thought to measure itself against that which, sustaining us from the beginning, scarcely consents to let itself be said.

In this, Heidegger is referring to a "state of mind," if we may call it that, in which the world is "given" to us tacitly, that is, without the subject acting, pointing, or explicitly indicating anything or anyone.

Something similar happens in meditation. The one who meditates enters a state of passivity that is precisely the "mood" that allows them to relate to what surrounds them, but at a more primordial level, without objects or subjects undertaking actions or containing meanings that belong to objectifying understanding. In this sense, the notion of meditation we propose here leads us to a sphere of existence in which we remain open, predisposed to the world, but without this, leading us to its theorization or conceptualization. As Heidegger would say, our most intimate bond with the world is ontological and not epistemological. This pre-understanding state can perhaps be better explained through a different, poetic language, and not a technical one.

Ultimately, the "relationship" with the world and its objects is not intentional, that is, it is not based on the capacities of subjects nor on their efforts to understand. Passivity, or pre-understanding, indicates a "relationality" without relationship or poles, without subjects or objects. Meditation underlies every positionality of the subject facing the object, in both understanding and being understood. In meditation, there is no effort, because a certain tension invariably accompanies all effort. Also, in meditation, we understand that striving for full consciousness is equivalent to confronting oneself, a superfluous conflict. The true awakening one can achieve through meditation does not originate in effort, but rather emerges spontaneously through surrendering to the naturalness of Being. It is the fruit of liberation, of embracing acceptance and immersing oneself in a state of relaxation. To meditate is an invitation to adopt a posture of serenity and peace, without trying to intervene actively and being merely a witness to how consciousness manifests effortlessly. There is no need to force its appearance or invoke it from a realm external to us, for it will emerge from the depth of our interior, provided we maintain a genuine calm state. We must recognize that there lies an inherent complexity in this simplicity: the challenge of remaining still, anchored in stillness, while thoughts come and go incessantly.

However, and as paradoxical as it may seem, in the calm state of meditation, one must allow them to pass. The meditator should not conflict with their thoughts or try to dominate them or manipulate them with effort. They should simply allow them to exist, just as clouds flow freely in the sky, and permit them to move without barriers or any kind of restriction. This ultimately means avoiding adopting a defensive posture or passing judgment on their suitability.

Meditation demands becoming situated in a state of complete passive receptivity. In this state, one eventually discovers that thoughts, with their constant ebb and flow, influence us less. And by ceasing to see ourselves disturbed by them, they will fade away on their own, not through a deliberate effort to expel them, but thanks to the same calm and the deep state of relaxation in which one is immersed. Furthermore, meditation is not a method per se, just as it does not depend on any methodology that could be applied or implemented, but quite the opposite. Meditation is, rather, the art of remaining idle. Meditation emerges naturally and spontaneously when one learns to be without doing anything; therein lies the secret of meditation: the art of inactivity. The moment activity becomes impossible, meditation unfolds on its own. In passivity, energy is directed toward our core, reorganizing itself in the center. In contrast, activity disperses energy because it is the way outward; passivity is the way inward. Constant activity is a diversion. Every activity acts as a pretext or justification to avoid encountering ourselves. Humanity, in its ignorance and blindness, chooses to remain in that state, for delving into oneself is delving into an apparent disorder. Within each one resides a chaos we have generated, and it is essential to face and traverse it.

In a sense, meditation is nothing other than being captivated by one's own existence. It is a simple process, a state of consciousness in which absolute relaxation prevails, without engaging in any activity. In meditation, we are conscious without being conscious of anything in particular. The appearance of action, of the act of consciousness and its concrete object, introduces tension. With it, anxiety arises immediately due to the utilitarian attitude about achieving success or avoiding failure, as well as questions that project us to the future. Thinking, speculating, or reflecting are possible only about the known, the concretized, and the objectified as such. Our knowledge about our religion, Śiva, Allah, Kṛṣṇa, or Ha Shem may be the center of our reflection or speculation, but they will never lead us to the unknown, to the un-concretized.

Therein lies the issue that links meditation, with the consciousness of the un-concretized, and religion. For precisely the Divine, the sacred, is the non-objectivized and non-concretized, that is, the unknown, the enigma, the mystery. Meditation consists of simply being, of ceasing all action, free from expectations, thoughts, and emotions. Without meditation, without maintaining this openness to the givenness and revelation of Being, without concretizing it, there would be no subsequent possible concretization, for there would be no Being in which anything could become something before our consciousness, our thinking, our knowing. To meditate is to un-understand the world, not to carry out phenomenological reductions or self-reflect, but to allow oneself to be engulfed by that latent state of openness to Being. Ultimately, meditation avoids making consciousness or Being an end in itself, a goal or objective, for such an approach obstructs truly experiencing it. In this sense, we present meditation as an attitude of observation and calm that is the condition of possibility for the noumenal phenomenon that manifests insofar as it does not manifest to reveal itself. In other words, without meditation, the sacred could not be attended to phenomenologically.

The "spiritual reduction" of the phenomenology of the hidden

Meditation is surrendering to relaxation, disengaging from our objects and our own individuality, letting thoughts pass in a simple way, and even letting time pass, almost literally. The meditation presented in these terms allows us to suggest that we are faced with a new reduction. This "reduction of the phenomenology of the hidden," as we might call it, unveils a state of existence that underlies all intentional consciousness, that is, all consciousness that constitutes meaning, objectifying and subjectivizing.

However, remaining immersed in the field of phenomenology, this reduction unveils a new phenomenon, a new level of consciousness that we should perhaps describe as pre-conscious, as the genesis of all consciousness, and, as such, hidden. Because, in the field of meditation, of authentic passivity, what "appears" is revealed, but without even being a concrete "thing. In the meditative state, what "appears" does not even have a stable (*morphê*) form and, therefore, is not eidetic, nor consequently intelligible through understanding, that is, through concepts and categories. In the state of complete passivity, of pure calm, what "appears" is given and revealed without calling it, naming it, or even seeking it, pointing to it, that is, without thinking it. That "that" is a "noumenal phenomenon" that simply gives itself, reveals itself even without being actively perceived as something concrete and individualized.

This genesis state of all subsequent consciousness, this meditative or passive state, is not reached or accessed through intention, for, as such, it does not respond or allow itself to be objectified or thought. The reduction of the phenomenology of the hidden is not the result of action, but rather of passivity. The path marked by effort does not lead to, nor penetrate, the oceans of passivity. It is not

Chapter 25: Phenomenology of the Hidden

through willpower or rigorous discipline that one achieves a "vision" of full attention, love, or full pre-understanding. The tendency to obsess does not offer a clear path to resolution. True grace, which is how we can define this meditative state that underlies all other subsequent states of consciousness, does not manifest in the one who exerts effort without measure, but in "one" who opens themselves entirely to the experience of surrender. Grace is discovered in the recognition of absolute surrender, in accepting a bond of total devotion toward the beloved. It is not the object of love that grants this grace, but rather, it is this grace itself that liberates the loving subject. Thus, the distinction between lover and beloved disappears, for this state lies deeper than any relationship between two poles. The degree of this surrender will reflect the depth of our devotion. It is important to understand that life provides a spiritual guide, but only when one is prepared to receive that guidance. Only the one who has contemplated and lived the divine experience possesses the true ability to instruct.

In this scenario, the phenomenon assumes a special dimension due to its innate capacity for unveiling, which is is independent of the observer's disposition, and because its nature transcends the limits of human perception and cognition. The excessiveness of the phenomenon lies in revealing aspects that transcend ordinary perception. The phenomenology of the underlying emphasizes aspects such as a softened intentionality, or almost a pre-intentionality, and essential characteristics of affection and openness that are tied to the exact moment of perception, but without being reduced to it. Parallel to this, for the phenomenon we here call "hidden" to reveal itself in its Being, a distinctive process of reduction is required. This process is no longer merely phenomenological or transcendental, but perhaps spiritual. It will prove fundamental for receiving that which manifests as hidden—without defined form or circumscribable categories.

As we have stated, the phenomenon in question cannot be approached directly in an intentional manner. As phenomenologists, we carry out a "reflection," but in quotation marks, because it is different from other levels of phenomenological inquiry, due to its particular disposition of passivity that allows one to position oneself in a way that enables capturing what is revealed. As we have pointed out a few paragraphs above, this passivity in the "reflection" is not a strategic passivity that, in the end, hides an effort. On the contrary, this reflection that occurs in terms of "spiritual reduction," as we propose to call it, is a surrender, a "letting go" without an object, without anything concrete to let go of.

Contrary to this passivity, this letting go or surrender, all effort originates in the subject, who is an intrinsic component of the observed phenomenon. The act of making an effort introduces, by default, a concept of duality, as it presupposes the existence of a space to be overcome between the observer and the object of observation, a space that the subject must cross. Effort creates conflict, conflict creates disorder, disorder creates chaos, and the latter prevents clear observation. That is why attaining calm becomes essential to begin perceiving clearly that "something" which is given, whose revelation is invisible because it lacks a form in which to appear.

In this sense, we propose that this "reflection" is not an effort, but rather a surrender, a complete letting go. It does not conform to any act of significance that arises from the decision to turn inward upon oneself. It does not create a space of separation where subjects distance themselves in order to relate to their own objects. "Spiritual reduction" does not create spaces or dualities and, therefore, does not constitute any intentional object. It would be like closing your eyes and abandoning yourself to sleep, in which the "that," which manifests without appearing, appears as amorphous and overflows us.

The noumenal phenomenon underlying all consciousness

The "spiritual reduction," would be similar to what Jean-Luc Marion calls "anamorphosis," which, according to him, is indispensable for the emergence of the hidden phenomenon. Marion uses this term to invite us to think of the phenomenon from different perspectives. He moves us away from the mere consideration of the phenomenon as an object and reveals other angles from which to explore it as a givenness and a manifestation of the hidden. In this way, he opens a path toward a deeper phenomenology. This phenomenon, which we call "noumenal" and which Marion also calls "saturated," although it is not perceived at first glance, does make itself known, but not through traditional senses.

To consider this phenomenon, which we could equate with what Heidegger calls "Being," it is essential to approach it from other perspectives that allow its unveiling. A specific disposition and a particular mode of positioning the subject's consciousness are required. This implies de-subjectivizing oneself and abandoning oneself, as we mentioned earlier. This process is achieved through a reduction that we call "spiritual," and its manner of proceeding is not an act, but an abandonment that opens the door to the field of meditation.

Without this explicitly passive surrender of consciousness, the subject will remain the same intentional subject operating through intentional acts. Therefore, the subject will not be able to capture that which reveals itself as hidden, amorphous, and pre-eidetic. This is the phenomenon of relationality without relation, of love that is not reduced or explained through the opposite poles of the lover and the beloved. "That" which reveals itself, "that" which appears as hidden, does not respond to noetic-intentional structures of consciousness. Therefore, it cannot be apprehended as an intentional object. In this sense, the hidden phenomenon has burst the seams of all intentionality and the acts of consciousness.

In fact, phenomenologically speaking, the intentional subject is incapacitated from turning upon itself in a self-reflective manner and directing its intentions toward the hidden. This is not due to the nature of a particular experience, but to the essence and existence inherent to experiences as such. By directing our intentions toward the hidden and attempting to address the amorphous intentionally, we incur its objectification, as we grant it a concrete form that erroneously transforms it into another objectual experience. By doing so, we load it with structures of experience that are foreign to it and do not belong to it, thus perverting it.

This problem is inscribed in the field of the phenomenology of the hidden, which is deeply intertwined with previous methodologies and perspectives. Husserl himself even intuited some of these, as we have mentioned on occasion, utilizing and expanding upon his developments. This phenomenological approach allows us to a deeper question of phenomena that appear hidden. That is, of all that underlies and, in a certain sense, "is" without "being conceptualizable," extending beyond the merely perceptible.

In this sense, the phenomenology of the underlying addresses a new dimension of experience or reconstructs the parameters of what we had until now understood as "consciousness." At the same time, it allows us to question the prior stages of the discipline and investigate aspects of non-hidden phenomena that, nonetheless, surpass our perception.

However, one does not occasionally decide to enter a state of meditative passivity. On the contrary, and as Heidegger warns by calling it "ontological pre-understanding," the hidden state accompanies consciousness throughout its entire active life. If the meditator can allow themselves to be imbued, to surrender to meditation, it is precisely because the meditative state already pulses within the subject at a pre-intentional level. Heidegger suggests with the expression "ontological pre-understanding," similarly to how Husserl refers to "prereflective intentionality," that all life and activity of consciousness cannot be reduced to its acts, intentionality, ideas, categories, forms, and its corresponding intelligibility of reality. Underlying all of this is a hidden dimension, a "reality" of phenomena, which we call "the passive state of meditation," which makes any subsequent knowledge possible. In other words, to perceive and know something, we must first maintain an underlying connection, a "relationality" with it, and be unconsciously aware of its apparent non-appearance, of its afenomenic phenomenicity.

Furthermore, this "underlying" not only affects consciousness as a non-intentional phenomenon, but it is also integral to every intentional phenomenon. For example, although one tends to think that objects of our experience, such as a stone, silence, the now, or nothingness, do not exceed our perceptual capacities, in reality, all of them can reveal dimensions of their essence that go beyond our immediate understanding. However, as such, they remain hidden from our cognitive powers. This is because, by attempting to apprehend these phenomena fully, we somehow transform them, altering their essence. One example of this is the wave in the ocean. It ceases to be recognized as such by dissolving into it, even when perceiving its oceanic nature.

Expressed in this way, the phenomenology of the hidden allows us to delve into a dimension of consciousness, of existence, to say it with Heidegger, that overflows the limits of the structures of thought and reason, and enriches our understanding of consciousness itself and its generative dimension. Moreover, this phenomenology of the hidden also has the virtue of showing us that the hidden underlies everything. This means that phenomenology must rethink itself, as the hidden phenomenon, which appears without revealing itself to the powers of perception and understanding, always overflows the intentional character of all knowledge.

However, this is not new, as it has accompanied phenomenology from its beginnings. In fact, the phenomenological study has always addressed the crumbling of modernity and the relevance of the conceptual framework. Within this complex environment, novel concepts have emerged, such as the various reductions we have described, and the one we have proposed in this very chapter. Each one has had implications for intentionality, as well as for the exploration of subjective experiences that differ from one's own. All of this development, of which the phenomenology of the hidden is a part, emphasizes that phenomenology transcends the analysis of isolated and personal actions, extending its focus to a broader understanding of the horizon in which experiences develop. This approach reaffirms the expansive nature of phenomenology, which seeks to understand the entirety of human experience, beyond individual and subjective limitations.

CHAPTER 26

RELATIONALITY AND THE APPEARANCE OF BEING AS THE SACRED

The Heideggerian notion of *ereignis*: concealment and clarity

We finished the previous chapter by linking the hidden phenomenon, as the primordial and genetic dimension of consciousness, with the hidden nature of all phenomena. In this sense, we argued that the phenomenology of the hidden has the virtue of addressing both the hidden phenomenon underlying all conscious life and our experience, as well as uncovering the hidden in every intentional phenomenon of consciousness. In other words, the hidden resides in every phenomenon, whether it is a passive dimension of all experience that does not lend itself to any form of perception or knowledge, or a dimension of the very acts of intentional consciousness that static phenomenology describes without, seemingly, too many problems.

This hidden dimension of every "hidden" phenomenon, and therefore phenomenologically describable, has been one of the main topics that Heidegger himself discussed at length. Addressing the issue from a unique perspective, the author of *Being and Time* introduces the concept of surplus, or *Überschuss* in German, with which he sought to denote a peculiar phenomenon that emerges when perceiving and attempting to understand something as an object. According to Heidegger, in every process of perception, a surplus manifests—a dimension that goes beyond the apparent or perceptible. This surplus is not a simple addition to our understanding but is rather revealed in such a way that it differs from the visible. For example, when observing an apple, we perceive its obvious characteristics, such as its color, shape, and size. However,

Heidegger suggests the existence of a deeper aspect, a hidden quality inherent to the very essence of the apple. This hidden facet is not merely a complement to the visible but is a completely distinct dimension. The appearance of this dimension of the phenomenon, which is a phenomenon in itself, is not something spontaneous and thus requires to be unveiled or facilitated in some way—not being a natural or automatic process.

This phenomenological requirement to unveil the hidden in the intentional phenomenon opens the door to new ways of seeing, perceiving, and intuiting. In the face of this phenomenological necessity, Heidegger introduces a new way of seeing, parallel to sensory intuition, whose goal is to enter the realm of phenomena that are not immediately evident.

This approach opens up a new panorama in the way we perceive and understand the world, extending even to spheres that are not visible or immediately manifest. This proposal invites us to a deep reflection on the complexity of our perception and experience of the world. It suggests the existence of elements beyond what our senses directly capture. As Heidegger will suggest, this other way of seeing, of intuiting, that transcends the powers of the senses, enriches the very perceptual experience, opening doors to levels of meaning beyond the superficial, the obvious, and the apparently given.

In his reflections on the inapparent, Heidegger emphasizes the importance of the Being remaining hidden in order to enable its unveiling, an idea that underscores the depth of the phenomenological experience and our understanding of the world. In his work *Vorträge und Aufsätze*, Heidegger delves into this idea and introduces the notion of *ereignis*, a term that can be translated as "event" or "occurrence," and which will prove crucial in understanding the reciprocal relationship between human beings and Being. Similar to how we expressed in the previous chapter, describing the hidden phenomenon of unconscious consciousness as a "relationality without relation," Heidegger uses the term "event" to describe the process of the revelation of Being. This highlights the premise that Being remains hidden in its primordial state. *Ereignis* is conceived as the realm where the human being and Being intertwine and coexist, transcending the identity of both. This "relationality" acts as the configuring principle of the various forms of Being, granting it existence and transforming it into a manifestation of the event that emerges in perceptible reality.

This link, this relationality without relation, as we have called it in this study, allows Being to express and actualize itself through humanity, thus suggesting an intimate dialogue between the human condition and the very nature of Being. In this, both interweave and define each other, unveiling crucial elements of both objective reality and our subjective perception of existence.

Ereignis symbolizes the critical moment in which Being and the individual converge, facilitating a new opening toward the understanding of Being. This shows that the conditions of possibility for all understanding and meaning emerge at a level where there is still no relationship between subject and intentional object of consciousness, but there is a relationality, an occurrence, a being-in-the-world that underlies all experience, chiseling in the darkness all possibility of meaning. It is important not to confuse the notion of *ereignis*, of event, or occurrence, with a mere sum of the human being and Being, as if they were two entities that approach each other and, upon uniting, accumulate. On the contrary, the occurring, the "relationality," is the hidden phenomenon, and not the presence of anything. Occurring is not becoming present in the traditional sense of the term, but flowing. In this sense, it can be understood as a dynamic that shapes the stage where Being pulses in the human being, manifesting and asserting itself. *Ereignis* is not a phenomenon of static presence but a dynamic occurring where Being and the human being mutually define each other in a relationality of appropriation and continuous belonging.

In *On the Way to Language (Unterwegs zur Sprache)*, Heidegger explores the essence of *ereignis*, a concept that, as we have begun to outline, transcends the idea of the revealed, the revealer, and the recipient of the revelation, focusing on the dynamic interaction between these elements. In this sense, Heidegger characterizes *ereignis* as "It is itself the most inconspicuous of inconspicuous phenomena, the simplest of simplicities,"¹¹³ highlighting its quality of sub-subjective givenness manifested in the notion of "there is." This asubjectivity arises from its lack of a concrete subject, reducing itself to the existence of a "there is" that expresses an existence, a having, a being, whose "appearance" demands no action nor subjective entity to articulate it. Moreover, what Heidegger is sketching here is a notion of manifestation that is defined by concealment. What is manifested, precisely, is the constant disappearing with which he underscores an existential background in which Being is primarily manifested through its tendency toward concealment.

However, Heidegger links this dimension of inapparency with the concept of *lichtung*, that is, "clarity." Here, the concealment of Being makes way for a space of clarity that rises in opposition to darkness, suggesting an essential differentiation in the manifestation of Being. Heidegger seems to point to a "relationality" that fluctuates prior to any relation, where Being shows its underlying concealment. Paradoxically, that concealment is its clarity, its "light," which is neither seen nor perceived, but without which we would not see, perceive, or understand anything. This light that does not show itself but illuminates and enables the seeing of everything else is what Heidegger understands as the Divine, the sacred—namely, that which manifests itself through the excess of Being that withdraws and conceals itself. *Ereignis*, as we have presented here, urges philosophy to emerge as an effort to understand the position of the human being in relation to this excess of the "present," in which God, Being, and *ereignis* itself coexist in a realm of inapparency that fosters the appearing of the sacred.

Being as the radical Other

In contrast to Edmund Husserl, whose genetic phenomenology never fully divorces itself from its static phenomenology, Heidegger introduces a methodology focused on unraveling the inapparency of

---

113. Martin Heidegger, *On the Way to Language (Unterwegs zur Sprache)*, trans. Peter D. Hertz (Harper & Row, 1971), 128.

Being without remaining anchored in conventional structures. For Heidegger, the problem with Husserl's phenomenology is that every genetic dimension is always anchored in the static dimension, that is, in the intentional consciousness that perceives and understands. Heidegger's project is to rid itself of this anchor in order to set sail and attend to Being and the sacred, allowing human beings to think and understand themselves philosophically with greater depth.

In this context, Heidegger's post-Husserlian approach underscores the importance of the ontological difference, that is, the distinction between "being an object" and "Being" itself. Although semantically close, these concepts contain profound ontological differences. This distinction is crucial for understanding the complexity of Heidegger's thought, which seeks to transcend the limitations of the traditional conceptualization of Being and delve into a philosophical territory where the essence of Being is revealed in its relationship with concealment, event (*ereignis*), and clarity (*lichtung*). Thus, a richer and more precise ontological understanding is configured—one that transcends the epistemological plane, as we develop in these chapters.

Husserl's phenomenology persists in an interpretation of Being grounded in the objectification or intentionality of consciousness, attributing to it a fixed identity, whether objective or subjective. Heidegger, however, proposes a radically different perspective. This is a crucial turning point in philosophical thought, returning to the foundational interpretations of Plato and Aristotle, who linked Being indissolubly to the notion of *parousía*, or "presence." Such a perspective has dominated metaphysical discourse throughout history, exerting a profound and lasting influence on the understanding of Being, which has persisted—according to Heidegger—until Husserl himself.

In his work *Seminare*, Heidegger articulates this critique by declaring that the trajectory of metaphysics has been essentially characterized by a history of Being of the entity, thus questioning the validity of the "metaphysics of presence" defended by Husserl. For Husserl, the authenticity of Being is confirmed through its perceptible manifestation. In contrast, Heidegger proposes that the true essence of Being transcends its mere physical appearance. As we have seen in this chapter, this implies its form, perception, and subsequent conceptual apprehension.

Heidegger refutes the equivalence between Being and presence (*ousia estin parousía*) that has underpinned the foundations of Western philosophy. He challenges the notion that Being exhausts itself in its visibility or manifestation before us—that is, that Being is merely an object-pole that only makes sense as an opposing pole to a subject that perceives and thinks of it as an intelligible object. For Heidegger, this philosophical conception of Being is fundamentally inadequate. Being, in its manifestation, does not reveal its deepest essence, but its very inapparency, that is, its concealment. This argument is explicitly laid out in *Being and Time*, where it is maintained that Being does not communicate its authentic reality as it presents itself before our eyes.

Therefore, Heidegger's contribution to philosophy transcends Husserl's significantly, offering a more complex and nuanced perspective. Heidegger rejects the simplistic interpretations of Being as a merely visible or identifiable entity and, therefore, knowable through intentional acts of consciousness. Although Husserl does not limit his phenomenology to intelligibility and acts of consciousness, Heidegger holds that he never entirely leaves them behind. Even when exploring passive genesis, Husserl remains within the limits of epistemology.

In response to this, Heidegger urges a profound reconsideration of ontology as "first philosophy," aiming to understand Being beyond its immediate presence. This opens us to an appreciation of its hidden depth and ontological meaning. This reorientation invites a richer and more detailed exploration of Being, emphasizing the need to overcome the limitations imposed by previous conceptions and revealing the more intricate and elusive layers of ontological reality. In *Seminare*, Heidegger argues that:

> *als Da-sein verstanden, das heißt, von der Ek-statik aus, der Mensch nur ist, indem er von sich bis zu jenem ganz anderen als er selbst kommt, das die Lichtung des Seins ist.*

[...] and thus to see that, understood as *Da-sein* (that is, from the *ek-static*), the human only exists in coming from itself to what is wholly other than itself, in coming to the clearing of being.[114]

For Heidegger, Being, as it is not a mere object, cannot be subjected to such a structure of transcendence within immanence proposed by Husserl, but instead corresponds only to a state of ecstasy, from the Greek *ekstasis*, meaning "pure exteriority." In this sense, *Dasein*, as being-in-the-world, transcends its personal confines to meet that which is completely alien, other, to its own existence. Furthermore, the authenticity of human beings is revealed in their capacity to transcend themselves and encounter the absolutely Other, that which radically distinguishes itself from their own essence. This moment of genuine openness toward the different, illuminated in the clearing (*lichtung*) of the event (*ereignis*), marks the instant in which human beings fully realize themselves. The true essence of humanity as being-in-the-world only emerges through "relationality" with the "radically Other"—as Levinas will later say—that is, with that which calls upon it and invites reflection on the world and on itself. Therefore, Heidegger, in his *Letter on Humanism*, argues that the essence of humanism does not reside in the exaltation of humans, but in their capacity to open up to Being, living in a constant reference or "relationality" to it.

Being as Truth

As we have seen in previous sections, Heidegger defines this "relationality" of openness to Being in terms of *ereignis* and *lichtung*, issues that refer us to the foundations of philosophy. Heidegger guides us in this return through a reflection on Parmenides, seeking to transcend what he identifies as the "But there was not yet in Being and Time a genuine knowledge of the history of being, hence the

---

114. Martin Heidegger, "Seminar in Zähringen 1973," in *Four Seminars*, trans. Andrew J. Mitchell and François Raffoul (Bloomington: Indiana University Press, 2003), 73.

awkwardness and, strictly speaking, the naïveté of the 'ontological destruction.'" (*die Ungeschicklichkeit und strenggenommen Naivität der' ontologischen Destruktion*)[115], an approach he criticizes in *Being and Time* as a primitive stage in the history of Being. Heidegger delves into a detailed analysis of the first verse of Parmenides' poem. This thinker, along with Anaximander and Heraclitus, stands as a fundamental pillar in the study of Being, linking Being with the topic of Truth (*alétheia*).

In contrast to Parmenides, Plato, and Aristotle orient their philosophical inquiry toward the entity rather than toward Being in its pure essence. Their concept of "truth" is restricted to the parameters of the beings, i.e., their empirical facticity and calculability, and to subjective capabilities limited to intelligibility and reason. From this critical perspective, Heidegger's definition of *alétheia* emerges as a dynamic event of the unhiddenness of Being.

This "unconcealment" event, while surrounding the existent with "presence," should not be understood as an act of full presencing. What unconcealment reveals is what lies at the periphery or surrounds presence without constituting presence itself. Put differently, what appears in unconcealment is Being as existence without objectification. This implies that it has no empirical characteristics of an being present to consciousness and, therefore, cannot be the object of an act that thinks of it in a calculated way.

By not fully manifesting as presence, Being offers itself while remaining hidden in the asubjective relationality of meditative calm. Being is that light or clarity that surrounds presence, giving it visibility. It is precisely its absence of presencing that allows the entity to reveal itself by itself. For this reason, such concealment, far from being manifest, always escapes any empirical verification, as it is not discernible through methods exclusively based on empirical knowledge. In his argument, Heidegger again refers to the verse from Parmenides (DK 28B1.28), which has been translated as:

---

115. Ibid., 78.

nötig ist, dass du die Erfahrung von allem machst

It is necessary that you experience all things.[116]

Heidegger interprets this quote from Parmenides to mean that the essence of what is observed is revealed through an experience. What is hidden transcends any epistemological framework based on sensible perception and the intelligibility derived from it. He argues that attempting to demonstrate the existence of Being through scientific methods—that is, epistemological parameters designed to comprehend beings—does nothing but ontify Being.

In contrast to objectifying and ontifying epistemology, Heidegger directs us toward contemplation and observation as the preferred path. The calm attitude opens up that "relationality" without relation, without ontification, which allows *Dasein* to remain linked to Being without ontologizing it, without making it an object of thought. As we said earlier, it is a state of meditation as a stage of existence, of consciousness, as Husserl would say, in which "relationality" can take place before the emergence of any object, but also of any subject. Had Heidegger been more familiar with this notion of meditation, he would surely have proposed it as the path to express what we call "relationality" with Being.

The importance of meditation, or contemplation as Heidegger would say, is that it opens a new notion of thought that does not depend on the traditional epistemological structures, which were born with Plato and lead to Husserl's phenomenology. Although Husserl provided us with a new conceptual map to study the origins of experience and knowledge, Heidegger still sees his approach as anchored in the philosophical tradition, even Cartesian, that needs to be surpassed. His main criticism concerns the notion of intuition, a concept that Husserl called "the principle of all principles." Because of intuition, Husserl's phenomenology fails to clearly distinguish between the genetic and static dimensions, that is, between what is generated and what remains fixed.

---

116. Ibid., 80.

Intuition in Husserl's phenomenology

For Heidegger, the problem with the concept of intuition in phenomenology arises from its conceptualization as a direct relationship between manifestation, appearance (phenomenon), and Being, expressed as "as much appearance, as much Being." That is, within the parameters of Husserl's philosophy, what *is*, is what appears. Or, in other words, there is no Being beyond the phenomenon of consciousness, so any possible conception of Being is restricted to the limits of the phenomenon.

Moreover, as we have stated in previous chapters, if the phenomenon is *its* appearing, *its* own manifestation (and not the manifestation of any other reality that precedes it), this would be equivalent to affirming that Being is its phenomenal manifestation. Therefore, there is no Being without manifestation. In this context, the concept of phenomenological intuition becomes a problem.

According to Husserl, especially the early Husserl of *Logical Investigations* and *Ideas I*, intuition is the complement of intentionality and perception, through which we confer meaning to every object of consciousness. The act of perception presents the object of intention to consciousness as an object still stripped of all meaning—that is, as a raw object that is almost undetermined. Intuition, in turn, is that other act which discerns amid the rough edges of the raw object and offers it to consciousness as an intelligible object. Perception, by itself, neither incorporates nor confers any meaning upon the object of intentionality. It merely encounters it as an object of consciousness and renders it a potential object-with-meaning. It offers it to the intuitive gaze, which subsequently envelops and shapes it as an object of our understanding. We might say, then, that without perception there would be nothing to see and without intuition, nothing to understand.

However, intuition should not be understood as an entirely independent act from intentionality or perception in which the object appears in consciousness. Intuition, as an act attached to perception, satisfies or frustrates what consciousness focuses on in the intentional act. Perception presents us with the "thing" that is the object of our attention. Along with perception, one begins to intuit its essences. At first, one sees it as something "with color" and "with shape," without yet being fully aware of the intentional object perceived. But gradually one intuits the material and formal categories that define it, such as the concepts "box," "red," and "square."

The intuition of essences and categories are not "additional" acts to perception; rather, and even though they are different acts, they are all intertwined acts that jointly and synthetically constitute the same experience with different moments. In this sense, for Husserl, intuition is the constitution of the intentional object, the object toward which consciousness is focused in the first moment. In every moment in which intuition acts, the object reveals a new dimension of itself and becomes an intentional object constituted by consciousness. Intuition is the synthetic act that perceives, abstracts, and reflects on the different dimensions of what presents itself to consciousness through perception.

From this point of view, for Husserl, intuition is the dimension of consciousness that allows what is given in consciousness to be understood in its own terms, in its own essence, revealing itself in its ideality and structural existence. In other words, intuition is the framework of all meaning, and for this reason, Husserl calls it, as we said, "the principle of all principles":

> *jede originar gebende Anschauung eine Rechtquelle der Erkenntnis sei, daß alles, was sich uns inter Intuition originär ... darbietet, einfach hinzunehmen sei, als was es sich gibt.*

> Every originary presentive intuition is a legitimizing source of cognition, that everything originarily [...] offered to us in "intuition" is to be accepted simply as what it is presented as being. [117]

---

117. Edmund Husserl, *Ideas Pertaining to a Pure Phenomenology and to a Phenomenological Philosophy*, trans. Fred Kersten (The Hague: Martinus Nijhoff Publishers, 1982), §24, 44.

Husserl says that everything that reveals itself to us in its Being, in its essence—that is, through its general, material, and categorial essences by means of intuition—is what it *is*, and what it *is* (Being) is that which is given (manifestation). This is where the problem lies for Heidegger: for no matter how infinite the synthesis of acts might be within the constitutive process of knowing an object, Being never exceeds its givenness. Moreover, by being confined to the powers of intuition, Being ultimately becomes a mere correlate of consciousness and, therefore, an object of it.

For this reason, Heidegger insists on the need to dismantle the Husserlian edifice of consciousness, where Being is always ontologized, and aims to situate ontology as the fundamental philosophy underlying all epistemology. The problem of Being, its ontologization, lies in the fact that all experience is reduced to the parameters of intentional consciousness and its cognitive abilities. In contrast to this, Heidegger maintains that, prior to any knowledge of an object through the filter of intuition, *Dasein* is already open to Being. Now, Being is not understood as a mere correlate of consciousness but as *ek-static* existence, that is, as purely exterior, radically Other, and irreducible to any act of knowledge.

This openness toward Being, which Heidegger describes as a response to the problem of ontologizing and epistemologizing experience and the sense of human being, amounts to an original predisposition toward the manifestation of Being, but without filtering it through cognitive intuition. Heidegger calls this disposition the true sense of Being. The analogy might be that of tuning into a specific station that broadcasts a particular piece of music; it is only possible to capture it in the frequency that the station chooses to transmit. Similarly, the relationality with Being is achieved exclusively through the mode or frequency in which it manifests, beyond the conceptualizations that consciousness may impose upon it. It is impossible to tune into that melody at any frequency, but only at the specific one the station transmits.

Bibliography section VI

- Aristotle. *De Anima: Books II and III, with Passages from Book I*. Translated with Introduction and Notes by D. W. Hamlyn, with a report on recent work and a revised bibliography by Christopher Shields. Clarendon Aristotle Series. Oxford: Clarendon Press, 1968; rev. ed., 1993.
- Heidegger, Martin. *Being and Time*. Translated by John Macquarrie and Edward Robinson. Oxford: Blackwell, 1962.
- Heidegger, Martin. *Introduction to Phenomenological Research*. Translated by Daniel O. Dahlstrom. Bloomington: Indiana University Press, 2005.
- Heidegger, Martin. "Letter on Humanism." In *Pathmarks*, edited by William McNeill, translated by Frank A. Capuzzi. Cambridge University Press, 1998.
- Heidegger, Martin. "Phenomenology and Theology." In *Pathmarks*, edited by William McNeill. Cambridge University Press, 1998.
- Heidegger, Martin. "Seminar in Zähringen 1973." In *Four Seminars*, translated by Andrew J. Mitchell and François Raffoul. Bloomington: Indiana University Press, 2003.
- Heidegger, Martin. *On the Way to Language (Unterwegs zur Sprache)*. Translated by Peter D. Hertz. New York: Harper & Row, 1971.
- Husserl, Edmund. *Formal and Transcendental Logic*. Translated by Dorion Cairns. The Hague: Martinus Nijhoff, 1969.
- Husserl, Edmund. *Ideas Pertaining to a Pure Phenomenology and to a Phenomenological Philosophy, First Book: General Introduction to a Pure Phenomenology*. Translated by Fred Kersten. In Collected Works, vol. 2. Dordrecht: Kluwer Academic Publishers, 1982.

- Inverso, Hernán Gabriel. *Fenomenología de lo inaparente*. Buenos Aires: Prometeo Libros, 2018.
- Janicaud, Dominique. *Heidegger in France*. Translated by David Pettigrew and François Raffoul. Bloomington: Indiana University Press, 2015.
- Zahavi, Dan. *Husserl's Phenomenology*. Stanford, CA: Stanford University Press, 2003.

Section VII

From ontology to (post)phenomenology

Chapter 27

The saturated phenomenon

The call of Being

As we have mentioned previously, and as Michel Henry also argues, in our perception, the visible is inherently linked to the invisible, the manifested to the unmanifested, and the given with the non-given. Following Heidegger's critique of Husserl, any givenness is presented to us as incomplete, limited by unexplored horizons, and surrounded by unfulfilled possibilities. Michel Henry suggests that in life, *tout est là tout entier à chaque instant*, meaning "everything is there, whole at every instant."[118] This implies that the ultimate givenness, or the final act of receiving or perceiving, of intuiting, as Husserl would say, is not segmented into different parts or goals to achieve. Each human perception refers to what is not perceived, and each given thing suggests what is non-given. In other words, the givenness integrates within itself the non-givenness, just as the apparent encloses within it the non-apparent. That is, the phenomenon does not extinguish itself in the visible and apparent. In this sense, the phenomenon is, as Jean-Luc Marion maintains, "a saturated phenomenon," which means that appearing also involves the hidden, always overflowing any possible knowledge of it. This allows us to affirm that the phenomenon, Being, is not fully known, since it always transcends all possible knowledge.

To speak of the phenomenon, or Being, in these terms— through this appearance that implies its non-appearance, through

---

118. Michel Henry, *De la phénoménologie, t.1: Phénoménologie de la vie* (Paris: Presses Universitaires de France, 2003), 91. Translation mine.

a givenness that includes the hidden, or the visible that encloses the invisible—leads us again, and now with greater clarity, to the issue of the symbol. A symbol consists of something visible that refers us to the invisible, to the imperceptible, to what always exceeds and overflows, and, as such, remains always hidden, revealing itself to all knowledge and visualization of it. This means that the donation of the saturated phenomenon occurs through symbolic means. Therefore, all donations are revealed as precarious, (un)framed by unattainable horizons and possibilities yet to be realized. Due to the inherent polysemy of the symbol, no exegesis can be confined strictly to a single dogmatic interpretation of it. Unlike what we might call "poor phenomena," saturated phenomena present a paradoxical nature in which the object of phenomenological study exceeds the abstract to delve into an eminently human and concrete reality: emotion, pathos. Therefore, at its core, the saturated phenomenon reveals absolutely nothing. Contrary to perspectives that dissociate or fragment their object of study, an emotive approach is offered. This view focuses not on what is external to the phenomenon, but on a complete and radical immanence to the phenomenon itself, to the non-apparent, to the hidden, as genuinely inherent to the given and visible. According to Henry, it is in this immanence where the essential key is found, asserting that:

> *non seulement elle n'oublie ni ne retranche rien mais que c'est par elle seulement que ce qu'elle a mis entre parenthèses reçoit ses propriétés particulières, tandis que le voir, l'intuition, l'évidence laissés à eux-mêmes ne les expliquent nullement.*

Not only does it not omit or subtract anything, but it is only through it that what it has placed in parentheses receives its particular properties, while seeing, intuition, and evidence left to themselves do not explain them in any way.[119]

---

119. Ibid., 92.

Chapter 27: The Saturated Phenomenon

Everything is given to be perceived, but what must be perceived is non-given. The revelation is donated; the phenomenon manifests as a givenness, but when we interpret it, it turns out there is nothing because the revelation simply reveals itself by hiding. We see an object, for example, a bottle. We perceive its glass, its label, the paper, the colors, what it contains, the metal of its cap, its roundness, its transparency. Although these elements, these material and categorical essences, to use Husserl's terms, direct us toward the bottle, the curious thing is that the bottle itself is elusive. In essence, within the set of elements to which we refer as the bottle, it is precisely the bottle that we cannot identify. Similarly, when delving into the microcosm to the tiniest particles or exploring the macrocosm to the most distant galaxies, we never really find something tangible. Behind the branches, the wood, the trunk, the leaves, the green color, the flowers, and the fruit, we do not find any element that we can clearly define as a tree, although all these aspects point toward it.

The phenomenon, understood as its own manifestation or revelation hiding itself, shows us that, in reality, nothing is definitively something and no one is definitively someone. Although accessible to our perception, vision, and intuition through the acts of consciousness, these are not revealed through perception or intuition. Henry supports this path with Marion's ideas, whose themes of "the call" and "the claim" subordinate Being, the essence of what is given, to something even more essential, affirming that:

> *L'appel de l'être, c'est tout simplement son surgissement en nous, c'est l'étreinte en laquelle il se donne à nous en même temps qu'il nous donne d'être. Ainsi n'y aurait-il rien sans cette irruption triomphale d'une révélation qui est celle de l'Absolu.*

The call of Being is simply its emergence in us; it is the embrace in which it gives itself to us at the same time that it gives us to be. Therefore, there would be nothing

335

without this triumphant eruption of a revelation that is that of the Absolute.[120]

The topic of the "call," according to Marion and Henry, leads us to redefine the underlying "relationality" with Being, understood by Heidegger as a "relationality" of pure exteriority, to understand it as one of pure immanence in which Being bursts into us, into our innermost interior, as the Absolute. That is, if the underlying "relationality" equals the ground in which Being can reveal itself in beings, Marion and Henry's approach shows us how Being bursts into us as the starting point for any possible identification as subjects, through which the human being can open itself to its cognitive objects. This eruption of Being into us, this embrace, as Henry describes it, is not an act of self-reflection, for it does not proceed from the subject, but from Being itself, which, by giving itself to us, makes us be ourselves.

What is given in this eruption of Being is a subjective anonymity that can only be understood through a plurality that is not the calculable result of singularities. One way of explaining this notion of givenness in terms of eruption or call is through the figures of the ocean and the waves. The immense ocean extends beyond human visual perception, proposing a scale and depth that surpass understanding, a domain whose immensity is elusive to our imagination. The complete reality of the ocean escapes our full comprehension; we tend to underestimate its magnificence, distancing ourselves significantly from its true extent. Within this vastness, the waves continuously manifest as natural expressions of the sea. Although they are named and considered distinct, in their essence, the waves are inseparable from the ocean, embodying the same substance. However, we often forget this essential reality: we share, like the waves, a common and universal essence that connects us with the great ocean of consciousness, neglecting our fundamental connection with the totality of Being.

---

120. Ibid., 96.

These reflections, from Husserl to Heidegger, and now more specifically from Marion and Henry, allow us to refer to a notion of consciousness that we might understand as that basic unity from which all emerge, that is, our genuine original essence. Such consciousness and unity, which integrates and coordinates the whole of existence, can be compared to the ocean in its limitlessness and vastness. We, as human beings, resemble the waves, mistakenly identified with our personalities, until we forget our authentic oceanic condition. This collective forgetting leads us to consider ourselves isolated, like a jar submerged in the ocean, without remembering that we remain part of the ocean despite the boundaries of the vessel. The fallacy of separation, grounded in the belief in our corporeal restrictions, prevents us from admitting that, fundamentally, we are and remain the ocean.

In this sense, the triumphant manifestation of the saturated phenomenon constitutes the essence of everything; without such manifestation, of the visible and the invisible with it, we would find ourselves facing non-existence itself. The multiplicity of objects we detect in our surroundings amounts to "nothing" until we identify it as such emptiness in our inner being, at which point we understand its true "existence." We are referring to the primordial essence of all that exists, asserting that the foundation and essence of this objectual multiplicity are unified in a single Being, an Absolute. This figure, intimately linked to boredom, emerges as the possibility of ignoring the call. Thus, Henry presents the concept of "radical reduction" as an act of temporarily withdrawing attention from Being itself and listening to the *forme pure d'appel*, or "pure form of the call." He describes the pure form of Being as:

> *a fulguration d'un apparaître qui nous submerge et qui, en tant qu'il fulgure, nous fait être en même temps que lui.*

Section VII: From Ontology to (Post)Phenomenology

> A fulguration of an appearing that submerges us and that, as it fulgurates, makes us be at the same time as it.[121]

The essence of life manifests in its ability to deeply move us, a truth Marion explores meticulously in his work *Being Given: Toward a Phenomenology of Givenness* (*Étant donné: Essai d'une phénoménologie de la givenness*). Here, and following the line of phenomenology, Marion presents a radical methodological alternative, proposing a voluntary limitation of subjective action to allow a purer manifestation of what appears to us. Criticizing the standard methodology for constraining the dynamism of the subject and thus strengthening the visibility of the manifest, Marion argues that such approaches stifle the spontaneity necessary for true revelation. The complexity of his argument lies in how to assign a solid foundation to a method that intrinsically requires withdrawal from action. For Marion, abandoning any pre-established methodology and passively accepting what is revealed constitutes the only valid practice. Losing initiative means being constantly thrown into the embrace of Being. This passivity, that letting oneself be imbued, which we have described as meditation, calm, aligns with Heidegger's "pathos of waiting" and immerses us in a constant disposition toward Being that does not involve initiating any action. However, and paradoxically, Marion emphasizes that achieving full passivity entails a significant effort, requiring and therefore proposing to take activity to the extreme in order to truly not act. In order to achieve doing nothing, much must be done; to reach the state of doing nothing, it is necessary to push doing to its maximum.

Michel Henry delves deeper into this matter that "Every originary presentive intuition is a legitimizing source of cognition."[122] He introduces the matter of language, positing that the act of expressing oneself about what is revealed to us has an

---

121. Ibid., 100.
122. Edmund Husserl, *Ideas Pertaining to a Pure Phenomenology and to a Phenomenological Philosophy*, trans. Fred Kersten (The Hague: Martinus Nijhoff Publishers, 1982), §24, 44.

inherent justification. It is not merely capricious or condemnable to speak of the revealed in us. An inalienable right to express ourselves about what has been unveiled is established, as this act of revelation justifies expression by itself, particularly by the one in whom the revelation has occurred directly. There is a right to speak of it because it was manifested, and the only one who truly has the right to speak of the revelation is the one in whom it has occurred. In reality, as we will see later, the Phenomenology of the Sacred is only for the enlightened beings.

New phenomenological principle: from intuition to givenness

One of the first questions that arises regarding the issue of the saturated phenomenon is: how can phenomenology account for such invisibility and justify that the saturated phenomenon is, indeed, a phenomenon? To answer this question, Marion introduces an important consideration concerning the axiom of intuitive perception in Husserl. According to phenomenological standards, intuitive perception is the principle of all principles as the vehicle through which phenomena are granted the right to be phenomenal, especially when they are subject to the condition of ecstasy and transcendence. In this regard, following Heidegger more than Husserl, Jean-Luc Marion interprets intuition, understood as the "source of right" of all phenomenality, in all instances where phenomena are in a relation of *ek-stasis* and transcendence. The term *ekstasis*, from the Greek ἔκστασις (*ek stasis*), which translates as "to be outside of oneself," evokes a state of being that goes beyond the egoic phenomenon or the separate "I." *Ek-stasis* suggests a deepening into Being, in which only the one who immerses themselves in the emotional experience of Being can receive the givenness of Being. In this sense, what is ecstatic transcends us in that it surpasses us, as it resides beyond our personal realm.

This first consideration leads Marion to highlight a certain ambiguity in situations where intuition might not play any role and, therefore, the action of granting or donating would occur without the mediation of intuition. In other words, Marion asks whether this process of givenness occurs, or can occur, "without surpassing the limits in which it is given."[123] He argues that the problem might lie in the fact that until now, givenness had been understood within boundaries that respond to the restrictions imposed by intuitive perception and not to the characteristics of givenness itself.

As Marion points out, highlighting the existence of an intrinsic paradox, if, on the one hand, our perceptions are finite, the essence of giving, on the other hand, is infinite; if intuition has limits, givenness, by its nature, does not. A simplified givenness, that is, freed from additional elements, is delivered absolutely, totally, fully, and unconditionally. Givenness, therefore, does not adjust to the parameters or the norms of intuition that the subject of knowledge has devised. According to Marion, phenomenology explores what is given within the confines in which it is given. However, these limits are influenced and predelimited, by our perceptive abilities more than by the properties of givenness itself and, more specifically, as we have seen before, by the givenness of the saturated phenomenon, that is, the phenomenon that, when given, also integrates what is hidden and not shown.

Marion does not call into question phenomenology, but rather discerns between different types of phenomena, that is, different "appearances" or givennesss. Therefore, according to Marion, the restrictions of phenomenology, especially the Husserlian one, do not apply to the revealed phenomenon but to the perceiving subject. This meticulous discernment is essential to identify the differences between the levels or strata of experience and phenomenological investigation. What is sought here is to emphasize that the dynamic between intuition and givenness differs and varies significantly; while perception and intuition belong to the domain of the subject, the "act" of giving emanates from Being.

---

123. Jean-Luc Marion, *Being Given: Toward a Phenomenology of Givenness*, trans. Jeffrey L. Kosky (Stanford University Press, 2002), 218.

CHAPTER 27: THE SATURATED PHENOMENON

This clarification of Marion is important because, in a way, it frees phenomenology itself from the limits it had imposed on itself, that is, the limits always marked by transcendental subjectivity. In a certain sense, and following Heidegger, Marion suggests that phenomenology can still exist without limiting itself to the intuition of the transcendental subject, now placing the emphasis on the givenness of the pure exteriority of the phenomenon.

This approach of Marion is complemented by the analysis carried out by Henry on another of the principles of Husserl's phenomenology, denoted by the need to return "to the things themselves," which emerges as the most invoked principle to define the epistemological approach of phenomenology. Following Marion, Henry questions whether givenness without intuition can be understood as an epistemology. As Heidegger already asked in his deep analysis in *Prolegomena to a History of the Concept of Time*, to which entities exactly does Husserl refer? It would seem that the reference is to "the phenomena," which emerge as the correlate of an intentional act.

However, by shifting the phenomenological focus from the intuitive subject to givenness, and therefore putting intuition in parentheses, we recognize that there are realms where this manifestation adopts various forms and structures. Phenomena emerge in different ways depending on the configuration of consciousness, or also according to their own way of being or manifesting, without the intuitive capabilities of subjective consciousness as a conditioning factor. This argument does not corner consciousness as the field of givenness, but rather frees it from the limits intuition imposes on it.

The great phenomenological leap that Marion and Henry take, under the auspices of Heidegger, is to reduce or suspend intuition, the concept of understanding or comprehension on which transcendental philosophy has been based since Kant, to uncover another level of consciousness that is now pre-epistemological and in which the phenomenon can be given in all its breadth, without perceptual limitations. This means that not only is the phenomenon not reducible to intuition, but consciousness is also not reducible to its intuitive capacities. This phenomenological reduction of intuition that Marion carries out does not dissolve phenomenology; rather, it opens it to other confines.

The paradoxical ethical principle of phenomenology

It is precisely in this context that Janicaud's criticisms of the "theological turn" in phenomenology, which we have discussed in previous chapters, make full sense. In this light, the same French phenomenologist asks: "How can we continue to call phenomenology phenomenology, once we have stripped it of its principle of all principles (intuition) and its epistemological dimension?"[124]

In *Philosophy as a Rigorous Science*, published in 1910, Husserl himself argues that "the impulse to research must proceed not from philosophies but from things and from the problems connected with them."[125] A. Zirión interprets this stance as an epistemological call of an ethical nature, promoting a summons for the autonomous use of thought and inquiry free from preconceived notions or biases. Ethics emerges as an essential component of phenomenology, repudiating the premise that there are predetermined paths for understanding. The stimuli for research must originate not in philosophical dictates but in the objective manifestation of things and the problems they present. The focus of interest must be the object of study itself, not philosophy, avoiding the influence of prejudices inherent in any philosophical system. These reflections urge us not to be led solely by the known or the understood, but to exercise independent critical thought at all times.

In his analysis, Zirión revisits the interpretation that Waldenfels gives to the Husserlian axiom, linking it to the notion of the "impulse toward the objectivity," or *Zug zur Sachlichkeit*, conceiving it as an

---

124. Translator's Introduction, in Dominique Janicaud et al., *Phenomenology and the "Theological Turn": The French Debate* (New York: Fordham University Press, 2000), 4–5.

125. Edmund Husserl, "Philosophy as Rigorous Science," trans. Quentin Lauer, in *Phenomenology and the Crisis of Philosophy* (New York: Harper & Row, 1965), 146 [Hua XXV, 61].

essential element. Zirión argues that Waldenfels proposes "Something more than a purely formal concept of thingness (*Sachlichkeit*) is needed to be able to affirm, as Waldenfels does, that phenomenology has to thematize always, along with the thing-content (*Sachgehalt*), the way-of-access (*Zugangsweise*), or that it searches for the *logos* of *phenomena*."[126] This impulse toward thingness commits us to the thing as it shows itself, as it appears, beyond a formalist interpretation.

We are not bound to the thing mentioned by the concept but to the concrete reality or the thing itself. Thus, the call "to the things themselves" suggests a rejection of preconceived notions of things in favor of direct contact with the thing. This impulse is crucial to assert that phenomenology must always analyze not only the objective content, that is, what the thing shows us, but also the appropriate way to approach it. The thing, in revealing itself, not only shows what it is but also how we should know it. When something is revealed, it shows both what it is and how it can be known. The thing itself reveals how it can be accessed.

The approach to reality is dictated by the essence of what is sought to be understood, which grounds the objection to establishing a universal phenomenological method or phenomenon. The imposition of a single methodology for phenomenological study would mean denying each entity both its expressive peculiarity and its way of showing itself. For example, the approach used to explore a cell differs substantially from that used to appreciate a melody. To claim that the approach for interpreting a poem is the exclusive model for understanding the environment would be a grave error.

Phenomenology focuses on how the phenomenon manifests itself, leaving aside the predispositions of the observer. This is precisely the aim of the phenomenological and transcendental reductions that Husserl himself carries out throughout his investigations. The reduction, as we mentioned before, is implemented to suspend prejudices, preconditions, and

---

126. Bernhard Waldenfels, "Ph¨anomenologie in Deutschland: Geschichte und Aktualit¨at," Husserl Studies, vol. 5 no. 2 (Aug. 1988): 149. Translation Alfredo Zirión Quijano.

assumptions. In fact, the reduction could be understood as the antidote to all dogmatism, as A. D. Smith argued in his book on Husserl's *Cartesian Meditations*. Likewise, as J. Siles i Borràs also debates extensively in *The Ethical Character of Husserl's Phenomenology*, Husserl himself invokes in several of his writings the principle of "self-responsibility" (*Selbstverantworlichkeit*) as the ethical criterion by which phenomenological research must always be guided in order to account for its own process and reorient itself if necessary in light of its new discoveries.

Thus, Marion can continue invoking phenomenology, because it is not restricted or limited to any of its principles. It should always question itself, its limitations, principles, and doctrines to allow the object of its study to be given, to show itself, in its own nature or being. The work of Heidegger, Marion, and Henry, among many others, is the most vivid expression of this. This "phenomenological self-responsibility," as we might call it, and which Husserl himself identifies as an "inner call," does not stop in the field of academic research. It should be understood as a universal principle that is not content with any bookish knowledge.

However, in Marion's view, this very Husserlian proposal of self-responsibility as the essence of all phenomenological action has important consequences that phenomenology itself must not overlook. Specifically, Marion writes:

> *Le paradoxe initial et final de la phénoménologie tient précisé- ment à ceci qu'elle prend l'initiative de la perdre. Certes comme toute science rigoureuse, elle décide de son projet, de son terrain et de sa méthode, prenant ainsi l'initiative (...), mais, à l'encontre de toute métaphysique, elle n'ambitionne que de perdre cette initiative le plus tôt et le plus complètement possible, puisqu'elle prétend rejoindre les apparitions de choses dans leur plus initiale originarité.*

The initial and final paradox of phenomenology stems precisely from this: that it takes the initiative (to perceive what is manifested) in losing it. To be sure, like all rigorous science, it decides its own project, its own terrain, and its own method, thus taking the initiative as originally as possible; but, counter to all metaphysics, it has no other ambition than to lose this initiative as quickly and completely as possible , seeing as it claims to connect the apparitions of things in their most initial originarity to the so-to-speak native state [...].[127]

From Marion's point of view, it is only through this foundational paradox that it is revealed that the initial methodological approach of phenomenology establishes the grounds for its own dissolution in the process of self-manifestation. The task of phenomenology lies in its resolution to abstain from any initiating action by the subjective polarity, allowing reality to emerge in its purest state. This implies liberating the object of study, letting it simply be, without intervention, for it is through an intervention that the subject imposes its method onto the object, distorting its true essence.

This is the task of the various reductions that Husserl, Heidegger, Marion, Henry, or ourselves with meditation, have implemented in our respective studies. However, it is precisely here that the paradox emerges: phenomenology takes the initiative with the explicit aim of abandoning it. This contradiction manifests in the fact that, although phenomenology initially adopts an active stance by defining its project, field of study, and methodology, its ultimate intention is to rid itself entirely of this active attitude in order to achieve a genuine understanding of reality as it truly is.

This process involves establishing the conditions for an ontological disappearance that allows the essence of Being to reveal itself. It is, therefore, a radical transition from what is presumed or believed to be toward what one truly is. Thus, the effort to unveil the essence of Being paradoxically entails a process of ontological disappearance.

---

127. Jean-Luc Marion, *Being Given: Toward a Phenomenology of Givenness*, trans. Jeffrey L. Kosky (Stanford University Press, 2002), 9.

Section VII: From ontology to (post)phenomenology

The phenomenological methodology, with all its essential self-responsibility, will, therefore, be characterized by its self-dissolution. For this reason, Marion states:

> *La méthode n'avance pas devant le phénomène, en le pré-voyant, le pré-disant et le pro-duisant, pour l'attendre d'emblée au bout du chemin qu'il entame á peine (metà hodós); désormais, elle marche justa u pas du phénomène, comme en le protégeant et lui dégageant le chemin.*

> The method does not run ahead of the phenomenon, by foreseeing it, predicting it, and producing it, in order to await it from the outset at the end of the path (*meta-hodos*) onto which it has just barely set forth. From now on, it travels in tandem with the phenomenon, as if protecting it and clearing a path for it [...].[128]

In ontological terms, nothing can precede Being, for it underlies everything, even the language that Being itself inhabits and in which it reveals and conceals itself simultaneously. If any method were able to foresee, predict, or accelerate it, it would precede Being, which means it would predispose it, the consequence of which would be that Being would cease to be Being and would become a product of a method. In this context, we must consider Marion's stance toward the phenomenological method and read it in the light of Heraclitus. Heraclitus asserts that only in renunciation is there the possibility of expecting the unexpected: "If (he) doesn't expect (the) unexpected, (he) will not discover (it); for (it) is difficult to discover and intractable."[129]

Thus, the primary requirement of phenomenology is renunciation of action in order to maintain a state of passivity that allows for the purest observation. This task, which might appear trivial and simple, is, in reality, one of the most significant challenges in research. The greatest challenge for phenomenology—as well as for philosophy and the various sciences—is to renounce any

---

128. Ibid.
129. Heraclitus, *Fragments: A Text and Translation with a Commentary*, trans. T.M. Robinson (Toronto: University of Toronto Press, 1987), (fragment 18, DK 22B18).

activity that might predispose the object to present itself in a particular mode and with specific characteristics. Marion points to the necessity of remaining in a state of stillness and silence that focuses exclusively on fine-tuning our capacity to perceive without falling into the temptation to act.

By remaining calm and avoiding making judgments about the darkness, without defining it as something harmful or beneficial, we avoid the turbulence generated in our minds. It is precisely this mental serenity that has the power to dissolve the shadows. In this sense, it becomes crucial to adopt an attitude of attentive, distant observation, passive, without prejudice or preconceived frameworks, similar to someone standing on top of a hill watching a valley covered in shadow and letting it embrace them. In this, letting oneself be embraced, and as meditative consciousness intensifies, opening up to what happens, paying attention without trying to conceptualize it, the darkness evaporates on its own. Then the observer perceives within himself a light that, by its very nature, radiates outward and reveals the shadow as shadow, dispelling the twilight.

In this process toward meditation, personal merit does not occur and, therefore, cannot be claimed as such. In the meditative state, the ego and any impulse to organize or regulate the understanding of what overwhelms us are absent. All that exists is a universal norm, a way of Being, that governs the internal domain. The key lies in accepting and submitting to this norm to allow it to operate freely without interventions. Any interference on our part only creates obstacles and hinders what is given to us, what overwhelms and overcomes us from the purest otherness at the deepest level of Being.

This is precisely what Lao Tzu called "action through non-action," and Zen, "effort without effort." As we have outlined thus far, the essence of this effortless action and of action without effort lies in the manner in which the inner light of Being shines forth. That eternal light illuminates the darkness as darkness itself and allows us to embrace otherness without needing to think about it. At the depths of our being resides perfection; there is no need to change anything. Although corruption may reign all around, we at the center remain in purity. Our true ultimate essence is the eternal light of Being. In this context, the Retroprogressive Path of meditation consists, precisely, in the recognition of our own luminosity.

As we noted in earlier chapters, this view of meditation aligns with Marion's phenomenological methodology. It also resonates with Heidegger, as it involves an inner disposition that allows us to sink into our own Being, into the most absolute pre-consciousness, so that the phenomenon—or the givenness—may reveal itself as it truly is, beyond our subjective capacities.

Now, all meditation techniques are merely introductory. True meditation begins with the recognition that activity constitutes an obstacle. Inactivity, or the abstention from any activity, is what allows existence to transform us and renew us. Unfortunately, society educates the human being for activity, condemning inactivity to ostracism and labeling it as laziness and fruitless. This conception may hold true in relation to the external objectual reality, but it should never be understood in this way with regard to the internal.

It is precisely passivity and inactivity, understood as non-agency, that opens the correlation with God. This does not mean that we choose inactivity in an attempt to turn someone into a worshiper of a celestial personal God who, at its core, is nothing more than an illusion, a creation of our own activity. On the contrary, the passivity of meditation is what opens us to the inner God, the Absolute that underlies everything and at all times. True reality resides within oneself, and to discover the foundation of life and all existence, it is enough to direct one's gaze inward, toward one's own Being. As Husserl himself wrote at the end of his *Cartesian Meditations*, quoting Saint Augustine in *De vera religione* (39, 72), regarding the inscription that could supposedly be read at the gates of an Oracle: *Noli foras ire, in teipsum redi; in interiori homine habitat veritas* that is, "Go back into yourself; the truth dwells in the inner man."[130]

---

130. Edmund Husserl, *Cartesian Meditations: An Introduction to Phenomenology*, trans. Dorion Cairns (The Hague: Martinus Nijhoff, 1960), 157. Here, Husserl quotes Augustine in Latin words asserting, "*Noli foras ire,*" "*in te redi t, in interiore homine habitat veritas.*"

The methodology proposed here of "entering into oneself" does not constitute nor should it be understood as any type of active action; it simply requires one to position oneself in tranquility, and thus one will gradually discover how to enter into their essence, possibly guided by a kind of magnetic attraction. Unconditional surrender to this pull, to this "call," as we have referred to it earlier following the terminology of Husserl, Heidegger, or Marion, is advised.

Meditation is to be engulfed by the inner reality, by the light of Being that shines within, in the very heartbeat of life, without resistance, without opposition, and moreover, without aspiring to surpass or transcend it. Meditation is also to disregard the siren songs of the ever-hungry egoic subjectivity that arises to control, conceptualize, and, with its lantern, dull the pre-egoic and pre-agential inner light. On the contrary, to let oneself be engulfed is not the result of any fervent aspiration, nor a desire or primordial will that always belongs to the subject, but of waiting, observing, and patience.

Meditation as a methodological element of phenomenology

Marion, in his conceptual revision, approaches the method from a renewed perspective, distinct from the one presented initially in *Reduction and Givenness*, where the idea of a negative phenomenology was considered. In this new phase, the method is oriented toward revealing the phenomenon, with the specific purpose of demonstrating how the independent "I" or ego allows something to manifest in its authentic presence. The focus is on a postponement of the egoic phenomenon as the manifestation of the essence of Being. This process is justified because it lays the foundations for its own annulment, becoming essential in phenomenology. It does not produce or synthesize, but rather prepares the ground for the phenomenon to emerge.

According to this view, the essence of givenness determines that nothing precedes the phenomenon except its autonomous manifestation, implying that the phenomenon emerges without an external origin to its own existence. Marion here partially takes up Husserl's position in *The Idea of Phenomenology* and he quotes him: "absolute givenness is a [last] term."[131] It acquires a definitive character when the act of manifestation occurs, confirming the essence of the given phenomenon through the process of reduction.

In this study, we propose meditation as a means of developing and clarifying phenomenological methodology. This represents a paradigm shift both for phenomenology as a field of research and for epistemological conception. In the realm of knowledge, the subject, the object, and the act of knowing are distinguished. In the classical conception of the theory of knowledge, the object is considered passive, what is known, while the subject acts as the active knowing agent. Based on this, any attempt to transcend the limitations of this structure is destined to fail from the outset, because the root of the effort is always the egoic phenomenon, regardless of the nature or orientation that the research may take.

This structure, grounded in egoic effort, presents a separate, independent, and free "I," embarking on a search to obtain more, to acquire more, to procure more, to seek more outside itself. This epistemological structure has soaked the entire conception of the "I." This is the same "I" that longs for more wealth, a larger house, a more luxurious car, a more attractive partner, more of this and much more of that.

The problem with epistemology is that it is not innocent. On the contrary, epistemology has been responsible for drawing the parameters of Western reality, and now no longer just Western. That is the egoic reality. However, the ego is not limited to this aspect, for it can also adopt an alternative strategy and allow serenity and peace to free it from its epistemological activity, so it can surrender to meditation to be embraced by the light that shines within it and achieve sanctity. This is, again, the same game but played in a different domain. The same ego that once sought to

---

131. Jean-Luc Marion, *Being Given: Toward a Phenomenology of Givenness*, trans. Jeffrey L. Kosky (Stanford University Press, 2002), 18. Quoting Edmund Husserl, *Die Idee der Phänomenologie. Fünf Vorlesungen*, ed. Walter Biemel, Husserliana III (Den Haag: Martinus Nijhoff, 1950), 9

adorn itself with material attributes now desires to beautify itself with religious and spiritual qualities, but in order to do so, it must suspend its activity and surrender, be engulfed, by its own pre-egoic dimension.

This is the key to the issue: if the goal is to transcend oneself, the ego condemns itself to its own effort. Driven by its own craving, the ego seeks to improve itself and become someone different. Yet that very notion of change is its own invention. Recognizing the ego as the true obstacle paves the way for genuine conversion, as Husserl points out in section 35 of *The Crisis of the European Sciences and Transcendental Phenomenology*. There, he argues that transcendental phenomenology proposes the most radical existential transformation—one that can only be compared to a "religious conversion." Conversion, from the Latin *conversio*, means turning toward oneself, in contrast to revolution, from the Latin *revolutio*, which implies an external change.

"Religious conversion" is radical (from the Latin *radicalis*), meaning a change at the root (*radix*). The term "religious" (from the Latin *religio*) is understood in its literal translation—that is, as "scrupulous consciousness." The turn toward the root of interiority is undertaken scrupulously and without the mediation of prejudices or presuppositions, as is the case with all false religion. This conversion arises naturally in the process of unraveling, of setting aside and suspending, the machinations of the ego.

This call to passivity, meditation, and calmness contrast with our contemporary society, where there is a dominant inclination toward constant activity. From an early age, we are instructed and forced to act. This teaching has permeated our lives so deeply that now it seems unusual and atypical to take a few minutes of the day simply to do nothing. Most people find themselves caught in an incessant whirlwind of tasks and commitments. In those scarce moments of respite between our numerous obligations, we anxiously seek some form of occupying those empty intervals, whether by lighting a cigarette, checking the phone, watching television, playing on the computer, or engaging in any other recreational activity. The intention behind these actions is to avoid, at all costs, the emptiness of inactivity. This phenomenon has become a distinguishing feature of our time, where the inertia of constant activity dominates our lives. Social and cultural pressure pushes us to always stay busy and to consider inactivity as something unproductive and, therefore, undesirable. This obsession with perpetual occupation leads us to see pauses and rest not as essential needs for human well-being, but as lapses that must be immediately filled with some form of distraction. As we navigate our days, laden with responsibilities and commitments, we rarely allow ourselves a moment for contemplation or the simple act of doing nothing. This absence of time for personal reflection and authentic rest creates a culture where the value of stillness has been lost. Consequently, our ability to enjoy serenity and calm is compromised, as we have been conditioned to see these moments as deficiencies that must be quickly remedied with some form of occupation. This drive toward constant activity and aversion to the void of inactivity highlights a transformation in the way we live and experience time. In a world where success and productivity are measured by the number of activities we can accomplish in a day, inactivity has become a luxury that few allow themselves. The pressure to stay occupied at all times deprives us of the opportunity to experience true rest and inner peace, which can only be found in moments of stillness.

It is crucial to recognize and question this tendency toward hyperactivity that defines our current society. Inactivity is not synonymous with laziness or unproductiveness, but rather is a necessary part of human life that also allows for mental and emotional regeneration. By learning to value and incorporate moments of authentic inactivity into our daily routines, we can recover a balance that allows us to live more fully and consciously. True wisdom lies in finding value in the pause and silence, thus allowing us to rediscover the power of the simple act of doing nothing.

Unlike the West, where passivity has been vilified under the auspices of certain traditional currents, the East has always valued peace, tranquility, and the enjoyment that resides in the simplicity of doing nothing. The great mystic of Zen Buddhism, Basho, expressed this with great wisdom when he said: "Sitting quietly, doing nothing, spring comes, and the grass grows by itself."

The passivity, or inactivity, we are discussing here should not be confused with what is often called "having positive thoughts." Many believe they would be happy if their thoughts were positive, as if their well-being depended on the quality of the content of mental activity. However, the problem does not lie in the content of thoughts, but in the act and the activity of thinking itself. The mind is an activity and, therefore, it would be more appropriate to refer to it as "mentation" rather than as "mind." Literally speaking, one could say that in "menting," the mind lies, and that, consequently, all that is "mented" is lied.

This process is similar to dancing. Dancing occurs when the dancer dances; if the dancer stops, the dance ceases. We cannot say that, if the dancer simply sits down, the dance has stopped. The dancer has legs and the faculties to dance but is not dancing. The legs may dance, but if they stop, then the legs and the faculties are there, but not the dance. In this sense, consciousness is like the dancer's legs, while the mind is the dance. If the movement stops, the mind disappears. Just as the dancer possesses legs and the capacity to dance, even while remaining still, the human being remains, in a certain way, conscious—even in the absence of the mind. This state of consciousness, which also includes dimensions such as preconsciousness or unconscious consciousness mentioned earlier, and which is not reducible to the mind, constitutes the essence of Zen Buddhism.

In saying that "the grass grows by itself," Basho suggests that the emergence of that transcendental state beyond the mind occurs effortlessly and arises spontaneously. It is possible to water and care for the grass, but it is impossible to force its growth because it is autonomous. Obviously, it is impossible to access a state of inactivity through active effort. In a certain way, we are faced with a dilemma because the goal is to meditate, but without engaging in any activity that leads us to it. Therefore, we have previously spoken of surrendering or being consumed. Only in these terms does the wisdom of Basho's phrase make sense.

Something similar happens with sleep or relaxation, which cannot be forced, but only allowed, surrendered to. We can buy a good bed with a comfortable mattress, turn off the lights, and close the windows, but it is impossible to force ourselves to sleep. The more we try to sleep, the more elusive sleep becomes. The same happens with relaxation: the more one tries to relax, the more tense one will be. It also happens with love for another person. We play no role in the gestation of love. It manifests within us, independent of our will—like vegetation that grows without intervention in fertile soil.

The fear of love arises from its untamable nature and resistance to being domesticated. This feeling is often attributed with blindness, criticizing it for its supposed lack of guidance; however, it is precisely in this state where a deep perception of reality is revealed. Love is the only lens capable of revealing a genuine understanding of Being, though many may deem it feverish or delusional. This perception of losing control indicates that existence itself takes charge. Love, like truth, arises from a sacred core, and thus, it is no coincidence that transcendental figures such as Jesus have proclaimed that "God is love" or an equivalent expression "Love is God." Both emanate from a common source, springing up naturally without requiring our intervention as subjects for their blossoming.

In this context, Marion shifts attention from the Husserlian dynamic, which privileges the subject's action in knowledge, to the dynamic of the object that reveals itself when being known. Unlike Husserl, for whom the cognizing subject plays a central role, Marion emphasizes the manifestation of the known object in its disposition to be discovered. In his framework, the phenomena called "poor" do not require intense participation from the subject, due to their limited predisposition. In contrast, the "saturated phenomenon" demands a high degree of openness from the subject for its full understanding. Once the saturated phenomenon has been experienced, it is considered that no further reality remains to be discovered, positioning it as the pinnacle of phenomenological revelation. Marion proposes transforming the phenomenological method into what some have called an anti-method. This has generated a wide range of criticisms that point to a risk of passivity in the cognizing subject, which could compromise their ability to act effectively within the phenomenological framework. The concern lies in the possibility that, in the absence of a structured method and the inactivity of the subject, there is uncertainty about the nature of the ongoing cognitive activity.

This issue holds significant relevance since the practice of meditation, intrinsically, is not subject to the implementation of specific techniques or methods. However, the adoption of methods seems imperative to eliminate the barriers obstructing the path to deep meditation. It is essential to clearly understand that the essence of meditation is not found in the technique, but in consciousness devoid of effort. Alertness, attention, observation, as well as unconscious awareness, are not techniques, but natural states of being. However, the path to this observation is riddled with obstacles that countless generations have accumulated over millennia and that need to be eradicated. By its very nature, meditation lacks the capacity to dissipate such obstacles, thus the need for a methodology to facilitate their removal. Therefore, the function of meditative techniques lies merely in smoothing the path toward meditation.

It is crucial not to confuse techniques with meditation itself. The spiritual market sells meditation techniques but not meditation itself. Those who preach that techniques are unnecessary for meditation must offer an alternative to address the obstacles inherent in the process. The issue of whether it is possible to delve into the depth of meditation without resorting to pre-established methods uncovers a hidden axiom: the true essence of meditation lies beyond technique, emerging as the only path toward authenticity. Meditation stands as the intrinsic essence of our Being, an inner radiance eager to rise and merge with infinity and eternity.

However, our mind imposes itself as a curtain that darkens the celestial dome. Techniques, then, assume the role of mystical keys, intended to pull back the curtain that hides the celestial sphere, thus opening gaps through which light can filter. They function as the antidote to self-imposed blindness, finally allowing us to glimpse the immeasurable beauty of the moon and stars. At this culminating point, meditation unfolds in its full splendor, freed from the need for any artifices. To define meditation as a conscious presence is to speak of an inherent state of wakefulness, an effortless awakening, an unconscious consciousness. However, given the mind's tendency to wander through temporal labyrinths, lost in the echoes of the past and the shadows of the future, the adoption of techniques that anchor it in the present, the only truly tangible moment, becomes indispensable. Once this temporal bastion is conquered, the use of techniques becomes obsolete, thus revealing the distilled essence of meditation, purged of all superfluousness. It is about developing the pathos of waiting.

The dynamic of waiting manifests differently when experienced in solitude compared to when it is lived collectively. In the silence of solitude, waiting transforms into a deeply personal experience, where the anticipation of a significant event is felt in an intimate and particular way. In contrast, when waiting is shared, it takes on a collective nature; for example, the shared longing of a community waiting for the conclusion of an important sporting event or a significant political change creates an atmosphere of solidarity and connection. Ludwig Landgrebe, in his studies, pointed out how waiting alters our perception of time, leading us to a state where the present seems to dissolve between what has passed and what we expect to happen. This alteration in the flow of time makes it difficult for us to be present in the now, as we find ourselves mentally projected toward anticipated futures, ignoring the present.

Being in waiting introduces a peculiar state where the current moment seems to elude us, concentrating our attention on what is to come. Even when we try to distract ourselves with other activities, we are internally aware that these attempts are merely ways of circumventing the anxiety that waiting brings with it. This idea is exemplified in a person who, while waiting for a phone call, distracts themselves by reading a book, demonstrating that, despite trying to focus on another task, waiting remains the center of their attention. In conclusion, waiting has the power to disconnect us from the present, whether in moments of isolation or in company, while another present absorbs the past and future that pass through it. Despite our efforts to manage this sensation in different ways, waiting has a unique capacity to fix our attention on what is to come, relegating the experience of the current moment. In the upcoming chapters, we will revisit the issue of waiting and its relationship with the notion of time.

CHAPTER 28

THE DIVINE MANIFESTATION

The interdependence between Being and knowledge

The debate initiated by Marion and Henry allows us to clarify what phenomenology is and how its method operates. Moreover, it helps us to reconsider essential questions within Western thought. Controversy arises when considering whether objects are revealed according to our intention toward them or whether, on the contrary, their manifestation requires a specific type of attention. In other words, do we adapt our perception to the way the object is presented to us, or does the object adjust itself to our perception? Formulated phenomenologically, the question would be: what prevails, the intentionality of consciousness or the givenness of the object? Is there a fit between our disposition and the manifestation of the object, or must we align our perception to the way the object reveals itself?

The response must be approached on two levels. From the sphere of Being, or genetic phenomenology, what prevails is the authentic manifestation of the object. From the sphere of knowledge, what prevails is our disposition to know it. It is crucial to differentiate between both spheres. In the realm of Being, the reality that manifests itself is defined by its authentic existence, just as divinity manifests itself to the human being in its own divine essence. However, to make itself accessible and visible, it takes on a human form, thus facilitating its understanding by human beings. This dynamic, which is obvious in Christianity with the figure of Jesus Christ, is also comparable to the notion of Iśvara in Vedanta or to the various divine incarnations. Divinity, in its essence, cannot be fully apprehended by us unless it reveals itself in comprehensible terms, taking on a human form. Therefore, since the divine nature prevails over how it is presented to our knowledge, it opts to manifest itself in a way that resonates with human cognitive experience, through its avatars, or even through a spiritual master, thus allowing for a deeper connection and understanding.

The *Aditya Purana* says:

अविद्यो वा सविद्यो वा गुरुरेव जनार्दनः ।
मार्गस्थो वाप्यमार्गस्थो गुरुरेव सदा गतिः ॥

avidyo vā sa-vidyo vā
gurur eva janārdanaḥ
mārga-stho vāpy amārga-stho
gurur eva sadā gatiḥ

Whether ignorant or learned, the spiritual master is God Himself. Whether he follows the path or not, the spiritual master alone is always our refuge.

(*Aditya Purana*, 15.33)

The *Bhāgavata Purana* says:

आचार्यं मां विजानीयान्नावमन्येत कर्हिचित् ।
न मर्त्यबुद्ध्यासूयेत सर्वदेवमयो गुरुः ॥

ācāryaṁ māṁ vijānīyān
nāvamanyeta karhicit
na martya-buddhyāsūyeta
sarva-deva-mayo guruḥ

One should know the *ācārya* as Myself and never disrespect him in any way. One should not envy him, thinking him an ordinary man, for he is the representative of all the gods.

(*Bhāgavata Purana*, 11.17.27)

The same idea is conveyed in the New Testament, in the book of John precisely, where we read:

I and the Father are one.
(John, 10:30)

Whoever has seen me has seen the Father.
(John, 14:9)

The same idea is expressed again in the *Bhāgavata Purana*:

कृष्णवर्णं त्विषाकृष्णं साङ्गोपाङ्गास्त्रपार्षदम् ।
यज्ञै: सङ्कीर्तनप्रायैर्यजन्ति हि सुमेधस: ॥

kṛṣṇa-varṇaṁ tviṣākṛṣṇaṁ
sāṅgopāṅgāstra-pārṣadam
yajñaiḥ saṅkīrtana-prāyair
yajanti hi su-medhasaḥ

In the Age of Kali, intelligent persons perform congregational chanting to worship the incarnation of Godhead who constantly sings the names of Kṛṣṇa. Although His complexion is not blackish, He is Kṛṣṇa Himself. He is accompanied by His associates, servants, weapons, and confidential companions.
(*Bhāgavata Purana*, 11.5.32)

In the order of Being, God, or consciousness, shows itself constantly. In the order of knowledge, it shows itself as a poor or saturated phenomenon, depending on our way of knowing. In other words, in the former, it manifests itself unceasingly, while in the latter, it reveals itself through phenomena, whether poor or saturated, according to the human approach to knowledge. This dual facet that the givenness of Being and the cognitive capacity express in order to understand Being phenomenologically is also present in philosophical and religious traditions.

According to the Vedantic tradition, for example, an avatar, though human in form, is recognized as the incarnation of divinity itself. Mahatma Gandhi, in his commentary on the Bhagavad Gita, states that as this divine essence intensifies and consolidates within an individual, they move away from their human condition. In the highest expression, they are considered a divinity incarnate or a deity who has taken on human form. To the extent that we are more spark, we are less human, and if someone is fully this spark, it is because they have practically transcended their humanity.

This differentiation between limited or full phenomena is connected to how divinity is perceived through knowledge. According to Marion, any phenomenon can be considered poor or saturated depending on the perspective from which it is approached. Therefore, it would be Being showing itself according to knowledge, because it is not the act of revelation that limits, but rather the disposition with which consciousness approaches the phenomenon. Taking as an example the statement that God is Jesus and that the only true church is the Catholic one, the one who closes themselves off to this sole interpretation experiences divinity as a poor phenomenon due to their inability to recognize it in its fullness. In contrast, the one who perceives divinity as a full and saturated phenomenon recognizes that the divine manifestation transcends any limit imposed by individual perception, accepting that divinity can reveal itself through every enlightened being of any religious tradition. That is, the perception of the saturated phenomenon opens us to the multifaceted way in which God shows Himself. Those who are in the fullness of the saturated phenomenon recognize that God is not exhausted in what I may perceive of Him. Therefore, the challenge lies not in the nature of the revelation but in the intentionality with which consciousness approaches it.

The "new" phenomenon: wonder and repetition

The closed consciousness only knows the poor phenomenon. The opening of consciousness toward the phenomenon reveals a dimension of knowledge that transcends the mere surface. Being presents itself as human from the ontic perspective in order to serve as a support for the ontological. Divinity, in its interaction with human perception, manifests itself in such a way that it acts as a link toward a deeper ontological understanding. This process is illustrated in the words of Jesus, where He self-identifies as "the way, the Truth, and the life; no one comes to the Father except through Me" (John, 14:6). The traditional interpretation of Christianity, which focuses exclusively on the figure of Jesus, overlooks the essence of His message: to serve as a path toward a transcendental reality (the Father).

The saturated phenomenon in its fullness is offered in a simplified form to constitute a symbol, through which, from a limited ontic perspective, access to ontological transcendence is made possible. This concept extends to the recognition of the master as a divine manifestation; it is a saturated phenomenon that, when simplified into a symbol, allows the human being to transcend toward the ontological. Without this understanding, the true nature and purpose of the master remain hidden. Chaitanya Mahāprabhu embodies this principle, presenting himself as a devotee to guide others on the path of devotion and, in this way, access the ontological.

From the subjective perspective, the interaction with the Divine involves a receptivity that transcends mere personal choice regarding how the phenomenon will manifest. The way the divinity reveals itself is intimately linked to our disposition to receive it. If we determine ourselves to receive it from the depth of the saturated, it manifests as Being. On the contrary, a predisposition toward the phenomenologically "poor," limits our experience to manifesting ontically, that is, as an objectified entity.

The daily devotional practice of Hinduism, with the worship of Kṛṣṇa through the offering of flowers and incense, exemplifies how our receptivity shapes the manifestation of the Divine. By honoring, worshiping, or venerating these figures, an ontic connection with the divinity is established, manifesting in the realm of the concrete. Idolatry occurs when the divine essence is confused with physical representations, that is, when Being is confused with the entity.

This point now allows us to return to the discussions surrounding the phenomenology of the hidden, highlighting the notion of the "new phenomenon" or "never-before-given." This notion emphasizes the debate over "the things themselves" and their applicability or not to the objects of research in scientific disciplines. According to Marion, we are confronted with a degree of phenomenality that could be considered "poor." Both the phenomena experienced in daily life and those studied by science are categorized as "poor phenomena." The "new phenomena," on the other hand, are those capable of propelling us toward new interpretations of Being, not yet assimilated. A "new phenomenon," or "never-before-given" phenomenon, is one that has not yet been ontified but can be ontified; that is, it has not yet been fully integrated into our understanding of Being but has the potential to be integrated. What we have already integrated and understood is considered an "entity" because it has already been assimilated, that is, conceptualized and thought of as the intentional object of consciousness.

The new phenomenon, on the other hand, is "the Last God," or that deity still unpossessed, unthought, or unconceptualized, destined to remain on the threshold of the unfathomable. The manifestation of existence is conditioned by its ability to reveal itself in a new and unprecedented way. In other words, the only way for Being to show itself is for it to show itself "again." This aspect of the "novel" is important because it allows us to delve deeper into the notion of relationality with Being, which we have been describing throughout our study, now linking it to two other important issues: wonder and repetition.

First, the novel as such is linked to the question of "wonder" as the foundation of philosophy, understanding wonder as the ability to discern novelties within the perpetually identical. *Taumatso*, or "wonder," is the ability to discover something new in the same old thing. This issue is especially addressed in the philosophy of Søren Kierkegaard. The first words of his famous work, *Repetition*, say:

Chapter 28: The divine manifestation

When the Eleatics denied motion, Diogenes, as everyone knows, came forward as an opponent. He literally did come forward, because he did not say a word but merely paced back and forth a few times, thereby assuming that he had sufficiently refuted them. When I was occupied for some time, at least on occasion, with the question of repetition—whether or not it is possible, what importance it has, whether something gains or loses in being repeated—I suddenly had the thought: You can, after all, take a trip to Berlin; you have been there once before, and now you can prove to yourself whether a repetition is possible and what importance it has. At home I had been practically immobilized by this question. Say what you will, this question will play a very important role in modern philosophy, for repetition is a crucial expression for what "recollection" was to the Greeks. Just as they taught that all knowing is a recollecting, modern philosophy will teach that all life is a repetition. The only modern philosopher who has had an intimation of this is Leibniz. Repetition and recollection are the same movement, except in opposite directions, for what is recollected has been, is repeated backward, whereas genuine repetition is recollected forward. Repetition, therefore, if it is possible, makes a person happy, whereas recollection makes him unhappy—assuming, of course, that he gives himself time to live and does not promptly at birth find an excuse to sneak out of life again, for example, that he has forgotten something.

Recollection's love [Kjærlighed], an author has said, is the only happy love. He is perfectly right in that, of course, provided one recollects that initially it makes a person unhappy. Repetition's love is in truth the only happy love. Like recollection's love, it does not have the restlessness of hope, the uneasy adventurousness of discovery, but neither does it have the sadness of recollection—it has the blissful security of the moment. Hope is a new garment, stiff and starched and lustrous, but it has never been tried on, and therefore one does not know how becoming it will be or how it will fit. Recollection is a discarded garment that does not fit, however beautiful it is, for one has outgrown it. Repetition is an indestructible garment that fits closely and tenderly, neither binds nor sags. Hope is a lovely maiden who slips away between one's fingers; recollection is a beautiful old woman with whom one is never satisfied at the moment; repetition is a beloved wife of whom one never wearies, for one becomes weary only of what is new. One never grows weary of the old, and when one has that, one is happy. He alone is truly happy who is not deluded into thinking that the repetition should be something new, for then one grows weary of it.[132]

Repetition, conceived as a return to the familiar but in a new disguise, is essential for sustaining interest. When something completely new is presented, it may cause a feeling of fatigue or disinterest. Therefore, the act of repeating involves returning to previous experiences, even if they are presented in a different setting. For example, there is an anecdote in which a karate apprentice asks their mentor how long they will have to keep practicing the same *kata*, a term referring to a set of movements in sequence. The master's response is revealing: they tell the apprentice that they do not need to practice the same kata, arguing that, had the disciple paid careful attention, they would have understood that they never repeated exactly the same sequence of movements twice. The essence of the teaching lies in full consciousness during the execution of the kata, emphasizing the idea that it is impossible to perform the exact same sequence more than once. This perspective invites reflection on the depth and constant renewal in practice, stressing the uniqueness of each execution and the continuous learning it entails. As Garth Stein, wrote in his novel *The Art of Racing in the Rain*: "People, like dogs,

---

132. Søren Kierkegaard, *Fear and Trembling/Repetition*, trans. Howard V. Hong and Edna H. Hong (Princeton: Princeton University Press, 1983), 131-132.

love repetition. Chasing a ball, lapping a course in a race car, sliding down a slide. Because as much as each incident is similar, so it is different."[133]

Taumatso, for its part, refers to the ability to experience wonder at what has already been experienced, without which, renewal would be impossible, as faith would turn into weariness and memory. The term *taumatso*, therefore, highlights the depth and richness that can be found in repetition and in the careful observation of what has been lived. As in the case of the devotee, approaching past experiences or knowledge with a renewed perspective awakens a sense of wonder and discovery that often goes unnoticed in daily life. Moreover, it is the wonder sparked by repetition that, in turn, invites subsequent philosophical reflection, through which we gain a deeper appreciation of aspects of life that might seem ordinary or routine at first glance, revealing their inherent complexity.

From concrete knowledge to absolute love

We can obtain knowledge about people, similar to the understanding dentists, mail carriers, or merchants have of our lives. In this line, the dentist is only familiar with the characteristics of our teeth; the mail carrier, for their part, recognizes exclusively our residential location, while the merchant understands our consumption preferences. At the same time, there are those who seek an understanding of divinity analogous to this approach, meaning they aspire to identify God through the apprehension of distinctive elements like His name, the language specific to Him, His inclinations, desires, and His location. However, if we truly wish to know a person, we should not ask what they think, but rather what they love. Our passions speak more eloquently about our reality than logical or rational constructions. Therefore, to access true knowledge, it is necessary to turn to the heart and not to the mind. In the book of Deuteronomy, we read:

---

133. Garth Stein, *The Art of Racing in the Rain* (HarperCollins, 2008), 17.

וְיָדַעְתָּ הַיּוֹם וַהֲשֵׁבֹתָ אֶל לְבָבֶךָ כִּי ה' הוּא הָאֱלֹהִים בַּשָּׁמַיִם מִמַּעַל וְעַל הָאָרֶץ מִתָּחַת אֵין עוֹד:

(דברים ד' ל"ט)

And you shall know this day, and set it to your heart, that the Lord, He is God, in the heavens above and on the earth below; there is no other.

(Deuteronomy, 4:39)

This verse begins with the Hebrew word *yadata*, which is the conjugation of the verb "to know or to be aware" in the past. Here, it is preceded by the letter *vav* (ו), meaning "and," transforming the word into the future. It is followed by the word *hayom* (היום), meaning "today," indicating the present. Therefore, *ve'yadata hayom* (You shall know today) implies "you knew, you know, and you will know," indicating that the knowledge of God is eternal, and as such, we can say that it was, is, and will always be. This knowledge consists of *ein od* (אין עוד), meaning "there is no other." In other words, outside of God, there is nothing, or only and truly God is. But it is important to understand that, in this context, to know or to be aware is to love, because in Hebrew, the terms for knowing and loving are used interchangeably, as we see in this verse:

וְהָאָדָם יָדַע אֶת חַוָּה אִשְׁתּוֹ וַתַּהַר וַתֵּלֶד אֶת קַיִן וַתֹּאמֶר קָנִיתִי אִישׁ אֶת ה':

(בראשית ד', א')

And the man knew Ḥavvah, his wife, and she conceived and bore Cain. And she said: "I have acquired (*kanithi*, like 'Cain') a man with the [help of the] Lord."

(Genesis, 4:1)

For to truly know is not to know us as our dentist, postman, or pharmacist knows us, but as the one who loves us. Those who love us know our moods just by looking into our eyes, and they truly know us. It is not only the person who studies veterinary medicine who is a good veterinarian, but the one who, above all, loves animals. If one wishes to hire a good gardener, they must look for someone who, before anything else, loves plants and flowers. The one who loves the sea truly knows how to appreciate the waves, tides, navigation, and marine weather. Only one who loves humanity can know something of God.

भक्त्या त्वनन्यया शक्य अहमेवंविधोऽर्जुन ।
ज्ञातुं द्रष्टुं च तत्त्वेन प्रवेष्टुं च परन्तप ॥

bhaktyā tv ananyayā śakya
aham evaṁ-vidho 'rjuna
jñātuṁ draṣṭuṁ ca tattvena
praveṣṭuṁ ca paran-tapa

My dear Arjuna, I can be understood as I am, only through devotion, only then will you be able to penetrate the mystery, O conqueror of enemies!

(Bhagavad Gita, 11.54)

To know the Self is to love and surrender to mystery. We should always keep in mind that contemplation, thought, or speculation about God, the soul, or the afterlife may lead us to believe that we possess some knowledge about Him. However, this belief is deceptive. The very notion of knowing "about" God is meaningless; the term "about" or "concerning" is itself a contradiction. True connection with God transcends the possibility of knowledge "about" Him, as this precept "about" is based on superficial knowledge. It is possible to experience love, but it is not viable to acquire knowledge "about" love, because "about" implies that knowledge comes from others. Opinions, theories, beliefs, and concepts accumulate, and it is proclaimed: "I know something about God." Any knowledge defined as "about" is inherently equivocal and represents a risk, for there is the possibility of being seduced by it. In other words, God is not knowable and, therefore, not intelligible, as Kierkegaard showed us through the episode of Abraham and Isaac. When, for whatever reason, we claim to have any knowledge of God, what we understand is only the concept that intentional consciousness has created of God, turning Him into a domesticated god, made in the image and likeness of the conceptual and the ontic, stripped of His radical transcendence.

It is possible to experience God, to experience love, and to understand oneself, but one must relinquish that "about" that forms the basis of a mistaken philosophy that confuses the entity with Being, and a conceptualized god with the God who transcends us, whose relationality pulses through all existence and subsequent thought. Sacred texts offer statements, but these will become mere speeches, talks, addresses, and discourses "about," unless they are transformed into personal experience; otherwise, their value will be null, wasted.

This principle is of utmost importance, for the tendency to reflect, think, or speculate persists and never abandons us. The mind is such that it can lead us to meditate "on" meditation, think about revelation or enlightenment. Meditation can become a mere object of your thoughts. The problem is that even reflecting "on" it will not bring about any change. Wandering through the world of thoughts distances you from your roots, and the further away you are, the less likely you are to resolve anything. You may not have noticed, but when you reflect, you isolate yourself. Everything in the present fades away. Your mind enters a maze of dreams. One word leads to another, one thought to another, going deeper and deeper. The more you immerse yourself in thought, the further you distance yourself from reality. Thinking is an act of distancing, a journey through a world made up of concepts. Return to the concrete. Life's problems can only be solved by rooting yourself in existence.

CHAPTER 29

Manifestation and concealment: phenomenon, time, and language

The phenomenon as revealed truth

In *The Reversal of Phenomenology*, included in his work *Incarnation*, Michel Henry addresses the central topic of phenomenology and one of our focal points in this study: the phenomenon of appearing. By referencing the seventh paragraph of *Being and Time*, Henry highlights how Heidegger defines the phenomenon, meticulously distinguishing between the content of a phenomenon and its manifestation. Husserl, for his part, had also delved into this distinction when speaking of "objects in their mode of givenness," directing the focus not toward their content but toward the way in which they are given.

Based on these positions, the phenomenon is understood as the way in which Being gives itself. As we have seen throughout this study, phenomenology does not concern itself with the supposed specific contents of beings but with how these beings appear, manifest, give themselves, reveal themselves, and conceal themselves without assuming any origin, objective reality, or content beyond that revelation. Even when phenomenology studies the content of phenomena, it must always approach them within the scope of their very givenness as such. That is, it must approach them in the acts of consciousness, which would be within the epistemological realm, or in the relationality with Being, which would be in the ontological realm. As we suggested earlier, from the perspective of phenomenology, the phenomenon is its own givenness, and all truth (*alétheia*) is equivalent to its unveiling as such.

From this perspective, Heidegger links the givenness of Being, or we might say Being as givenness, that is, as phenomenon, with the issue of truth, which he simply conceives as the capacity to reveal itself. In this context, he critiques the historical habit of confusing the most original phenomenon of truth with the objects themselves, pointing again to the ontological difference between Being and beings, or, put in phenomenological terms, between givenness and the "possible" content or objective reality of the phenomenon. Upon observing our surroundings, we notice that this apparent diversity is, in reality, nothing; it is a "multiplicity of multiplicities," as Alain Badiou puts it.

This is why Heidegger points out the historical tendency to confuse the fundamental phenomenon of truth with the things themselves, thus emphasizing the essential ontological distinction. Truth does not lie in the thing-in-itself, but in its revealing, which, as we introduced earlier, also includes its own concealment. Being reveals itself precisely insofar as it conceals itself, thus generating a paradox that redefines the very notion of phenomenon (*phainómenon*). This later allowed Marion to develop the notion of the saturated phenomenon: that which unites the visible with the invisible, what is revealed with what remains hidden. This unveiling, or appearing, understood as a dual movement of manifestation and concealment at once, is clearly defined in both Husserl's and Heidegger's works, but in terms of temporality.

The phenomenon as temporality

In his book *The Phenomenology of Internal Time-Consciousness*, Edmund Husserl defines the phenomenon of the appearance of the object in intentional consciousness through a becoming divided into three "moments": protention, now, and retention. These three moments or dimensions are not attributes or characteristics that constitute the unity of the object in time. Rather, they are the temporal extension, the duration, in which the intentional object gives itself or is perceived in consciousness. Thus, Husserl argues from the very beginning that, since every intentional object of consciousness can only be given or appear in consciousness, the object of intentional phenomenology will be nothing other than that very temporality of the object, not its attributes. In the terminology Husserl used in *Ideas I*, the being of an object, the phenomenon, is the temporal givenness in which the object itself emerges as such in consciousness and can be perceived and intuited gradually in time, in its durability.

Husserl turns to the example of the tones of a melody to show that it is never perceived as an immediate totality. The melody, like any object, emerges gradually in consciousness, unfolding tone by tone. Each note appears in sequence, becoming a melody within the consciousness that holds it and allows it to arise imbued with meaning. Just as with the melody, we can also think of a sentence when we read or hear it. We will never read or hear the entire sentence at once, but we will read its words, linking them gradually one after another, and as we do so, the sentence acquires meaning in consciousness. Moreover, we do not perceive all the sounds of words at once. We hear syllable after syllable, gradually—that is, temporally. However small or brief an object may be, a letter, a tone, that very object will also be given in consciousness gradually, which leads Husserl to define every object by its temporality as it is given in consciousness.

Although, for explanatory purposes, Husserl introduces the terms we have mentioned earlier of now (present), retention (past), and protention (future), he will ultimately argue that the givenness of the object in consciousness must be understood not as the perception of small static and independent units of one another, but as flows that run into each other. In the example of a melody, we perceive tone A first, which continues sounding, while tone B appears, pushing tone A into the past, remaining or being retained in consciousness as tone A, prior to tone B, which in turn is pushed into the past as tone C appears, making tone A pass as a past prior to the past, which is now B in relation to C. This explanation illustrates that the awareness of melody entails both retention and protention. That is, the recollection of the tones already heard and the anticipation of the tone about to sound, as if such anticipation were already opening an expectation around the next tone.

371

Thus, the temporality of perception plays out in a constant flow between memory and anticipation, between past and future, intertwining. Moreover, Husserl emphasizes that none of these moments takes precedence over the other, to the point of asserting that none could be without the others. There is no possible anticipation without memory, that is, no future without past. Likewise, there is no memory without anticipation, that is, no past without openness to the future. The phenomenon, understood as givenness, is nothing other than its pure temporality. Appearing, giving itself, donating itself, is to temporalize itself. Nevertheless, Husserl argues that for this to be possible, for the object to appear as it temporalizes itself, there must be an inherently temporal structure in consciousness capable of receiving and harboring such temporalization. In other words, what allows the tones of a melody, or any other object of consciousness, to appear or be given gradually is the temporal structure of the very consciousness. Time, in other words, is the backbone of consciousness in which reality acquires its meaning.

As we advanced in Chapter 3 of this study, Heidegger's notion of time follows a similar pattern. In *Being and Time*, Heidegger introduces the idea of "the projection of exteriority," with which he interprets the appearing, the phenomenon, in terms of temporality. Appearing is revealing itself temporally. Or conversely, temporality is equivalent to giving itself, to appearing. Following Husserl, Heidegger defines the arising of the phenomenon in a tripartite movement that encompasses protention, perception, and retention, combining into an intentional triad that shapes our internal understanding of time and, by extension, unravels the essence of our primordial subjectivity. Thus, time is not an autonomous, foreign entity, but an emanation toward what is to come. Or, to put it more directly, Being is its temporality, in whose givenness it shows and hides itself at the same time, just as the melody sounds, showing itself, appearing, and fading before us.

This notion of temporality not only refers to the manifestation and concealment of Being but also, for Heidegger, plays a fundamental role in the nature of *Dasein* itself. Heidegger, who was probably

Chapter 29: Manifestation and Concealment: Phenomenon, Time, and Language

the first to read, and edited Husserl's writings on time, gave an existential dimension to Husserl's postulates about temporality. He emphasized the moment of protention, or anticipation of the future, which he interpreted as the fear of one's own death. For Heidegger, human beings, *Dasein*, always live being unconsciously aware of the inexorability of their own death as a future event (*ereignis*). All their experiences are framed and filtered, in a sense, by this underlying predisposition or openness to their inexorable future, within which memory and the meaning of everything lived are created. *Dasein* is characterized by this dynamic of tension between projection toward what is to come and retention of what has been. Being-in-the-world would be, in a certain way, being-in-the-world by temporalizing it in our experience. If the phenomenon, Being, is the same temporalization of the givenness, it is because that temporalization appears and finds shelter in another temporality, which is the underlying openness of *Dasein* to its future death.

It is in this notion of the temporality of *Dasein* in Heidegger, or of the intentional consciousness of Husserl, both understood as pure temporality, that the world unfolds and acquires existence as a world full of meaning for *Dasein*, for the human being. In the world of being-in-the-world, that is, a world of meaning, the issue of truth also emerges. Thus, the most fundamental revelation of truth takes shape as the manifestation of the world, appearing as *ek-stasis*, a projection in which world, experience, being, and time are inextricably fused.

This idea that the world, time, and Being all belong together is already outlined in the Old Testament. In the biblical context, what we might recognize as consciousness hides itself by disappearing into an objective reality called *'olam*, which means "world" in Hebrew. It comes from the root 'a.l.m (ע.ל.מ) which contains both the concept of place and the idea of time: *le'olam* means "forever" and *me'olam* means "since always." The term *he'elem* is derived from *'olam* and means "disappearance or concealment"; therefore, *'olam*, or "objective reality," is not a positive creation that *aggregates* or *creates* something, but the opposite. Objective reality is the concealment of consciousness. Therefore, consciousness becomes

Section VII: From Ontology to (Post)Phenomenology

the universe by concealing itself, which allows becoming without exchanging. Consciousness achieves its objectification through its self-concealment or voluntary withdrawal. God, called in Hebrew *Alufo Shel 'Olam*, or "The Lord of the world," hides in you, as you.

אֶת־הַכֹּל עָשָׂה יָפֶה בְעִתּוֹ גַּם אֶת־הָעֹלָם נָתַן בְּלִבָּם מִבְּלִי אֲשֶׁר לֹא־יִמְצָא הָאָדָם אֶת־הַמַּעֲשֶׂה אֲשֶׁר־עָשָׂה הָאֱלֹהִים מֵרֹאשׁ וְעַד־סוֹף:

(קהלת ג', י"א)

[God] has made everything to pass precisely in its time, and He also set in their heart the *olam* (can be translated as "world, eternity, or concealment") so that no one can fathom the work which God had done from beginning to end.

(Ecclesiastes, 3:11)

Midrash Rabbah on this verse says:

"אֶת־הַכֹּל עָשָׂה יָפֶה בְעִתּוֹ גַּם אֶת־הָעֹלָם נָתַן בְּלִבָּם" (קהלת ג', י"א) אָמַר רַבִּי אַחְוָה בְּרֵיהּ דְּרַבִּי זֵירָא: "הָעֹלָם" – הָעֶלֵם מֵהֶם שֵׁם הַמְפֹרָשׁ. וְאָמַר רַבִּי טַרְפוֹן: פַּעַם אַחַת שָׁמַעְתִּי וְנָפַלְתִּי עַל פָּנָי. הַקְּרוֹבִים שֶׁכְּשֶׁהֵם שׁוֹמְעִין אוֹתוֹ, נוֹפְלִים עַל פְּנֵיהֶם וְאוֹמְרִים: "בָּרוּךְ שֵׁם כְּבוֹד מַלְכוּתוֹ לְעוֹלָם וָעֶד". אֵלּוּ וָאֵלּוּ לֹא הָיוּ זָזִין מִשָּׁם עַד שָׁעָה שֶׁנִּתְעַלֵּם מֵהֶם, שֶׁנֶּאֱמַר (שמות ג', ט"ו): "זֶה שְּׁמִי לְעֹלָם", לְעַלֵּם כְּתִיב. וְכָל כָּךְ לָמָּה? "מִבְּלִי אֲשֶׁר לֹא יִמְצָא הָאָדָם אֶת הַמַּעֲשֶׂה אֲשֶׁר עָשָׂה הָאֱלֹהִים מֵרֹאשׁ וְעַד סוֹף"(קהלת ג', י"א).

(קהלת רבה ג', י"א)

He made everything beautiful, in its time. Also, the world (*ha'olam*) [can also read "of what is hidden"], He placed in their heart (Ecclesiastes, 3:11). [...] Rabbi Aḥva, son of Rabbi Zeira, said: "The world (*ha'olam*)—the explicit name was concealed (*ho'alam*) from them." [...] And Rabbi Tarfon said: "One time I heard it [the name] and I fell on my face. Those nearby, when they hear it, fall on their faces, and say: 'Blessed be the name of His glorious kingdom for ever and ever.' These and those would not move from there until the time when it was forgotten (*shenit'alem*) from them, as it is

Chapter 29: Manifestation and concealment: phenomenon, time, and language

stated: 'This is My name forever (*le'olam*)' (Exodus, 3:15), it is written: *le'alem* [the word *le'olam* is written without a vowel, so it can be read as *le'alem*, which means "to hide"]. Why? 'so that no one can fathom the work which God had done from beginning to end' (Ecclesiastes, 3:11)."

(*Kohelet Rabbah*, 3.11)

Absolute reality hides behind illusions such as time and space but is revealed by transcending them in the now and here.

אָמַר רַבִּי בּוּן: מַאי דִכְתִיב (משלי ח', כ"ג) "מֵעוֹלָם נִסַּכְתִּי מֵרֹאשׁ מִקַּדְמֵי אָרֶץ"? מַאי מֵעוֹלָם? שֶׁצָּרִיךְ לְהַעֲלִימוֹ מִכָּל עָלְמָא. דִכְתִיב (קהלת ג', י"א): "גַּם אֶת הָעֹלָם נָתַן בְּלִבָּם", אַל תִּקְרָא הָעוֹלָם אֶלָּא הֶעְלֵם.

(ספר הבהיר, סימן י')

Rabbi Boon said: "What is the meaning of the verse: 'I was set up from everlasting (*me'olam*), from the beginning, before ever the earth was' (Proverbs, 8:23). Why *me'olam*? Because He needs to conceal it from everybody. As it is written: 'He also set in their heart the *olam*' (Ecclesiastes, 3:11), do not read *ha'olam* (world), but *he'elem* (concealment)."

(*Sefer HaBahir*, 10)

הִנֵּה בְּרִבּוּי הַהִשְׁתַּלְשְׁלוּת נִתְהַוָּה מִזֶּה צִמְצוּם גָּמוּר וְהֶעְלֵם גָּדוֹל שֶׁנִּתְעַלֵּם בְּחִינַת כֹּחַ הָאֱלֹהִי הַמְחַיֶּה אֶת הָעוֹלָם וְנִתְלַבֵּשׁ בִּלְבוּשִׁים רַבִּים וַעֲצוּמִים, כִּי עוֹלָם הוּא מִלְּשׁוֹן הֶעְלֵם כַּנּוֹדָע.

(האדמו"ר הזקן, ליקוטי תורה, פרשת שלח, ב', ד')

And with the advancement of the emanation, there was a complete contraction and great concealment, in which the quality of divine power, which vitalizes the world, concealed itself and clothed itself with many great garments, as it is well-known that the word *olam* conveys also *he'elem*.

(The Alter Rebbe, *Likkutei Torah*, "Shlach," 2.4)

Section VII: From ontology to (post)phenomenology

This brief commentary on the etymological root of the term, and how it has been used in Hebrew, leads us to suggest that *Alufo Shel Olam* is concealed as the world insofar as it consists of time and space. Phenomenology, therefore, investigates how perceptions are linked within the temporal flow, emphasizing that these perceptions occur within that flow.

This approach to the issue allows us to present the dilemma of the mutual exclusion between Being and manifestation, a paradox in which, in turn, language emerges as the vehicular medium. Deeply rooted in phenomenology, language shapes the logos as the channel that unequivocally guides us toward the phenomenon. This mutual exclusion between Being and manifestation, as presented by Parmenides, holds that what manifests is not, and what is, does not manifest, for what is, when manifested, does so in the manner of an entity, remaining concealed as Being. This would mean that Being does not exhibit itself, but rather donates itself. If it were to be exhibited, it would cease to be Being and become an entity. From this, it follows that Being cannot simply manifest, but must offer or give itself. What Being grants us is not an image, but a word or language, as Being does not reveal itself visually, but through language.

Michel Henry, in *Incarnation*, argues that the foundation of our discourse on any object rests in its prior manifestation; thus, phenomenicity and logos constitute an indivisible unity in which language plays an essential function, highlighting the intrinsic deficiency in the manifestation of the world and mimicking its structure. This is because, although language serves as a vehicle for revelation, it lacks the intrinsic capacity to bestow existence, as it refers to an external referent which, in itself, lacks foundation. In other words, although it is through language that the world acquires its meaning, this does not imply that existence, that reality, is merely a result of language. Language does not invent the world *ex nihilo* but rather endows it with its own possible significance.

Paradoxically, the exhibition of the world through language nullifies or undoes the reality of its own presentation. Just as Being manifests in language, it is also in language that Being conceals itself. Both movements happen simultaneously, and it could not be otherwise. If Being were to manifest in the world in its complete fullness, it would cease to be Being; and if the world were to be revealed as such, it would no longer be the world. Therefore, manifestation implies offering what is not, since Being and appearing are, by default, antagonistic. The underlying maxim is that nothing can reveal itself as it truly is; for if it revealed itself as it truly is, it would no longer be as it appears, having to present itself through language. What can be shown is only the temporal dimension of what is, that is, the time of Being, which inexorably implies that all revelation carries within it concealment. We call it concealment because showing what is manifest is hiding its unmanifest or eternal aspect. The paradox shines brightly because the phenomenon, the appearing (*phainómenon*), and Being exclude each other while also including each other, pulsing one within the other through language.

The affective self-revelation: origin of all temporality

As we have argued previously, the phenomenon of an object of consciousness is, at its core, the object itself. We cannot assume any objective reality beyond the field of consciousness, in which the object is always an intentional object. This would apply to Husserl, but in a certain way, also to Heidegger, who substitutes consciousness with existence, with Being. In both cases, the phenomenon, Being, always exceeds our perception and intuition of it due to its temporal dimension. In *Ideas I*, Husserl himself admits that intuition is overwhelmed when, upon reflecting on the temporality of consciousness, we are only revealed the manifest concealment of our own transcendental subjectivity, that which structures and articulates consciousness, that is, the temporality in which reality appears and acquires meaning.

When we apprehend and describe our own acts of consciousness and understand that all of them synthesize into a vital flow, what chains them disappears as soon as we try to make it the intentional object of our thought and intuition. That is why Henry argues that every phenomenon implies its own concealment, that is, that Being manifests itself insofar as it is concealed. Put another way, what really appears, deep down, is the constant disappearance of what appears.

In this context, we can understand that, for Heidegger, all beings always unfold within the restrictions imposed by time and space, as Kant had already warned, manifesting as a defined and limited entity. This manifestation implies, for the entity that reveals itself, an acceptance of the inherent limitations of its existence as an entity in our experience. Unlike the entity, Being is that which pulses limitlessly in every entity, in every experience of the entity, in every *Dasein*, and, therefore, is what allows entities to reveal themselves and show themselves. As such, it cannot appear before *Dasein*'s attention as if it were an entity. In this context, the notion of the unlimited is intrinsically opposed to the limited; the former cannot enclose its essence within restricted confines, while the latter cannot aspire to infinity.

In the realm of the infinite, only one singular presence can exist, excluding the possibility of multiplicity. This framework also applies to what Henry has called the "impressional" or "sensory impressions," which follow the same laws observed in phenomena characterized by their excessive or saturated nature, thus marking the limit of the hidden, the Absolute, and revelation. The term "impressional" refers to anything capable of generating impressions in our perceptual faculties, establishing that each entity acts as a model, an archetype, within which a saturated phenomenon exemplifies the paradigm of all phenomena and, consequently, of phenomenology itself. In its essence, objective reality is presented to us as an unconditional gift.

Michel Henry links the impressional with affectivity and posits that, through passivity, through "relationality with Being," the impression arises spontaneously, allowing us to move toward the understanding of the "coming to itself of life." The impression, which for Henry lies deep within all consciousness or all existence, summons itself, and what impacts our senses is what offers itself freely or gives itself. This notion translates into a direct and unmediated experience of life, which manifests as an authentic self-revelation. Henry asserts that if both Husserl and Heidegger can speak of a certain element of understanding of the phenomenon and of Being, respectively, which appears and disappears, it is because before any thought, perception is already experiencing itself through the human being.

Husserl speaks to us of horizontal intentionality, understood as a tacit, unmediated self-perception, which is not in itself an act but is inherent in all acts of consciousness, and as such, it is the self-temporalization of consciousness in which all acts synthesize as "my" acts. Similarly, now Henry speaks to us of an affective perception that allows life to experience itself passively in a state of pathos, or original and pure affectivity. This affectivity, which must be understood as transcendental and not merely empirical, has the singular capacity to be experienced without mediation, without distance, which leads it to constitute the phenomenological pillar that determines the essence of self-revelation and, by extension, the essence of life itself. Through this notion of original affectivity and the emergence of life as an immediate and primary experience, Henry argues that, prior to all intentional consciousness and even all relationality with Being, transcendental affectivity already pulses inexorably within the human being. This allows it to "live itself" without the need for identity or agency and, therefore, without the need for self-knowledge either. In fact, if phenomenology can proceed and reflect upon our own transcendental subjectivity, it is because the human being, without identity or agency yet defined, already lives itself in the most absolute stillness and prior to all temporality.

This is Henry's argument, that the impression transcends mere temporality, understood as the structure of consciousness and of all possible knowledge, to become an essential and enduring affectivity. The essence of the very identity and subsequent agency of the human being, of any possible subject, is rooted in affectivity. This not only refers to Husserl's intentional consciousness but also to relationality with Being. Every act of consciousness integrates within itself a latent self-revelation of affectivity that enables meditation and subsequent acts of intentional consciousness. This implies that, at its deepest core, every emotion, in its quality of self-experience, acts as a manifestation of the "I" that is not yet. Every sensation, when experienced as an introspective perception, allows for the existence and reveals the essence of Being. In this sense, affectivity underlies the constitution of our individual identity and becomes the vehicle through which Being makes itself apparent and defines itself. This process of self-revelation through affectivity underscores the fundamental importance of emotions as generative and revelatory elements of the "I," playing a crucial role in the articulation and understanding of our individual existence.

Henry's positioning regarding self-affectivity, understood as the pre-cognitive origin of all transcendental "I," is obviously related to Husserl, Heidegger, and Marion. But, it also maintains a strong link with Descartes, for whom *cogitatio*, or life as understood by an individual, acquires its full meaning within this affective framework. Any impression or sensation we experience comes from the outside, integrating into our being in multiple forms. Some may call this profound affectivity God, while Descartes refers to it as *cogitatio*, though both terms point toward the same transcendental reality seeking to manifest through us. We refer here to those impressions that go beyond what is merely perceptible, to those aspects that transcend ordinary perception. Michel Henry, interpreting Descartes' second meditation on the proofs of the existence of God, highlights that the essence of *cogitatio* lies in its capacity for self-revelation. Through Henry's lens, Descartes seems to defend this view, finding in his work a questioning of the intentional structure suggested by the hypothesis of the evil genius, which opens the door to considering a false perception. A relevant aspect of the *Meditations* is expressed in the phrase *at certe videre videor*, or "But certainly I seem to be seeing," which breaks down the act of seeing into two interrelated dimensions.[134] On one side, we have the term *videre*, which refers to the unfolding of the world, and on the other side, and simultaneously, the term *videor*, which highlights the process of self-revelation within the framework in which the world unfolds before the *cogito*.

In this conceptual framework, Descartes' introduction of the evil genius invites us to question the reliability of our sensory perceptions,

---

134. René Descartes, *Meditations on First Philosophy: With Selections from the Objections and Replies*, trans. and intro. Michael Moriarty (New York: Oxford University Press, 2008), 21 (§§29–30).

suggesting that what is perceived through them may be illusory. Therefore, it is only through individual consciousness, or cognitive capacity, that it is possible to access Being, offering the only true way to perceive reality: the eyes of the soul or true vision. Being, therefore, does not manifest to the senses, but reveals itself in cognitive potential. That said, and here lies Henry's reading, for Being to be given to us as truth through cognition, the "underlying" affectivity in which the *cogitatio* pulses incessantly opens us "affectively" to the other, to the world, but also to the very subject who then thinks and understands.

It is true that, for the reasons explained above, Descartes did not reach the philosophical depths that Heidegger would later explore; however, the introduction of the evil genius notion proved to be a critical tool, demonstrating the impossibility of placing full trust in sensory perceptions, while indirectly affirming the existence of a primordial sensory affectivity within the human being. Similarly, Kant criticizes the stance of those who accept as dogma the reality of what is captured by the senses, categorizing them as dogmatic. This perspective underscores a fundamental skepticism regarding the reliability of our senses to discern the Truth, a line of thought that questions the authenticity of sensory experience as a vehicle for attaining accurate knowledge.

Bibliography section VII

- Descartes, René. *Meditations on First Philosophy: With Selections from the Objections and Replies.* Translated with an introduction and notes by Michael Moriarty. New York: Oxford University Press, 2008.
- Henry, Michel. *The Michel Henry Reader.* Edited by Scott Davidson and Frédéric Seyler. Translated by Leonard Lawlor, Joseph Rivera, George Faithful, Michael Tweed, Peter T. Connor, and Karl Hefty. Evanston, IL: Northwestern University Press, 2019.
- Henry, Michel. *The Essence of Manifestation.* Translated by Girard J. Etzkorn. The Hague: Nijhoff, 1973.
- Henry, Michel. *Material Phenomenology.* Translated by Scott Davidson. New York: Fordham University Press, 2008.
- Heraclitus. *Fragments: A Text and Translation with a Commentary.* Translated by T. M. Robinson. Toronto: University of Toronto Press, 1987.
- Husserl, Edmund. *Cartesian Meditations: An Introduction to Phenomenology.* Translated by Dorion Cairns. The Hague: Martinus Nijhoff, 1960.
- Husserl, Edmund. *Aufsätze und Vorträge* (1911–1921). Edited by Thomas Nenon and Hans Rainer Sepp. Husserliana XXV. Dordrecht: Kluwer Academic Publishers, 1987.
- Husserl, Edmund. *Phenomenology and the Crisis of Philosophy.* Translated by Quentin Lauer. New York: Harper & Row, 1965.
- Janicaud, Dominique, Jean-François Courtine, Jean-Louis Chrétien, Michel Henry, and Jean-Luc Marion. *Phenomenology and the "Theological Turn": The French Debate.* New York: Fordham University Press, 2000.

- Kierkegaard, Søren. *Fear and Trembling/Repetition*. Translated by Howard V. Hong and Edna H. Hong. Princeton: Princeton University Press, 1983.
- Marion, Jean-Luc. *Being Given: Toward a Phenomenology of Givenness*. Translated by Jeffrey L. Kosky. Stanford, CA: Stanford University Press, 2002.
- Marion, Jean-Luc. *Reduction and Givenness: Investigations of Husserl, Heidegger, and Phenomenology*. Evanston, IL: Northwestern University Press, 1998.
- Prášek, Petr. "A Theological Turn in Phenomenology? Janicaud and Contemporary French Phenomenology." *Studia Phaenomenologica* 23 (2023): 351–75.
- Stein, Garth. *The Art of Racing in the Rain*. New York: HarperCollins, 2008.
- Zirión Quijano, Alfredo. "The Call 'Back to the Things Themselves' and the Notion of Phenomenology." *Husserl Studies* 22, no. 1 (2006): 29–51.

Section VIII
Phenomenology of Time

CHAPTER 30

A GENEALOGY OF TIME

When addressing the topic of waiting that we have previously introduced, we must inevitably consider time as a crucial element. Only by understanding the flow of time can we truly appreciate the greatness and meaning of what is timeless and authentic. Furthermore, the issue of affectivity, which springs tacitly and spontaneously prior to any formation or subjective constitution, as Henry has so aptly demonstrated, brings us back to the question of temporality and the need to rethink it in order to understand our experience of Being better. Although we have examined the topic of time in various sections of this study, especially in relation to Husserl and Heidegger, time is not an exclusive concern of phenomenology, but has been a central preoccupation of philosophy since its inception.

We will offer a brief philosophical genealogy of the concept of time. This fascinating intellectual journey spans from the earliest reflections on change and movement to the complex theories of quantum physics and relativity. Finally, we will return to the topic of timeless waiting, which is of particular interest in this study. We begin by outlining the main developments:

- The pre-Socratics introduce us to the idea that the foundation of reality is constant change, with Heraclitus asserting that "everything flows," placing time at the heart of the becoming of the world. Heraclitus' example, when he writes that we never bathe in the same river, clearly reflects the position of the philosopher from Ephesus.

- Plato elevates the concept, proposing a distinction between eternal time and the time of the world, linking the latter with the stars and considering it a manifestation of eternity in the sensible realm.
- Aristotle, for his part, offers a more structured perspective that leads him to define time as the measure of movement according to before and after, anchoring time in the concrete experience of change.
- St. Augustine introduces an introspective dimension, considering time as an entity that only exists in the consciousness of the individual, with the past and future living solely in memory and anticipation.
- During the Middle Ages, St. Thomas Aquinas fused these ideas with the Christian theological framework, maintaining that God, as the eternal Being, transcends time, which is seen as part of the divine creation.
- The Renaissance and the Enlightenment marked the beginning of the modern conception of time, particularly with Isaac Newton, who introduced the idea of absolute time, a framework that seems independent of the events of the universe.
- Immanuel Kant moves the debate into the sphere of human perception, arguing that time (and space) are a priori forms of sensibility, essential for structuring our experience of the world.
- Contemporary physics, particularly through Albert Einstein, revolutionizes our understanding of time, showing it to be relative and inseparably linked to space, challenging the notion of a universal and absolute time.
- In the 20th century, philosophers such as Henri Bergson and Martin Heidegger delve deeper into the subjective and existential experience of time, exploring its implications for identity, memory, and existence. Beyond phenomenology, even Wittgenstein asked: "Where does the present go when it becomes past? Where is the past?"

- Contemporary theories continue to challenge and expand our understanding of time, exploring its relationship with quantum mechanics, cosmology, and consciousness in an effort to understand the most fundamental bases of reality.

This genealogy demonstrates how the concept of time has been and continues to be central in our quest to understand the nature of the universe and our own existence. The questions that philosophy raises in relation to time indicate that we are dealing with a fundamental and omnipresent issue. In the odyssey of human life, time permeates everything from the learning of skills and means of survival to the deepest layers of our self-understanding as beings endowed with a transcendental and spiritual dimension. Each stage reflects an advance in philosophical and scientific thought, as well as a mirror of the concerns existing in its cultural context. Time continues to reveal new dimensions of reality, maintaining its place as one of the most intriguing and fundamental topics to keep exploring.

CHAPTER 31

TIME ACCORDING TO ARISTOTLE

Aristotle: time, movement, and soul

One of the authors whose study of time has had the greatest impact on philosophy is Aristotle, for whom time surrounds us, encompassing everything we do and are. According to the Stagirite, time is related to movement and change, and if we notice the passage of time, it is because we perceive the movement and change of things. Time is, therefore, like a vertex that connects a before and an after, what has happened with what will happen. This view of time laid the foundations for the concept of linear time, that is, time as a line in which we move. In *Physics*, Book IV (217b 29), Aristotle embarks on an inquiry into the nature of time, initially establishing the topics and problems to be addressed, following his usual method. This exploration focuses first on determining whether time truly exists and, if so, what its essence is. In other words, he begins by questioning the existence of time and investigates its nature.

Aristotle initially proposes that time is conceived as being composed of two parts: the past and the future. Excluding the present, as it is not considered a proper part, he argues that time does not exist in an absolute sense, but rather in a relative and confused way. The future is something that will be, but is not yet, and the past is something that was and, therefore, is no longer. This perspective casts doubt on the existence of time, as it is problematic to affirm the existence of something made up of parts that are not, or that are non-existent, or, phenomenologically speaking, that no longer appear or manifest, and thus are hidden. To affirm the existence of something divisible into parts, Aristotle points out that two conditions must be met: that some or all of its parts exist, and that these parts contribute to a measure of the whole, meaning that they have some extension within the continuum to which they belong. Since time, for the reasons mentioned, does not fulfill the first condition, the second condition faces serious difficulties. The only aspect of time that can be considered existing, the present or the "now," cannot be seen as an extension and, therefore, as part of time.

Next, Aristotle proceeds to delve into the discussion about the nature of the "now," questioning whether it can always be the same or, on the contrary, must always be considered different. The conclusion is that each "now" is unique and cannot coexist, as they do not represent temporal extensions, but act as limit points, inextensible and indivisible, of time. The solution to the dilemma of the identity and otherness of the "now" lies in the distinction between the "now" as a specific moment and its nature as a continuous substrate that allows the succession of events. Just as each stage of a movement is different from the others, but participates in continuous movement, the "now" is understood in a double sense: as a unique instant in time and as the constant substrate that facilitates the transition between these moments.

Aristotle reinforces this understanding with an analogy between the "now" and the "mover" (219b 15 – 220a), suggesting that the "now," just like the "mover" in motion, remains constant as a substrate while manifesting differently in each phase of movement or time.[135] This analogy clarifies that the "now," and, by extension, time, has a dual nature: it is, in essence, constant but changing in manifestation. Based on the above, Aristotle proceeds to address the problem of the existence of time without attempting to offer a definitive solution. He emphasizes that the analysis of the "now" and its modes of being provides fundamental guidelines for addressing the nature of time. Following his methodology, he first examines the views of his predecessors on the subject, a method that allows him to lay the foundations for his own definition.

---

135. Aristotle, *Physics*, trans. R. P. Hardie and R. K. Gaye, in *The Complete Works of Aristotle: The Revised Oxford Translation*, ed. Jonathan Barnes (Princeton: Princeton University Press, 1984), book 4, part 13.

Chapter 31: Time according to Aristotle

The Stagirite considers and then refutes two previous conceptions of time: the first, that time is the movement of the whole, specifically the rotation of the celestial sphere; and the second, that time is the celestial sphere itself. He rejects the first idea, arguing that time can be considered even in fragments of the movement of the sphere, not exclusively in its totality. He points out that the hypothesis of multiple worlds with their own movements would imply the existence of simultaneous times, which is erroneous according to this view. Against the second conception, he argues that thinking of time as the celestial sphere is a simplification, as it confuses the notion of being "in time" with being "in the sphere." Aristotle clarifies that, while time is related to movement, it is not identical to it. Movement affects only what changes, whereas time concerns all things. Moreover, while movement can vary in speed, time cannot, as speed is measured in relation to time. This leads to the conclusion that time is not movement, but is intrinsically related to change. The perception of time depends on the perception of change by the soul.

The relationship between time and movement is clarified by considering that movement occurs in a "continuum," which, for Aristotle, is primarily space. The continuity of movement gives rise to the continuity of time. Knowledge of time arises from the soul's ability to distinguish between "nows," identifying what is prior and what is subsequent in movement. Aristotle then defines time as "the number of movement according to the prior and the posterior," establishing a distinction between the concept of "number" as what is counted and the act of counting. In this definition, time does not number movement per se, but rather the breadth of the movement between two points in time, the "nows." From this, Aristotle proposes that if the greater and the lesser are measured by number, and if movement (whether greater or lesser) is measured by time, then time functions as a kind of number. This does not imply an absolute identification between time and movement, but rather that time is related to movement in terms of its quantifiable aspect. This approach emphasizes the role of time as a measure of movement, highlighting its quantitative aspect and its independence from the concrete nature of movement itself.

In conclusion, it is essential to emphasize that the similarity previously noted between the concept of the "now" and the "mover" transcends mere coincidence of being identical under certain circumstances and different under others. This similarity extends to the role both play as gateways to the understanding of the "continuum" to which they belong. On the one hand, it is maintained that our understanding of movement derives exclusively from the "mover." On the other hand, if we refer to the previously established definition of time, as "the number of movement in relation to the prior and the posterior," and understand that the "prior" and the "posterior" refer to two temporal instances or "nows," then it is concluded that our knowledge of time also proceeds from the "now."

Based on Aristotle's analysis, the following paragraphs will address the consequences arising from the interactions between time-soul and time-world. In this regard, it is relevant to revisit the concepts (although not necessarily the analyses) proposed by Paul Ricoeur in *Time and Narrative*, concerning the two perspectives from which our issue is examined. On the one hand, there is an approach that we might call psychological, focused on the inquiry into the relationship between time and the soul. On the other, we face a vision that we would qualify as cosmological, aimed at exploring the connection between time and the world. Through this approach, we seek to demonstrate that, although the measure of movement by the soul is established as the moment when the existence of time acquires meaning, this relationship does not absolutely constitute the condition for the possibility of the existence of time.

From the outset, Aristotle seeks to eliminate any clear distinction between the existence of time and its perception. However, his own definition of time implies the existence of the soul. We propose that a careful analysis in this regard will allow us to project a conception of time independent of its link with the soul (cosmology of time). This is because even in the absence of the soul, one can speak of a "substrate of time" to facilitate the examination of the time-world relationship. Afterward, we will discuss the relevance and function of the "Unmoved Mover" in terms of the cosmological foundations that establish the notion of temporality in Aristotle.

Chapter 31: Time according to Aristotle

To elucidate the role of the soul in its relationship with time, it is useful to revisit the previous discussion on the connection between time and movement. Although Aristotle does not directly equate time with movement, it is clear that he identifies an immediate connection between these two "continuums." He maintains that our knowledge of time originates in movement, and vice versa, our understanding of movement is grounded in time. This interdependence is clearly evidenced in his definition of time as "For time is just this – number of motion in respect of 'before' and 'after.'"[136] When addressing the concept of "number," Aristotle distinguishes it in two senses: as the number that is counted (the counted) and as the number with which one counts (the counter). In his conceptualization of time, the notion of counted number explicitly operates, that is, that which is "measured." This measurement undeniably requires an entity that performs the act of counting, and it is here that the soul assumes a crucial role within Aristotle's conception of time. The soul, or more specifically its intellectual faculty, facilitates the conception of time as the number of movement by distinguishing two "nows" in time—the prior and the posterior in movement—and recognizing that these moments are distinct from what lies between them.

In light of this conception, we might then ask, after defining time as the number of movement, whether it is feasible to consider it as something that can exist independently of the soul. Aristotle poses this question in the following way: Would time exist in the absence of the soul? To which he himself responds that if there were no one to count, there would also be nothing to count, and therefore, there would be no number, since a number is either that which is counted or that which is countable. Aristotle's response to this dilemma is concise and grounded in his definition of time. Since time is the number of movement, the presence of an entity capable of counting that movement is essential for time to manifest effectively. Thus, "but if nothing but soul, or in soul reason, is qualified to count, there would not be time unless there were soul, but only that of which time

---

136. Ibid., book 4, part 11.

is an attribute," as would be the case with a movement that persists without a soul.[137] Suppose we disregard time as the numeration of movement, and consider what time numerates. In that case, we obtain something that, although not time per se, does constitute its substrate, that is, the movement that is potentially countable.

Alejandro Vigo has pointed out that the discussion extending from 223a21 to 223a29 in *Physics* has presented interpretative complications. This is largely due to the modern perspective from which it has been read, involving categories such as realism and idealism. Vigo argues that the real challenge lies in the fact that Aristotle's approach to the relationship between the soul and movement, and by extension, with the world, does not easily fit into these categories. An idealist interpretation fades upon considering that Aristotle does not suggest that time occurs within the soul or that the soul constitutes it, but rather emphasizes that time, being the number of movement, is intimately linked to the act of counting. On the other hand, a realist interpretation, which assumes the real existence of the objects of knowledge independently of the cognizing subject, might rely on Aristotle's words in *Metaphysics* IV, 5, where he discusses the existence of the sensible in the absence of living beings. This perspective supports the view that the object of knowledge has an existence independent of the determinations the soul might perceive.

In this framework, it is essential to differentiate between the primary objects of perception, which do not currently exist independently of perception, and the substrate of these perceptions, which can exist independently of the soul's perceptual activity, as it is what allows the manifestation of the sensible. Thus, we recognize that time is not a substantial entity or a substrate independent of the soul, but a determination of those substantial entities in movement. Its existence, as the affection of movement, is intrinsically linked to the soul's perception of movement. This is the essence of Aristotle's assertion that time emerges when the "before" and "after" moments in change can be counted. Consequently, Aristotle maintains that

---

137. Ibid., book 4, part 14.

time is not reduced to mere observation by the soul nor to a simple determination of movement, but represents the point of convergence between the soul's capacity to count and the movement's capacity to be counted. What Aristotle proposes does not absolutely deny the existence of time independent of the soul, as time, being a "counted" number of movement, and the counted can also be considered "countable." This allows us to speak of time even in the potentiality of being counted, without it necessarily being realized in act. This reflection, however, opens the door to what we might call a "cosmology of time."

Aristotle: time, cosmos, and God

In Aristotle's thought, as in the general Greek conception, the universe is considered eternal and indestructible, dismissing the possibility of creation *ex nihilo* or an absolute transition from being to non-being of the cosmos. However, it is in the specificity of his arguments that the most significant divergences with Plato are observed. In the myth told in the *Timaeus*, Plato conceives the world as an entity formed and organized by a Demiurge from a preexisting prime matter within a framework of chaotic and indefinite time. However, Aristotle maintains that the world and all its constituent elements, including space, movement, and time, are co-eternal with a first and eternal reality, which occupies this preeminent place over Being, the first cause of movement. In this regard, it is imperative to examine the foundations that led Aristotle to postulate the existence of an Unmoved Mover, an entity that, although not directly interacting with the cosmos, allows for its persistence.

For Aristotle, the idea that the world was generated contradicts logic. The most eloquent explanation of this conception is found in *Physics* VIII, where, although it focuses on the eternity of motion, this reasoning can be extrapolated to the eternity of time and the material or spatial world. This extrapolation is possible due to the continuous nature of space, motion, and time: the continuous is defined by having a before and an after. First, the before and after are conceptualized in terms of spatial position, since in spatial magnitude, exists a before and an after, motion, by analogy, must also have a before and an after. Similarly, time contains a before and an after, as it follows motion. Thus, while time is inherent to motion (it is impossible to conceive one without the other), motion depends on spatial magnitude, as it involves the displacement of something in space, not motion in itself. Therefore, by asserting the eternity of motion, we simultaneously affirm the eternity of time and the cosmos.

Aristotle poses the dilemma in this way: Was motion ever generated, without having existed previously, and will it one day be destroyed, ceasing all motion? Or was motion never generated, nor will it be destroyed, having always existed and always to exist, thus belonging to the immortality and permanence of things? The options posed can be summarized as follows: 1) Was motion (and, therefore, the world) ever created only to end? or 2) Is it eternal, without beginning or end? To address this issue, which also holds great interest in the debate between paganism and Christianity, Aristotle primarily resorts to logical-causal arguments. The Stagirite is correct in noting that, regardless of the position taken on the finitude or eternity of the world, nearly all philosophers who have developed cosmogonies have acknowledged, explicitly or implicitly, the existence of motion. This is because such cosmogonies address processes of generation and corruption, which are manifestations of change. The nature of motion is analyzed in detail in *Physics* III, where it is defined as "the actuality of what is in potential, as such." This concept suggests that motion is the effective realization of a potential.[138] Under this conceptual framework, when it is argued that motion had a beginning in time, without having existed previously, two possibilities are presented.

The first possibility suggests that the world was generated and then began to move. This scenario implies that generation itself is already a form of change, as, if something does not exist and has the potential to exist, its emergence or generation involves the actualization of that potential. This, according to the Aristotelian definition, constitutes motion. This argument suggests that motion

---

138. Ibid., book 3, part 1.

would be prior to the supposed beginning of motion. Moreover, to assert that the world was generated "together with motion" wrongly presupposes a prior time in which neither the world nor motion existed, which is contradictory because time is inseparable from motion. The second possibility considers it absurd to think that the world, being eternal, could experience a beginning of motion. If it is assumed that motion had a beginning, we would necessarily have to postulate the existence of a first mover and a first cause. However, for something to function as a cause, it must possess motion, which can only be imparted by another cause, leading this reasoning to an infinite regression of causes and motions.

These reflections led Aristotle to reject the idea of a temporal beginning for motion and the conception of a world generated independently of it. Aristotle's conclusion emphasizes the fundamental interdependence between motion, time, and the very existence of the cosmos, which strengthens his argument for the eternity of the world and motion. This position resolves the paradoxes and establishes a firm foundation for the concept of an eternal universe, where change and motion are intrinsic and coeternal with the existence of the cosmos.

Aristotle's denial of the generation of motion leads us to the need to identify a first cause that explains its eternity without falling into an infinite regress. This is based on the principle of causality, which holds that everything that moves must be moved by something. According to our definition of motion, every being capable of inducing change must be in actuality; for example, a body is heated by the action of another body that is already hot. Here arises an aporia: it seems that everything in actuality once had a potential (that is, the thing that heats was not always hot, but acquired its heat from another body), but potential does not necessarily lead to actuality, as the potential may not be actualized. Thus, potentiality would seem to precede actuality. If this were the case, then nothing that exists would be, as the potential would not necessarily materialize into actuality. This dilemma resonates both with the theological idea that everything emerged from darkness and with the conception of the philosophers of nature that "everything was together"; both scenarios face the problem of how motion could have arisen without a cause in actuality.

Section VIII: Phenomenology of time

Since motion is eternal, a mover is required that is always in actuality, that is, pure actuality, because if it possessed any potential, eternal motion would be at risk, as the potential might not be realized. Therefore, the first cause of eternal motion must be an eternal, immaterial actuality (since materiality implies potentiality), and free from any potentiality. This first cause, being pure actuality, cannot interact or be affected by anything other than its own perfection, thus avoiding any contamination with potentiality. The attributes of the first mover include being eternal, immaterial, pure actuality, and immobile, which leads us to the question of how the Aristotelian God, who does not act as an efficient cause due to his separation from the material world, can be the eternal cause of motion.

One possible way to approach this topic is to pay attention to the distinction between Greek and Christian thought, with the latter being grounded in the doctrine of creation *ex nihilo*, in contrast to the Aristotelian conception. While the Christian God is seen as the efficient cause of the world, creating it out of nothing just as a craftsman works with matter, the God of Aristotle acts as the final cause, moving the world in an analogous way to how the beloved moves the lover. Thus, the Aristotelian unmoved mover avoids any contact with the material. Aristotle, in fact, maintains that the world cannot have an efficient cause, as this would imply an infinite regression of causes. However, he argues that it is possible to conceive of a first cause that is not first in a chronological sense, if it is understood that the eternity of this cause is coeternal with the eternity of time and the world. This approach allows Aristotle to offer a coherent explanation of the eternity of motion without falling into the logical complications of a temporal beginning or end to motion itself.

CHAPTER 32

TIME AND ETERNITY ACCORDING TO SAINT AUGUSTINE

The paradox of time

The commentaries that Saint Augustine dedicated to the topic of time served as a point of reference for later studies, especially in the field of philosophy. In order to address the position of the philosopher from Hippo regarding this subject, we will focus on the reading of Book XI of his famous work *Confessions*. There he argues, in a manner somewhat similar to Aristotle, that only the present has real existence, while the past and the future exist only in the mind. Furthermore, he defines time as a measure of movement, indicating that this concept is also a divine creation that arises with the act of creation itself, not preceding it, positioning God as prior to time, but not in a chronological sense. Saint Augustine argues:

> For what is time? Who can easily and briefly explain it? Who even in thought can comprehend it, even to the pronouncing of a word concerning it? But what in speaking do we refer to more familiarly and knowingly than time? And certainly we understand when we speak of it; we understand also when we hear it spoken of by another. What, then, is time? If no one ask of me, I know; if I wish to explain to him who asks, I know not. Yet I say with confidence, that I know that if nothing passed away, there would not be past time; and if nothing were coming, there would not be future time; and if nothing were, there would not be present time.

Section VIII: Phenomenology of Time

Those two times, therefore, past and future, how are they, when even the past now is not; and the future is not as yet? But should the present be always present, and should it not pass into time past, time truly it could not be, but eternity. If, then, time present — if it be time — only comes into existence because it passes into time past, how do we say that even this is, whose cause of being is that it shall not be — namely, so that we cannot truly say that time is, unless because it tends not to be?[139]

Whence it appeared to me that time is nothing else than protraction; but of what I know not. It is wonderful to me, if it be not of the mind itself. For what do I measure, I beseech You, O my God, even when I say either indefinitely, This time is longer than that; or even definitely, This is double that? That I measure time, I know. But I measure not the future, for it is not yet; nor do I measure the present, because it is extended by no space; nor do I measure the past, because it no longer is. What, therefore, do I measure? Is it times passing, not past? For thus had I said.[140]

In you, O my mind, I measure times. Do not overwhelm me with your clamour. That is, do not overwhelm yourself with the multitude of your impressions. In you, I say, I measure times; the impression which things as they pass by make on you, and which, when they have passed by, remains, that I measure as time present, not those things which have passed by, that the impression should be made. This I measure when I measure times. Either, then, these are times, or I do not measure times.[141]

---

139. St. Augustine, *Confessions*, trans. J. G. Pilkington, in Nicene and Post-Nicene Fathers, First Series, vol. 1, ed. Philip Schaff (Buffalo, NY: Christian Literature Publishing Co., 1886), Book XI, chapter 14, §17.
140. Ibid., Book XI, chapter 26, §33.
141. Ibid., Book XI, chapter 27, §36.

But what now is manifest and clear is, that neither are there future nor past things. Nor is it fitly said, There are three times, past, present and future; but perchance it might be fitly said, There are three times; a present of things past, a present of things present, and a present of things future. For these three do somehow exist in the soul, and otherwise I see them not: present of things past, memory; present of things present, sight; present of things future, expectation. If of these things we are permitted to speak, I see three times, and I grant there are three. It may also be said, There are three times, past, present and future, as usage falsely has it. See, I trouble not, nor gainsay, nor reprove; provided always that which is said may be understood, that neither the future, nor that which is past, now is. For there are but few things which we speak properly, many things improperly; but what we may wish to say is understood.[142]

These things do I within, in that vast chamber of my memory. For there are near me heaven, earth, sea, and whatever I can think upon in them, besides those which I have forgotten. There also do I meet with myself, and recall myself — what, when, or where I did a thing, and how I was affected when I did it. There are all which I remember, either by personal experience or on the faith of others. Out of the same supply do I myself with the past construct now this, now that likeness of things, which either I have experienced, or, from having experienced, have believed; and thence again future actions, events, and hopes, and upon all these again do I meditate as if they were present. I will do this or that, say I to myself in that vast womb of my mind, filled with the images of things so many and so great, and this or that shall follow upon it. Oh that this or that might come to pass! God avert this or that! Thus speak I to myself; and when I speak, the images of all I speak about are present, out of the same treasury of

---

142. Ibid., Book XI, chapter 20, §26.

memory; nor could I say anything at all about them were the images absent.[143]

Saint Augustine delves into the complex issue of time, presenting reflections that challenge common intuition. This famous quote encapsulates the difficulty of defining time: "What, then, is time? If no one asks me, I know; but if I try to explain it to the one who asks me, I do not know." Time is a familiar concept in daily experience, but elusive when one seeks to conceptualize it. Contrary to the general notion that divides time into past, present, and future, Saint Augustine proposes that only the present possesses tangible reality, while the past and future exist only in the mind, as memories or expectations. The past no longer exists, and the future does not yet exist. Similar to Aristotle, this conclusion leads to the non-reality of both the past and the future, posing the dilemma of how it is possible to measure something that does not exist. Measuring time, therefore, seems to refer to a quality that has no entity outside of our perception and mental conception.

In addressing the measurement of time, Saint Augustine points to the impossibility of asserting that a past time was long, since it cannot be measured either as past (since it has ceased to exist) or as present (since the present has no extension). This reasoning leads to the conclusion that only the present is real, although it would be, at the same time, a present without extension and, therefore, without measurable duration. To illustrate this point, Saint Augustine uses the example of a hundred years, in which he shows that we can only consider the year currently passing as present, while the others are either future (and thus nonexistent) or past (and no longer exist). This division continues until the conclusion that the present is indivisible. The present, according to Saint Augustine, is a fleeting instant that does not allow any division into smaller parts without falling into the category of past or future.

The Augustinian reflection on time is noted for its philosophical depth, offering a perspective that challenges linear and segmented

---

143. Ibid., Book X, chapter 8, §14.

conceptions of time. By considering time not as an independent and divisible entity but as a subjective and momentary experience marked by consciousness, Saint Augustine contributes to the philosophical discussion on the nature of being, perception, and divine existence. This approach to time, viewed as something that escapes objective definition and is rooted in subjective experience and consciousness, invites reflection on how we understand and live temporality in our daily and spiritual lives.

Saint Augustine delves into the apparent contradiction between the non-existence of the past and future and our ability to speak and know about them. While he initially holds that only the present truly exists, he acknowledges the need to admit some form of existence for the past and future, in order to explain how historical knowledge, prophecy, and anticipation of the effects of our actions are possible. To resolve this apparent paradox, Saint Augustine suggests that, although the past and future do not exist in the reality of things in a tangible sense, they must have some mode of existence that allows for their knowledge and measurement. He argues that, if the future did not exist at all, it would be impossible for prophets to predict it, and if the past had no existence, it would be impossible to remember it or narrate it truthfully.

In this regard, Saint Augustine proposes that both the memory of the past and the anticipation of the future occur in the present. Memories of the past are not the actual events that have already occurred, but rather images or traces of those events stored in memory, which manifest in the present when accessed. Similarly, the premeditation or planning of future actions occurs in the present, even though the actions themselves have not yet happened and are, therefore, future. Regarding the prediction of future events, Saint Augustine clarifies that what is truly seen or known are the present causes or signs that indicate what will happen, not the future events themselves. These causes or signs exist in the present and allow us to infer or imagine what will happen in the future. This analysis leads Saint Augustine to firmly maintain that only the present has real existence, while recognizing that the past and the future have an existence in the mind, in "some place" where they manifest as present for the observer. This conception refines his initial understanding of the nature of time, allowing him to reconcile the real and unique existence of the present with our experience and knowledge of the past and future.

In confronting the dilemma of how we measure time, if the past and future do not exist in reality and the present has no duration, Saint Augustine explores the relationship between time and movement. The duration of the movement or rest of a body is measured by time, indicating that, although time is not movement itself, it acts as the measure of the duration of both movement and rest. This analysis leads Saint Augustine to conclude that we measure time in its passage, meaning that we measure neither the future (since it is nonexistent), nor the present (since it has no extension), nor the past (since it has ceased to exist). However, despite these limitations, time is measured in relation to movement, suggesting that time is a measure of movement and, by extension, of rest.

Based on the above, Saint Augustine advances his reflection by arguing that time not only measures movement but also measures itself. This manifests in how the duration of different time intervals is compared, for example, measuring the duration of a long syllable in relation to a short one. This ability to measure intervals of time against each other leads Saint Augustine to a significant conclusion about the nature of time: time is a distension. This conceptualization of time as distension, or extension, implies that time is something more than a mere succession of instants or a framework in which events occur. Rather, time is understood as a continuity that allows the experience of change and movement. This distension encompasses the sequence of events and also the internal extension of our consciousness, where the memories of the past and anticipations of the future reside, thus enabling the measurement of time.

Therefore, the Augustinian explanation of how we measure time, despite its apparent contradictions, reveals a profound understanding of the temporal nature as intrinsically linked to human experience, movement, and consciousness. Time as distension encapsulates the continuity of our internal experience, uniting the physical world with human perception and thought.

Time as the possibility of experience

Saint Augustine intrinsically links the existence of time, understood as the continuity of the experience of subjective consciousness, with the presence of movement. He argues that time can only exist where there are material beings capable of movement. This idea reflects an understanding of the universe where time and movement are codependent, and both are subject to the existence of matter. In this context, Saint Augustine argues that in order for movement to occur, there must be beings composed of matter and form, since in matter without form there can be no movement.

This position is reinforced in his commentary on the biblical passage of Genesis (1:2), where the earth is described as "formless and empty" and covered in darkness. Saint Augustine interprets the "formless and empty earth" as a reference to primordial matter without form, from which God would have formed the earth as we know it. This interpretation leads Saint Augustine to conclude that formless matter, lacking form and order, is not counted by the Scriptures among the days of creation. For him, where there is no form or order, there is no change, and where there is no change, there is no time or succession of temporal spaces. Saint Augustine delves even further into this idea by affirming that time originates from the changes in things, through variations and successions of forms over matter. This perspective highlights that time is intrinsically tied to the existence of material beings and the changes that occur in them. In other words, the Augustinian conception defends that time is a construct related to order, form, and change in the material universe.

This analysis provides an in-depth view of how Saint Augustine understands creation and the nature of time, linking it to physical aspects, such as movement and matter, as well as to metaphysical concepts such as form and order. Thus, the relationship between time, movement, and matter is fundamental for understanding the physical universe, but also reflects a spiritual and theological dimension in the interpretation of the divine creative act. In his deep reflection on the nature of time in the *Confessions*, the philosopher of Hippo reaches the conclusion that time, more than an external and objective entity, is experienced and measured within the human spirit. This perspective develops from the observation that, although we seem to measure objective times such as the past or the future, in reality, we measure our impressions, that is, our internal perceptions and memories of those times. For Saint Augustine, time is measured in the spirit through the impressions that things leave as they pass, and which remain even after they have passed.

This Augustinian perception of time is based on three faculties of the spirit: memory, through which we retain the past; attention, through which we experience the present; and expectation, by which we anticipate the future. The example of uttering a prolonged voice illustrates how the spirit operates with these three temporal dimensions. Before uttering the voice, its duration is premeditated in thought, entrusting this premeditation to memory. As the voice is uttered, the present intention moves what was in the future into the past, in a process where the future is reduced and the past accumulates, all managed by the memory, attention, and expectation of the spirit.

This understanding of time as something that is lived and measured internally resolves the paradoxes of its nonexistence and its lack of extension and explains how it is possible to speak of long or short times. A "long future" is nothing more than a long wait for what is to come, and a "long past" is a long memory of what has been. Saint Augustine, therefore, offers us a profoundly introspective and subjective view of time, anchored in the human spirit's internal experience, which underscores the central role of human consciousness in the perception and measurement of time. This Augustinian conception of time as a distension of the spirit, and its measurement as an act of memory, attention, and expectation, reveals an understanding of time that transcends its physical manifestation, placing it in the domain of subjective and spiritual experience.

Identifying time with subjective consciousness excludes it from the creative dimension of God. In the same Book XI of the *Confessions*, Saint Augustine addresses precisely the complex relationship between God, time, and creation, offering a profound reflection on the nature of time and its divine origin. For him, the question of what God was doing before the creation of the world makes no sense, as time itself is a creation of God. This perspective implies that time did not exist before the creation of the universe; therefore, there was no "before" in the temporal sense where God was inactive. The Bishop of Hippo resolves the problem of the eternity of the world by arguing against the idea that the world must be coeternal with God to avoid changes in the divine will. He asserts that time, being a creation of God, does not precede the material creation, which means that there is no need for the world to be eternal, nor does it imply a change in the substance or will of God to create the world at a specific moment, as such a decision and action lie outside the framework of created time.

The precedence of God over time is understood not in chronological terms, but from the perspective of God's eternity, which is always present and surpasses both past and future times. God knows all times simultaneously, without temporal limitations, and moves temporal things without being subject to the movements of time. Saint Augustine emphasizes that no creature, even those "superior to time" such as angels, is coeternal with God. All created beings, regardless of their nature, have a beginning established by God, although it may not be a temporal beginning in the case of spiritual beings. This reinforces the idea that only God is eternal, existing outside and before time and creation.

Finally, Saint Augustine suggests that the experience of time is linked to the dual nature of human beings, composed of spirit and matter. While the pure spirit can be considered superior to time, it is the incarnation of the spirit in matter that introduces us to the experience of time, marked by movement and change. This analysis highlights the connection between spirituality, materiality, and our perception of time, showing how our embodied existence places us in the temporal flow, in contrast to the immutable eternity of God.

The analysis of time allows Saint Augustine to carry out an exploration of eternity and time, through which he establishes a fundamental distinction between the nature of God and human temporal experience. By comparing eternity with the present, he illustrates how the human concept of time, defined by successions and changes, contrasts with divine eternity, where everything is permanently present and nothing is transitory. This comparison seeks to highlight the difference between the temporality of creation and the atemporality of God, without suggesting that God's eternity is simply an extended present in the human sense. Divine eternity should not be understood as an extended present, but as a reality where temporal succession does not occur, and where everything exists in a state of constant and complete presence. In contrast, human time is characterized by the impossibility of simultaneously experiencing the past, present, and future, as we are always in motion, traversing successive moments.

Although Saint Augustine acknowledges the influence of the soul or spirit on the perception of time, arguing that the soul is necessary for time to exist as we experience it, he also affirms the importance of physical movement. In this sense, his view does not exclude a real foundation of time in material things, recognizing that movement—a material phenomenon—is essential for the existence of time. Therefore, although his conception of time has a significant component related to the spirit or soul, it does not deny the objective reality of time manifested in the material world.

St. Augustine's approach to time and eternity reflects the depth of his thinking and his ability to integrate philosophical reflections on the nature of God, the soul, and the material universe. He reached conclusions similar to those of Aristotle on the relationship between time and movement without having had direct access to his books. In addressing these issues, Saint Augustine significantly contributes to the philosophical tradition, offering a perspective that transcends its historical context and continues to influence contemporary philosophical debate, especially in the field of phenomenology.

CHAPTER 33

TIME ACCORDING TO KANT, HUSSERL, AND HEIDEGGER

The Kantian revolution: time as a priori knowledge

In the 18th century, Immanuel Kant's philosophy sparked the so-called "Copernican revolution." The origin and reason for all knowledge shifted from the reality of the experienced object to the subject who experiences reality.
Kant's philosophy, which denies the positions of Descartes on one side and Hume on the other, radically breaks with certain principles of the philosophical tradition and inaugurates a new starting point upon which modern philosophy will be founded. Kant is said to have marked a turning point in the history of philosophy.

Kant explores the nature of knowledge, questioning whether it derives entirely from sensory experience or whether there is knowledge that is a priori, that is, that precedes all empirical experience. He questions whether time and space are learned experiences or inherent conditions of our cognitive structure. Kant's answer is clear when he defines time not as another object of experience and knowledge but as a necessary prior condition for any experience.

Before Kant, the conception of time had evolved from Aristotle and Saint Augustine, through the conceptual changes introduced by Christianity, to the philosophical debates between Newton and Leibniz. These historical dialogues laid the groundwork for Kant's revolutionary approach, which questioned the reliability of the senses in capturing reality as it truly is, illustrated by the phenomenon of optical illusions and mirages. Kant distinguishes between empirical knowledge, subject to the variability of experience, and a priori knowledge, which is universal and necessary, such as the principles of geometry. Human understanding organizes sensory information through cognitive structures. This means that our perception of reality is an interpretation of sensory data filtered through these innate structures, such as time and space.

Specifically, Kant argues that, along with space, time is the form of intuition, which simply means that it is a necessary a priori condition for all experience, indispensable for organizing and understanding phenomena. What Kant is essentially saying, in a manner similar to what Husserl will later argue, is that objects of sensory experience are given to us temporally, not all at once. This perspective posed a challenge both to the Newtonian view of time, which considers time as an absolute independent of observers, and to the Leibnizian perspective, which sees it as a relation between events. For Kant, time does not exist outside of human capacity to perceive and structure experience, emphasizing that it is the a priori form of our sensitivity. This understanding of time as a necessary condition for experience forces us to rethink the conception of change, moving away from traditional paradoxes and applying principles such as the Law of Conservation of Mass-Energy. Kant argues that what changes is not the fundamental existence of things but the manner in which these existences manifest. This new view of time and space involved a radical reconfiguration of how philosophy approached these issues and, more importantly, of the conception of our own relationship with the world and the nature of knowledge.

In summary, time, according to Kant, is not an external entity that affects objects but an essential dimension of our experience, possessing an a priori character inseparable from the human condition, that is, from the subject of experience. This view connects us with a universe where time, although fundamental to our existence, is not independent of our perception and cognition. Substance, eternal through change, highlights the interconnectedness between our perception of time and our ability to interact with reality, placing time at the center of our epistemological and existential understanding.

From Husserl's remembrance to Heidegger's *ereignis*

This paradigm shift concerning the subject and time will serve as the starting point for both Husserlian and Heideggerian conceptions. As we have seen before, and in line with Kant, Husserl ends up identifying time and consciousness to the point of suggesting, as we have done, that time is the backbone of all intentional consciousness; therefore, it is through time that any possible form of transcendental subjectivity emerges or can emerge. At the same time, Husserl himself wonders how the phenomenologist can "grasp" or "perceive" time as the internal time of consciousness, if he himself, in posing the question, remains anchored in the very same flow of consciousness. That is to say, he asks what type of reflection is deployed and under what type of intuition phenomenology can perceive what overflows the same intentional reflective act. The time of consciousness cannot be taken as another object given to us within consciousness, as time is consciousness itself from which the question is formulated. In this sense, Edmund Husserl's problem and conception radically contrast with everything philosophy had proposed until his time. For, unlike Kant, for whom time is a priori form of sensitivity that allows knowledge of the thing through succession, what really interests Husserl concerning time is the experiential (*erlebnis*) component of time itself. In other words, what Husserl seeks to describe, beyond the temporalized structure of a passive consciousness, is precisely how I become aware of what is called "time."

Let us recall that, in response to this question, Aristotle argued that we perceive time insofar as we perceive change, while Saint Augustine said that if we perceive time, it is because we can measure it. Husserl, for his part, argues that the consciousness of time emerges when we are able to detach ourselves from the very continuity of the temporal flow, much like how a machine stops. This stopping allows us to recognize our insertion in time, transforming it into something perceptible, an element of the world that is felt and experienced.

In this framework, Husserl introduces two crucial notions for his analysis of time: retention and reminiscence. Retention is understood as immediate memory, which we have already discussed, while reminiscence refers to second-order memory, or what we might call the memory of a memory. Through the experience of a sound that emerges, persists, and fades away, this phenomenon becomes an "object" that can be understood because it allows us to grasp it, even though, as such, it slips away from us, transcending all limits of intuition. The same happens with consciousness itself as an "object" of reflection.

We can define and even describe the temporal structure of the acts of consciousness, as we have seen in previous chapters. However, when focusing our attention on the innermost interiority of this structure, which is the time of temporality, it fades away, much like Heidegger's Being. Time, therefore, reveals itself in its concealment, overflowing and surpassing the limits of any intentional act. For this reason, Husserl places so much importance on reminiscence, understanding it as a comet that we observe passing by, being only aware of its trail. This second-order memory is characterized by its complete detachment from the present, shifting toward a very distant past. For Husserl, reminiscence is that dimension of the very structure of the act of consciousness that allows the act to overflow and go beyond itself, opening itself up beyond the limits of presence and actuality, and by doing so, it allows us to "realize" time as simultaneously flow and structure.

At this point, Heidegger explores the topic of time in relation to Being. To do so, he first argues that the conception of time as an absolute or relative parameter and as a succession of present moments emerged with the Greek philosophers. From his perspective, it still prevails in modern theories, including non-Euclidean geometries and the Theory of Relativity, and has obstructed the understanding of time in its primordial sense, which he calls "temporality." Starting from Husserl, Heidegger argues that temporality must be understood as a unity where the past, present, and future do not constitute distinct moments but interrelate as *ekstases*, that is, as forms of stepping outside of themselves. Therefore, they are intertwined in an essential manner, as a future projected toward which we are thrown, while simultaneously sinking into a past that evaporates.

It is precisely between the protention of consciousness and the retained consciousness that *Dasein* resides in containment. Containment consists in being tensioned both toward the past and the future. Heidegger's analysis will focus on the relationship between these three moments or dimensions. More specifically, and reading Kierkegaard through Husserl's phenomenological method, Heidegger interprets the past as "guilt" and the future as "fear of death," understanding these two phenomena as aspects of consciousness through which time unveils itself as a horizon for understanding Being. According to Heidegger, Being is a "presenting coming-forth that is continuously having been." "Coming-forth" corresponds to the protended consciousness, "presenting" to presence, and "having been" to retained consciousness.

Dasein, in its temporality, inhabits the future or the past, which tension it in both directions, dissolving any possible connotation of stable presence, which, in future texts, will lead Heidegger to say that it is even necessary to strike out *Dasein* with an X. In Being and Time, Being unfolds from time, but in the third Heidegger, Being does not unfold from time but from *ereignis*.

Chapter 34

The transcendence of time

Beyond chronological and psychological time

Human beings understand that every personal achievement or evolution requires time; whether it is learning a language or the natural progression from youth to old age, each of these is inscribed within a temporal dimension. Ambitious aspirations like space conquest underline time as an equivalent of distance and expansion, highlighting its critical role in our reality. To deny its influence would be to ignore an undeniable truth of our existence. However, we are unclear whether psychological time consists of an objective reality or if it is merely a mental construct in our search for purpose and change. I recognize myself as prone to envy, greed, and violence; nevertheless, I harbor the hope that the passage of time will allow me to shed these chains, leading me toward inner peace. Is it possible to consider this process as a measurable reality, akin to the distance between two points?

For Aristotle, time is the measure of movement according to a prior and a subsequent, and only beings move. If chronological time measures movement, only beings that move suffer temporality, but since Being does not move, it is not subject to temporality. Is there another modality of time that offers the same objectivity as space and distance? Ultimately, can we confirm the existence of psychological time with certainty? This reflection invites us to consider the nature of time beyond its physical manifestations, questioning its reality and our perception of it within the framework of human experience. While we recognize its presence and are immersed in its flow, one may ask whether time constitutes an objective reality. We accept without reservation that both chronological and psychological time are real phenomena, with doubt emerging over whether the latter is essential for a clear and direct perception of our surroundings. It is necessary to elucidate whether time is indispensable for understanding the nature of desire, envy, and the pain these emotions generate, and to perceive Truth in its purest form. Perhaps the mind invented the concept of psychological time as a strategy to navigate the complexity of existence, postponing confrontations and evading the pressure of the present moment.

Thus, time becomes a refuge for a mind that clings to passivity. It is that mind, resistant to change, that hides behind time to justify its inertia; the one that postpones action under the pretext of needing more time to meditate and proceed. Conservatives cling to the past, and progressives cling to the future. Both traditionalists, who wish for everything to remain unchanged, and those who advocate for total transformation, fail to understand the true nature of time. Some long for the past, and others have hopes for the future, but both are living prisoners of a time that becomes and, like Kronos, devours itself. This conception is precisely what gives rise to the notion of the "ought to be," an idealization that contrasts with tangible reality, creating an abyss between what is and what is longed for. And in the face of this, we are compelled to ask: Is this ideal of the "ought to be" a palpable truth, or merely a mental subterfuge to prolong our responsibilities and avoid transformation?

Ultimately, each person yearns to achieve fulfillment and spiritual enrichment. A life saturated with meaning, constituting the highest longing for authentic happiness, is freed from temporal bonds. Like love, such existence transcends time; to grasp the eternal, we must shift our gaze from the clock and immerse ourselves in its true essence. We must not use time as a means to achieve or understand the timeless. However, this perpetual challenge of life consists of unraveling time in the search for the perpetual. Understanding time in its complexity, not merely in fragments, presents a challenge for our development. Therefore, it is crucial to explore the essence of time, convinced that it is possible to liberate ourselves from its dominion.

CHAPTER 34: THE TRANSCENDENCE OF TIME

The contemplation of our existence, intimately intertwined with the flow of time, incites meaningful introspection. We are not referring solely to the mechanical succession of seconds, minutes, and years, but rather to an experience deeply rooted in our temporal consciousness, which manifests through memory. Our lives are inexorably tied to time, sculpted by its passage. The mind, nourished by a series of past experiences, acts as a mirror of the moments lived. In fact, according to Paul Ricoeur, even forgetting is a temporal phenomenon, and precisely because of this, the individual must distance themselves from the historical fact to be able to remember it. But to remember it, it is essential to forget it, that is, forgetting is fundamental to memory. Thus, the present is but a bridge between what was and what will be, imbuing every aspect of our being with the essence of time.

Without this temporal dimension, thought would lose its context, as it is nourished by the sequence of accumulated experiences stored in memory. Memory, therefore, reveals itself as a direct projection of time, which leads us to distinguish between two variants of it: chronological time, observable on the clock, and psychological time, anchored in memory. In contemplating the nature of time, we do not discern chronological time, that measured by calendars, a cultural construct rooted in conventions that define units like hours, minutes, days, and years. Such collective consensus enables the coordination of our actions, allowing us to adhere to commitments and engage in the mechanisms of society. Chronological time is defined by the movement of the hands on the clock, acting as a quantifiable measure at the service of humanity to organize the duration of its actions and natural cycles. Ignoring the chronological aspect would be a fallacy, as it would imply relearning existence at every moment.

Psychological time, for its part, emerges as a construct of our own psyche. In the absence of reflection, time fades away, transforming into an echo of what once was, a fusion of yesterday and now that shapes tomorrow. Psychological time resides in the internal sphere of each individual, framing their thoughts, aspirations, nostalgias, and memories. This constitutes the thread that connects each reflection, places ideas in time, and guarantees uninterrupted continuity. Past experiences and conceptions influence our current thinking and shape our expectations. This psychological time manifests both in hope and fear, functioning as a catalyst to materialize our desires while simultaneously evoking the fear of death, abandonment, and exclusion, thereby establishing a perpetual struggle between the desire for hope and the avoidance of fear. That is why Heidegger will say in *Being and Time* that fear (of death, of one's own death) binds human beings to the future, while guilt condemns them to the past, that is, to finitude.

Moreover, psychological time acts as a transformation mechanism, driving changes in our way of life, character, and social interactions. It translates into mental goals whose realization is indefinitely postponed, relegating to the future what "ought to be" in the present. Therefore, it encompasses the past, present, and future. Essentially, psychological time operates as an imaginary construction that allows us to justify our actions, find comfort, or defer decisions. It becomes a subterfuge to detach us from immediate reality, allowing us to retreat into a self-constructed, personalized ideal. In harmony with the present, the act of remembering gives rise to the future, shaping the course of thought, a path forged by our consciousness. The development of thought involves a progression through psychological time; however, true happiness transcends the past and the future, for it resides in the eternal now, a domain free from time.

It is possible to observe that, in moments of pure joy and pleasure, when we experience full happiness, the notion of time dissolves, with only the present moment prevailing. The mind reappears when it tries to survive and perpetuate itself. However, in the now, the mind disappears, and thus the egoic phenomenon fades away. In the Bhagavad Gita, it is said:

न त्वेवाहं जातु नासं न त्वं नेमे जनाधिपाः ।
न चैव नभविष्यामः सर्वे वयमतः परम् ॥

na tvevāhaṁ jātu nāsaṁ
na tvaṁ neme janādhipāḥ
na caiva na bhaviṣyāmaḥ
sarve vayam ataḥ param

Chapter 34: The transcendence of time

> Never was there a time when I did not exist, nor you, nor all these kings; nor in the future shall any of us cease to be.
> (Bhagavad Gita, 2.12)

In this verse, the individuality of Kṛṣṇa, Arjuna, and all the kings is mentioned in relation to both the past and the future. However, no individuality is mentioned in the present moment. Because, in the now, the mind, and thus the individuality of the *ahaṅkāra*, evaporates. By renouncing all attachment to the mind, positioning ourselves as mere spectators at the summit while the mind remains immersed in the shadowed valleys, we enter into that state of being in which all questions dissipate. By assuming solely the role of observer, thought dissolves. We disappear when we remain on the sunlit peaks, unbound to anything—be it good or bad, sacred or profane, spiritual or material. We become no one, without a past and stripped of any future, and thus, without a present. However, in its attempt to prolong those moments, the mind interferes in the present with memory and desire, accumulating new experiences and generating time with them. Thus, time is configured through our constant search for "more," being both an acquisition and a detachment that, ironically, continues to be a mental conquest.

Therefore, the mere act of submitting the mind to the temporal framework, of placing thought within the limits of memory, does not succeed in revealing the timeless dimension. The prevailing conviction among us holds that time is a crucial factor for growth and personal metamorphosis. We begin from a state of being toward a desired goal, firmly believing that time is a fundamental component of this process. We are trapped by greed, which drags us into states of confusion, opposition, dispute, and suffering; consequently, to evolve into a state of "absence of greed," we consider time an indispensable resource. It is assumed that time serves as a catalyst for development, to transform us into something different from what we are.

However, we face the dilemma that, by nature, we are beings marked by violence, greed, envy, anger, vices, and passions. We seek to change because our present situation is unsatisfactory; it generates conflict and agitation. In the face of this discontent with our current state, we wish to attain a higher, nobler, more ideal stage. The motivation to transform arises from pain, discomfort, and discord. However, if we postulate that time is the solution to the conflict, we remain trapped in its spiral. One might argue that it will take twenty days or twenty years to overcome the conflict and change our being, but throughout that time, we will remain submerged in the conflict; thus, time does not create transformation. Using time as a tool to achieve a particular quality, virtue, or state of being is equivalent to postponing or evading the reality of what is. It is crucial to understand this point.

The problem arises because when we practice nonviolence for a period of time, we reveal a constant attempt to avoid conflict. This is what Heraclitus means when he says that to have hope, one must renounce time. It is argued that it is essential to resist conflict to overcome it, and time is required for such resistance. But this resistance itself constitutes a form of conflict. Energy is invested in opposing what is called greed, envy, or violence, thereby maintaining the mind in a state of conflict. Therefore, it is crucial to recognize the illusion of depending on time to overcome violence. Only when we accept violence as an integral part of ourselves can we free ourselves from this cycle. No psychological disturbance fades by striving to make it disappear, but only by embracing it deep within.

The time of meditation

The key to unraveling any dilemma, whether human or scientific, lies in having a serene mind. A mind open to understanding is required, not one that closes or tries to force concentration, for the latter is simply another form of resistance. My mind plunges into a calm state when I genuinely want to understand something. This mental stillness is similar to what we experience when listening to music that pleases us; in those moments, our mind does not wander, but fully concentrates on the auditory experience. In the same way, when we face conflict without depending on time, confronting reality as it is, our mind calms automatically, reaching a state of tranquility and peace. By abandoning the idea of using time as a mutational vehicle and recognizing the futility of such an approach, we face reality directly. True understanding will remain elusive as long as the mind remains trapped in conflict, busy criticizing, resisting, and condemning. A sincere interest in understanding reality as it is naturally leads to a profound mental stillness. When the mind ceases its resistance, its evasion, its rejection or condemnation of reality and remains passively attentive, it is then, and only then, that delving into the problem brings about a transformation.

In our objective perception, we interpret time as the process of moving from one location to another. In the physical context, this translates into a change of position within space. The nonexistence of space negates the possibility of external movement. However, mental displacement occurs in a different sphere: that of time. Without the presence of time, internal movement becomes unfeasible. Time, then, functions as a mental space in which we move from one instant to another, from one day to the next, in a continuous flow of moments. Thus, time becomes the stage of our inner world. An introspection will reveal a constant navigation between the past and the future, in a balance between what was lived and what is desired, what is remembered and what is longed for. This swaying uses the present moment merely as a threshold, a provisional means. For the mind, the present has no inherent entity; it is simply a transition point to the past or the future. The mind is perpetually projected toward other times, unable to reside in the current moment.

It is essential to understand that the present is static, a temporal point where mobility does not exist. The now is always a unique instant, and we never coexist in more than one moment. There is no "here" and "there" in the present; there is only "here." This reality of the present time emphasizes that our existence unfolds invariably in a single continuous instant, trapped in an uninterrupted sequence of moments without the possibility of internal movement. The mind, dependent on the dynamics of movement for its functioning, is thus incapable of acting in the present. The mind can return to the past, an immense deposit of memories and experiences. Similarly, it can project itself into the future, which is nothing more than a recreation of our past experiences, filtered by our desires for repetition or evasion. For example, the desire to relive a past love becomes a future hope. In this way, the future is erected as a projection of our past, facilitating our navigation through it. But the mind is not limited to the future of this life; it extends its projections beyond death, imagining utopias and future existences. Dissatisfied with a limited future, the mind extends the notion of time beyond earthly life and all its concepts and boundaries.

Both the past and the future present themselves as broad domains accessible for mental displacement. However, in the present, this movement halts. Stillness becomes the essence of being in the now, which constitutes the second dimension of peace. A state of absolute calm is attained by remaining in the present instant, in the here and now. There is no alternative nor another path to complete tranquility. Internal transformation is only possible in the now, not in the future; renewal must occur in the present moment, and it cannot be postponed. If one experiences what has been described, one discovers that instant regeneration occurs, and something new and fresh emerges; this is so because the mind remains serene when it is genuinely interested in understanding.

Many of us fear that understanding will completely transform our lives. That is why we resort to time or ideals as a defense mechanism to resist change. The great Lutheran theologian Ebeling once said that the human being breaks with productive capitalist time through the concept of "moment." The moment has no measure; thus, by living by moments, the human being breaks with that logic of productive time.

Thus, genuine transformation never occurs in the future or in a defined, delimited, and measurable future. It is only possible in the present, the moment, which is not measurable. Those who rely on time as the path to happiness are actually deceiving themselves, for they remain in a state of ignorance and, therefore, in perpetual conflict. As long as time is considered a tool to achieve goals, such as the understanding of truth, divine knowledge, or revelation, the mind will remain trapped in its own constructions. Only a mind that has been renewed and stripped of the concept of time, that is free from any projection and immersed in profound internal silence, can transcend its limitations. On the other hand, those who understand that time does not resolve our conflicts and who relinquish illusions naturally draw closer to deep understanding. Then the mind, without methods or effort, enters into genuine stillness, free from escape or resistance. When the search for answers ceases, and the flight from questions ends, inner regeneration becomes possible. In that meditative serenity, the recognition of Truth can occur. And it is the Truth—not the yearning for freedom—that truly liberates us.

Thought, with its load of memories, prejudices, hopes, and isolations, encapsulates our lived experience of time. In aspiring to a timeless dimension, an inescapable question arises: can the mind completely free itself from experience, from knowledge, and from past images that together constitute time? Therefore, time reveals itself as thought, thought as memory, memory as echoes of the past, and the past, in essence, as nonexistent. All of this forms time: mere illusions woven by the mind. The subject must live in this tension, which only disappears in the temporality we spoke of before. This dual dimension of time, one being psychological time and the other time in the sense of temporality, corresponds to two types of givenness: givenness according to knowledge and givenness according to Being, respectively. The former would be the givenness in the subjective polarity, while the latter would take place from and in Being. For this to be given in knowledge, the givenness must adapt to the intuitive limitations of the subject. It is there where the givenness must be given in humanized terms: the limited must be limited, the infinite must be finitarized. If one aspires to givenness in its pure form, the subject must adapt to Being. In this context, and as we will see next, waiting is situated in the eternal now of Being.

CHAPTER 35

THE ART OF WAITING

The negative waiting

In his books *The Genealogy of Morals* and *Beyond Good and Evil*, Nietzsche criticizes the act of dividing human actions into simply good or bad, an attitude he defined as an oversimplification that avoids the complexity of human existence.[144] Let us imagine that our decisions are like a boat sailing down a river, which is time. We can let the current take us, or we can row in our own direction. If we believe that time does not change, our decisions will seem to lack true significance. But if we believe that we can influence how time flows, then our actions will become much more relevant.

Nietzsche criticizes religions that present time as rigid and immutable. When we conceive of time as motionless and wait passively, we feel lost, like prisoners in a dead-end corridor. The resulting inactivity distances us from ourselves and exiles us from the present. Thus, time becomes meaningless and transforms into a sterile succession, incapable of sustaining our experience.

To prevent waiting from paralyzing us, Nietzsche proposes two paths. The first consists of ignoring it, adopting an automatic attitude that frees us from the feeling of being trapped in waiting. The second involves facing it directly, taking the helm of the boat with which we sail down the river of time. The first option can make us indifferent, causing us to lose track of time. The second, on the other hand, allows us to use that time and our actions to shape our lives. Nietzsche urges us not

---

144. Friedrich Nietzsche, *On the Genealogy of Morality*, ed. Keith Ansell-Pearson, trans. Carol Diethe (Cambridge: Cambridge University Press, 2007), I, §§10–11, 20–22.

to let waiting dominate us, but rather to take control of time and live according to our unique perspective and what we truly value.

According to the Gospels, Jesus taught:

> Be dressed for action and have your lamps lit; be like those who are waiting for their master to return from the wedding banquet, so that they may open the door for him as soon as he comes and knocks.
>
> (Luke, 12:35–36)

The way Jesus spoke of waiting in his stories is very different from the common idea of simply doing nothing, feeling boredom or anxiety. Waiting is not just sitting and dreaming about the future; seeing the present as something that hinders us from achieving what we desire. We can call this notion of waiting "negative waiting," as it denies and avoids the present, as well as the meditative state in which only *Being* and the sacred can be lived. Contrary to this negative waiting, Jesus spoke of a very special kind of waiting, which requires being completely alert and ready for anything that might happen at every moment. If we are not fully focused and calm, we may miss the unexpected.

This type of waiting implies an openness or total predisposition to the now, a surrender without distractions, without thinking about the past or the future. In this authentic waiting, there is no place for guilt, stress, or fear, only a clear consciousness of the moment. In this state, the entire complexity of who we are, with our past and our future plans, fades away, although this does not mean that we lose our value. In reality, the opposite occurs: in that present clarity, we experience—perhaps for the first time—the essence of our being and the true richness of the present moment.

Jesus tells a story about five women who were not prepared because they did not have enough oil to keep their lamps burning, which means they were not truly present or aware. Because of this, they missed an important celebration. In contrast, the other five women were ready and attentive. Similarly, Judaism introduces the same idea. We read in Habakkuk:

Chapter 35: The art of waiting

כִּי עוֹד חָזוֹן לַמּוֹעֵד וְיָפֵחַ לַקֵּץ וְלֹא יְכַזֵּב אִם יִתְמַהְמָהּ חַכֵּה לוֹ כִּי בֹא יָבֹא לֹא יְאַחֵר:

(חבקוק ב', ג')

For the vision is waiting for the appointed time. It speaks of the end and will not prove false. If it tarries, wait for it, because it will certainly come and will not delay.

(Habakkuk, 2:3)

הַיְסוֹד הַשְּׁנֵים עָשָׂר, יְמוֹת הַמָּשִׁיחַ. וְהוּא לְהַאֲמִין וּלְאַמֵּת שֶׁיָּבוֹא, וְלֹא יַחְשֹׁב שֶׁיִּתְאַחֵר, "אִם יִתְמַהְמָהּ חַכֵּה לוֹ" (חבקוק ב', ג'). וְלֹא יָשִׂים לוֹ זְמַן, וְלֹא יַעֲשֶׂה לוֹ סְבָרוֹת בְּמִקְרָאוֹת לְהוֹצִיא זְמַן בִּיאָתוֹ.

(רמב"ם, הקדמה לפרק חלק, משנה סנהדרין, פרק י')

The twelfth principle, "the messianic era," is to believe and to confirm that he will come and not to think that he is late. "If he tarries, wait for him" (Habakkuk, 2:3) and do not give him a [set] time and do not create analyses from the verses to extrapolate the time of his coming.

(Maimonides, Introduction to *Perek Ḥekek, Mishnah Sanhedrin*, chapter 10)

אֲנִי מַאֲמִין בֶּאֱמוּנָה שְׁלֵמָה בְּבִיאַת הַמָּשִׁיחַ, וְאַף עַל פִּי שֶׁיִּתְמַהְמֵהַּ, עִם כָּל זֶה אֲחַכֶּה לוֹ בְּכָל יוֹם שֶׁיָּבוֹא.

(סידור התפילה, י"ג העיקרים, עיקר י"ב)

I believe with complete faith in the coming of the Messiah and even though he may tarry, nevertheless, I yearn every day for his coming.

(Book of Prayers, The 13 principles, principle 12)

אָמַר רַבִּי שְׁמוּאֵל בַּר נַחְמָנִי אָמַר רַבִּי יוֹנָתָן: תִּיפַּח עַצְמָן שֶׁל מְחַשְּׁבֵי קִצִּין שֶׁהָיוּ אוֹמְרִים כֵּיוָן שֶׁהִגִּיעַ (אֶת) הַקֵּץ וְלֹא בָא שׁוּב אֵינוֹ בָא. אֶלָּא חַכֵּה לוֹ שֶׁנֶּאֱמַר (חבקוק ב', ג'): "אִם יִתְמַהְמָהּ חַכֵּה לוֹ". שֶׁמָּא תֹּאמַר: אָנוּ מְחַכִּין וְהוּא אֵינוֹ מְחַכֶּה? תַּלְמוּד לוֹמַר (ישעיהו ל', י"ח): "וְלָכֵן יְחַכֶּה ה' לַחֲנַנְכֶם וְלָכֵן יָרוּם לְרַחֶמְכֶם". וְכִי מֵאַחַר שֶׁאָנוּ מְחַכִּים וְהוּא מְחַכֶּה– מִי מְעַכֵּב? מִדַּת הַדִּין מְעַכֶּבֶת. וְכִי מֵאַחַר שֶׁמִּדַּת

Section VIII: Phenomenology of time

הַדִּין מְעַכֶּבֶת– אָנוּ לָמָּה מְחַכִּין? לְקַבֵּל שָׂכָר. שֶׁנֶּאֱמַר (שם): "אַשְׁרֵי כָּל חוֹכֵי לוֹ".
(תלמוד בבלי, מסכת סנהדרין, צ"ז, ב')

Rabbi Shmuel bar Naḥmani says that Rabbi Yonatan says: "May those who calculate the end of days be cursed, as they would say: since the end of days that they calculated arrived and the Messiah did not come, that he will no longer come at all." Rather, the proper behavior is to continue to wait for his coming, as it is stated (Habakkuk, 2:3): "If it tarry, wait for it." To say: "We are expectantly awaiting the end of days and the Holy One, Blessed be He, is not awaiting the end of days and does not want to redeem His people?" Another verse (Isaiah, 30:18) teaches us: "And therefore will the Lord wait, to be gracious to you; and therefore, will He be exalted, to have mercy upon you; for the Lord is a God of judgment; happy are all they who wait for Him. And seemingly, since we are awaiting the end of days and the Holy One, Blessed be He, is also awaiting the end of days, who is preventing the coming of the Messiah? It is the divine attribute of judgment that prevents his coming. And since the attribute of judgment prevents the coming of the Messiah and we are not worthy of redemption, why do we await his coming daily? We do so to receive a reward, as it is stated: 'Happy are all they who wait for Him.'"

(*Talmud Bavli*, "*Sanhedrin*," 97b)

We spend much time waiting negatively for things in our lives, from short waits like standing in line or being stuck in traffic, to long waits like wishing for a vacation, achieving success at work, or finding deeper meaning in life. In this negative waiting, which only focuses on and alludes to concrete triumphs, we postpone living in the present moment, thinking that our "true" life will begin after these big things we are waiting for happen. This feeling, rooted in the future and in dissatisfaction with the present, prevents us from fully enjoying the life we are living now.

However, true wealth has nothing to do with what we expect to achieve in the future, but with feeling grateful and valuing what we have right now. Realizing how good we have it in our current life, such as where we are, who we are, what we do, and what we have, awakens gratitude for our existence and our possessions. This recognition and enjoyment of the present is what it truly means to be rich. To enjoy the present reveals a true wealth we already possess. Moreover, this disposition draws blessings we did not foresee.

When we feel dissatisfied or upset by what we lack, we may give in to the desire to get more money, thinking it will make us happy. But even with much money, we can still feel empty inside, as if something is missing that money cannot buy. The things we buy with money may be exciting for a moment, but that happiness does not last, and soon, we want more. If we do not live in the present and appreciate what life offers us now, we miss experiencing true fulfillment. When we notice that we are actively waiting for what we have conceptualized, we must return to the present and, quite simply, live and delight in being who we are. Being in the current moment removes the need to wait negatively for what we lack. Impatient waiting is always related to desire and dissatisfaction. In authentic waiting, however, if someone is late for an appointment and makes us wait, we will not feel that we were left waiting, but rather, we will enjoy moments in which we simply are living ourselves in an auto-affective way.

Our mental states, such as daydreaming about the past or the future, are ways in which our mind tries to escape the present. These tactics often go unnoticed and become a normal part of our life, creating a kind of constant dissatisfaction that is always there, in the background. If we pay more attention to how we feel mentally and emotionally, we can realize that when our mind strays toward these thoughts, it takes us away from the current moment and from ourselves. This helps us return to the present and set aside those distractions.

But we must be careful, because our ego, that part of us that feels dissatisfied, always desires immeasurably and is defined by our thoughts and how time passes. It sees the present as a danger to its existence and will try by all means to distract us from the now, taking us back to that illusion that time is the most important thing. To recognize that the present is the only moment in which the ego loses its power over us allows for a life of authenticity and connection with the true self. To wait authentically is to expect nothing, because it is in that expectation of nothing that we live our lives to the fullest.

From waiting to the dichotomy of the multiple and the One

In many spiritual and religious practices, such as meditation, there is a sort of waiting, a preparation to receive the transcendental, but it should not be understood as a series of actions meant to hasten its manifestation. The focus does not fall on the actions or methods to provoke the manifestation of a divinity, but on preparing ourselves adequately for it. This conception, which could be mistakenly interpreted as an invitation to "passivizing" inaction, arises from the complexity of the Greek term *páscho*, historically used to form the concept of passivity. Such complexity is evidenced in the duality of its meaning, which, on the one hand, implies "to suffer," and, on the other, applies technically to the grammatical voice of "passive." This double interpretation of the term has been crucial in the conceptualization of passivity throughout history. In a sense, we can say that a dynamic interaction is established between the concept of *pragmatón*, referring to the actions an individual carries out, and pathos, which alludes to the experiences one suffers or the situations one undergoes. *Pragmatón* encompasses all activities generated by personal will and execution, while pathos represents the circumstances or events that impact the individual externally, without them necessarily playing an active role in their occurrence. It is crucial to understand that *páscho*, in the sense of pathos, refers to the sensitivity necessary to receive environmental impressions. This becomes evident in its derived noun, pathos, which itself evokes the notion of "affection" and represents the reception capacity.

Therefore, a pathos disposition does not suggest passivity, but rather an integral openness to full revelation, a willingness to be permeable to the essence of Being. It is worth noting, however, that the Greek term *páscho*, meaning "passivity," carries the dual meaning we have mentioned of *pragmatón* and pathos, establishing a dialectical or continuous interaction between the agent and the events that affect them, highlighting how human experience is shaped both by personal actions and external influences.

This concept gains greater depth when contemplating complex cognitive processes, such as reference, combination, and relation, elements that Husserl suggests in *Aufsätze und Vorträge* are integrated by consciousness into a coherent and uncomplicated objectivity. To delve into these more sophisticated aspects of cognition, it is necessary to turn to epistemology, or the theory of knowledge, to understand how these cognitive processes form part of a complex understanding structure. This branch of philosophy examines how the individual achieves an integrated and synthetic understanding of the world. It emphasizes the importance of receptivity and openness in the process of knowledge, in contrast to a mere passive accumulation of information.

In his work *The Degrees of Knowledge*,[145] Jacques Maritain offers a deep perspective on the structure and hierarchy of knowledge. In this conception, basic cognitive functions such as physical sensations and thoughts are distinguished from higher cognitive functions or spiritual understandings, including reference, combinations, and relations. These elements are not understood as isolated entities, but as parts of complex structures integrated within the unity of consciousness that constitutes a synthetic and simple objectivity.

Cognition is articulated on a sort of scale that ranges from diversity, at its lower end, to pure unity at its pinnacle. This scale symbolizes a progressive transition from the perception of multiplicity toward the apprehension of unity. The lower cognitions, located near the start of this scale, are linked to sensory perception and capture the objective diversity of the phenomenal world. In contrast, higher cognitions, or intelligible perceptions, are associated with the higher steps of the scale and are capable of perceiving the unity underlying this diversity. This model suggests that our ability to perceive unity in multiplicity increases as we ascend in

---

145. Jacques Maritain, *The Degrees of Knowledge*, trans. W. T. H. Jackson (London: Geoffrey Bles, 1937).

the cognitive hierarchy. At the pinnacle of this hierarchy is absolute perception, which manages to grasp absolute unity, reflecting the unity of consciousness at its highest level.

This gnoseological categorization by Maritain is directly related to the introduction of the concept of substance as the supreme genus of all things, which, as such, marks a crucial moment in the philosophical tradition, with roots already found in the thought of Plato and Aristotle. Later, in the 3rd century CE, the Neoplatonic philosopher Porphyry expanded this conceptual framework with his own explanatory model, known as the Tree of Porphyry. This model presents a hierarchical structure in the form of a tree, where all of existence is organized in a spectrum from the most general to the most particular. Within this scheme, three fundamental concepts are employed: genus, species, and individual, establishing a progression from broad and encompassing categories to singular and concrete entities. The Tree of Porphyry serves as a tool to understand how different categories of being relate to one another, providing a method for classifying and understanding reality in terms of its levels of generality and particularity.

The Tree of Porphyry represents a significant advancement in the philosophical and classificatory understanding of reality, incorporating a nominalist perspective that holds that general concepts do not exist independently of things, but are merely names used to designate sets of properties grouped in things. This approach marked a turning point in the way the relationship between concepts and observable reality was conceived. In constructing his classification of existence, Porphyry reinterpreted and synthesized the views of Plato and Aristotle. From Plato, he took the general notion of substance, while from Aristotle, he adopted the analysis of categories, applying them specifically to the idea of substance. This fusion of ideas contributed to the creation of a referential model for philosophy and the natural sciences, influencing future taxonomies in the study of nature.

Porphyry distinguished two primary categories of substance: composed and simple. Composed substances refer to bodily entities, which are further divided into animate and inanimate. In turn, animate bodies are classified as sensitive or insensitive, with an example of the former being an animal's body. At the top of this hierarchy, animals are distinguished as rational and irrational, placing humans as rational animals. This classificatory system is based on dichotomies and Aristotelian logic, operating through a series of subdivisions that define the properties an entity may or may not possess. Thus, the identity of a specific individual is understood through a chain of underlying logical concepts that define them in terms of rationality, animality, sensitivity, animation, vitality, and composition. All these notions are integrated under the broad concept of substance. Therefore, this model establishes a relationship of subordination that allows for an understanding of the complexity of Being in terms of an ordered and logically coherent structure.

This approach is crucial to understanding how we conceptualize our experience of the world and underscores the importance of hierarchy in our cognitive faculties. "Lower cognitions" deal with tangible phenomenal reality, recognizing an objective reality defined by names and forms. "Higher cognitions," on the other hand, transcend the sensible and apprehend reality in an integrated and holistic manner. They seek the unity underlying the apparent diversity of the world, perceiving the subtler aspects of reality until they reach "absolute cognition," which is the perception of the unity of consciousness.

It is worth noting, however, that the apprehension of the absolute unity of consciousness requires both sensory perception and cognition that transcends the sensible. As is often the case in meditation, by directing our attention first to sensations such as the breath and then to thoughts or emotions, it is possible to approach perception itself. It is a process in which the pinnacle consists of attention resting upon attention itself, perception self-perceiving, or consciousness being conscious of itself.

This idea of complicity between physical and bodily sensitivity on the one hand, and transcendental intelligibility on the other, also appears in the Old Testament and the Talmud. Specifically, we will focus on what is traditionally called "Jacob's dream," which,

Section VIII: Phenomenology of Time

according to certain interpretations, allows us to think about how the apprehension of absolute unity, that is, of God, is not foreign to sensory perception. In other words, absolute unity is apprehended from multiplicity, which in turn is perceived and understood through absolute unity.

וַיִּפְגַּע בַּמָּקוֹם וַיָּלֶן שָׁם כִּי־בָא הַשֶּׁמֶשׁ וַיִּקַּח מֵאַבְנֵי הַמָּקוֹם וַיָּשֶׂם מְרַאֲשֹׁתָיו וַיִּשְׁכַּב בַּמָּקוֹם הַהוּא: וַיַּחֲלֹם וְהִנֵּה סֻלָּם מֻצָּב אַרְצָה וְרֹאשׁוֹ מַגִּיעַ הַשָּׁמָיְמָה וְהִנֵּה מַלְאֲכֵי אֱלֹהִים עֹלִים וְיֹרְדִים בּוֹ: וְהִנֵּה ה' נִצָּב עָלָיו וַיֹּאמַר אֲנִי ה' אֱלֹהֵי אַבְרָהָם אָבִיךָ וֵאלֹהֵי יִצְחָק הָאָרֶץ אֲשֶׁר אַתָּה שֹׁכֵב עָלֶיהָ לְךָ אֶתְּנֶנָּה וּלְזַרְעֶךָ: וְהָיָה זַרְעֲךָ כַּעֲפַר הָאָרֶץ וּפָרַצְתָּ יָמָּה וָקֵדְמָה וְצָפֹנָה וָנֶגְבָּה וְנִבְרְכוּ בְךָ כָּל־מִשְׁפְּחֹת הָאֲדָמָה וּבְזַרְעֶךָ: וְהִנֵּה אָנֹכִי עִמָּךְ וּשְׁמַרְתִּיךָ בְּכֹל אֲשֶׁר־תֵּלֵךְ וַהֲשִׁבֹתִיךָ אֶל־הָאֲדָמָה הַזֹּאת כִּי לֹא אֶעֱזָבְךָ עַד אֲשֶׁר אִם־עָשִׂיתִי אֵת אֲשֶׁר־דִּבַּרְתִּי לָךְ: וַיִּיקַץ יַעֲקֹב מִשְּׁנָתוֹ וַיֹּאמֶר אָכֵן יֵשׁ ה' בַּמָּקוֹם הַזֶּה וְאָנֹכִי לֹא יָדָעְתִּי: וַיִּירָא וַיֹּאמַר מַה־נּוֹרָא הַמָּקוֹם הַזֶּה אֵין זֶה כִּי אִם־בֵּית אֱלֹהִים וְזֶה שַׁעַר הַשָּׁמָיִם: וַיַּשְׁכֵּם יַעֲקֹב בַּבֹּקֶר וַיִּקַּח אֶת־הָאֶבֶן אֲשֶׁר־שָׂם מְרַאֲשֹׁתָיו וַיָּשֶׂם אֹתָהּ מַצֵּבָה וַיִּצֹק שֶׁמֶן עַל־רֹאשָׁהּ: וַיִּקְרָא אֶת־שֵׁם־הַמָּקוֹם הַהוּא בֵּית־אֵל וְאוּלָם לוּז שֵׁם־הָעִיר לָרִאשֹׁנָה:
(בראשית כ"ח, י'-י"ט)

And he came to the place and he spent the night there, for the sun had set. And he took of the stones of the place and set them under his head, and he lay down in that place. And he dreamed, and, behold, a ladder set in the earth, and its top reaching the heavens, and, behold, angels of God ascending and descending upon it. And, behold, the Lord was standing over him, and He said: I am the Lord, the God of Abraham your father, and the God of Isaac. The land on which you lie, to you shall I give it, and to your descendants. And your descendants will be as dust of the earth, and you will burst forth, west and east and north and south. And all the families of the earth will bless themselves in you and in your descendants. And, behold, I am with you, and I shall keep you, wherever you go, and I shall return you to this land; for I shall not forsake you until I have done what I have spoken concerning you. And Jacob awoke from his sleep and he said: In truth, the Lord is in this place, and I did not know it. And he feared and he said:

Chapter 35: The Art of Waiting

How awesome is this place! This is none other than the house of God, and this is the gate of heaven. And Jacob arose early in the morning and he took the stone that he had placed under his head and he set it up as a monument and he poured oil on its top. And he called the name of that place Beth-El ("the house of God"), whereas Luz had been the name of the city in the beginning.

(Genesis, 28:11–19)

The *Gemara* explains another verse from Jacob's dream.

"הָאָרֶץ אֲשֶׁר אַתָּה שֹׁכֵב עָלֶיהָ" וְגוֹ' (בראשית כ"ח, י"ג). מַאי רְבוּתֵיהּ? אָמַר רַבִּי יִצְחָק: מְלַמֵּד שֶׁקִּפְּלָהּ הַקָּדוֹשׁ בָּרוּךְ הוּא לְכָל אֶרֶץ יִשְׂרָאֵל וְהִנִּיחָהּ תַּחַת יַעֲקֹב אָבִינוּ וכו'.

(תלמוד בבלי, חולין צ"א, ב')

"The land upon which you lie [...]" (Genesis, 28:13). [The *Gemara* asks]: "What is the greatness of this promise?" [i.e., why is it expressed in this way despite the fact that in a literal sense Jacob was lying on a very small amount of land?]. Rabbi Yitzḥak says: "This teaches that the Holy One, Blessed be He, folded up the entirety of the Land of Israel and placed it under Jacob, our patriarch, etc."

(*Talmud Bavli*, "*Hullin*," 91b)

The *Gemara* cites another exposition of Rabbi Yitzḥak to explain an apparent contradiction between two verses pertaining to this incident.

כְּתִיב "וַיִּקַּח מֵאַבְנֵי הַמָּקוֹם" וּכְתִיב "וַיִּקַּח אֶת הָאֶבֶן" אָמַר רַבִּי יִצְחָק מְלַמֵּד שֶׁנִּתְקַבְּצוּ כָּל אוֹתָן אֲבָנִים לְמָקוֹם אֶחָד וְכָל אַחַת וְאַחַת אוֹמֶרֶת עָלַי יַנִּיחַ צַדִּיק זֶה רֹאשׁוֹ תָּנָא. וְכֻלָּן נִבְלְעוּ בְּאֶחָד.

(תלמוד בבלי, חולין צ"א, ב')

It is written: "And he took of the stones of the place" (Genesis, 28:11). And it is written: "and he took the stone"

(Genesis, 28:18). [The first verse indicates that Jacob took several stones, whereas the latter verse indicates that he took only one stone]. Rabbi Yitzḥak says: "This teaches that all those stones gathered to one place and each one said: 'Let this righteous man place his head upon me.' And it was taught: And all of them were absorbed into one rock."

(*Talmud Bavli*, "*Hullin*," 91b)

That is to say, God situates diversity in the One.

The expectation of the unexpected

In his later writings, Husserl directly addressed the problems that his phenomenology encounters as it progresses. One of them is related to time, and which we have already introduced in previous sections, can now be reformulated as follows: How can Husserl's phenomenology account for that transcendental dimension of consciousness, understood as time itself, when the internal time of consciousness, as an object of knowledge, always exceeds the limits of intuition? In other words, how can consciousness apprehend itself if, when it attempts to turn upon itself to apprehend itself, what is given cannot be given to us as a phenomenon, but rather stands out because of its excess beyond it? Precisely due to this problem, Marion introduces the notion of the "saturated phenomenon," that is, a phenomenon that not only appears (*phainómenon*) but, in appearing, also incorporates what overflows and exceeds the phenomenon.

In response to this, in his essay *Zur phänomenologischen Reduktion* (included in *Husserliana* XXXIV), Husserl guides us toward the transcendence of a mere reduction to the depth of consciousness, promoting an approach to the vital core of a "present" through what he calls "radical reduction." In this framework, and in light of the phenomena of ordinary experience, now seen as phenomena that become saturated and surpass any meaningful anticipation, intuition is revealed as insufficient. This excess implies that Being always contains more than what is accessible to the reflective consciousness of the phenomenon. This concept is illustrated by an anecdote told by Saint Augustine. A child dug a hole in the sand on the beach. With his small bucket, he tirelessly carried water from the ocean to fill it. His father asked him what he was trying to do. The child replied, "I'm transferring the ocean into this hole." The father smiled and told him it was an impossible task. Then the child looked at him with wisdom and said, "It is just as futile as your attempt to understand God through speculation."

Similarly, revelation is presented as an open process, without an established canon, free from orthodoxies, high priests, or a priestly caste. Revelation stands out precisely because it is indeterminate and inexhaustible, and thus transcends the limits of intuition, that is, the "principle of all principles" of phenomenology, as Husserl had defined it. This step, already outlined by Husserl himself, is of great importance. By not restricting itself to intuition, and accepting revelation and the saturation of the phenomenon, phenomenology accepts transcending its own epistemological limits, opening itself to new terrains and pathways that lead us to accept the impossibility of fully knowing what is revealed. Therefore, it exposes the need to relate to it in ways that do not restrict themselves to the parameters of epistemology.

Opening up to revelation implies, however, suspending all phenomenal objects as we had understood them up until now and accepting the mode in which they give themselves. At the same time, this openness should not be confused with any kind of belief or anticipation. Holding a preconceived belief about the nature or content of revelation in itself obstructs the possibility of truly encountering the Being that reveals itself as such in the revelation. By clinging to personal concepts, the very subject limits the capacity for perception, preventing the necessary openness for the Being to manifest in all its richness.

As we have already mentioned, in one of his most well-known poems, Rilke emphasizes this very idea when he asserts: "While you do not collect what you yourself cast, everything will be just skill and insignificant loot." The expectation or anticipation of what revelation must or can be leads us away from true waiting, directing us toward our own notions, beliefs, and fantasies with which we then predesign what is expected. Contrary to anticipation, the authentic waiting of meditation is one that waits without expecting anything or anyone specific, thought or imagined. This is the authentic wait, which precedes every "I," as Heraclitus has rightly pointed out when he states, "If (he) doesn't expect (the) unexpected, (he) will not discover (it) [...]."[146]

"Waiting without waiting for anything" is rooted in the renunciation of all expectation and action. It is a way of waiting free from the anticipation of a "I" that harbors expectations and becomes frustrated when they are not fulfilled. For the subject, however, as a subject, it is impossible to expect the unexpected or the saturated phenomenon without first renouncing both oneself and the very saturated phenomenon. The habitual attitude of anticipation is characterized by the expectation of something absent, not present, which already contains within itself a preconception that distorts the wait as such.

This reasoning highlights the paradox inherent in human nature: the search for completeness or the attainment of existential fullness is often based on the mistaken premise that we lack that primordial essence, when, in reality, this very essence constitutes our intrinsic nature. Unlike the lack upon which anticipation rests, waiting occurs in the astonishment that enables an open disposition to the unexpected of Being.

This position in relation to the waiting for the unexpected, which precedes the "I" and its expectations, imaginations, memories, and fantasies, and thus, all actions of intentional consciousness, does not imply a denial of the latter. R. Walton, for example, speaks of excess and intentionality as realities that coexist through their open, indeterminate, and inexhaustible horizons, in contrast to the tendency of institutionalized religion and organized faith, which have always sought to delimit, exhaust, and dogmatize this relationship, turning revelation into an exclusive and commercial product tied to principles and clouded by dogmatism and fanaticism.

---

146. Heraclitus, *Fragments: A Text and Translation with a Commentary*, trans. T.M. Robinson (Toronto: University of Toronto Press, 1987), (fragment 18, DK 22B18).

The eternal "present"

This complicity between the intentionality of consciousness and the presubjective and pre-egoic wait must be understood, however, as a necessity. In this context, *nous*, or "understanding," with its capacity to reflect upon the intelligible, seeks to transcend the merely sensory. Its goal is to delve into, understand, and, as Henry mentions in *Incarnation*: "lost in the contemplation of the Intelligible, the soul will, like the Intelligible, be eternal." (*s'abîmer avec lui dans la contemplation de l'intelligible, et elle sera éternelle comme lui*).[147] The soul and understanding, intertwined in their complicity, distance themselves from the perishable, the sensory, to enter into the profound contemplation of the intelligible. Thus, they achieve a fusion that transcends temporality and, at the same time, opens up a "present" that overflows and does not respond to temporal or sensory limits. This quest for the intelligible over the sensory underscores a yearning for transcendence and union with the eternal, with which Henry emphasizes the importance of reflection and contemplation in the process of knowledge and revelation.

Transcending and distancing oneself from the sensory does not mean separating from it and alienating it, but transcending its limits. We separate from sensory knowledge without discarding the senses. Just as, when we focus on our own physical breathing, we open ourselves to the deep contemplation of the intelligible without ceasing to breathe. In this separation, consciousness is transfigured, reaching a dimension of eternity similar to that of Being itself and merging with Being to contemplate eternity. Thus, the temporal and spatial limitations of the sensory are transcended in a "present" that is not enslaved by future anticipations nor by the melancholy of the past.

The question that arises for us at this moment is: what is this connection, this complicity, between meditative waiting and intentional thought? Or, in other words, how do presubjectivity

---

147. Michel Henry, *Incarnation: A Philosophy of Flesh*, trans. Karl Hefty (Evanston, IL: Northwestern University Press, 2015), 22.

in meditation and the ego of intentional thought coexist? Henry himself confronts these questions through self-affection, especially when he writes with great beauty:

> *Aucune Vie n'est possible qui ne porte en elle un premier Soi vivant en lequel elle s'éprouve elle-même et se fait vie. Aucune vie sans un vivant mais, de même, aucun vivant en dehors de ce mouvement par lequel la Vie vient en soi en s'éprouvant soi-même dans le Soi de ce vivant, aucun vivant sans la vie.*

> No life is possible that does not carry within itself a first living Self in which it experiences itself and becomes life. No life without a living being, but likewise no living being outside of this movement by which Life comes into being by experiencing itself in the Self of this living being, no living being without life.[148]

In this relationship between life and living being, as Henry describes it, it is established that life cannot exist without a living being to experience it and through which life knows itself. That is, present itself, affirm itself, without being exhausted or limited by time structures. Henry understands life as an external concept and the living being as its internal counterpart. Life needs the living being to comprehend itself, while the living being uses life to exist. Both—life and living being—form a unity composed of two aspects of the same reality. They are intrinsically interdependent.

This analysis extends to the Christian phenomenon, which is characterized by its transcendence beyond the limitations of horizontality, offering a revelation that is both infinite and intangible. We can identify two types of phenomena: the Greek and the Christian. The Greek phenomenon is associated with a human transcendence that seeks to understand the world in terms of proximity, not superiority, symbolizing a horizontal

---

148. Michel Henry, *Incarnation: A Philosophy of Flesh*, trans. Karl Hefty (Evanston, IL: Northwestern University Press, 2015), 35.

transcendence that extends laterally. On the other hand, the Christian phenomenon represents a vertical transcendence that is perceived as a givenness descending from above. In this context, Michel Henry states:

> *Ce qui permet à tout être de se manifester, de devenir 'phénomène', c'est le milieu de visibilité où il peut surgir à titre de présence effective. Le déploiement d'un tel milieu, en tant qu'horizon transcendental de tout être en général, est l'oeuvre de l'être lui-même.*

> What allows any being to manifest itself, to become a "phenomenon," is the medium of visibility where it can emerge as an effective presence. The unfolding of such a medium, as a transcendental horizon for every being in general, is the work of being itself.[149]

From Henry's perspective, there exists a Being that seeks self-knowledge and manifestation, residing in an external realm that transcends our human capacities and faculties. We can only come to know it if it decides to reveal itself, using symbols—visible means through which it makes itself present and known. The symbol is the phenomenon that transforms the invisible into the visible. By giving itself as Being in itself, the symbol encompasses the imperceptible in the perceptible. Our knowledge of what exceeds our perceptual capacities is achieved through a givenness from Being, motivated by its desire to manifest itself and its longing for self-knowledge. The subject cannot undertake any action that precipitates the appearance of Being, as if it were a magician pulling a rabbit out of a hat.

These descriptions, however, can only be understood through the self-givenness of life through the topic of affectivity, which, unlike all action, is a permanent affective experiencing through which life affirms itself in the living being and the latter gains presence

---

149. Michel Henry, *The Essence of Manifestation*, trans. Girard Etzkorn (The Hague: Martinus Nijhoff, 1973). Translation mine.

through life. This positioning of waiting that underlies everything has its roots in phenomenology, but in this case, in Hegel. Thus, Michel Henry writes similarly to Hegel's words in *Phenomenology of Spirit* when he asserts that: "In the manifestation of Being, life captures life":

> *Or à l'apparazîre du monde s'oppose trait pour trait, selon nous, la révélation propre à la vie. Alors que le monde dévoile dans le 'hors-de-soi', en sorte que tout ce qu'il dévoile est extérieur, autre, différent, le premier trait décisif de la révélation de la vie est que celle-ci, qui ne porte en elle aucun écart et ne diffère jamais de soi, ne révèle jamais qu'elle-même. La vie se révèle. La vie est une autorévélation. Autorévélation, quand il s'agit de la vie, veut donc dire deux choses : d'une part, c'est la vie qui accomplit l'œuvre de la révélation, elle est tout sauf un processus anonyme et aveugle. D'autre part, ce qu'elle révèle, c'est elle-même. La révélation de la vie et ce qui se révèle en elle ne font qu'un.*

At the appearance of the world, there opposes exactly, according to us, the revelation proper to life. While the world reveals itself in the *"out-of-itself,"* in such a way that all it reveals is external, other, different, the first decisive trait of the revelation of life is that it, which implies no distance and never differs from itself, never reveals anything but itself. Life reveals itself. Life is a self-revelation. Self-revelation, when it comes to life, therefore means two things: on the one hand, it is life that accomplishes the work of revelation, it is anything but an anonymous and blind process. On the other hand, what it reveals is itself. The revelation of life and what is revealed in it are one and the same.[150]

Let us examine this quote more closely. "At the appearance of the world, there opposes exactly, according to us, the revelation

---

150. Michel Henry, *Fenomenología de la vida I. De la fenomenología*, trad. Javier Teira, Gorka Fernández y Roberto Ranz (Salamanca: Ediciones Sígueme, 2010), 196. Translation mine.

proper to life" refers to the idea that the world, in already Hegelian terminology, is the "not-I." Consciousness is divided into the "I," or that which resides within the bodily limits and consists solely of sensations, and the "not-I," which is referred to as the "world." Therefore, everything objective, observed, or perceived is regarded as external.

Henry also asserts that "the first decisive trait of the revelation of life is that it, which implies no distance and never differs from itself, never reveals anything but itself." This sentence suggests that the difficulty in recognizing consciousness lies in the absence of distance between the observer and the observed. In reality, there is no difference whatsoever between oneself and life, and therefore, the self-givenness of life involves no mediation or act. Life, by being life, gives itself immediately. To properly understand this issue, we can return to Jean-Luc Marion, when he writes that:

> *Une phénoménalité de la givenness peut permettre au phénomène de se montrer en soi et par soi, parce qu'il se donne, mais une phénoménalité de l'objectité ne peut que constituer le phénomène à partir de l'ego d'une conscience qui le vise comme son noème.*

> A phenomenality of givenness can allow the phenomenon to show itself in itself and by itself because it gives itself, but a phenomenality of objectivity can only constitute the phenomenon from the ego of a consciousness that targets it as its noema.[151]

According to Marion's quote, the phenomenon can be perceived in two ways. The first is as an object constituted or imagined by the ego, which only gathers what it has previously projected. The second is as a phenomenon that reveals itself on its own, without the intervention of subjective constitution, and without having been previously conceived in thought, fantasy, or desire. The

---

151. Jean-Luc Marion, *Being Given: Toward a Phenomenology of Givenness*, trans. Jeffrey L. Kosky (Stanford University Press, 2002), 32.

phenomenality of givenness enables the phenomenon to manifest in its own essence, while the phenomenality of objectivity depends on the ego constituting the phenomenon through its own projections, understanding this as its noema or concept. In other words, only what has not been fabricated by the individual, but what is a pure self-affectivity, can be genuinely considered donated.

If we now return to Henry, we will understand in what sense life is immediate self-givenness, without mediation of acts or egos or subjects that design or name it. Life gives itself to the living being without the latter thinking about it or imagining it. Life self-reveals itself, because it is the life that beats underlyingly in the living being to whom it is revealed. In other words, consciousness, now understood as a living being, is inherently aware of itself, not because the ego of consciousness desires it, seeks it, or needs it, but because the itself of consciousness cannot but reveal itself in every consciousness.

This self-revealing of life, therefore, does not respond to intentional acts, but to an affectivity that emerges latent in the waiting of meditation. Through meditation, Being pulses without being the object of any thought or subject. This immediately raises the question of how to distinguish whether an experience, such as one arising in meditation, is an egoistic construction or an authentic reality. Based on what has been said so far, if the meditator actively seeks the experience, it could be considered an invention, since it is the same meditator who precipitates the experience or phenomenon due to an objective they seek to achieve, whatever that may be. On the other hand, that which arises spontaneously, without expectations, is accepted as a givenness, a real and true self-revelation. In authentic meditation, meditators allow themselves to be absorbed in waiting, in the most absolute openness and readiness, prepared to receive. Without projecting themselves or expecting anything, they remain absorbed in an eternal "present."

Bibliography section VIII

- Aristotle. *Physics*. Translated by R. P. Hardie and R. K. Gaye. In *The Complete Works of Aristotle: The Revised Oxford Translation*. Edited by Jonathan Barnes. 2 vols. Princeton: Princeton University Press, 1984.
- Canullo, Francesco Paolo. "Michel Henry: From the Essence of Manifestation to the Essence of Religion." *The Heythrop Journal* 56, no. 2 (2015): 176–86.
- Heraclitus. *Fragments: A Text and Translation with a Commentary*. Translated by T. M. Robinson. Toronto: University of Toronto Press, 1987.
- Henry, Michel. *The Essence of Manifestation*. Translated by Girard J. Etzkorn. The Hague: Nijhoff, 1973.
- Henry, Michel. *Fenomenología de la vida I. De la fenomenología*. Translated by Javier Teira, Gorka Fernández, and Roberto Ranz. Salamanca: Ediciones Sígueme, 2010.
- Henry, Michel. *Incarnation: A Philosophy of Flesh*. Translated by Karl Hefty. Evanston, IL: Northwestern University Press, 2015.
- Maritain, Jacques. *The Degrees of Knowledge*. Translated by W. T. H. Jackson. London: Geoffrey Bles, 1937.
- Marion, Jean-Luc. *Being Given: Toward a Phenomenology of Givenness*. Translated by Jeffrey L. Kosky. Stanford, CA: Stanford University Press, 2002.
- Nietzsche, Friedrich. *On the Genealogy of Morality*. Edited by Keith Ansell-Pearson. Translated by Carol Diethe. Cambridge: Cambridge University Press, 2007.
- Sandywell, Barry. *Presocratic Reflexivity: The Construction of Philosophical Discourse c. 600–450 B.C.* Logological Investigations, vol. 3. 1st ed. London: Routledge, 1996; eBook, 2002.

- Scruggs, Jonathan. "Flesh, Body, World: Michel Henry on Incarnation." *Religions* 14, no. 9 (August 2023): 1109.
- St. Augustine. *Confessions*. Translated by J. G. Pilkington. In Nicene and Post-Nicene Fathers, First Series, vol. 1, edited by Philip Schaff. Buffalo, NY: Christian Literature Publishing Co., 1886.

SECTION IX
PHENOMENOLOGY OF THE SACRED

CHAPTER 36

THE SATURATED PHENOMENON IN THE LIGHT OF HERMENEUTICS

Hermeneutics as clarification of the saturated phenomenon

To express in different terms what was said in the previous chapter, in the exploration of what is revealed to us, it is fundamental to recognize that the nature of givenness is manifested in the complexity of what is given. Thus, any phenomenon, no matter how ordinary, is inextricably linked to the act of givenness. Moreover, as we suggested earlier, the phenomenon is nothing other than its own givenness. This implies that the phenomenon and givenness are indistinguishable, since there can be no phenomenon that either gives itself or does not give itself to consciousness. It is not that we perceive or grasp the universe directly; rather, the universe is given to us, and this giving happens in consciousness, not merely through the senses nor directly before our eyes. It is as if a curtain is drawn, allowing us to access the essence of the objective world.

In this conceptual framework, in which we link self-affectivity with meditation, and the latter with the intentional structure of consciousness, Marion revisits the work of Husserl, and also of Kant, evoking the Kantian distinction between phenomenon and noumenon. Kant defines the phenomenon as that which manifests and is understood.[152] However, what manifests and is understood (the phenomenon) is not the thing in itself. The thing as it is in itself (the noumenon) remains hidden from our cognitive faculties

---

152. Immanuel Kant, *Critique of Pure Reason*, ed. and trans. Paul Guyer and Allen W. Wood (Cambridge: Cambridge University Press, 1998), A249/B305, 346.

due to the limits of human comprehension. In this context, Marion identifies in the saturated phenomenon an inherent tension between the manifest and the hidden, between the phenomenon and the noumenon, to use Kantian terms. He suggests that what is revealed is not precisely identical to what remains veiled. That is, the phenomenon and the noumenon are not simply identifiable, nor is the former an imperfect copy of the latter. At the same time, however, this condition presupposes a disposition toward passivity, which facilitates that the hidden in the manifest may reveal itself in its authenticity. This conceptual map that brings together Kant, Husserl, and Marion is perfectly embodied in hermeneutics, especially in the work of Hans-Georg Gadamer, thanks to which everything said so far makes greater sense.

Hermeneutics is the art of interpreting texts with the aim of understanding their meaning—whether complex or hidden—either within the text itself or as intended by its author. In this context, hermeneutics maintains that it is impossible to assign arbitrary meanings to texts, since our consciousness is fully integrated with the written material. In proceeding to the drafting of a text, we surrender ourselves to this process until we merge with the final product. Thus, the foreign interpretation should not distort the original meaning. If someone interprets an author's words without attending to their context and essence, they will be corrupting the text by projecting their own conceptions onto it. Therefore, rather than the work serving as a portal to a different reality, it merely reflects the reader's subjective universe.

Despite this, the task of objectifying the psyche, which might suggest a shift toward the unconscious, turns out to be feasible, though intricate, according to Dilthey. This process of objectification is based on the objectification of life itself, the starting point for any understanding. Thus, the individual projects their mind outward, acquiring self-perception through alterity. This mechanism of constructing oneself "from the outside in" allows the world reflected by consciousness to acquire an objective character through self-objectification.

CHAPTER 36: THE SATURATED PHENOMENON IN THE LIGHT OF HERMENEUTICS

From the point of view of hermeneutic understanding, to understand what resides within us, it is essential to project our internal essence outward, through the creation of a text or a work of art. When painting, we spill our being onto the canvas and, by analyzing the resulting work, we study ourselves. That work is nothing but the material representation of our Being, transforming us into an object of study. Consequently, the act of creating art becomes the process of objectifying ourselves, of making ourselves an object, "expelling ourselves" in order to be filled with life.

In essence, everything that exists outside is likewise found inside. What is perceived in the environment, identified as objects, has its correspondence within oneself. This reflection highlights the deep interconnectedness between individuals and their environment, suggesting that the barrier between the "I" and the "other" is more permeable than we think. Moreover, understanding of the world and of oneself are intrinsically linked processes. Knowledge of oneself, therefore, is obtained indirectly, through signs and creations, a principle that later influenced Cassirer.

What has been said so far indicates that hermeneutics clearly distinguishes between "explanation," which is always direct and aligns with the natural sciences, and "understanding," which requires mediation and is linked to the sciences of the spirit. The objectification of understanding does not lie in the textual content per se, but in what the text expresses, that is, life performing its own exegesis. For this reason, Wilhelm Dilthey states that life captures life, because it is when we read our own text that our life captures life itself. In any text that speaks of Being, it is the life of Being capturing the life of Being. In philosophy, Being captures Being itself, or, in other words, the spirit knows itself through the history of philosophy. Hegel considered that existence is a historical sequence and said, "life understands life."[153] This idea was vehemently criticized by Nietzsche. In reality, the perceived objective world is nothing but an objectification of our psyche. That is, the world—under the gaze of

---

153. G. W. F. Hegel, *Phenomenology of Spirit*, trans. A. V. Miller (Oxford: Oxford University Press, 1977), 482–93.

hermeneutics—is nothing but objectified consciousness. Everything we perceive around us is our own consciousness projected in which we endow ourselves with meaning.

However, a third party is involved: the reader who interprets the text. The Pietists were the first to emphasize the importance of a psychological interpretation, suggesting that the feelings of the interpreter must resonate with those of the author to achieve true understanding. This notion of hermeneutic empathy, influenced by Pietism, was further developed by Schleiermacher and Dilthey. Gadamer, on the other hand, argues that each era uniquely interprets texts, pointing out that the true meaning of a text, as revealed to the interpreter, is not limited by the circumstances of the author or their original audience. According to him, an author may not be fully aware of the real meaning of their writings, allowing the interpreter, on many occasions, to reach a deeper understanding than the author themselves. This perspective emphasizes that the meaning of a text transcends its creator, an idea that Gadamer considers not only occasional but a constant.

The interaction between text and interpretation becomes evident when recognizing that, often, it is an interpretation that drives the critical creation of the text. This positions Gadamer in line with Derrida's proposal to Heidegger on the *intentio lectoris*, where the text serves merely as a catalyst for subjects to perform a hermeneutics of themselves. In this context, Gadamer takes a step further and questions whether the meaning of a text is limited solely to the "intentional" purpose of the author, or whether understanding involves a recreation of the original work. He suggests that the interpretation by the artist is not a mere reproduction but a new creation that expands the original meaning intended by the author. Gadamer seems to suggest that it is the interpretation of the text that allows the manifest to reveal itself by itself and that, with it, the hidden also emerges; that is, what the authors themselves were not aware they had narrated. A similar idea arises in various Talmudic studies, where we can read:

רַבִּי יוֹחָנָן דִּידֵיהּ אָמַר: "אָנֹכִי", נוֹטָרִיקוֹן: אֲנָא נַפְשִׁי כְּתָבִית יְהָבִית.
(תלמוד בבלי, מסכת שבת, ק"ה, א')

Chapter 36: The saturated phenomenon in the light of hermeneutics

> Rabbi Yoḥanan himself said that the word *anochi* (that begins the Ten Commandments) is an abbreviation for: I, my own Self, wrote and gave [*ana nafshi ketavit yehavit*].
>
> (*Talmud Bavli*, "Shabbat," 105a)

The Rebbe of Lubavitch explains the meaning of the words of Rabbi Yoḥanan:

> פֵּרוּשׁוֹ שֶׁהקב"ה הִכְנִיס אֶת עַצְמוּתוֹ בַּתּוֹרָה, וְכָךְ הוּא גַּם בַּצַּדִּיקִים, שֶׁהֵם עַצְמָם,
> בְּכָל עַצְמוּתָם וּמַהוּתָם, נִמְצָאִים בְּתוֹרָתָם.
> (האדמו"ר מליובביץ, תורת מנחם, י"ב, שנת תשי"ד חלק ג', שיחת ש"פ
> נצבים, כ"ז אלול)

> Meaning, that The Holy One, Blessed be He, inserted his own being in the Torah, and it is the case also with the saints, who, themselves, with all their being and essence, exist in their teachings.
>
> (The Admor of Lubavitch, *Torat Menaḥem*, Volume 12, Year of 5714, part 3, talk of *Parashat Nitzavim*)

What these readings reveal is that we are written letters, a teaching also expressed in the Second Letter to the Corinthians, where we read:

> Our letters are you, written in our hearts, known and read by all men; being manifest that you are the letter of Christ, delivered by us, written not with ink, but with the Spirit of the living God; not in tablets of stone, but in the fleshly tablets of the heart.
>
> (2 Corinthians, 3:2–3)

These two quotes now show us, on a divine level, that "that" which pulses in the human being is Being. In pulsing, Being manifests as such, that is, manifesting and veiling itself at the same time. From a phenomenological perspective, Gadamer's proposal significantly reconfigures the Husserlian vision. He asserts that intentionality itself—where the phenomenon is manifested in consciousness—

encloses an excess: the hidden, that which intentionality itself did not know about. This surplus is more of a necessity than a problem, thanks to which the intentional object, the text, never ceases to offer us meaning, significance, its own life, and ours with it. In fact, as Gadamer himself affirms on several occasions, and as Derrida will later remind us: we are the text, outside of which there is nothing. Gadamer's hermeneutics, in this sense, enriches the phenomenon by keeping it within the limits of intentionality, while at the same time opening it to that dimension of the phenomenon that overflows it and makes it unpredictable, unforeseeable, and hidden within the manifest.

Gadamer's argument now allows us to see that, if we define the horizon by which the manifest must reveal itself, then what is revealed does not do so in its true essence, but rather reflects our own subjectivity. However, by allowing the manifest to reveal itself by itself, we eliminate the distinction between the manifest and the hidden, as well as the distinction between the manifest and ourselves. As a result, we come to be one with what manifests, overcoming the limitations of our own subjectivity to merge with reality as it is.

The condition of impossibility of the sacred

This reading of Gadamer, which in a certain way already opens the door to the notion of the saturated phenomenon that Marion will later expand upon, allows us to delve even further into the act of givenness or the phenomenon as appearance, and its relationship with what it hides. In this context, it should be emphasized that the phenomenon—the text, in Gadamer's terms—is a symbol in which lies whatever cannot be made visible. Meaning, that which, despite being of a phenomenal dimension, cannot manifest itself on its own. That is to say, the invisible, while part of the visible, exceeds it and, as such, remains always invisible.

A second important issue in relation to this is what we might call "the absence of reciprocity." In the perspective of the "subject" that it offers, the gift of revelation is characterized by its nature of not requiring either reciprocity or an active response, but simply being received. Furthermore, the gift must not be retained in memory or considered as evidence of a sacrifice or a symbolic representation, since any symbol carries with it the implicit expectation of compensation. This is also understood in the New Testament, especially in the Letter to the Corinthians, where we read:

> For who makes you differ from another? And what do you have that you did not receive? Now if you did indeed receive it, why do you boast as if you had not received it?
>
> (1 Corinthians, 4:7)

> Every good gift and every perfect gift is from above, and comes down from the Father of lights, with whom there is no variation or shadow of turning.
>
> (James, 1:17)

Symbols should not be kept in memory because they are assumed to be constantly renewed; there is always a new delivery. This concept is reflected in the words of Lamentations, where it speaks of the mercy of the Lord, which is renewed every morning, evidencing His inexhaustible faithfulness:

> חַסְדֵי ה' כִּי לֹא־תָמְנוּ כִּי לֹא־כָלוּ רַחֲמָיו:
> חֲדָשִׁים לַבְּקָרִים רַבָּה אֱמוּנָתֶךָ:
>
> (איכה ג', כ"א-כ"ב)

> By the mercies of the Lord, we are not consumed, because His mercies never fail. They are new every morning; great is Your faithfulness.
>
> (Lamentations, 3:22–23)

This principle is also illustrated in chapter 16 of the Book of Exodus, which recounts how God provided manna from heaven, instructing the people of Israel to gather only what was necessary for the day, without storing any excess for the future. This divine instruction, intended to teach the people's daily dependence on

God's provision, contrasts with the human tendency to retain and accumulate. Despite the divine command, the people's disobedience in storing manna for the next day resulted in the food spoiling, symbolizing the futility of attempting to contain or preserve what is meant to be a perpetual and renewable gift. Likewise, when Jesus asks the Father for "our daily bread," He underscores the importance of trusting in daily provision and not accumulating for the future. It resembles givenness, which should be experienced in the present without clinging to it in memory. This approach to givenness and receiving emphasizes liberation from expectations and openness to the constant renewal of grace.

Revelation also transforms our understanding of temporality. The recognition of our true essence dispels the illusion of past and future, revealing that only the present is real and tangible. Our memories of the past, as well as our expectations for the future, are experiences that occur only in the now, making the present moment the only possible stage for an authentic encounter with reality or life.

By remembering a revelation, we inadvertently relegate it to the past, and any attempt to relive it does not constitute a connection with the present reality but rather with a version of the past that shapes our expectations. Revelation, always present, demands that we refrain from memorizing, storing, or preserving. Authentic revelation is not remembered as a past event, for it is not an act of conventional recollection but a perpetual phenomenon. It is a door that remains unchangeably open to those who wait, predisposed, without projections or expectations, thus challenging the notion that it can be an event confined to the past.

The response to such a gift involves an ontological presence that reflects the action and identity of the ego. Any reaction, no matter how minimal, denotes the egoic presence of action. At the same time, every reaction causes more concealment. In acting, the subject cannot help but project itself onto the phenomenon, further obscuring what is hidden and blurring the phenomenon as a whole under the subjective mantle. Therefore, instead of reacting, the receiver should immerse themselves in passivity, accepting the revelation without trying to possess or define it. We cannot cling to revelations as if they were childhood garments that we try to continue wearing into adulthood. The door to revelation is always open, but the saturated phenomenon it reveals is constantly renewed. The essence of revelation remains unaltered, yet its manifestations are never identical. That is why we depend on its constant revelation to know its nature.

The discussion about the inherent limitations of the concept of the gift, and the subsequent questioning of the philosophical foundations behind the act of thinking and its subject-object logic, marks a deepening critique of traditional structures of thought. Despite Heidegger's attempts to distance himself from these frameworks through his proposals on meditative thinking, the leap, and tautological thinking, these reflections do not fully detach from conventional parameters. This analysis highlights a fundamental challenge in philosophy: to find a mode of thinking that truly transcends the established dynamics and allows us to address the complexity of the gift beyond the restrictions of traditional subject-object logic. We can clearly see this in what Derrida says in dialogue with Marion in the Villanova Talk, when he states:

> I never said there is no gift. No. I said exactly the opposite. What are the conditions for us to say there is a gift, if we cannot determine them theoretically, phenomenologically? It is through the experience of impossibility, that its possibility is possible as impossible.[154]

The reflection on the impossibility of the gift challenges the conceptual frameworks from which it has traditionally been addressed. It highlights the limitations both of the anthropological approach centered on economic exchange and of phenomenology in its conventional form. The proposal to explore the gift through the expansion of phenomenological limits, through existential reduction and orientation toward givenness, as we have done in

---

154. Jacques Derrida and Jean-Luc Marion, "On the Gift," in *God, the Gift, and Postmodernism*, ed. John D. Caputo and Michael J. Scanlon (Bloomington: Indiana University Press, 1999), 60.

this study, seeks to enrich the philosophical exercise. However, these approaches face difficulties in fulfilling their objectives, as they cannot adequately address the dissemination of meaning and the structure of "trace of trace," remaining trapped in nostalgia for the original.

This discussion extends to the concept of the "saturated phenomenon," which becomes conceivable only when the limit of impossibility is reached. The question about the possibility of knowing concrete objects, such as a stone, illustrates that the need for the gift arises precisely when perception and direct experience become impossible. Contrary to Kant, who investigates the conditions of possibility of experience, here the focus is on the condition of impossibility, closely linking it with passivity and the impossibility itself. This issue is precisely the object of reflection in the Gospel of Luke, where we read:

> A certain ruler asked him, saying, "Good Teacher, what shall I do to inherit eternal life?" Jesus said to him, "Why do you call me good? No one is good but One, that is, God. You know the commandments: Do not commit adultery; do not murder; do not steal; do not bear false witness; honor your father and your mother." He said, "All these I have kept from my youth." So when Jesus heard these things, He said to him, "You still lack one thing: Sell all that you have and distribute to the poor, and you will have treasure in heaven; and come, follow me." But when he heard this, he became very sorrowful, for he was very rich. And when Jesus saw that he became very sorrowful, He said, "How hard it is for those who have riches to enter the kingdom of God! For it is easier for a camel to go through the eye of a needle than for a rich man to enter the kingdom of God." And those who heard it said, "Who then can be saved?" But He said, "The things which are impossible with men are possible with God." Then Peter said, "See, we have left all and followed You." So He said to them, "Assuredly, I say to you, there is no one who has left house or parents or brothers or wife or

children, for the sake of the kingdom of God, who shall not receive many times more in this present time, and in the age to come, eternal life.

(Luke, 18)

Accessing Being does not involve obtaining, acquiring, or gaining something, but on the contrary, involves shedding or relinquishing everything. Therefore, the question is about what must be done for Being to be revealed. But there is nothing that the human being can do for Being to be revealed, for only Being can reveal itself.

In the Letter to the Romans, we also read:

What shall we say then that Abraham our father has found according to the flesh? For if Abraham was justified by works, he has something to boast about, but not before God. For what does the Scripture say? Abraham believed God, and it was accounted to him for righteousness. Now to him who works, the wages are not counted as grace but as debt; but to him who does not work but believes on Him who justifies the ungodly, his faith is accounted for righteousness.

(Romans, 4:1–7)

To him who works, the wages are not counted as grace but as debt. And the givenness of Being is not debt but grace. Therefore, any human work does not precede it, and no technique or method can precipitate or accelerate the revelation of Being.

This perspective suggests that Being is not an external object nor does it occupy a place in space. When we seek it through the senses or the mind, we distance ourselves from its essence. Only by recognizing our powerlessness does a passivity arise that makes the impossible possible. This approach urges us to reconsider the relationship with knowledge and experience, suggesting that in the acceptance of our limitations lies the possibility of a genuine encounter with reality and with that which overflows, namely, the sacred.

We know in which direction to move depending on what we desire. However, we do not know where or how to move if we desire to access our authentic nature or what we truly are. For this purpose, only relaxation and calmness is needed, which allows us to enter the field of meditation. As said in religious terms, the search for God is posed as an exploration toward the impossible, where the very act of searching does not guarantee the encounter but rather makes it even more impossible. If God could be found through seeking, it would imply that God could be possessed. This would reduce the Divine to the property of the seeker and, therefore, render it a mere projection of the individual who seeks it.

The notion of possessing the infinite or eternal presents itself as a contradiction, an absurdity. However, it is argued that the beginning of the search is necessary to understand this absurdity. The search for God is, therefore, a process of longing for the impossible, a march toward an inevitable defeat where the seeker and his will to find and possess dissolve. It is in this defeat, in the dissolution of the ego and the will, where transformation and authentic surrender take place. The senses and knowledge prove insufficient to comprehend the Divine, the sacred, invisible and hidden. But from them, from philosophy, we begin the journey that will lead us to understand the impossibility of knowing the Divine. At the same time, it allows us to accept the need for a new approach, to continue unveiling other realms of the human being through which we may attend to the Divine, to the Being in all its Being, perhaps without having to understand it as we understand any object.

This perspective emphasizes that only in passivity and acceptance of the impossible can the doors to the absolutely transcendent be opened. The authentic experience of the Divine, or of any reality that transcends human comprehension, occurs only within the framework of what is ontologically impossible for the human being. Therefore, the Divine or the infinite is situated beyond conventional human experience, accessible not through effort or will, but in surrender and the acceptance of our limitations. That is why it is important to repeat the words of Heraclitus that we mentioned earlier: "only in renunciation can the possibility of waiting for the unexpected exist."¹⁵⁵ The revelation of Being is only possible in the waiting that expects nothing concrete, in the infinite predisposition and openness to what transcends us.

From impossibility to the experience of the sacred

This relationship based on the condition of possibility of the impossible opens the door to a mystical and profound conception of communion with the divinity, as articulated by Meister Eckhart, who highlights the spiritual fusion of the soul with the divinity. More specifically, Eckhart emphasizes a direct and personal connection with the sacred that transcends the conventional theological boundaries between innate humanity and the divine gift of grace. The premise that "in the consummation of the sacred, duality is transformed into unity" captures Eckhart's thought on the ultimate experience with the divinity, where the line that separates the human condition from divine grace fades away. For him, at the beginning of the spiritual journey, the human and the Divine appear as separate spheres. The sphere of nature symbolizes human limitation and predisposition to error; the sphere of grace represents divine benevolence aimed at the redemption and elevation of the human being.

Nevertheless, at the peak of the mystical journey, upon achieving total communion with the divinity, the distinctions between the human and the Divine, between nature and grace, cease. This state of sublime union does not entail the literal annulment of these realities or their devaluation; rather, it suggests that, in the face of the overwhelming magnificence of the Divine, such differentiations become obsolete. The soul, then, does not perceive the divinity as a distant or external entity, but experiences a profound fusion, where the individual being amalgamates with the divine infinitude. Eckhart proposes this principle to deepen the potential of the human-divine relationship, the supreme end of which transcends mere acceptance

---

155. Heraclitus, *Fragments: A Text and Translation with a Commentary*, trans. T.M. Robinson (Toronto: University of Toronto Press, 1987), (fragment 18, DK 22B18).

of grace without blurring the distinction between the giver and the receiver. Through this experience, according to Eckhart, the soul recognizes that its essence and the Divine are inseparable, leading to an understanding beyond the ordinary conception of nature and grace as distinct entities. This discernment, imbued with philosophical and theological richness, invites us to contemplate union with the Divine not as the culmination of grace received in opposition to our nature, but as the recognition of a shared identity with the divinity, thereby eclipsing the previous dualities.

CHAPTER 37

HEIDEGGER'S UNDERSTANDING OF THE SACRED

Heidegger and the Divine

Heidegger, in his *Letter on Humanism*, urges us to embark on a journey into the depths of our essence and the environment surrounding us, before attempting to embrace concepts of such magnitude as the Divine, the sacred, and the very definition of God. He proposes that the beginning of this understanding lies in the recognition and understanding of the truth of Being, the foundation upon which the totality of the existent stands. This foundation allows us, gradually, to unravel the meaning of the sacred, to deepen our interpretation of the Divine, and, ultimately, to come closer to the understanding of God. Heidegger emphasizes the need to approach these notions with moderation and depth, avoiding falling into hasty or superficial interpretations. He maintains that it is futile to debate the proximity or distance of God without first having acquired a solid foundation in the essential concepts of Being and the sacred. Furthermore, he highlights that, in his time, the connection with the sacred has faded, a situation he deems alarming. Nevertheless, he clarifies that his interest in the truth of Being does not imply a call to theism or atheism. His proposal is more ambitious: it focuses on clarifying the limits of our thinking and what is truly possible to know about Being. Essentially, Heidegger challenges us to go beyond traditional beliefs in order to achieve a deeper understanding of both our own existence and the divine sphere.

The philosophical proposal outlined here suggests that the essence of phenomenality lies in givenness, understood as the capacity to reveal the phenomenon in its pure and strict giving, without the need to invoke an external efficient cause or a transcendental recipient. This view holds that the phenomenon is characterized by its nature of being irrevocably given, based solely on the experiences of giftability—attributed to Being—and acceptability—attributed to the human being. The sacred is defined by its quality of being unchangeable, accessible only to the individual who is fully aware of this characteristic of intangibility. This understanding highlights the special relationship between the consciousness of Being and the sphere of the sacred, suggesting that only through a deep recognition of the sacrality inherent in certain aspects of existence can one truly "touch" or connect meaningfully with the Divine or transcendental, respecting its unchangeable essence.

The evolution of the human being and the emergence of the sacred run parallel, preserving essential traits of its ancestral nature. In the face of the increasing uniformity and automation of contemporary life, concerns arise as to whether we are witnessing a decline, not so much in the practice of religious rites, which may survive in a ceremonial framework, but in the experience of the Divine, which historically intertwined with these practices.

Today, it could be said that a distancing from the religious prevails in many facets of society, a phenomenon Nietzsche highlights in *The Gay Science*, particularly through the figure of the "madman." This character, still in search of the Divine, sees himself and society as responsible for the "death of God," a symbolic act reflecting a significant change in our relationship with the transcendent. The declaration of the "madman" does not stem from a lack of interest in the sacred but from a reflection on the deterioration of cultural foundations, manifested as a lament for the contemporary disconnection from the spiritual and its effect on culture and collective spirituality.

In delving into the sacred in our time, Heidegger found in Nietzsche's dialogue an indication of an awakening toward a more authentic thinking and a liberation from the constraints of reason. In his analysis of Nietzsche's phrase "God is dead," he suggests that the authenticity of this cry invites us to question whether we have remained indifferent to its true resonance. He warns that true thinking begins only when we recognize that reason, long venerated, has hindered the depth of thought. In light of this, Heidegger himself invites us to reconsider the principles of Western thought and seek a more existential knowledge, overcoming the barriers of overly structured logic.

For Heidegger, and in line with what we have argued throughout this study, the sacred is found in immersion within contemplative or meditative silence, a state where words and actions no longer have a place. In this tranquility and absence of sound, the indispensable conditions for the manifestation of the ultimate divinity are found. This approach emphasizes the importance of stillness and withdrawal from worldly distractions as a means to achieve a spiritual connection. Heidegger views this silence not as a mere absence of noise, but as a space full of potential for an encounter with the transcendent, where the Divine can reveal itself in its purest form without mediation.

Frequently, we exalt reason by attributing to it a noble lineage, forgetting that its roots are far from being as elevated or altruistic as we assume. The word *reason* derives from *ratio*, a Latin term meaning calculation, which refers to the stones used by Roman merchants in balances to weigh their goods. Therefore, the origin of this concept is essentially pragmatic and worldly. This act of measuring by merchants is similar to our reasoning process, evaluating pros and cons to make decisions.

However, this mental activity does not coincide with what Heidegger understands by thinking. He proposes a "thinking-other," or *denken-danken* in German, which primarily refers to the contemplation of Being. He maintains that this other thinking (*denken*) transcends mere intellectual or logical activity. In his perspective, the act of thinking in its most authentic form is an openness to Being, a meditation that seeks to unravel the meaning of existence. *Denken* means "to think," and *danken* is "to thank." Heidegger uses this etymological relation to delve into the intrinsic connection between thought and gratitude. That is, to think is to thank for what has been given, rather than projecting a calculation, prediction, or forecast. This *denken-danken* suggests that an attitude of gratitude must accompany true thinking.

Section IX: Phenomenology of the Sacred

Denken is a type of thinking that requires meticulous attention and reverential care toward Being, a willingness to listen and respond to the call of Truth. *Danken*, on the other hand, is not simply an expression of gratitude, but a thanksgiving that represents sincere appreciation for Being. It involves an attitude of respect and reverence toward the world and our own existence within it. It is recognizing that Being has been given to us, and our responsibility is to correspond to this gift. Heidegger maintains that to think authentically means to recognize and value Being and its mystery.

The "thinking-other" in Heidegger's philosophy invites us to a type of thinking that does not center on rational, logical, or scientific analysis, but rather on a more essential reflection on our relationship with Being. Heidegger critiques the Western metaphysical tradition for its tendency to categorize Being, reducing it to mere objects of analysis and control. The "thinking-other" seeks to transcend these limitations, opening new possibilities for understanding and relating to Being. This type of thinking involves an attitude of listening and openness. Instead of imposing pre-defined concepts and structures onto reality, the "thinking-other" strives to listen to the silence in which Being itself expresses what it has to say. It is a type of receptive attention that seeks to be guided by Being, rather than trying to dominate it.

Unlike calculative and technical thinking, the "thinking-other" is contemplative in nature. Heidegger emphasizes the importance of meditation as a means of approaching Being more authentically. This approach requires patience and a willingness to accept the mystery and indeterminacy of Being. Rather than considering Being as an object separate from the subject contemplating it, the "thinking-other" recognizes the fundamental interconnection between Being and thinking. This type of thinking seeks to understand how we are already immersed in Being and how our own existences are intertwined with the world. Ultimately, the "thinking-other" changes thinkers themselves. By adopting an attitude of openness and receptivity, thinkers become more aware of their own existence and their relationship with the world. This transformation is essential for accessing a deeper and more authentic understanding of Being.

Contrary to the idea that the human being is a rational animal, Heidegger would argue that this definition is transcended precisely by the human's capacity to think about the yet-unknown if they are confronted with the experience of the sacred. This capacity for awe before the unknown and the transcendental distinguishes the human being from other forms of life and challenges the traditional conception of reason. According to Heidegger, true thinking arises not from logic or calculation, but from openness to the sacred, which can profoundly transform our understanding of the world and of ourselves. Heidegger, aligning with Nietzsche in his critique of calculative rationality, privileges a form of thinking that at least glimpses the experience of the sacred. However, this does not imply that Heidegger defends any specific religious ideology. On the contrary, he views ideologies as closed systems that exclude the diverse or contradictory, labeling them as erroneous or false. Heidegger seeks to transcend these ideological and theological limitations, pointing toward a more open and reflective thought that allows the emergence of the sacred, free from the restrictions imposed by dogmatic structures. His approach promotes a profound exploration of Being, beyond the confines of instrumental rationality and conventional religious conceptions.

According to this approach, the individual is not the one who creates or projects the phenomenon, but the one who receives, accepts, and thanks it. Therefore, what human beings possess is a pure capacity for reception in the face of the pure givenness of the phenomenon. The distinction between phenomenon and object is established through the subject's attitude: an object becomes such when the subject interprets and defines it, whereas a phenomenon reveals itself when it is allowed to manifest as it is. Thus, the stone may be known as an object—when interpreted by the subject—or as a phenomenon, when it shows itself on its own.

The task of givenness, then, is to make the given appear as entirely phenomenal, and the phenomenon as entirely given. The philosophical reduction implied suggests that everything is phenomenon and that every phenomenon is given, shifting the perception of an external world that is merely sensory to a reality given in consciousness. Consciousness, always given, often remains unnoticed, but it is the field in which the phenomenal manifests. This conceptual framework emphasizes the centrality of givenness and reception in the phenomenological experience. It highlights an ontology where the appearance of the phenomenon is independent of the voluntary action of subjects and resides in their ability to receive and accept what is presented to them.

In *Being and Time*, and as we have already outlined, Heidegger situates *Dasein*, or "being-there," as the entity whose ontological structure gives it the unique capacity to question its own Being and, by extension, Being in general. Thus, the responsibility to understand Being falls upon *Dasein*, as it is the only one capable of carrying out this inquiry consciously and reflectively. The *kehre*, or "turn," in Heidegger's thought, marks a transition toward a perspective where the focus of inquiry about Being shifts from *Dasein* to Being itself. This change emphasizes that it is Being that reveals or conceals itself, rather than *Dasein* actively discovering or unraveling Being. In this sense, the responsibility for the revelation of Being shifts from human effort toward understanding to the way in which Being manifests in itself and by itself. The *kehre* reflects a profound change in Heidegger's approach to ontology, emphasizing a more passive and receptive relationship of the human being toward the self-revelation of Being. If in *Being and Time* the responsibility lay with *Dasein*, in the *Letter on Humanism*, it lies with Being.

We can open a fruitful intercultural dialogue between Western and Eastern philosophy. Heidegger's *Dasein* emphasizes the unique existential condition of human beings with their inherent capacity for self-awareness and reflection on existence and Being. For its part, the *ahaṅkāra* of Vedanta identifies the ego, or sense of "I," as an illusion of separation of the true Self (Ātman) from the universe (Brahman). While Heidegger uses *Dasein* to delve into temporality, finitude, and the confrontation with human mortality, Vedanta posits that *ahaṅkāra* is an obstacle to achieving spiritual enlightenment by confusing the temporal Being with the eternal Being. Despite their distinct philosophical contexts and goals, both concepts provoke profound reflection on the nature of Being, identity, and the possibility of transcending the limitations of our existential understanding. This comparison reveals a rich diversity of thought about the human condition and its relation to Being.

The saturated phenomenon and its witness

The concept of the saturated phenomenon, which we have addressed in our study, challenges traditional approaches to knowledge and perception, while also bearing a clear resemblance to the way Heidegger defined the sacred and the significance this holds for the understanding of Being and the human being. By definition, the saturated phenomenon, like the sacred, is unpredictable; that is, it cannot be anticipated or mentally conceived before it occurs. Unlike phenomena that can be quantified or broken down into predictable parts, the saturated phenomenon presents itself in its entirety immediately and without prior warning, making it impossible to foresee, forecast, or mentally construct. This characteristic, underscores its unique nature and its capacity to surprise and challenge our expectations and preconceived notions. Therefore, the sacred is revealed, and this revelation is only possible under certain conditions, which we have already introduced with the notions of waiting, wonder, and the timeless present, and which we will revisit in greater detail in the following paragraphs.

Wonder, as a trait that defines meditation as a presubjective and pre-egoic state with which the "non-I" waits without expecting anything or anyone, perfectly illustrates this impossibility of anticipation. Descartes already understood that wonder affects us before we can fully know the thing that causes it or precisely because we do not know it. This state of surprise is disruptive because it interrupts our prejudices and expectations, forcing us to confront reality in a new, unfiltered manner. Wonder is an opening toward the revelation of the unknown, the impossible, that which is veiled and shows itself for the first time without any expectation.

On its part, the saturated phenomenon, being anamorphic, lacks a defined form or size that can be measured or quantified. Everything that is susceptible to measurement or quantification is considered objectual, existing within the dimensions of space and time. However, the saturated phenomenon transcends these limitations, presenting itself in a "mysterious time" that does not follow a linear sequence and cannot be accounted for in minutes or seconds. In contrast, the revelation of the saturated phenomenon is characterized by a presence that could be defined by its timelessness and infinitude. These terms allow us to situate the sacred as a saturated phenomenon, beyond any conventional notion of time. This underscores its complete immeasurability and its resistance to being understood or controlled through traditional techniques. In other words, the saturated phenomenon challenges conventional logic and invites us to experience its reality directly, free from the restrictions imposed by our usual conceptual and temporal structures.

This notion of presence or timeless present emerges from the distinction between the concepts of *chrónos* and *aión*, which is fundamental for understanding the measurement of time in relation to beings and Being, respectively. *Chrónos* represents measurable time associated with beings, where measurement and sequentiality are possible and relevant. In contrast, *aión* reflects the time of Being, which is intrinsically immeasurable and cannot be divided into successive parts. The totality of Being is revealed in an absolute unity, undoing any distinction between parts, moments, or differences. This revelation emphasizes the omnipresence of Being, suggesting that God, transcendental and timeless, resides everywhere, challenging the conceptualization of Being in spatial or temporal terms. Being manifests itself and hides in its own "mysterious time," in a timeless present.

On the other hand, as Marion explains in *Being Given: Toward a Phenomenology of Givenness* (*Étant donné: Essai d'une phénoménologie de la donation*), the experience of the phenomenal is framed in representation, which requires a necessary connection between perceptions, as discussed in the references to the analogies of experience. These analogies presuppose a unity of experience that allows for the phenomenological manifestation within a pre-established coordinated framework, though this framework only applies to a portion of the spectrum of phenomenality, leaving

CHAPTER 37: HEIDEGGER'S UNDERSTANDING OF THE SACRED

phenomena such as historical ones outside its reach. It is argued that, although the analogies of experience seek to regulate unity, their phenomenological application is limited, especially when comparing quantitative analogies in mathematics with qualitative ones in philosophy.

The transition from externally perceived experiences to their assimilation and transformation within individual consciousness constitutes a central phenomenon in the evolution of self-consciousness. This phenomenon illustrates a critical shift from perception that resides outside of us to an understanding that is rooted within us. Such a process highlights the Aristotelian perspective on the nature of knowledge, which emphasizes how the object of knowledge amalgamates with the subject that knows, merging with the essence of its being. For Aristotle, knowing is experiencing a deep fusion between the subject and the object, in which the object is incorporated by the subject, becoming part of their subjective sphere. This process signals knowledge as a form of profound personal transformation, where the known transcends mere external understanding to be absorbed, reconfiguring the ontological structure of the individual.

Therefore, acquiring knowledge transcends the simple collection of data or information, constituting rather a process of growth and development of Being, in which each new understanding intertwines with the individual's consciousness, remodeling their identity and perception of the environment. This conception unravels the profound connection between the act of knowing and the essence of Being, postulating that knowledge possesses an inherent transformative power. Each learning experience strengthens this bond. Furthermore, it reveals that our view of the world and our inner selves is constantly evolving, shaped by every experience we absorb. These experiences redefine our understanding of ourselves and our existence.

In the case of a saturated phenomenon, it exceeds the conventional categories of quantity and attributes, presenting itself as a pure event that disconnects from all established relations, as it does not share a common measure with any known or expected term. This characterization highlights the singularity of the saturated phenomenon, its resistance to being boxed into the traditional limits of phenomenology, and its ability to challenge our understanding and perception of reality. It cannot be categorized within the traditional ontic time and entity categories, space, possession, passion, or relation. Since there is no category that can explain it, the saturated phenomenon is supracategorical. The third assumption regarding the unity of experience suggests that it develops against the backdrop of time, considered as the ultimate horizon for phenomena. However, there are saturated phenomena that transcend this horizon in various ways, receiving intuitions that exceed any pre-established conceptual framework. At the same time, they surpass boundaries by articulating several horizons at once, as Spinoza proposes with his idea of a single substance. These phenomena provoke a saturation that prevents any articulation of horizons, making the phenomenon as a whole intractable. This last case, as Marion emphasizes, implies that the phenomenon may not find a space to manifest in a comprehensible way within the existing thought structures.

In relation to the categories of modality, these do not directly define objects or their interrelations, but rather their relationship to thought in general, pointing toward the cognizant I. This approach alienates the phenomenon, associating it with an objectifying intentionality. The saturated phenomenon, therefore, challenges the cognitive capacity of the "I," generating a disagreement between what could potentially be perceived and the subjective conditions of experience, resulting in a phenomenon that cannot be objectified. This non-objectifiable phenomenon is characterized by being inapprehensible, a quality that distinguishes it and makes it appear exceptionally, but at the same time contradicts the conditions associated with a more conventional or "poor" phenomenality.

Marion himself describes this contradiction in *Being Given: Toward a Phenomenology of Givenness*, as a counter-experience, defined by the inaccessibility of the phenomenon to objectification. The paradox manifests when the advent of the phenomenon exceeds what was previously known or anticipated, suspending and eventually reversing the domain relationship of the "I" over the phenomenon. This approach underscores a dimension of the phenomenological experience that resists being captured by traditional structures of knowledge, challenging our understanding and expectations about the nature and accessibility of reality.

In this same analysis, the subject transforms and passes from being a transcendental, constitutive agent to merely a witness of the experience, constituted by the experience itself. It ceases to be a Kantian transcendental subject and becomes a transcendent that transcends its own experience. From being the active subject that shapes experience, it becomes that which surpasses its own limitations. Is it like going from being the filmmaker who directs each scene to merely becoming a spectator in the theater, losing control over the plot and simply immersing yourself in it. This transformation occurs because such experiences are so powerful or impactful that they exceed our ability to describe them with the language and concepts we usually employ, as happened to Kierkegaard's Abraham. This transformation occurs because the intuition experienced surpasses what any hermeneutics of the concept could interpret as meaning, placing the "I" in a position where no dominant perspective prevails over the intuition that surrounds it.

Thus, the "I" loses its priority as an egological pole, and the figure of the witness becomes more appropriate to describe its role. The "I" no longer initiates the manifestation of the phenomenon nor does it conceive of it as an intentional object. It cannot perceive the phenomenon in its entirety nor is it capable of interpreting the excess of intuition that characterizes it. When addressing the nature of revelation and its theological association with saturated phenomena, Marion explores how these phenomena carry an inherent sacred and theological connection. However, this link poses a challenge, as it activates a dimension of belief that seems incompatible with the neutral attitude Marion proposes for the reception of phenomena. Although Marion explicitly rejects any association with theology, we might argue that it is impossible to maintain neutrality in the face of phenomena of revelation. Saturated phenomena transform phenomenology into theology, complicating the distinction between the two and reducing the former to the latter. Perhaps it is for this very reason that Marion himself, in his essay *God without Being* (*Dieu sans l'être*), states that "God must be emancipated from Metaphysics," which would be something akin to Buddha's task of liberating God from humanity.[156]

The reflection we have carried out throughout the last chapters concerning the philosophical method, particularly focused on phenomenology and more briefly on hermeneutics, has led to a significant expansion of its horizons, now encompassing what has traditionally been considered imperceptible, indefinable, indescribable, and sacred. This methodological evolution has involved a reorientation toward aspects of reality that escape direct sensory perception and conventional definitional categories. In this context, a phenomenology of the hidden has been proposed, a novel approach that, unlike classical phenomenology focused on studying the visible and accessible manifestations of reality, concentrates on those aspects that remain veiled or are intrinsically elusive. This "phenomenology of the hidden" marks a turning point in the discipline, as it challenges the fundamental premise that phenomenology must be limited to the study of what becomes present and knowable to consciousness. Instead, the phenomenology of the hidden delves into the realm of what does not become evident, what resides beyond or beneath the perceptible surface, attempting to articulate and understand the essence of what is withheld from direct apprehension—that is, the sacred.

In this framework, the role of the master also undergoes a significant transformation, becoming someone endowed with the extraordinary ability to describe the indescribable, to give voice to that which, by its very nature, defies linguistic expression. This ability requires exceptional sensitivity and openness to subtler and deeper dimensions of reality and a mastery of language that allows for the communication of the ineffable, which constitutes a true philosophical and pedagogical prowess.

---

156. Jean-Luc Marion, *God Without Being*, trans. Thomas A. Carlson (University of Chicago Press, 1991), 83.

CHAPTER 38

INTENTIONALITY IN THE REVELATION
OF THE SACRED

The Other and the sacred according to Husserl and Henry

This phenomenological relationship with the sacred, which we have gradually articulated throughout our study and presented as a relationality that transcends epistemological cognizability, still requires further description. One of the key aspects, as we might put it, is that it refers to a relationality that "takes place" or happens (*ereignis*). However, it is not reducible to a relationship of perceptibility or knowledge through concepts or categories. Thus, the sacred phenomenon, though saturated by its own dimension of invisibility, incomprehensibility, or unknowability, is nevertheless a phenomenon, insofar as it gives itself, it reveals itself in consciousness precisely as imperceptible, invisible, and unknowable. Therefore, and paradoxically, we are asserting that the non-visible reveals itself and appears as the surplus of the visible and cognizable. In this regard, we can ask the following: how can we affirm that the invisible or incognizable reveals itself if its nature is precisely to transcend our faculties of perception and intuition, which are the ones that allow us to see and know?

The resource of meditation has allowed us to outline a state of consciousness that underlies all active notion of agency. It has opened a path to a dimension in which consciousness, prostrated in waiting that expects nothing in particular, opens as a witness to receive, but without knowing or understanding. This meditation has also given rise to a relationality without relation that transcends the polarization of experience in terms of subject and object. In meditation, the one who waits is not the subject but the witness of a phenomenon that cannot be objectified. Husserl addresses this topic in his *Cartesian Meditations*, where he discusses the issue of the Other. Let us link the topic of intentionality with the issues of givenness and the sacred. Henry examines how the study of the experience of alterity, proposed by Husserl in the fifth of the *Cartesian Meditations*, is based on two fundamental premises. The first is:

n'y a un autre pour moi que si j'en ai une expérience, que si, sous quelque forme ou sous aspect que ce soit, l'autre m'est donné, en sorte que je le trouve daris ma propre vie et que, d'une certaine façon, il est en moi

The first presupposition is that there is an other for me only if I have an experience of the other, only if, in whatever form or manner, the other is given to me, such that I find the other in my own life and that, in some way, the other is in me.[157]

This first assumption refers to the Epicurean argument about death, which considers it "nothing for us" because, being an impossible contact, we would not even have its idea. At the same time, Henry interprets that this notion resonates with Husserl's statement:

Diese Erfahrungen und ihre Leistungen sind ja transzendentale Tatsachen meiner phänomenologischen Sphäre

These experiences and their works are facts belonging to my phenomenological sphere.[158]

The second assumption, which is not specifically detailed in the fifth of the *Cartesian Meditations*, but which permeates Husserl's work

---

157. Michel Henry, *Material Phenomenology* (New York: Fordham University Press, 2008), 101.
158. Edmund Husserl, *Cartesian Meditations: An Introduction to Phenomenology*, trans. Dorion Cairns (The Hague: Martinus Nijhoff, 1960), 90, §42 [Hua I, 121].

as a whole, relates to the way in which the Other is given to me through the structure of intentionality. Henry asserts:

> To say that the other enters into my experience means that the other enters into this primordial Outside into which intentionality casts itself, into this place of light where intentionality reaches and sees all that it sees.[159]

Husserl delves into the idea that our understanding and perception of the objects and phenomena of the world are the result of constitutive mental processes. However, he establishes a crucial distinction when it comes to other people. According to Husserl, unlike inanimate objects such as a stone, which we can perceive and conceptualize through mental construction, the encounter with another human being, with another consciousness, occurs in terms of "givenness." This means that we recognize the Other not as a mere construction of our mind, but as an entity endowed with its own subjectivity. That is, the Other thinks, feels, and experiences the world from their own unique perspective. Our interactions with other human beings differ from our relationship with inanimate objects. With people, we enter a space of exchange and mutual recognition, where the Other manifests not as an objective entity defined by our mental constructs, but as a living subject with their own agency and perspective.

Michel Henry says that we can only affirm the presence of the Other in our lives if, in some way, we have had an experience with the Other, which allows it to manifest itself within us. In other words, the appearance of the Other in me marks a different kind of non-constitutive experience in which the Other acquires my recognition without constituting it. This point is important because Husserl's *Cartesian Meditations* does not include the Meditation on God carried out by Descartes in his *Meditationes de prima philosophia*, but instead includes a meditation on the Other.

---

159. Michel Henry, *Material Phenomenology* (New York: Fordham University Press, 2008), 101-102.

Henry's reading of Husserl's fifth meditation contrasts with the view of St. Thomas, for whom Being (*Esse*) is conceived as separate and subsistent by itself (*Esse Separatur*), indicating an autonomous existence of Being in itself. This idea reflects a conception where God is understood as an entity absolutely distinct and separate from His creatures, marking a deep metaphysical discontinuity between the Creator and the created. In this framework, God transcends the physical world and everything that exists since its nature is entirely other, that is, "otherly everything." This implies that His essence and mode of being cannot be fully understood or assimilated by the creatures within their own ontological and epistemological reality. This insurmountable transcendence emphasizes the idea that no matter how creatures try to approach, understand, or explain God through the resources of reason or experience, there will always be an impassable abyss separating God from His creatures, highlighting His total otherness and mystery.

However, for Henry, just as for Descartes, according to Henry's interpretation, Being, as the Other in Husserl, is realized and given in individual experience; the substance of Being is founded in and inseparable from personal experience. Without this experience, Being would lack meaning or substance. The reference to "me" implies a notion of Being that is distinct from oneself, while also suggesting that Being is found within the individual, or "it is in me." This idea resonates with Paul's words in Galatians, when he says:

> I have been crucified with Christ; and it is no longer I who live, but it is Christ who lives in me. And the life I now live in the flesh I live by faith in the Son of God, who loved me and gave himself for me.
>
> (Galatians, 2:20)

What Paul emphasizes in this verse is the integration of the experience of the Other, in this case, Christ, the sacred, into the individual's own existence, thus expressing a profound internal transformation.

In accordance with Paul's words, from Henry's phenomenological perspective the discussion returns to intentionality, reveals how it profoundly connects the subject with the external world, essentially intertwining the interiority of the subject with the exteriority of Being, of the Other, of the sacred. The key to this relationship lies in the concept of intentionality. Intentionality is the act by which the subjectivity, or the consciousness of the subject, is projected toward Being, and, in turn, the act of showing in which Being reveals or projects itself toward the intentionality of the subject. Henry suggests that the process of showing finds its place in intentionality, and vice versa; intentionality finds its foundation in the act of showing. Thus, a cycle of interdependence is created, where Being exists for the subject because the subject exists in Being. Henry defends the existence of a relationship that, although it transcends knowledge, cannot fully transcend intentionality. Without it, Being itself would lack meaning and could not even be given. Therefore, Being reveals itself through the subject's intentionality, while the subject opens to Being through their intentionality. This intertwining of Being and consciousness, of givenness and intentionality, underscores a mutual co-belonging, a transcendence within immanence, as Husserl would say. As we have reiterated throughout this study, revelation is conceived as the moment when the subject's intentionality and the givenness of Being meet and complement each other.

In a way, Henry's argument can be understood as a return to Husserl and an attempt to correct Heidegger and Marion, for whom the phenomenological experience of the sacred transcends and bursts the seams of all intentionality. For Henry, however, the sacred, as impossible, is still impossible within the horizon of intentionality, for this is the only horizon where reality, of any kind, possible or impossible, thinkable or unthinkable, can make sense. As Husserl already warned, there is no possibility of even speaking of experience and the sacred outside the structures of intentionality. Henry argues that intentionality is not reducible to a subject-object relationship but is even deeper and more original than any knowledge. Thus, in contrast to Heidegger and Marion, he argues that revelation takes place in the space of intentionality, illuminating the intrinsic and reciprocal relationship between the intentional agent and Being.

This emphasizes how the fundamental structure of our consciousness and our ability to direct ourselves toward the world are not merely subjective acts. They are intrinsically linked to the way in which Being offers or gives itself, or permanently reveals itself in and to us. Our intentional relationship with Being transcends a mere subject-object interaction to become an active participation in the process of the revelation of Being. Just as the wave exists in the ocean, and the ocean in the wave, this co-participation or correlation reflects a singular intentionality inherent to consciousness. This relationality symbolizes the integration between intentionality and givenness, through which intentionality represents the subject's openness, while givenness is associated with the revelation of the object. In this framework, the intentionality of beings is characterized by their passivity, in contrast with the activity inherent in givenness, as we will see next.

Following Henry through the previously discussed quotes in this section, we can now assert that the essence of my Being is immersed in existence itself, and when it is expressed "that it enters into my experience," it refers to that transcendent realm where intentionality unfolds. Henry refers to that illuminated space from which everything visible is perceived and understood. Here, the notion of "I am in Being" is articulated, which differs from the statement "Being is in me." Both propositions, although distinct, are intertwined in their meaning. In this context, intentionality is better understood as a "launching." That is, a "throwing oneself" even toward something, without implying any personal purpose on the part of the agent.

Within Henry's interpretation, which, as we now see, follows Husserl more closely than one might have initially thought, it would be a mistake to equate "intentionality" with "intention" in a strict sense. Instead, it would be more accurate to conceive it as a "tension" or an extension of something. Thus, the term "intentionality" could be appropriately replaced with "launching," or "throwing," maintaining the depth of its original meaning. In this way, Husserl and Henry preserve intentionality without it implying any form of constructivism, but rather an ongoing openness to Being, which is immanent yet transcendent to it.

This interpretation of intentionality in the field of phenomenology dispels the conventional differentiation between subject and object, paving the way for an interaction defined by the terms of givenness and intentionality. Givenness describes the way the object manifests or "projects" itself toward the subject, while intentionality captures the reciprocal dynamic, that is, the throwing of consciousness outward. This duality of movements emphasizes a reciprocal interaction of recognition and encounter. The "object" becomes present to consciousness, which, in turn, directs its attention and being toward the object in a continuous process of exploration and attribution of meaning. Thus, instead of treating the "subject" and the "object" as separate and immutable entities, the phenomenology of Henry and Husserl proposes understanding them as components of an interactive and dynamic process, mutually involved in their existence and definition. As Hegel's phenomenology proposed long before, we are not faced with two distinct entities but with two facets of a single reality. The apparent duality is, in essence, an illusion, because what we actually have are two roles played by the same unaltered consciousness. In a certain sense, it would be comparable to the two faces of a coin. Essentially, what is discussed is a single pure consciousness that adopts, and unfolds as such, in two modes of expression at once: on the one hand, intentionally projecting itself, and on the other, manifesting itself.

Religion, God, and the Other

Unlike Hegel, for whom spirit manifests exclusively within the philosophical sphere, for Henry, the manifestation of Being, of the sacred, extends into the religious realm, transcending the limits of reason, but in no case of intentionality. This difference rests on the fact that Hegel, as a rationalist, considers that only what falls within the limits of reason can be valid, while religion, being based on the domain of faith, is placed outside these limits. According to Hegel, in its origins, spirit operated through faith, but over time, evolved into a state of greater knowledge, rendering religion unnecessary and leaving philosophy as its sole need. Interestingly, Hegel does not speak of "philosophy" in general terms but specifically refers to "my philosophy."

According to Henry and Marion, revelation can also take place within the religious context, which they regard as the stage where the words of the Divine resonate. Hegel states that Being reveals itself through philosophical concepts and not through the words of the gods. On the contrary, Marion argues that it is precisely in religions that we are spoken about God through their sacred texts. Thus, the reading and understanding of the spirit (to say it hermeneutically) of these sacred scriptures open a path toward the Divine, allowing us to access the sphere of the sacred.

This argument that links religion with the revelation of the sacred must be seen in the light of alterity. As we have previously said, in his *Cartesian Meditations*, Husserl dedicates the fifth meditation to the Other and leaves out the topic of God, which Descartes had addressed in his Third *Meditatio*. Although we cannot address what this implies here, it is important to note that it is not a mere coincidence. From Husserl's phenomenology, the experience of the Other is what opens the door to the experience of the sacred, although always within the "limits" and "parameters" of intentionality and givenness, beyond which no experience or revelation of meaning would be possible. That is why Henry emphasizes that, "instead of problematizing the givenness that precedes explication in a radical way..." Husserl chooses to explore another path.[160] This decision suggests the relevance of expanding our understanding in this specific domain, leading to the conclusion that the study of alterity transcends the simple analysis of:

> It is a matter of knowing how this intentional object, which belongs to me, can yet be more than "a point of intersection belonging to my constitutive synthesis" (Hua I 135/105). It is a matter of knowing how the other, in some respect,

---

160. Ibid., 107.

CHAPTER 38: INTENTIONALITY IN THE REVELATION OF THE SACRED

can be irreducible to my own being, really other than me, transcendent in relation to me.[161]

Henry shows us the need to develop a phenomenology of that which does not manifest itself directly. To elucidate the most convincing aspects of his contribution, it will be necessary to set aside criticisms and refocus them as clarifications of the aspects that would complement Husserl's analyses, especially those derived from the exploration of the inapparent.

Delving deeper into alterity goes beyond understanding how an intentional object, being mine, can still represent something more than "the point of intersection of my constitutive syntheses." It involves the understanding that the truly Other can be, in some way, inassimilable to my essence, truly distinct and transcendent in relation to me. Alterity, defined as "the Other" or "the Otherness," implies that, although the Other manifests in me and through me, it constitutes more than my individual being. It resembles how the ocean reveals itself in a wave, yet exceeds its singularity. The terms of Henry himself ("truly other than I," "transcendent in relation to me") point out that, despite manifesting in me, the Other overwhelms me in existence, highlighting a dimension of transcendence immanent to which Husserl himself had already pointed.

This notion of immanent transcendence takes on a dual dimension in that, on the one hand, it opens a vertical relationship that elevates us toward the Divine, and on the other, a horizontal one that extends us toward our neighbor. While God is situated on a plane of superiority in relation to us, the neighbor presents itself as our equal, though it also transcends us by going beyond the limits of our own subjectivity. This transcendence of the Other lies in its complete otherness; it is not a mirror of ourselves, but a distinct entity that challenges us to recognize and respect its uniqueness, with which, at the same time, we live the world. We cannot simplify the other to already known terms; instead, we are called to embrace its

---

161. Ibid.

mystery with love. The otherness of the neighbor carries an essential irreducibility, turning it into a perpetual enigma that escapes our total comprehension.

This enigmatic phenomenological otherness is not only applicable to the other human being but also pulses in our relationship with ourselves. Every individual is the bearer of an intrinsic mystery that transcends them from their innermost interior. Derrida articulates that we conceive ourselves as an entity behind a mask, under the belief that behind it resides our authentic "I." However, behind this first mask, we discover successively another and another. In trying to unveil this "I" by removing the mask that hides it, we find only more layers, other masks. This suggests that consciousness generates a mistaken or false consciousness of itself, which in turn generates another, and so on, in an endless process of self-deception and an incessant search for authenticity. The Other is not an addition or a complement, but a necessity that lies and beats immanently in the same consciousness of intentionality, which opens and throws itself toward what is not itself. The Other, therefore, can be understood as the Divine, the sacred, which transcends us from the innermost immanence. Alterity, as understood from Husserl to Henry and Marion, would equate to the enigma of the hidden, whose underlying invisibility is revealed in everything without revealing itself as something.

This new conceptualization of alterity as that which transcends me from my innermost immanence, but which cannot appear by itself, not only redefines the phenomenon as such but also has important implications for phenomenology and its goal. The phenomenology of the sacred, of the hidden, of the underlying, places special emphasis on this idea of a "new phenomenon," highlighting that the debate about "the things themselves" to which Husserl wanted to return is situated within the realm of its possible extension to the objects of study of the sciences. That is, it lies within a framework of phenomenality that can be considered limited or conventional, employing the terminology proposed by Marion. However, by adopting an approach that contemplates the inapparent, as is the case with alterity, the revealed "things themselves" multiply in

CHAPTER 38: INTENTIONALITY IN THE REVELATION OF THE SACRED

their diversity, thus allowing what remained hidden to manifest. Michel Henry emphasizes the relevance of adopting this broader perspective by stating:

> One might say that phenomenology mistrusts ultimate explanations and is attached primarily to problems of description. But a description that allows the "thing itself"—the pathos of every concrete intersubjectivity—to escape as it occurs cannot be justified, even on the level of facticity.[162]

From this perspective, phenomenology moves away from the task of describing the fixed or immutable essence of things, recognizing instead that what defines things is an identity in constant transformation. This introduces a dynamic in which only that which differs from me can truly be described. Nevertheless, if we consider that Being is found within me, any distinction between the subject and the object of description dissolves. If, on the contrary, we considered that Being is in me, and only in me, but is not understood as alterity, we would be dissolving any distance, any difference, which is what ultimately allows for description. If Being were solely immanent, any attempt to explain, reference, or define what is not separate from oneself would become an act of reification. This is why Heidegger conceives of Being as "nothing," referring to its absence of existence independent of us, which leads him to underline a fundamental principle of phenomenology that recognizes the interweaving between the observer and the observed, thus challenging traditional conceptions of objectivity and separation. The same idea is found in the Roman philosopher Cicero, when he wrote:

> What do you think of the Cyrenaic School? philosophers far from contemptible, who affirm that there is nothing which can be perceived externally; and that they perceive those things alone which they feel by their inmost touch, such as

---

162. Ibid., 117–118.

pain, or pleasure. And that they do not know what colour anything is of, or what sound it utters; but only feel that they themselves are affected in a certain manner.[163]

---

163. Cicero, *The Academic Questions, Treatise De Finibus, and Tusculan Disputations: With a Sketch of the Greek Philosophers Mentioned by Cicero*, trans. Charles Duke Yonge (London: George Bell & Sons, 1891), 58.

CHAPTER 39

THE ROLE OF THE OBSERVER

The reinterpretation and redefinition of intentionality and givenness, from Henry's perspective, have led Marion to reinterpret the concept of "I" through the lens of anamorphosis. This suggests adopting a new perspective facilitated by givenness that positions the individual in the role of observer rather than active protagonist. According to Marion, we should avoid an overly psychologistic view (which would arise from asking, "to whom is the givenness given?") or an overly neutral interpretation (which would result from asking, "to what is the givenness given?"). What is important is not "to whom" or "to what" it is shown, but "that it is shown."

In this framework, Marion introduces the figure of the addressee, which marks a transition from his metaphysical configuration. Unlike the subject, the addressee interacts without the intention to anticipate or generate the phenomenon, establishing a relationship devoid of dominance. In other words, the addressee is a witness and he waits. When discussing the notion of the addressee, Marion anticipates two potential criticisms from "metaphysical approaches," which emphasize the importance of the subject in ensuring the phenomenality in any act of representation. In response to this, Marion distinguishes between recognizing that no phenomenon remains outside the representation of the "I," which involves the notion of "I exist," and the idea that such representation implies a thought of the "I" that synthesizes and unifies.

This reveals the transcendence inherent in the act of communication, where the figures of the sender, the receiver, and the statement do not refer to a concrete and singular "I," but rather to the Being of the sender, which cannot be condensed or fully explained through any individual consciousness. In this dynamic, the "self" of the sender transcends the boundaries of a clearly defined identity, showing that the essence of the one who communicates is much broader and more complex than any simple individual identity could contain.

The transformation in the perception of the subject toward the role of the addressee is characterized by what could be called a "lowering or diminishment of intentional activity." The primacy of thought as a central paradigm is relegated to the background, favoring the model of affectivity as the underlying foundation of all subjectivity. In this sense, Marion proposes that Being should manifest primarily as "I am affected" and explains this transition by stating:

> The "self" of the phenomenon—as soon as it is established against objectness—transforms the I into a witness, according to a compulsory anamorphosis, because it first inverts the nominative (the subject, such as grammar posits it) into a more original dative, which designates (grammatically again) the "unto whom/which" of its receiver.[164]

The phenomenon, therefore, stands out through its self-affirmation, an opening that arises by opposing objectivity. In this scenario, there is no object, essence, thing, or being definable, because there is no subject that thinks, intuits, or defines it. The "I," in this sphere of experience, becomes an observer, no longer as the recipient of the givenness but as the witness to this giving, leading to a dynamic in which the "I" loses all centrality. The addressee or witness assumes the role of observer of the Being presented to him, thus differentiating themselves from the "me." Therefore, the "I" becomes a distinct entity, an external observer who, as we will see next, disappears in favor of observation and even loses its identity as a being, which dissolves into the very observation.

---

164. Jean-Luc Marion, *Being Given: Toward a Phenomenology of Givenness*, trans. Jeffrey L. Kosky (Stanford: Stanford University Press, 2002), 249.

Chapter 39: The role of the observer

In the experience of pure or ultimate consciousness, even the distanced "I" is regarded as just another object within the whole of reality. What one authentically is—the witness, the recipient, or the addressee—reveals itself beyond these transient identifications. This approach shifts the traditional understanding of the "I," proposing a view in which authentic Being transcends the limitations of both objective and subjective perception, emphasizing a state of being that lies beyond all individual cognition or affectivity.

According to Marion, the addressee enters into the essence of the phenomenon in its pure manifestation, facilitating the revealing of what is given exactly as it is delivered. Within this scheme, receiving becomes an act that transmutes the givenness into manifestation, positioning itself at an intermediate point between action and receptivity. Through the sensitivity of feeling, the givenness becomes manifestation. The addressee acts as a catalyst that allows the emergence of the first visibility, not because they actively seek to generate it, but as a result of their presence, of being-there, as Heidegger would say. This catalyst initially serves as the canvas on which the given becomes present, or as Marion himself explains:

> Before the not yet phenomenalized given gives itself, no filter awaits it. Only the impact of what gives itself brings about the arising, with one and the same shock, of the flash with which its first visibility bursts and the very screen on which it crashes. (*l'écran même où il s'écrase*).[165]

In this dynamic, thought is more associated with the reception of what is delivered than with its construction, and through this, it fosters its revelation:

> The response comes after (echoes, returns, corresponds), but for the I become a gifted.[166]

---

165. Ibid., 265.
166. Ibid., 265.

Thus, Marion dismisses the approach that prioritizes the knowledge of an object as that impressionistic dimension highlighted by Henry. However, he does agree that there is a stage that precedes constituted phenomenality. He refers to the attitude of givenness that precedes every figure bearing any sort of feature similar to and inherited from subjectivity. In other words, the given, the revealed, is what awakens the addressee, who, upon awakening, waits without knowing what is to come. Therefore, Marion argues in this same book: "The addressee echoes what is manifested, responding to what is given (*il répond à ce qui se donne*)."[167] In this context, we can assert, as Marion does, but also Derrida, that prior to all knowledge, perception, subject, receiver, object, and donor, there is only givenness in the process of phenomenization. Givenness underlies all entities that awaken when it occurs, bursting forth without being awaited or calculated by anything or anyone. This is how Derrida understands it when he talks about gift-giving, saying:

> *Le don non seulement ne doit pas être payé de retour, mais même gardé en mémoire, retenu comme symbole d'un sacrifice, comme symbolique en général. Car le symbole engage immédiatement dans la restitution. A vrai dire, le don ne doit pas même apparaître ou signifier, consciemment ou inconsciemment, comme don pour les donateurs, sujets individuels ou collectifs. Dès lors que le don apparaîtrait comme don, comme tel, comme ce qu'il est, dans son phénomène, son sens et son essence, il serait engagé dans une structure symbolique, sacrificielle ou économique qui annulerait le don dans le cercle rituel de la dette. La simple intention de donner, en tant qu'elle porte le sens intentionnel du don, suffit à se payer de retour. La simple conscience du don se renvoie aussitôt l'image gratifiante de la bonté ou de la géné- rosité, de l'être-donnant, qui, se sachant tel, se reconnaît cir- culairement, spéculairement, dans une sorte d'auto-reconnaissance, d'approbation de soi-même et de gratitude narcissique.*

---

167. Ibid., 288.

CHAPTER 39: THE ROLE OF THE OBSERVER

To tell the truth, the gift must not even appear or signify, consciously or unconsciously, as gift for the donors, whether individual or collective subjects. From the moment the gift would appear as gift, as such, as what it is, in its phenomenon, its sense and its essence, it would be engaged in a symbolic, sacrificial, or economic structure that would annul the gift in the ritual circle of the debt. The simple intention to give, insofar as it carries the intentional meaning of the gift, suffices to make a return payment to oneself. The simple consciousness of the gift right away sends itself back the gratifying image of goodness or generosity, of the giving-being who, knowing itself to be such, recognizes itself in a circular, specular fashion, in a sort of auto-recognition, self-approval, and narcissistic gratitude. And this is produced as soon as there is a subject, as soon as donor and donee are constituted as identical, identifiable subjects, capable of identifying themselves by keeping and naming themselves. It is even a matter, in this circle, of the movement of subjectivation [...]. The becoming-subject then reckons with itself, it enters into the realm of the calculable as subject. That is why, if there is gift, it cannot take place between two subjects exchanging objects, things, or symbols. The question of the gift should therefore seek its place before any relation to the subject, before any conscious or unconscious relation to self of the subject.[168]

When what is granted, what is given without expectation, awakens observation, and the phenomenon emerges, it presents itself, it reveals itself, as a saturated phenomenon. Its effect intensifies, transforming into an imperative and turning the recipient into a privileged addressee. The allusion to the "calling" evokes previous discussions influenced by Heidegger and Levinas. Contrary to Heidegger's proposals, Marion argues that the calling transcends the problem

---

168. Jacques Derrida, "Giving Time: The False Coin," in *Given Time: I. Counterfeit Money*, trans. Peggy Kamuf (Chicago: University of Chicago Press, 1992), 23–24.

of Being or the ontological difference. Rather, the calling and the demand are configured as central elements in the summoning of the addressee. This aspect is of particular interest for the analysis of changes in the "subjective" aspect within the phenomenology of the immanent, as the receptive disposition toward saturated phenomena is directly associated with an inversion of intentionality. This inversion was hinted at by Levinas when he introduced the notion of a "countercurrent consciousness" which outlines a "counter-intentionality" in his book *Otherwise than Being: or Beyond Essence*. This is a concept that defines the nature of all saturated phenomena by its capacity to invert intentionality and subject the addressee to the imposition of the calling.

All this leads us to a double conclusion. On the one hand, Marion redefines intentionality, transcending it and turning it into givenness from the perspective of the saturated phenomenon. On the other hand, and as a direct consequence of this, the intentional subject has taken the position of the assignee, the witness, giving rise to the manifestation of Being as an entity and, finally, clearing the path for the entity to dissolve into Being. Or, what would be the same, for God to become human so that the human may become divine. Therefore, Marion can say:

> Before the not yet phenomenalized given gives itself, no filter awaits it. Only the impact of what gives itself brings about the arising, with one and the same shock, of the flash with which its first visibility bursts and the very screen on which it crashes. (*l'écran même où il s'écrase*).[169]

This statement emphasizes the unpredictability and radicality of the given, underscoring how the initial revelation of any unexpected phenomenon simultaneously triggers both manifestation and the recipient's receptive capacity. Thus, Being reveals itself suddenly and surprisingly, like a lightning bolt no

---

169. Jean-Luc Marion, *Being Given: Toward a Phenomenology of Givenness*, trans. Jeffrey L. Kosky (Stanford: Stanford University Press, 2002), 265.

one anticipates. Its eruption occurs in moments and in ways completely unexpected to its own timelessness, in which there is still no present, past, or future, which are categories of the time of cognitive consciousness. This rupture is triggered in the medium where it strikes, for Being, upon revealing itself, does not merely present itself, but bursts forth with force, decomposing or collapsing the structure of the "I."

"It is the same revelation that, upon bursting forth, strips the subject, removing all its coverings and canceling it as a subject, turning it into a witness, into the addressee of the sacred that is revealed. The revelation of the sacred causes a profound transformation: "It is no longer I who live, but it is Christ who lives in me" (Galatians 2:20). This expression shows a "me" devoid of "I." If the revelation of the sacred did not dissolve the barrier of duality, it would remain merely a mystical experience, where the first glimpse on the screen of individual consciousness would be comparable to the marvelous spectacle of a lightning bolt. However, Being, upon striking, also disintegrates this mystical screen, eliminating any projection upon it and completely dissolving the subject-object dichotomy."

Our personal experiences and dramas are projected onto the screen of pure consciousness. With the appearance of Being, this screen also collapses. The revelation of the sacred is not about an additional projection on the screen. Before anything can be phenomenalized, and therefore before it can be considered a phenomenon, something else occurs. Marion emphasizes that "no filter awaits it or there is no screen," highlighting the importance of this "screen" as the stage upon which our lives, tragedies, and dramas are projected. The irruption of Being, instead of integrating itself into this narrative, breaks the illusion of the simulacrum. The Being always resides in me, for although one assumes the role of a king on the stage and says "I," referring to the monarch, one simultaneously refers to the actor, who is the underlying Being characterized by its latent revelation. Heidegger reflects on this condition, stating: "The drama of the West is that it seeks Being outside the cave, when in reality it was inside,"[170] that is, in the revelation of the sacred through which every agent, every subject, and every universe of phenomena is born. What Heidegger, and phenomenology, have ultimately shown is that the search for Being has been misdirected outward, when its essence and "presence" lie within us.

---

170. Martin Heidegger, "Plato's Doctrine of Truth," in *Pathmarks*, ed. William McNeill (Cambridge: Cambridge University Press, 1998), 155.

Bibliography section IX

- Cicero. *The Academic Questions, Treatise De Finibus, and Tusculan Disputations: With a Sketch of the Greek Philosophers Mentioned by Cicero*. Translated by Charles Duke Yonge. London: George Bell & Sons, 1891.
- Derrida, Jacques. "Giving Time: The False Coin." In *Given Time: I. Counterfeit Money*, translated by Peggy Kamuf. Chicago: University of Chicago Press, 1992.
- Derrida, Jacques, and Jean-Luc Marion. "On the Gift." In *God, the Gift, and Postmodernism*, edited by John D. Caputo and Michael J. Scanlon, 54–78. Bloomington: Indiana University Press, 1999.
- Hegel, Georg Wilhelm Friedrich. *Phenomenology of Spirit*. Translated by A. V. Miller. Oxford: Oxford University Press, 1977.
- Heidegger, Martin. "Plato's Doctrine of Truth." In *Pathmarks*, edited by William McNeill, 155–82. Cambridge: Cambridge University Press, 1998.
- Henry, Michel. *Material Phenomenology*. Translated by Scott Davidson. New York: Fordham University Press, 2008.
- Husserl, Edmund. *Cartesian Meditations: An Introduction to Phenomenology*. Translated by Dorion Cairns. The Hague: Martinus Nijhoff, 1960.
- Kant, Immanuel. *Critique of Pure Reason*. Edited and translated by Paul Guyer and Allen W. Wood. Cambridge: Cambridge University Press, 1998.
- Marion, Jean-Luc. *Being Given: Toward a Phenomenology of Givenness*. Translated by Jeffrey L. Kosky. Stanford, CA: Stanford University Press, 2002.
- Marion, Jean-Luc. *God Without Being*. Translated by Thomas A. Carlson. Chicago: University of Chicago Press, 1991.

- O'Murchadha, Felix. *The Time of Revolution: Kairos and Chronos in Heidegger*. London: Bloomsbury Academic, 2013.
- Sandywell, Barry. *Presocratic Reflexivity: The Construction of Philosophical Discourse c. 600–450 B.C. Logological Investigations*, vol. 3. 1st ed. London: Routledge, 1996; eBook, 2002.
- Spinoza, Baruch. *Ethics Demonstrated in Geometrical Order*. Translated by William Hale White. London: Teubner & Co., 1883.

Section X

In search of God

CHAPTER 40

ECHOES OF SPINOZA, HEGEL, AND SCHOPENHAUER ON GOD

The exposition we have made so far about the phenomenology of the sacred maintains important ties with certain authors, whom we would like to address here, even briefly. More specifically, we will examine Spinoza, Hegel, and Schopenhauer to clarify and further enrich some of the central points of our study.

In Spinoza's conceptualization of the Divine, we are presented with a notion of God that is deeply rooted in immanence, delineating God as the exclusive substance upon which reality is based, admitting the existence of nothing outside of it. Spinoza maintains that there is a single substance constituting reality, in contrast to the duality proposed by René Descartes of *res cogitans*, or "the mind," and *res extensa*, "or matter." This single substance is identified with God, who is infinite and possesses countless attributes and dimensions, of which we have only partial knowledge. In this view, both thought and matter are expressions, modes, or manifestations of this single substance, meaning that all that exists, including ourselves, is part of the divinity. For Spinoza, the soul is not an entity exclusive to the human mind but permeates everything, from stones to landscapes, which implies that everything is divine in a certain sense.

Therefore, for Spinoza, the differences typically made between the spiritual and the material are virtually nonexistent. Spinoza does not conceive of God as a personal entity that governs existence from the outside but rather as the totality manifesting both in extension and in thought. In other words, reality itself is God, expressing itself through nature, which is one of the specific ways it manifests. In this framework, God does not impose a purpose on the world; rather, the world is an extension of God. Spinoza himself describes this concept as "natura naturans," that is, the essence that originates various forms or "natura naturata," such as thought and matter.

For Spinoza, God is everything, and there is absolutely nothing outside of Him. In his work *Ethics Demonstrated in Geometrical Order*,[171] published in 1677, it is stated that God is a singular, eternal, unlimited, self-generated entity endowed with an infinity of aspects, which serve as means for His understanding. This conception gives God autonomy in causal, logical, ontological, and epistemological terms in relation to the rest of the cosmos, which manifests as variations or components within the same essence. In opposition to the Divine, understood as the primordial essence of and in everything, finite entities present themselves as manifestations, variations, or incidents of this totality. This idea is summarized in this proposition:

> Whatever is, is in God, and nothing can either be or be conceived without God.[172]

From Spinoza's perspective, therefore, the assumption of the existence of any being or entity independent of God would, by necessity, imply a restriction on the limitless nature of the Divine. The emergence of any reality outside of God would undermine the totalizing character of His omnipresence, as the presence of such entities would diminish the extent of His boundless domain. According to this doctrine, every being, everything that is, is immersed in God or, in other words, God is everything. This implies that the possibility of something external to this divine reality would directly contradict His essence of infinity. By His condition of infinity, God encompasses and constitutes the totality of all that exists, so that any manifestation of reality can only be interpreted as an expression or facet of the divinity itself. Therefore, there is no space for an existence that unfolds outside of this primordial and unlimited substance. This

---

171. Baruch Spinoza, *Ethics Demonstrated in Geometrical Order*, trans. William Hale White (London: Teubner & Co., 1883).
172. Ibid., Part I, Prop. XV, 14.

interpretation invites us to consider the totality of the cosmos and its manifestations as parts of the divine substance, with no elements or dimensions outside this sacred and infinite framework, thus ensuring a coherent and unified vision of existence.

The interpretation and classification of Spinoza's ideas by later thinkers have been varied, labeling him as pantheist, panentheist, and a proponent of absolute immanentism. Due to these classifications and his rejection of the notion of a personal and revealed God, he was ultimately accused of atheism. Because of his understanding of substance as causally determinative and excluding freedom, he was seen as a fatalist and nihilist. Spinoza's proposal of the Divine stirred controversy in significant sectors of subsequent philosophy, which initially repudiated it, only to later appreciate and integrate it, especially reinterpreting it in the era of German idealism. Philosophers such as Leibniz, Lessing, Fichte, Schelling, Hegel, Nietzsche, Bergson, and Deleuze have reflected Spinoza's conception of divinity in their works. Additionally, in fields outside pure philosophy, figures such as Albert Einstein, Sigmund Freud, and Antonio Damasio have recognized Spinoza's influence on their thinking, demonstrating the broad and profound impact of his ideas across various disciplines.

Another author to whom we wish to pay special attention in this chapter is Hegel. Although his view regarding God may have certain points of connection with Spinoza's position, the approach is radically different. In his *Phenomenology of Spirit*, Hegel writes:

> The bud disappears in the bursting-forth of the blossom, and one might say that the former is refuted by the latter; similarly, when the fruit appears, the blossom is shown up in its turn as a false manifestation of the plant, and the fruit now emerges as the truth of it instead. These forms are not just distinguished from one another, they also supplant one another as mutually incompatible. Yet at the same time their fluid nature makes them moments of an organic unity in which they not only do not conflict, but in which each is

as necessary as the other; and this mutual necessity alone constitutes the life of the whole.[173]

According to Hegel, spirit unfolds, transforms, and develops through an act of self-reflection, transcending from a phase of purely potential existence, or being-in-itself, toward a more conscious and self-determined manifestation, known as being-for-itself. This process of introspection brings with it a peculiar dialectic: in attempting to conceptualize itself and become the subject of its own contemplation, spirit faces alienation from itself. In this phenomenon of transformation, the spirit perceives itself as another. This game of self-exteriorization is necessary for spirit to reach genuine self-understanding. This can only materialize when spirit is able to see itself reflected in another, insofar as this other also represents an extension of its being. However, such reciprocal recognition can only be viable under the condition that the estrangement from itself, or self-alienation, is not total. If this self-alienation were total, there would be no recognition, but rather knowledge of something entirely external and different from spirit.

In the Hegelian philosophical horizon, the supreme purpose of spirit is its complete understanding and self-identification—a goal that is fully realized in the domain of philosophy. In this sense, the history of philosophy is interpreted as an evolution toward greater self-consciousness and spiritual self-realization. The culmination of this spiritual and intellectual journey, along with that of spirit itself, is achieved through a comprehensive philosophical understanding of spirit, an objective that Hegel claims to have reached in his own philosophical work. This landscape outlines a journey where philosophy not only narrates the development of spirit toward its full realization but also stands as the ultimate stage where spirit comes to understand itself in all its complexity and totality.

Within the conceptual framework proposed by Hegel, the "spirit" is understood as an entity that embodies both corporeality and

---

173. Georg Wilhelm Friedrich Hegel, *Phenomenology of Spirit*, trans. A.V. Miller (Oxford University Press, 1977), 2.

dynamism, as well as an extension of thought into tangible reality. Contrary to an immobile existence in a purely theoretical domain, spirit is saturated and energized by its interaction with the universe, emerging as the primordial force behind all being. In other words, for Hegel, the history of humanity is the history of spirit coming to understand itself—that is, comprehending its ultimate meaning in all the material extension in which it is reflected and without which it could neither self-unfold nor self-understand. In this sense, all thought, all historical stages, all philosophies, and movements are necessary steps of the same spirit, the result of a cumulative process of self-exploration and the historical evolution of thought.

Spirit, originally latent, reaches its fullness through this development, manifesting an intrinsic and fundamental displacement within Being, where the essence of spirit infiltrates and defines the nature of the object. Therefore, the object manifests as a projection of its synchronicity with spirit, highlighting the underlying logic of its development. This phenomenon underscores a moment of symmetry between the concept and its materialization, in which the universe encapsulates the bidirectional movement of thought toward Being and Being back toward thought. Spirit, therefore, transitions from the realm of the abstract to the concrete, a journey that gives rise to culture, civilization, physical practices, and the structuring of beings in time and space within a system. From this external manifestation, the structure of objectivity is generated. Thought, in its quest for self-discovery within this external domain, embarks on the process of incorporating activities and forms defined by its own logic. This path proposed by Hegel traces a complete circle, from theory to phenomenology and back again to the theoretical realm, thus outlining a dynamic of continuous exchange between intellect and physical reality.

In *The Phenomenology of Spirit* by Hegel, the concept of consciousness plays a fundamental dialectical role, characterized by its ability to contradict its own definition when there is a discrepancy between it and its corresponding object. This act of contradiction is decisive for the development of consciousness and, consequently, of reality itself. Only by identifying the truth of its knowledge does consciousness reach a deep understanding of its own essence and the environment in which it finds itself. The process of the evolution of consciousness that Hegel outlines is not the result of a spontaneous emergence but rather reflects a carefully elaborated progression from his initial writings to the culmination of its theoretical expression in this work. The persistence of consciousness throughout Hegel's work, from his early critiques to the consolidation of his philosophical system, establishes it as a critical element against modern philosophical doctrines and their views of the cosmos. Essentially, consciousness serves as the link that harmonizes Being with thought, addressing and resolving the dualism that has caused so much debate within philosophy, and which, in the eyes of Søren Kierkegaard, would be nothing but "the tragedy of knowing oneself" and "the anguish of despairing of oneself."

In analyzing revelation from the perspective of the Western philosophical tradition, one could discuss how the scheme or framework of phenomenology integrates with Schopenhauer's ontological conception. This philosopher postulates the existence of an actively desiring subject and an object that is desired, thus establishing the foundations of individual consciousness. The "I" is presented as an entity in constant search of satisfaction before a desired object. Schopenhauer argues that, after repeated attempts to placate his will through various entities or people, the subject comes to the realization that no external entity fulfills his expectations. He thus recognizes that no element of the external world has the capacity to soothe his perpetual longing. The individual, chained to his own desiring nature, may come to reflect that his desire is erroneous or that, in essence, the objects of his desire are mere illusions. This may then lead him to deduce that the objects of his yearning, in fact, lack the ability to satisfy his aspirations genuinely.

Upon becoming aware of this reality, the subject begins a process of distancing himself from things, understanding that they are nothing but manifestations of his will, created in a futile attempt to achieve satisfaction. In this sense, his will is reflected in the desirable objects, which have been conceived by the desire to reach a state of fulfillment. Upon discovering the illusory nature of the objects, the subject's will dissolves, as the existence of the will is intrinsically linked to that of the desired thing. With the object's disappearance, the subject finds himself incapable of desiring anything more. Schopenhauer calls this phenomenon of the dissolution of both the object and the will of the subject, *nirvāṇa*, or "liberation" in Sanskrit. This is a state in which the duality between desiring and the object of desire evaporates. Along with the object's disappearance, the subject also evaporates, for, as Kant already holds that there is no object without a subject.

CHAPTER 41

A PHILOSOPHICAL JOURNEY IN THE SEARCH FOR GOD

Historically, metaphysicians have taken on the task of assigning names to the Divine, defining it through concepts such as the idea of the good for Plato, pure reflection in Aristotle, or the One in Plotinus. Thus, they have established a correspondence between the Divine, later identified with the Christian God in scholasticism and a specific denomination. Aristotle introduces the concept of the Unmoved Mover as a purely actual entity, without potential, that moves the world without being moved, through the desire or love it inspires in other beings. Inspired by both Christianity and Platonism, Saint Augustine identifies God as the Supreme Good, the ultimate source of all goodness and existence. In his synthesis of philosophy and Christian theology, Thomas Aquinas describes God as Pure Act, without potentiality, perfect, immutable, and the first cause of everything that exists.

According to Baruch Spinoza, God is the only substance that exists, with infinite attributes, of which everything else is a mode or expression. Hegel conceptualizes God as the Absolute, the ultimate reality that manifests through the dialectical process of thesis, antithesis, and synthesis, reaching its full realization in absolute spirit. Meister Eckhart speaks of a "Groundless Godhead," a divine principle beyond God, incomprehensible and without attributes, where the true union of the soul with the Divine occurs. Søren Kierkegaard emphasizes the absolute transcendence of God, seeing Him as "The Absolutely Other," completely distinct from human existence and understandable only through a leap of faith that transcends reason, intellect, and even language. It is often represented in the episode of Abraham that we have previously discussed. Paul Tillich proposes that God is the "Ground of Being," the depth of Being in itself, which sustains all that exists and before whom one finds oneself in a state of "ultimate concern." On the other hand, Immanuel Kant refers to the existence of a supreme moral being, that is, God.

Formulating a principle or basis that describes the Divine does not pose a challenge for those accustomed to thinking about these matters. However, the legitimacy of such a nominal assignment to the Divine, made after the argument for the existence of God, where a particular concept is linked to the Divine in a somewhat veiled and seemingly obvious manner, could only be confirmed directly by God Himself. Therefore, the question about the existence of God is posed not at the beginning, but at the end of reasoning. At this stage, it is no longer enough for us to choose a concept or an entity to represent God. The need arises to validate that God Himself fully coincides with our choice.

Based on this, it can be argued that the five ways of Saint Thomas do not lead unequivocally to God. For example, the first leads us to the Unmoved Mover, regarding which Thomas points out that "this is what everyone understands by God." The second leads us to the primary efficient cause, named by all as "God"; and so on until the fifth, which identifies a final purpose, again described as "that which everyone recognizes as God."

In modern times, thinkers like Malebranche and Descartes have described the divinity in terms that refer to the Infinite, the unlimited Being, or a perfect and independent substance. Nevertheless, the essential question that emerges here is related to the one who determines the equivalence between the final concept obtained in the demonstration and the "God" universally recognized. It does not seem clear to determine the grounds and foundations of this reasoning to equate such a final concept with God Himself.

The attempt to encapsulate the nature of the Divine or of God within the narrowness of terms and definitions confronts us with a complex dilemma. For instance, Hegel suggests that religious revelation shows a fusion between the Divine and the human, which could imply an intimacy with the Divine, but at the possible cost of reducing it to an anthropomorphic image. In our effort to frame God within linguistic constructions, what we accomplish is distancing ourselves from His ineffable reality, forging a representation that does not correspond to His true entity and resembles more of a deity fabricated by the human mind.

In this endeavor to discern the Divine exclusively through logical analysis, we distance ourselves to the point of feeling in a spiritual void, as if the divine presence slips away between the fingers of our understanding. In the attempt to comprehend the divinity exclusively through intellect and human logic, we paradoxically move away from the essence of the sacred. It would be akin to the effort of holding water in our hands; the harder we squeeze, the more it slips away. By wanting to unravel God with definitions and reasonings, we weave a web of complexities that diverts and deprives us of a true spiritual encounter. In this rational search for the Divine, we strip away its presence, ending up in a void where its existence seems to fade.

The proposed reflection urges us to think about a warning from Leibniz: the fundamental distinction between our personal conceptions of God and His genuine manifestation. By addressing the divine understanding without anchoring it in the true essence of Being, we travel a path where the usual tools of comprehension lose effectiveness. It is vital to recognize that the inability to encapsulate God in precise definitions does not constitute a paradox or a failure; the essence of God transcends what can be conceived by the human mind. Nature, vast and divergent in our everyday experience, challenges any attempt at exhaustive description. This effort is not in vain but a recognition that certain aspects of the Divine exceed our comprehension, inviting us to accept the existence of unfathomable mysteries that foster a greater reverence and admiration for the sacred.

According to Leibniz, it is impossible to capture the essence of God solely with theories or concepts. Instead, he suggests that we should recognize that God is something that goes beyond our capacity to understand completely through language or logic. This does not mean it is a problem or a contradiction; rather, God is so great and complex that it defies any attempt to be completely defined or comprehended by our reason. Leibniz reflects on divine existence, arguing that if the impossibility of the coexistence of God's perfections cannot be demonstrated, then His possible existence must be contemplated. Under this reasoning, the mere possibility of God implies His real existence, as absolute perfection presupposes authentic existence. Leibniz also suggests that we should not limit ourselves to this idea, but remain open to further evidence of God's existence based on our observations of the world. This approach not only expands the spectrum of divine understanding but invites a continuous exploration of the sacred through empirical evidence and logic.

When trying to know or understand God, we face the limitation of not possessing a theoretical framework that can encapsulate His infinite magnitude. Marion presents us with a perspective where God surpasses any attempt to be pigeonholed within our notion of "Being." The philosophy of Jean-Luc Marion provides clues to answer those great questions that resonate in the confusion and void of our era. These clues question the limits set by modern metaphysics, which seems to be trapped in its own wear and tear or in failed attempts at revival. It aims to give fresh air to reason.

Marion suggests that reason should renew itself, allowing itself to be questioned and inspired by the topics of theology, in a journey toward the unknown and the new. In this intersection where metaphysics, theology, and phenomenology converge, Marion's position and the unique potency of his work truly stand out. His work focuses on challenging the fusion between God and a mere idea. More specifically, in attempting to fit "God" within the bounds of metaphysics, the French phenomenologist accuses modern philosophy of having led to what is referred to as "the death of God." However, according to him, what has really fallen is only an idolatrous concept of God, not the divinity itself.

This "death of God" speaks of a huge gap that no concept can encompass. By deconstructing the conceptual images we have mistakenly taken as divine, Marion invites us to an openness toward the unknown, allowing words and listening to be oriented toward a genuine transcendence. In this era, still resonating with Nietzsche, what dies is an idol, not the God of Abraham, Isaac, and Jacob. Marion advocates for a non-philosophical transcendence, in the style of Pascal, which does not renounce reason, but challenges it to confront what exceeds it, transforming it profoundly. From his early works, he addresses this tension, reinterpreting Descartes and critically dialoguing with Heidegger, seeking to free the living God from the constraints of an ontotheology. To confuse God with a supreme being turns Him into the cause of all that exists, trapping Him in a cycle of cause and effect where the miraculous becomes impossible. The real problem with this vision is that it ends up reducing the Divine to something manageable and predictable. In contrast, Marion proposes a vision where God is understood beyond these categories. He invites us to think of Him not as a being among beings, but as something completely apart, challenging traditional metaphysics and opening space for a more authentic and free relationship with the Divine.

Contrary to thinkers like Hegel, Marion proposes that a true self-exploration includes the religious and spiritual realm, indicating that the understanding of God transcends our capacity for reasoning. He suggests that, although it seems like a paradox, there is a possibility of approaching divine understanding, recognizing that certain aspects of the divinity will remain beyond our full cognitive reach. Thus, approaching the understanding of God involves delving into the realm of what our mind cannot fully grasp: a domain that exceeds both our understanding and the unimaginable for us. Although the immeasurable seems to be beyond our reasoning, it invites us to consider that; somehow, we may reach partial understanding within the limits of our thought, opening the possibility of approaching the Divine from a new perspective. Every intellectual effort to understand the divinity reveals the futility of our efforts to materialize it. Marion urges us to elevate our perception toward an understanding of God that goes beyond any human representation or idolatrous practice, encouraging us to adopt a distinctive marker that constantly reminds us of His nature beyond our most complex constructions.

Idols and concepts can act in the same way, serving as limited representations of the Divine. Throughout history, ontotheology has replaced true openness to the Divine with rigid concepts of "God." The succession of conceptions of God we see throughout history culminates in the critique of Feuerbach and Marx, who viewed the notion of "God" as a human conceptual construction. In contrast, the icon represents the Divine in a way that preserves its mystery and separation. According to Saint Paul, Christ is the "icon of the invisible God," showing the Divine without pretending to possess it:

> He is the image of the invisible God, the firstborn of all creation.
>
> (Colossians, 1:15)

While the idol reflects the subject, the icon acts as a prism that reveals the light of the Divine without reducing it to elements of the tangible world. The icon, then, is not a projection of the subject, but a window to transcendence, initiating a gaze that comes from beyond the human domain or understanding, marking a clear distinction between the self-indulgence of the idol and the transcendental openness of the icon, as Marion states when he affirms:

> [...] But the intention here issues from infinity; hence it implies that the icon allows itself to be traversed by an infinite depth. However, whereas the idol is always determined as a reflex, which allows it to come from a fixed point [...] the icon is defined by an origin without original.[174]

Many have tried to understand God, pigeonholing Him within concepts and theories, almost as if trying to package Him with a concrete definition. Marion, however, argues that this approach is insufficient, for God, by His very nature, transcends any attempt to be confined by our mental constructions. He points to Dionysius the

---

174. Jean-Luc Marion, *God Without Being*, trans. Thomas A. Carlson (Chicago: University of Chicago Press, 1991), 22–24.

Areopagite, who, inspired by Saint Paul's discourse on the "unknown God," quotes the Book of Acts and says:

> Because while I was passing and observing the objects of your worship, I also found an altar with this inscription: TO THE UNKNOWN GOD. For what you worship without knowing, this I proclaim to you.
>
> (Acts, 17:23)

Dionysius opens a path to understanding the Divine that goes beyond mere conceptualization. He describes God as the supreme Good, pointing toward an existence that transcends mere physical presence, inviting us to embrace a more expansive vision of the Divine. Similarly, Marion advocates for an exploration of God that is not limited to reductive descriptions, but instead employs a language capable of capturing His ineffable and sublime nature, without subjecting it to our limited categories.

Based on this, Marion emphasizes that the true approach to God is not achieved solely through intellectual efforts, but by living in a way that reflects the magnificence and divine love. According to Marion, it is this experience of love toward others that genuinely brings us closer to God, beyond any theoretical speculation. He urges us to free ourselves from the temptation to encapsulate God within our limited understandings and to live in a way that manifests divine love and glory. He believes that religion invites us to overcome our restrictive views of the Divine, teaching us to look beyond our own intellectual confines toward the true greatness of God. Far from diminishing the value attributed to the Divine, this approach invites us to deepen our appreciation of His magnitude, challenging the limits of our understanding. To achieve this, he incorporates the idea of the unthinkable into our reasoning in such a way that it truly becomes something we cannot conceive, encouraging us to reflect on our own cognitive abilities.

The essence of this message is not to call for the abandonment of our idea of God, but rather to invite a deeper introspection on the true meaning of the Divine in our lives. We are motivated to adopt a reflective and meticulous stance, phenomenologically speaking, regarding our perception and approach to what we consider supremely transcendent, that is, that which goes beyond the ordinary. This approach seeks to enrich our understanding of the divinity, urging us to question and delve into our relationship with the sacred. It encourages us to conduct an exhaustive analysis of how we understand and approach the notion of something that is supremely transcendent, motivating us to question and deepen our understanding and relationship with the divine concept:

> To cross out God, in fact, indicates and recalls that God crosses out our thought because he saturates it; better, he enters into our thought only in obliging it to criticize itself. The crossing out of God we trace on his written name only because, first, He brings it to bear on our thought, as his unthinkableness. We cross out the name of God only in order to show ourselves that his unthinkableness saturates our thought-right from the beginning, and forever.[175]

Jean-Luc Marion elevates love to the category of an essential principle for reflecting on God, emphasizing that "God is love, Agapè." This perspective radically distinguishes itself from metaphysical and Heideggerian interpretations by placing love as the central axis for avoiding idolatry in our perception of God, based on two essential reasons. First, because of its nature of selfless giving, love breaks the limitations of rational thought and pre-established expectations, offering an approach to God free of conditions and human limitations. This concept breaks the chains of idolatry, which relies on the need to establish conditions that attempt to assign to God a place worthy of His majesty. However, when God is understood from the perspective of love, all prior conditions dissolve, since divine love for humanity is unconditional. Divine love, grounded solely in the desire for reciprocity, dismantles every idolatrous

---

175. Jean-Luc Marion, *God Without Being*, trans. Thomas A. Carlson (Chicago: University of Chicago Press, 1991), 46.

construct about God. Marion addresses the concept of "idolatry" as the act of constraining God within the limits of our conceptions, images, or ideas, which are accessible and understandable within our capacity for reasoning. He argues that by attempting to define God purely based on our own terms and representations, we are actually fabricating "idols" instead of connecting with the authentic divine nature. However, idolatry is not limited to the worship of physical figures but is rather a conceptual restriction that traps God within the framework of our logical reasoning and preconceived notions.

Secondly, by imagining God through the lens of Agapè, we prevent falling into the trap of visualizing Him through tangible representations or unreachable ideals. This unconditional love allows us to distance ourselves from limited representations of the Divine, favoring a relationship with God, based on generosity and altruistic exchange. In contrast to concepts that seek to capture and limit, love is characterized by its desire to give itself unconditionally, establishing a dynamic where the act of giving and the gift are inseparable. This unlimited and unconditional love prohibits us from clinging to idols, promoting an understanding of the Divine free from any idolatrous attachment.

Thus, Marion asserts that the only way to transcend idolatry is to approach God from His fundamental requirement, which transcends any conceptual barrier imposed both by ontotheology and by the limitations inherent in thought based on ontological difference. God becomes accessible to human thought without incurring idolatry only when He is considered as a gift, a givenness of love bestowed upon humanity. To distance "God" from any idolatrous form, Marion invites us to approach Him from a perspective that avoids reducing Him to mere idolatrous concepts, thus freeing "God" from conceptual restrictions and allowing us to think of Him beyond the confines of metaphysics and outside the realm of Being.

Our Retroprogressive system finds resonance, precisely, in the theories of these prominent philosophers we have been discussing. Thanks to them, we have been able to argue how the Phenomenology of the Sacred is a philosophical framework that allows us to approach the Divine as a phenomenon. However, as we will soon see in the next lines, this Phenomenology of the Sacred is not an introspection that merely leads us to the innermost part of a subject with which we can decipher the sacred as just another phenomenon. As we pointed out in the previous sections, authors such as Spinoza and Hegel have already laid the foundations to help us better understand the sacred. Spinoza, for example, conceives God as the total sum, the only and absolute reality, arguing that outside of God, nothing else can exist. For Spinoza, the infinity of God implies that everything is contained within Him; any separate existence would limit His infinity, making Him finite, and thus contradicting His nature. Thus, he posits that all existence is a manifestation of God, of the sacred. That is, all search for the sacred is, as Hegel later states, an expression of God Himself.

It is for this very reason that Hegel sees God unfolding and reaching self-knowledge through the development of the history of philosophy. For Hegel, this process of becoming and self-knowledge represents the absolute spirit manifesting throughout history, with philosophy standing as the domain in which this process unfolds most fully. Marion takes this idea even further, suggesting that God also self-knows through the history of religions. In this framework, different religious traditions provide specific "masks" through which the Divine can be experienced and revealed to itself, particularly through sacred texts.

In light of the above, we refer to the Retroprogressive Path as the interpretive framework that encompasses both philosophy and religion. It offers an integrative vision of divine self-knowledge that transcends the limits of any specific discipline or belief, reflecting the underlying unity of all quests for knowledge and truth. Divinity reveals itself in the saturated phenomenon, beyond the philosophical and theological boundaries, emerging from the innermost of intimacies, but as the radical excess of the same and, therefore, as pure otherness in immanence.

This relationship between intimacy and otherness within it, so to speak, that we have reached through our phenomenological study of the sacred, arises from the phenomenological relationship of the intentional object, but to later transcend it. Thus, initially, and following the premises of Husserlian phenomenology, we have stated that every relationship between consciousness and the object occurs through intentionality and givenness. The process by which the object presents itself to the subject, offering itself as a gift to be discovered, establishes the premise that the object, in its essence of givenness, is ready to be known.

In contrast, the subject emerges as the intention focused on recognizing the object or the givenness itself. This implies that the consciousness of the subject is directed to knowing the donated object. The subject's consciousness is not pure, as the act of thinking cannot be dissociated from content, meaning there is no act of consciousness without an object of thought. There is no *cogito* without *cogitatum*.

Following Marion's approach, based on Spinoza, Hegel, and Schopenhauer, we have discovered that beneath the relationship between consciousness and intentional objects lies a sphere of life in which the sacred beats permanently. This allows transcendental consciousness to correlate with its intentional objects so that these, the phenomena, can be given in consciousness in the fullness of their phenomenality.

In other words, during the act of knowledge, an intersection of horizons occurs that, as a phenomenological process, initially allows us to distinguish between givenness and intentionality, and later culminates in the unification of both into a single phenomenon. A dual beginning that leads to the oceanic unity of pure consciousness. The source and origin of both givenness and intentionality, the metaphysical space where both meet, as well as the substance of both, is the same pure consciousness. In essence, the phenomenon represents the awakening of consciousness from its illusion of duality, in which the one without a second donates and intends itself, by itself, from itself, in itself, and toward itself. This same idea pulses alive in the following quote:

न निरोधो न चोत्पत्तिर्न बद्धो न च साधकः ।
न मुमुक्षुर्न वै मुक्त इत्येषा परमार्थता ॥

Section X: In search of God

na nirodho na cotpattirna
baddho na ca sādhakaḥ
na mumukṣur na vai mukta
ity eṣā paramārthatā

> There is no dissolution, no birth, none in bondage, none aspiring for wisdom, no seeker of liberation and none liberated. This is the absolute Truth.
>
> (*Māṇḍūkya-kārikā*, 2.32)

In addition to philosophy, however, religion plays a fundamental role that, even without saying so, has accompanied us throughout our study, in that the essence of religion lies precisely in the deep exploration of consciousness. Despite my affinity for rationalism, my philosophical approach exceeds it and I do not confine myself to it. Logic and reasoning are merely the threshold to an ascending journey that surpasses the limits of the rational. Transcendence to the suprarational domain is synonymous with access to the Divine. Diverging from conventional conceptions of an *entitative* god, deeply rooted in religious traditions, the reality of such an entity is revealed to us as merely an illusion or fiction. What permeates the universe is divinity or consciousness.

Recognizing this consciousness begins with the exercise of reason, from which, paradoxically, we are able to liberate ourselves from rational bonds. It is not the figure of a god that prevails, but rather divinity, universal consciousness, or that vitality reflected in each entity and in the fabric of existence. The notion of God, as conceived by religious traditions, does not embody a specific entity, but rather, in essence, all things and all beings constitute that divinity. To assert that the god personified by religions does not fit reality does not categorize us as atheists, for we recognize the divine nature of existence itself. This position places us beyond the classifications of fideism or atheism. Our perspective does not align with those who affirm or deny the existence of an entitative and personal god, for God is not something but everything; He is not someone but everyone.

Chapter 41: A philosophical journey in the search for God

According to my own experience, God, Being, or consciousness is revealed as the canvas on which every experience is drawn, standing as the primordial source of all experience and the medium through which all experience is and can be known. In other words, God is the fundamental substance from which all experiences are woven. This divinity, this Being, thus stands as the foundation and guiding thread of subjective reality, configuring the space in which all experiences unfold.

BIBLIOGRAPHY SECTION X

- Hegel, Georg Wilhelm Friedrich. *Phenomenology of Spirit*. Translated by A. V. Miller. Oxford: Oxford University Press, 1977.
- Marion, Jean-Luc. *God Without Being*. Translated by Thomas A. Carlson. Chicago: University of Chicago Press, 1991.
- Spinoza, Baruch. *Ethics Demonstrated in Geometrical Order*. Translated by William Hale White. London: Teubner & Co., 1883.

Section XI

Toward a Retroprogressive Phenomenology

CHAPTER 42

THE RETROPROGRESSIVE INVERSION

Intentionality and givenness in traditional phenomenology

In traditional phenomenology, the concept of givenness refers to the act by which Being manifests or gives itself to consciousness, while intentionality describes the movement of consciousness as it directs itself toward an object, or *cogitatum*. Intentionality is the thrust of consciousness toward a *cogitatum*. It is the demand that consciousness has to be conscious of something. Just as consciousness illuminates Being so that it becomes conscious of itself, we say that consciousness is the light of Being. Phenomenology is the study of this light, which is consciousness. According to Husserl's phenomenology, intentionality constitutes the very essence of consciousness, that is, the light of Being.

The term "intentionality" sketches a notion of consciousness that should not be understood as an empty or neutral box that we simply fill with objects through experience. Rather, intentionality describes consciousness as an impulse that is inherently directed toward an object. In turn, this object, far from being a mere passive datum, presents itself to consciousness as part of the same intentional structure that allows its apprehension from multiple perspectives or modes of appearance. These modes of appearance facilitate the perception of the object and the understanding of its essence, in a dynamic process that could be characterized as a phenomenological manifestation of Being, rather than a mere givenness of the phenomenon. Thus, the great discovery of intentionality in Husserl's work is that it makes clear that there is no object without consciousness, just as there can be no consciousness without an object that consciousness is conscious of. Consciousness is a *cogito* that, by default, asks for or demands a *cogitatum*. In other words, it is impossible to conceive of an act of thinking or any state of consciousness that is not directed toward a content, an object upon which that act is focused. Therefore, consciousness is not an abstract entity separate from the world; rather, it is continuously engaged with it, interacting with the objects presented to it, forming a perpetual movement of seeking and apprehending meaning.

Thus, in classical phenomenology, consciousness fully realizes itself by becoming aware of its own ability to intend, to project itself toward what is not itself, always seeking to transcend and understand the Being that is revealed to it. There cannot be thought without an object to attend to, nor perception without a perceived object. Every mental state—whether of thought, emotion, desire, or perception—is inherently linked to an object that shapes and defines it. This essential link is precisely what defines intentionality: consciousness is always "consciousness of something," and that "something" cannot be separated from the conscious act itself. Moreover, intentionality not only structures consciousness but also reveals its dynamic nature. Consciousness is not a passive entity that merely receives impressions from the world; rather, it is a constant activity that projects itself toward objects, exploring, interpreting, and assigning meaning to them. This active process is what allows consciousness to build a meaningful relationship with the external world. In its orientation toward objects, it not only perceives them but also configures them within a horizon of unique meaning to it.

On the other hand, "givenness" is the second essential concept in our phenomenological exploration, as it plays a crucial role in the interaction between Being and consciousness, outlining an active and fruitful process through which Being becomes present to it. Givenness characterizes the manner in which Being manifests and offers itself to consciousness, allowing it to assimilate it. This process is not merely passive or one-directional; rather, it constitutes a dynamic phenomenon in which Being, in its manifestation, exhibits an intrinsic generosity, unfolding before consciousness in an act of revelation.

In his dialectic of the Spirit (*Geist*), Hegel offers a radically different view from that of Husserl's phenomenology. In Hegel, Being does not present itself immediately or statically, but is understood as a historical and dialectical process that develops and reaches self-consciousness over time. In this framework, consciousness is not a given starting point, but the result of the self-reflection of Spirit in its historical unfolding. For Hegel, history is the stage on which Spirit recognizes itself as subject, progressing toward an absolute consciousness, in which Being is fully understood and realized. Thus, Being is not a fixed entity but a continuous process of self-knowledge and realization that culminates in absolute consciousness.

The notion of givenness that arises from these approaches is grounded in the idea that Being is not a static entity closed within itself, but is in a constant state of openness toward consciousness. This concept highlights Being's capacity to reveal itself, to make itself known through conscious experience. In this process, Being reveals or uncovers itself, allowing consciousness to access its deep essence. Therefore, givenness is not simply an act in which Being gives itself; it is also the process by which consciousness receives, assimilates, and responds to that offering of Being's manifestation. Thus, we can affirm that consciousness, with its intentional structure, is not a passive receptor, but rather an impulse that is always directed toward something, receiving and assimilating the givenness of its correlate, immersed in a constant search for meaning.

From this perspective, givenness establishes a deep bond between Being and consciousness, a bond that is both ontological and epistemological. It is ontological in that it defines the way in which Being relates to and opens itself to consciousness in all the acts in which consciousness participates. It is epistemological in that it structures the way consciousness knows and relates to Being. Givenness thus becomes a bridge that connects Being with consciousness, allowing consciousness to be constituted from the openness of Being. In phenomenology, this relationship invites us to reconsider Being not as a pre-given entity, but as that which reveals itself and presents itself continuously in lived experience, in an incessant process of revelation and understanding.

This phenomenological perspective, based on the concepts of intentionality and givenness, forcefully challenges the conceptions of consciousness as an isolated entity, closed within itself and limited to introspection. By emphasizing intentionality, phenomenology redefines consciousness as an entity that not only relates to the world but is precisely constituted through that relation. The *cogito* is not a solitary thought contemplating itself; it is an act that necessarily involves an openness to something beyond, to a *cogitatum* that provides it with content and purpose. Therefore, intentionality is not simply an added attribute of consciousness; it constitutes its very essence. By requiring a *cogitatum*, consciousness reveals both its active and directed nature and the fundamental structure that makes all experience and knowledge possible.

It is this intentional relationship with Being that allows the world to become present to consciousness and that Being, in all its diversity, manifests itself before it. Without this intentionality, consciousness would remain disconnected from reality, and the world would remain hidden and inaccessible. Through this constant orientation toward objects, consciousness constructs its experience of the world, enabling understanding, knowledge, and, ultimately, the very existence of the known being. This process culminates in a kind of phenomenological closure when intentionality and givenness integrate, that is, when both aspects unify in an indistinguishable experience. In this context, givenness is interpreted as the mechanism by which consciousness opens itself to the manifestation of the phenomenon, while intentionality corresponds to the receptive act of consciousness that embraces this manifestation.

Intentionality and givenness in Retroprogressive Phenomenology

Retroprogressive Phenomenology proposes an innovative reinterpretation in which these concepts are inverted: what was traditionally understood as intentionality is now conceived as givenness, and what was understood as givenness transforms into intentionality. By inverting the roles of intentionality and givenness of traditional phenomenology, Retroprogressive Phenomenology assigns to consciousness the role that belongs to Being and to Being the role that belongs to consciousness. Under this new optic, Being is the intentionality that seeks to be conscious of itself by recognizing itself as consciousness. Being intends consciousness and meditates because it wants to be known, while, for its part, consciousness donates itself, opening itself to reveal itself as the light of Being. In this way, the relationship between both is redefined, profoundly altering the classical structure of phenomenological analysis.

Within this traditional phenomenological context, we have just described, and which, even saving the distances between them, takes us from Hegel to Heidegger through Husserl, Being is characterized by a fundamental action of givenness. For its part, consciousness, in its traditional dynamic, stands as the movement of orientation toward Being, as if it were its intentional object. However, from the perspective of Retroprogressive Phenomenology, it is now consciousness that donates itself to assume the status of Being, while Being intends itself with the purpose of being apprehended by consciousness. Here, consciousness does not seek an external object to know, but rather constitutes itself as that known object. In other words, it is not that Being is an object that consciousness apprehends, but rather that consciousness itself emerges as such and knows itself through Being.

In this sense, Retroprogressive Phenomenology reveals an ontological inversion that finds an interesting parallel with Marx's critique of labor and commodity. In Marx's theory, the worker, by transforming their labor into the production of commodities, transfers to them their value, their life, and their vital effort. Matter, which in its natural state is an inert object without intrinsic value, is humanized through the labor process, assuming the characteristics of what is living and valuable that come from the worker. However, this process culminates in alienation, where the worker is deprived of their humanity, becoming reified, while the commodity, in turn, is elevated to the status of a valuable subject, personified by its exchange value in the capitalist economy. Here, in a sense, Marx identifies an ontological inversion: what was originally human and living becomes a thing, reified, and what was a thing becomes humanized, subjectivized. Just as in Marx's analysis, where the labor process reconfigures relations between the human and the material, Retroprogressive Phenomenology proposes a reconfiguration where the dichotomy between Being and consciousness crumbles, giving way to a unity in which Being is fully realized only in its self-consciousness. In both cases, the ontological inversion unveils profound implications about the nature of Being, value, and consciousness, revealing the underlying dynamics that transform and sometimes distort the reality in which we live.

Retroprogressive Phenomenology introduces a radical reinterpretation of these concepts: here, Being becomes intentionality through meditation, and consciousness transforms into givenness through illumination or revelation. The key to this inversion lies in the fact that Being, as it is known by consciousness, is revealed (*alétheia*), recognizing itself as consciousness. This suggests that consciousness donates itself, emerging as Being in the process of self-knowledge, where Being intends and consciousness recognizes itself as part of that process. When Being intends, it does so to be known by consciousness, thus asking that consciousness become aware of its own essence. This process culminates in the rupture of individual consciousness, which dissolves as it becomes Being, while Being assumes the form of consciousness by intending itself and donating itself to gather itself into its own Being.

In traditional phenomenology, consciousness maintains a posture of knowing Being, of intending toward something that exists beyond it, something that transcends it. That transcendence is the distance that allows the object to appear precisely as something distinct from the very consciousness, and, therefore, as an object of knowledge for that consciousness. In contrast, in Retroprogressive Phenomenology, this relationship becomes bidirectional and more intrinsic: Being transforms into consciousness, and consciousness is realized in Being. Thus, the dichotomy between Being and consciousness blurs, reaching a point where consciousness becomes Being, and Being becomes consciousness. This approach not only reconfigures the classical relationship between both terms but also proposes a profound fusion where existence itself is understood as a process of self-revealing consciousness, in constant becoming and self-identification.

The blurring of the dichotomy between Being and consciousness that occurs after the reinterpretation of Retroprogressive Phenomenology also involves the fading of the traditional distinction between subject and object, resulting in the unification of givenness and intentionality into a single reality. That is to say, the relationship between consciousness and Being that Retroprogressive Phenomenology redraws is not based on a play of polarities; that is, on a binary relationship. On the contrary, in the process of givenness, Being presents itself to consciousness, and it is assimilated by it, dissolving into its infinitude and vastness, thus completing the dissolution of Being (*katálysis* κατάλυσις).

As this duality disappears, consciousness identifies with Being, as it is fully conscious of itself. In this way, in this context, we can affirm that there is no distinction between Being and consciousness. Both manifest as expressions of a single reality that configures itself through intentionality and givenness. Being intends in meditation, while consciousness donates itself, revealing itself in a process that unfolds from itself and in itself. It is, therefore, an act of reciprocity in which intentionality and givenness are nothing but two facets of a single reality, a unique dance where the multiple is found in the unity of Being and consciousness.

CHAPTER 43

LIGHT AND CONSCIOUSNESS: A RETROPROGRESSIVE EXPLORATION

Light and consciousness in traditional phenomenology

What has been presented thus far regarding the study of phenomena and the sacred leads us to an interpretation in terms of Retroprogressive Phenomenology. As we have explored in previous sections of this study, the etymology of "phenomenology" unveils a deep and meaningful relationship with the notion of "light" by investigating its roots in the Greek language. The word phenomenon comes from the Greek term *phainómenon* (φαινόμενον), which has its roots in the verb *phaínesthai* (φαίνεσθαι), which can be translated as "to appear" or "to manifest." In turn, *phaínesthai* derives from the verb *phaínein* (φαίνειν), meaning "to make appear" or "to make visible." This verb is intrinsically linked to the Greek word *phôs* (φῶς), which translates as "light," from which the word *phosphor* and others are derived. Light, in its most fundamental sense, is that which allows visibility, that which makes objects and forms reveal themselves before our eyes. In other words, it is the principle that enables something to take form and "appear," or become manifest in our perception, thus acquiring its phenomenality, its "appearance" as something concrete. On the other hand, the suffix *logy* (λογία) comes from *lógos* (λόγος), which in the context of ancient Greek encompassed meanings such as "discourse," "reason," "science," or "study." In the framework of phenomenology, this component of the term refers to a systematic approach, to a discipline concerned with studying phenomena, that is, investigating and understanding what is shown or revealed to consciousness.

Thus, when we speak of phenomenology, we can understand it as the discipline dedicated to the study of what becomes visible, of that which is illuminated and unfolds before consciousness. This study is not simply an analysis of what appears in a superficial sense, but a profound inquiry into how and why phenomena manifest in the first place and why they do so in the way they do. Phenomenology explores how these emerge from darkness into the light of consciousness, allowing for a clearer and more complete understanding of reality as it presents itself to human experience. This philosophical approach does not limit itself to describing external reality as it might be in itself, but focuses on how such reality is revealed and experienced by the conscious subject.

In the first book of *Metaphysics*, Aristotle introduces a profound reflection on the role of the senses in knowledge, proposing that these constitute the first faculties through which the human being is able to grasp the differences (*diáforas*) between objects in the world. Aristotle's theory of perception is based on the idea that each of the senses has the ability to grasp specific and limited aspects of sensible objects, confined to a particular dimension of reality. Thus, touch perceives qualities such as hardness or softness, but cannot perceive color or smell. Similarly, smell deals only with aromas, while sight perceives color and form but cannot apprehend either sound or taste. This sensory specialization reflects the inherent fragmentation of perceptual reality, inasmuch as each sense focuses on an isolated facet of the object. Aristotle suggests that such fragmentation is essential for the senses to provide knowledge about the *diáforas*, that is, the differences that constitute the plurality of the phenomenal world.

Although the senses provide us with information about the diversity of the sensible, Aristotle acknowledges that the knowledge obtained through them is incomplete. By their nature, the senses cannot grasp the object in its entirety or essence. Each sense operates within a scope delimited by the inherent characteristics of sensible objects, leading to fragmented and limited knowledge, dependent on the contingent and subjected to appearances. Consequently, sensory perception offers a partial and superficial view of reality. In light of this inherent limitation of the senses, Aristotle introduces a fundamental distinction between sensible knowledge and intellectual knowledge. While the senses allow for grasping the multiplicity and phenomenal diversity, it is the *nous*, or "intellect," the faculty that transcends appearances and reaches the understanding of *ousia*, or the "essence of objects." Unlike the senses, the intellect can apprehend the first causes and universal principles underlying sensible reality, thus allowing for access to a unifying and coherent understanding of the world. This intellectual knowledge is therefore superior to sensory knowledge, as it is not limited to the particular and accidental, but is oriented toward the universal and necessary, revealing the rational order that governs Being.

In his phenomenology, Edmund Husserl offers a different perspective that resonates with certain aspects of Aristotelian thought, introducing the concept of *eidetic intuition*. For him, although the senses fragment reality by presenting a dispersed multiplicity of sensible manifestations, eidetic intuition allows consciousness to apprehend the essence of the object in its totality. This type of intuition does not stop at external appearances or accidental differences; rather, it seeks to penetrate the essential structure of Being, offering a deep and unified understanding of reality. In this sense, *eidetic intuition* surpasses the limitations of sensory knowledge; it is not merely a complement to sensory perception but a form of knowledge that transcends it. While the senses offer us a dispersed and partial view of the world, *eidetic intuition* unifies these diverse facets into a complete apprehension, revealing the unity underlying phenomenal multiplicity. For Husserl, this direct intuition of the indivisible essence of the object allows us to access a deeper and more complete knowledge of reality, one that is not subject to the restrictions of sensible perception.

This contrast between Aristotle and Husserl highlights two distinct approaches to the process of knowledge. Aristotle conceives of *nous* as the faculty that allows us to transcend perceptual fragmentation and access the essential unity of Being. Husserl, on the other hand, places this capacity in *eidetic intuition*, which allows consciousness to apprehend the unified essence of objects beyond the phenomenal divisions. Both, though from different perspectives, seek the underlying unity that transcends the diversity of sensible appearances and postulate the existence of a superior faculty that enables access to a deeper and more integral understanding of reality.

The Retroprogressive integration of the visible, the audible, and the tactile

From the heart of a properly phenomenological investigation, we must ask ourselves in what sense it is possible to speak of a phenomenology that goes beyond the pillars of perception and knowledge upon which traditional epistemology is based. Phenomenology, as it has traditionally been conceived in the West, and as we have shown throughout this study, has focused on the manifestation of objects through their appearance to the sight, given that truth has historically been associated with the adequacy of thought to what is shown visually. This approach has its roots in Greek and Roman philosophy, where truth is understood as a revelation through vision, a process of *erscheinung* ("appearance" in German) in which the hidden is revealed to the eyes. However, contemporary thinkers such as Jean-Luc Marion and Michel Henry have proposed an expansion of this phenomenological conception, suggesting that the phenomenon is not limited to manifesting itself through sight. In this sense, they argue that Being can also reveal itself through hearing via revelation, thus implying a revaluation of the auditory sense in phenomenological experience.

This idea resonates with the Semitic and Vedic traditions, in which the ear is considered the main channel for the perception of the sacred. The *Shema Israel* (Hear Israel), one of the central pillars of Jewish liturgy, transcends its merely religious and ceremonial function to become a profound philosophical reflection on consciousness, listening, and the ontological relationship with the Divine. Although in common translations it is simply rendered as "hear," the Hebrew verb *shama* contains a conceptual complexity that far exceeds the simple reception of auditory stimuli. In Biblical Hebrew, *shama* refers to a modality of integral attention, which not only involves the reception of a message but also its deep understanding, assimilation, and an active response. This nuance is key to understanding the philosophical and theological meaning of the *Shema*. Far from being a mere verbal proclamation about the oneness of God—"Adonai is one"—the *Shema* constitutes an invitation to an existential disposition toward the sacred. Listening, in this context, is not limited to a passive act of hearing words; it demands a complete openness of Being, a sustained state of attention. In essence, this active listening is an epistemological and ethical stance that demands both intellectual acceptance of theological truth about divine unity as well as its integration into the totality of life. In this sense, the *Shema* forms a call to recognize the centrality of God beyond the ritual sphere. The structure and content of the *Shema* reveal a demand for ontological alignment with the divinity, an imperative to live in complete alignment with the consciousness of the oneness of God. It is not merely about reciting a prayer but about an openness and surrender to the transcendent.

At this point, an analogy can be drawn with the notion of *alétheia* in Greek philosophy, especially in the work of Martin Heidegger, where truth is more than the correspondence between a proposition and reality: it is the unveiling of Being. The *Shema*, like *alétheia*, invites a constant revelation of Being in its relationship with the sacred. Therefore, the *Shema Israel* can be interpreted as an exhortation to live in a state of permanent attentive observation, where listening to the Divine is not a mechanical or sporadic operation but a latent way of being that involves the totality of who we are. This listening transforms us, as the affirmation of the oneness of God demands a dying and a rebirth. Thus, the *Shema* becomes a paradigm of active listening, a model for how the human being must relate to the Divine: not merely as a passive receiver of revelation but as a willing agent who transforms their life from that listening, giving rise to an ethical existence that reflects the unity and fullness proclaimed in the prayer.

In the tradition of *Sanātana-dharma*, the Vedas, which include the Upanishads, are grouped under the concept of *śruti*, a Sanskrit term meaning "what is heard." This concept refers to the divine revelation received by the ṛṣis, sages who accessed eternal truths in states of deep transcendental meditation. In Hinduism, the *ṛṣis* hold a place of deep reverence, being seen as those who attained a state of illumination and transcendental wisdom. Through the ascetic practice of meditation, known as *tapas*, they accessed eternal knowledge, encapsulated in the Vedic hymns that form the basis of the revelation. With the development of Hinduism, the role of the *ṛsis* evolved into figures venerated for their ability to access higher spheres of reality through strict meditative discipline, granting them unparalleled spiritual authority. This process of enlightenment involved an integral transformation of the being, through which they directly understood the universal laws and the cosmic order. *Ṛsi* is translated into Pali as *isi*. In Buddhism, it refers to individuals of elevated spiritual level, such as Buddhas, *pacceka-buddhas* (solitary Buddhas), or *arahats* (beings liberated from *saṃsāra*). Although the terms vary, the central idea of a sage who reaches the ultimate Truth through meditation and transcendental knowledge is shared in both traditions.

On the other hand, the Egyptian tradition offers a distinct perspective by emphasizing touch as a means to interact with the sacred, suggesting that truth and knowledge can be apprehended through physical contact, thus integrating a tactile dimension into phenomenology. The religious tradition of ancient Egypt, whose peak spans from approximately 3200 BCE to 30 BCE, assigns a primordial relevance to the sense of touch in interaction with the Divine. This conception fits into a worldview where no clear distinction exists between the material and the spiritual; rather, both dimensions form a unified reality. For the Egyptians, the physical sphere was not an autonomous realm or foreign to the Divine; they were direct manifestations of sacred powers. In this sense, objects, statues, and ritual symbols were not merely perceived as symbolic representations, but as tangible incarnations of the power and presence of the deities. The act of touching these sacred objects was essential to establish contact with the divinities, as through touch, divine energy was channeled, allowing the faithful to access transcendental spheres.

By decentering the vision and elevating hearing and touch to equal importance, a new phenomenological horizon is inaugurated, inviting a reconsideration of the ways in which the Being is presented and apprehended by consciousness, even before it can be thought of as consciousness. In this conceptual framework, a conception of enlightenment is introduced that transcends the merely physical to place itself in the realm of the metaphysical. It is no longer about a light that our bodily eyes can capture in the phenomenal world, nor about what our cognitive abilities can categorize and understand in the most traditional sense of the term. On the contrary, it is an enlightenment that operates on a higher plane, where the sacred is revealed with a deeper and fuller essence, so full that it appears as non-apparent, that is, invisible and incomprehensible.

Retroprogressive Phenomenology emerges as a current that seeks to integrate these sensory traditions—the sight, hearing, and touch—into a more holistic "understanding" of the phenomenon. The turning point of this proposal lies in dissociating enlightenment and the sacred from the sense of sight, which has dominated Western tradition, and in reorienting the focus toward a form of enlightenment that is not confined to the visible but extends to the experience of the non-apparent. Therefore, Retroprogressive Phenomenology deliberately distances itself from a phenomenology of the apparent—focused on what is revealed to the eyes—to venture into a phenomenology of the non-apparent, focusing on what is not shown to the eye but which nonetheless has the ability to illuminate. This form of enlightenment no longer seeks merely to clarify what is captured by the senses, but aims to illuminate consciousness itself, transcending sensory perception in favor of a deeper and more essential experience. Thus, Retroprogressive Phenomenology redefines the relationship between the sacred and its manifestation, proposing a phenomenology that encompasses the visible, the audible, and the tactile in a synthesis that seeks to capture the totality of the experience of the Being.

Light and consciousness in Retroprogressive Phenomenology

Traditional phenomenology, as it has been conceived, has never addressed the sacred as its main object of study; it has always focused on what clearly appears, leaving aside the non-apparent. In this sense, it has explored the essence of concrete objects, such as a plant, a dog, a table, or a chair, and how these reveal themselves qua objects clearly in the light of consciousness. Retroprogressive Phenomenology distances itself from the study of the objects that manifest in the light and how they manifest as objects, and instead focuses on the light that makes the appearance of those objects possible. The object of Retroprogressive Phenomenology is no longer the light of essence but the essence of light. This light is the Being itself, the ultimate reality of what we are. By focusing on the light that underlies the manifestation of objects, this phenomenological current seeks to unveil a deeper ontological dimension, one in which Being and the sacred intertwine in a single essential reality. Therefore, Retroprogressive Phenomenology is not merely an investigation of phenomena as they are shown through light, but an exploration of light in its quality as the manifestation of Being.

Retroprogressive Phenomenology establishes, therefore, a connection between the sacred and enlightenment. Its interest does not lie in what appears before the light, but in the light itself and in how the human being relates to this light on a plane that transcends vision and understanding. It is fundamental to distinguish between vision and that which allows vision. In this context, light is conceived as a clarity that illuminates the very ability to see, that is, a light that clarifies and amplifies consciousness beyond the reach of the perceptible. This inner light is not accessible through the bodily eyes, but is apprehended by the "eyes of the soul"; it does not direct itself toward the illumination of the external world, but toward the revelation of internal and transcendental truths. It is through this light of the soul that the Being manifests itself in its true essence, distancing itself from sensory appearances to enter into its most authentic dimension. Thus, the light of the soul ultimately discovers the soul of the light.

In this sense, Retroprogressive Phenomenology can, paradoxically, be described as a form of post-phenomenology. On one hand, it aligns with ontological phenomenology by investigating the Being in relation to consciousness; on the other, it transcends it by reflecting on consciousness itself, exploring how it is illuminated and revealed, emerging as such, without the mediation of external objects.

Chapter 43: Light and Consciousness: A Retroprogressive Exploration

Retroprogressive Phenomenology does not address consciousness merely as a phenomenon, but focuses on the *fos*, the primordial light from which all phenomena emerge, including consciousness itself as a phenomenon of study. Thus, it focuses on genesis, the origin (*bereshit*), in that essential light where both phenomena and their consciousness manifest.

In this framework, the Retroprogressive phenomenologist transforms into an explorer of the pure essence of the revealing light, which makes the appearance of any object possible, that is, which facilitates the phenomenality of something, rather than merely being a passive observer of objects illuminated by this light. In this context, light is not merely a means to know the entity, but the object of study in its own enigmatic depth. This phenomenology stands as an effort to unveil the Being before consciousness, discovering its essence directly and without intermediaries. This philosophical current asserts that the Being does not merely manifest to consciousness, but that its very reason for being is precisely this: to make itself present to it, providing meaning and guidance. Thus, the Being achieves its most essential purpose by becoming a cognizable object, allowing consciousness to become aware of itself.

In a sense, and in light of what has been said so far, we can define Retroprogressive Phenomenology as an ontological phenomenology of the sacred. This perspective redefines simple phenomenology, transforming it into an ontological investigation that does not focus on what is shown, but on the light that makes any manifestation possible and that is the foundation of all phenomenon. This "retroprogression" reflects the dynamics of religion, which is understood as *re-ligare*, that is, as the action of reconnecting with the Divine, with the origin. In religious traditions, this return to the source or to the sacred is not a simple backward movement, but a profound union that reconstitutes the totality of the Being.

> Once again, Jesus spoke to them, saying: "I am the light of the world; whoever follows me will never walk in darkness, but will have the light of life.
>
> (John, 8:12)

Section XI: Toward a Retroprogressive Phenomenology

This light, which is the very essence of the Being and the sacred, is the true object of study, taking the reflection beyond the analysis of phenomena to delve into the underlying principle that sustains and makes possible all experience. It is a return to the primordial source, a study of that light which is not perceived, but simply *is*, reflecting the reality of the sacred and of our most authentic nature.

The sacred, by its very nature, does not manifest with the same clarity and evidence. Being our authentic Being, it does not present itself directly or immediately, but through mediation. Human life is constituted by experiences that appear in the light of consciousness, and it is this light that makes the experienced present. However, it is crucial to recognize that the true foundation of all experience is not the object, but the light in which these objects appear and are experienced. While what is experienced depends on the light, the light does not need what is experienced to *be*, which allows us to affirm that, therefore, this light constitutes the foundation of all experience and, ultimately, of all phenomenon.

The light itself is nevertheless imperceptible in its essence; what we perceive are the forms and surfaces upon which it is projected. No one has ever observed the light as such, for when we speak of light, we ultimately refer to the necessary condition for vision to occur. Light is not a phenomenon that reveals itself by itself; its subtlety escapes the senses. Only through the perception of objects do we infer its presence, since, in complete darkness, nothing would be visible. Similarly, the notion of darkness only refers to the absence of vision, that is, to the inability to perceive the objects in the environment.

If, at this moment, a doctor were to ask you if you are conscious, you would undoubtedly answer "yes," thus immediately confirming your own consciousness. Consciousness, therefore, is not only evident in itself but also to us. Even if, paradoxically, we claimed to be unconscious, this very response would constitute proof of our consciousness, for only a conscious being can offer such a denial. This recognition of our being is inevitable and transcends any need for verification through the senses. We do not require the mediation of the eyes to affirm our existence; rather, this certainty is provided by an internal, deep, and direct intuition of our own nature. Just as in an illuminated space the light allows us to see the objects, in the realm of consciousness there exists an "illumination" not perceptible by the senses but which guides us and reveals our being infallibly. It is a light that does not belong to the physical realm, but to the sphere of self-consciousness, and its presence is as indubitable as it is immaterial.

Although this light does not manifest directly before our senses, the mere fact of being conscious of our existence implies that there is a source of light, not physical but internal. Even in the most absolute sensory darkness, we are able to affirm, without hesitation, the certainty of our own existence. The lack of external stimuli does not in any way weaken the evidence of our consciousness, for it remains unquestionable and self-evident to us. In fact, physical darkness does not annul the presence of an "inner" light, which is a direct manifestation of consciousness itself. As Kṛṣṇa mentions in the Bhagavad Gita:

न तद्भासयते सूर्यो न शशाङ्को न पावकः ।
यद्गत्वा न निवर्तन्ते तद्धाम परमं मम ॥

na tad bhāsayate sūryo
na śaśāṅko na pāvakaḥ
yad gatvā na nivartante
tad dhāma paramaṁ mama

Neither the sun shines there, nor the moon, nor the fire; having gone there they do not return; that is My supreme abode.

(Bhagavad Gita, 15.6)

The capacity to perceive ourselves reveals by itself the presence of light. To meditate is to attend to and recognize the light of consciousness, which is our authentic nature.

In the Islamic realm, *Nūr* stands as a concept of profound transcendence, symbolizing the "cold light of the night" or "light without heat," commonly associated with the soft glow of the moon.

Unlike sunlight, characterized by its intensity and heat, *Nūr* is evoked as a metaphor for divine guidance and spiritual knowledge. This moonlight, gentle and calm, is associated with the mercy of God, an illumination that does not scorch but rather guides with softness and calm, granting clarity without imposing itself with violence. *Nūr* is distinguished from *Nar*, which designates "fire, hot light, or sunlight." While *Nar* can imply judgment, severity, or the burning force of the sun, *Nūr* represents a form of illumination that is more delicate and spiritual, linked to knowledge that emanates directly from the Divine. This symbolism is deepened in the Qur'an, where it states:

> God is the Light of the heavens and the earth.
> The example of His light is like a niche within which is a lamp.
> The lamp is within a glass, the glass as if it were a pearly star [white],
> illuminated by [the oil of] a blessed olive tree,
> which is neither of the east nor of the west, whose oil would almost glow even if untouched by fire.
> Light upon light.
> God guides to His light whom He wills.
> And God presents examples for the people,
> and God is All-Knowing all things.
>
> (Qur'an, sura 24:35)

This statement emphasizes that *Nūr* is a manifestation of transcendent divine knowledge and points to the omnipresence of God, who illuminates both the material and spiritual dimensions, granting clarity and understanding in both realms. Thus, *Nūr* becomes an emblem of divine revelation that illuminates the believer's path and extends to all of creation.

In the Retroprogressive Phenomenology, we present here, a phenomenological line is followed which, from its beginnings, has been called to describe "a form of existence" that, although secretly inherent to us, allows us to "attend" to the light of the soul without seeing it or understanding it. This light, as the highest expression of the sacred, escapes any attempt at comprehension or perception. However, staying true to the fundamental principles of phenomenology, Retroprogressive Phenomenology does not deduce or presuppose the existence of that light. It seeks to describe the relationship of the human being with it, beyond the limits of perception and understanding. Far from denying perception or epistemology, this phenomenology attempts to penetrate its essence as tools that allow us to describe how and in what manner our relationship with the infinite light of the soul consists, a light we cannot see nor understand.

Perhaps following Kierkegaard again, we could say that what Retroprogressive Phenomenology seeks to explain is what we might call the Abrahamic experience: how "Abraham listens" to his God ("who He is," that is, Being) when He asks him to take Isaac to Mount Moriah to sacrifice him. Abraham does not see God, nor does he understand Him, but he listens to His call. This call is "brutal," not in a cruel sense, as some have suggested, but because it transcends reason and expresses the incomprehensible, the imperceptible. Despite this, Abraham responds in the most absolute silence, for this listening to the divine call also transcends language. He "responds" with all the weight of responsibility, and in doing so, he himself emerges as an ontological and ethical subject, as self-consciousness. What this episode narrates, and what Retroprogressive Phenomenology discovers, is that there is meaning beyond the limits of epistemology and language. As mentioned earlier, the Abraham of Kierkegaard responds without words because his relationship with the sacred, with the soul of the light, transcends language. The listening to Being does not imply hearing words, but rather being touched and allowing oneself to be touched by the light of the soul. It is in that instant, in that now, where the deepest meaning of existence emerges, renewed and perennial.

Life, in its totality, is only light; matter is but a mirage, an illusion that appears when vision is veiled. When seeing clearly, differences dissolve, leaving behind an infinite ocean of light, of which we are but ephemeral waves, emerging in a play of bubbles and foam.

> Beloved, now we are children of God, and it has not yet been revealed what we shall be; but we know that when He is revealed, we shall be like Him, for we shall see Him as He is.
> (1 John, 3:2)

Knowing this ocean of light requires the death of the old, the known, and the familiar, so that the new and fresh may be reborn. Only by recognizing ourselves as light can we experience life in its true luminosity. In the total absence of darkness, there is no death or suffering, but only eternal bliss.

לֹא־יִהְיֶה־לָּךְ עוֹד הַשֶּׁמֶשׁ לְאוֹר יוֹמָם וּלְנֹגַהּ הַיָּרֵחַ לֹא־יָאִיר לָךְ וְהָיָה־לָךְ ה' לְאוֹר עוֹלָם וֵאלֹהַיִךְ לְתִפְאַרְתֵּךְ:

לֹא־יָבוֹא עוֹד שִׁמְשֵׁךְ וִירֵחֵךְ לֹא יֵאָסֵף כִּי ה' יִהְיֶה־לָּךְ לְאוֹר עוֹלָם וְשָׁלְמוּ יְמֵי אֶבְלֵךְ:

(ישעיהו ס', י"ט-כ')

> No longer shall you need the sun, for light by day, nor the shining of the moon. For radiance [by night]; For God shall be your light everlasting, Your God shall be your glory. Your sun shall set no more, Your moon no more withdraw; For God shall be a light to you forever, And your days of mourning shall be ended.
> (Isaiah, 60:19–20)

The consciousness constitutes the primordial substance that penetrates and defines each Being, each experience, and outside of it, nothing possesses authentic existence. Furthermore, this reading of the relationship between Being and consciousness, as we have described at the beginning of this conclusion, allows us to turn this revelation into the beacon, the unshakable light (*fos*), that guides all existence, which leads us to suggest that reality, in its totality, that is, as everything, is nothing more than the manifestation of a single and vast consciousness. The recognition of consciousness brings with it a profound transformation in our perception of the world. Gradually, the objects that we once perceived as firm material realities will begin to become subtler, revealing in their place the presence of living beings, conscious emanations manifesting in every corner of the universe. Eventually, this perceptual change will reach a climax, where the totality of the world will reveal itself in its true state, dissipating the illusion of an inert environment that was nothing more than a reflection of the inherent insensitivity of a subject toward the surrounding life. Retroprogressive Phenomenology proposes to surpass the barrier of traditional epistemological perception that, not only in modern philosophy but already in Plato, had drawn the horizon of all possible understanding of reality and existence. By jumping over this epistemological barrier, what emerges is precisely a reality in which everything that surrounds us is not only alive but, in its innermost core, everything is pure and luminous consciousness.

APPENDICES

Prabhuji

H.H. Avadhūta Bhaktivedānta Yogācārya
Śrī Ramakrishnananda Bābājī Mahārāja

About Prabhuji

Prabhuji is a realized master, a universalist Advaita mystic, and an authorized representative of Hinduism. His profound religious dedication is expressed through his artistic work as a writer and painter. In recognition of his spiritual attainment, his guru has conferred upon him the title of *avadhūta*. He has developed the Retroprogressive Path, an original contribution rooted in the inclusive principles of *Sanātana Dharma*, an ancient tradition to which he maintains a formal and constant adherence.

His solid background includes a doctorate in *Vaiṣṇava* philosophy, awarded by the prestigious Jiva Institute of Vedic Studies in Vrindavan, India, and a doctorate in Yogic philosophy earned at Yoga-Samskrutham University. These doctorates reaffirm his commitment to traditional teachings and his connection to the spiritual roots of the Hindu religion.

Prabhuji has dedicated more than fifty years to the exploration and practice of different religions, philosophies, paths of liberation, and spiritual disciplines. He has absorbed the teachings of great masters, shamans, priests, machis, shifus, roshis, shaykhs, daoshis, yogis, pastors, swamis, rabbis, kabbalists, monks, gurus, philosophers, sages, and saints whom he personally visited during his years of searching. He has lived in many places and traveled the world, thirsting for Truth.

In 2011, with the blessings of his Gurudeva, Prabhuji adopted the path of a secluded *bhajanānandī* and withdrew from society to lead the contemplative life of a hermit. Since then, he has been living as an independent Christian-Marian Hindu religious hermit. His days have been spent in solitude, praying, writing, painting, and meditating in silence and contemplation. His *iṣṭa-devatā*, or "chosen deity," is Lord Yeshua, understood from the traditional Hindu perspective as the *avatāra*, the "incarnate God" in whom he centers his devotion. Unlike the interpretation of Western Christianity, his connection with Yeshua arises from the Semitic roots of the historical Jesus, within the original Hebrew horizon of his revelation.

Prabhuji is the sole disciple of H.D.G. Avadhūta Śrī Brahmānanda Bābājī Mahārāja, who in turn is one of the closest and most intimate disciples of H.D.G. Avadhūta Śrī Mastarāma Bābājī Mahārāja.

Prabhuji was appointed as the successor of the lineage by his master, who conferred upon him the responsibility of continuing the sacred *paramparā* of *avadhūtas*, officially appointing him as guru and ordering him to serve as Ācārya successor under the name H.H. Avadhūta Bhaktivedānta Yogācārya Śrī Ramakrishnananda Bābājī Mahārāja.

Prabhuji is also a disciple of H.D.G. Bhakti-kavi Atulānanda Ācārya Mahārāja, who is a direct disciple of H.D.G. A.C. Bhaktivedānta Swami Prabhupāda. We could say that Gurudeva Atulānanda affectionately assumed the role of guide during his initial stage of learning, and because he was Prabhuji's first guru, he is considered a fundamental part of his evolutionary process. For his part, Guru Mahārāja was Prabhuji's second and last guru and provided him with guidance during his advanced stage. Gurudeva acted as the primary educator at the dawn of his spiritual path, while Guru Mahārāja exercised with great diligence the role of master at the highest level, accompanying him until his realization.

Prabhuji's Hinduism is broad, universal, and pluralistic. Living up to his title of *avadhūta*, his lively and fresh teachings are not confined by any philosophy or religion, even his own. His teachings promote critical thinking and invite us to question our own convictions. The essence of his syncretic vision, the Retroprogressive Path, is self-awareness and the recognition of consciousness. For him, awakening at the level of consciousness, or the transcendence of the egoic phenomenon, is the next step in humanity's evolution.

Prabhuji was born on March 21, 1958, in Santiago, the capital of the Republic of Chile. When he was eight years old, he had a mystical experience that motivated his search for the Truth, or the Ultimate Reality. This transformed his life into an authentic inner and outer pilgrimage. He has completely devoted his life to deepening the early transformative experience that marked the beginning of his process of retroevolution.

From an early age, his father, Yosef Har-Zion ZT"L, and his mother, Frida Lazcano ZT"L, expressed a constant and unconditional love, independent of academic performance or achievements. Prabhuji's paternal grandfather was a distinguished senior officer in the Chilean police, who raised his father Yosef under a strict discipline. Marked by this, Yosef decided to raise his own children in an environment defined by freedom. Prabhuji and his sister were their parents' most cherished endeavors, guided by their trust in life itself as the compass for their choices.

In this context, Prabhuji grew up without experiencing any sense of urgency, demand, or external pressure. From a very young age, he noticed that the educational system prevented him from devoting himself to what truly mattered: learning about himself. At the age of eleven, he decided to stop attending conventional school and devote himself to autodidactic learning. When he chose to leave school in pursuit of his inner quest, his family responded with profound respect and acceptance. Yosef fully supported his son's interests, encouraging him at every step of his search for Truth.

From the age of ten onward, his father shared with him the wisdom of Hebrew spirituality and Western philosophy, fostering an environment of daily discussions that often extended late into the night. In essence, Prabhuji embodied the ideal of freedom and unconditional love that his parents had striven to cultivate within their home.

From a very young age and on his own initiative, Prabhuji began to practice karate and to study Eastern philosophy and religions in a self-taught manner. During his adolescence, no one interfered with his decisions. At the age of 15, he established a deep, intimate, and long friendship with the famous Uruguayan writer and poet Blanca Luz Brum, who was his neighbor on Merced Street in Santiago, Chile. He traveled throughout Chile in search of wise and interesting people from whom he could learn. In southern Chile, he met *machis* who taught him about the rich Mapuche spirituality and shamanism.

In June 1975, at the young age of 17, he earned his first certification as a Yoga Teacher under H.H. Śrī Brahmānanda Sarasvatī (Rāmamurti S. Mishra, M.D.), the founder of the World Yoga University, the Yoga Society of NY, and the Ananda Ashram.

At the age of 18, Prabhuji embraced the monastic discipline through long stays in various ashrams of different Hindu currents (*Gauḍīya* Vaishnavas, Advaita Vedanta, etc.) in Chile and Israel. There, he underwent rigorous training within the Hindu religion. Immersed in the strict observance of religious life, he received a systematic education, following traditional methods of monastic teaching. His training included the in-depth study of sacred scriptures, the practice of austerities, the fulfillment of strict vows, and participation in prescribed rituals, all under the guidance of masters or gurus. Through this intensive discipline, he internalized the fundamental principles of Hindu monastic life, adopting its values, codes of conduct, and contemplative practices. This allowed him to learn the theory and also to incorporate the ideals that characterize the spirituality of Hinduism.

Over the years, Prabhuji became a recognized authority on Eastern wisdom. He is known for his erudition on the *Vaidika* and *Tāntrika* aspects of Hinduism and all branches of yoga (*jñāna, karma, bhakti, haṭha, rāja, kuṇḍalinī, tantra, mantra,* and others). He has an inclusive attitude toward all religions and is intimately familiar with Judaism, Christianity, Buddhism, Islam, Sufism, Taoism, Sikhism, Jainism, Shintoism, Bahaism, Shamanism, and the Mapuche religion, among others.

During his stay in the Middle East, his esteemed friend and scholar, Kamil Shchadi, imparted to him profound knowledge about the Druze faith. He also benefited from his closeness to the revered and wise Salach Abbas, who helped him to reach a thorough understanding of Islam and Sufism. He studied Theravada Buddhism personally from the Venerable W. Medhananda Thero of Sri Lanka. He delved deeper into Christian theology with H.H. Monsignor Iván Larraín Eyzaguirre at the Veracruz Church in Santiago de Chile and with Mr. Héctor Luis Muñoz, who holds a degree in theology from the Universidad Católica de la Santísima

Concepción, Chile. His profound studies, his masters' blessings, his research into the sacred scriptures, and his vast teaching experience have earned him international recognition in the field of religion and spirituality.

Prabhuji's curiosity for Western thought led him to venture into the field of philosophy in all its different branches. He specialized in Transcendental Phenomenology and the Phenomenology of Religion. He had the privilege of studying intensively for several years with his uncle Jorge Balazs, philosopher, researcher, and author, who wrote *The world upside-down* under his pen name Gyuri Akos. Prabhuji pursued private studies in mythology and philosophy for four years (1984–1987) under Dr. Meira Laneado of Bar-Ilan University. He studied privately for many years with Dr. Jonathan Ramos, a renowned philosopher, historian, and university professor graduated from the Universidad Católica de Salta, Argentina. He also studied with Dr. Alejandro Cavallazzi Sánchez, who holds an undergraduate degree in philosophy from the Universidad Panamericana, a master's degree in philosophy from the Universidad Iberoamericana, and a doctorate in philosophy from the Universidad Nacional Autónoma de México (UNAM). He also studied privately with Santiago Sánchez Borboa, who holds a PhD in Philosophy from the University of Arizona, USA.

Prabhuji's spiritual quest led him to study with masters from different traditions and to travel far from his native Chile, to places as distant as Israel, Brazil, India, and the United States. He is fluent in Spanish, Hebrew, Portuguese, and English. During his stay in Israel, he furthered his Hebrew and Aramaic studies in order to broaden his knowledge of the sacred scriptures. He studied other languages intensively, such as Sanskrit with Dr. Naga Kanya Kumari Garipathi, from Osmania University in Hyderabad (India); Pali at the Oxford Center for Buddhist Studies; and Latin and Ancient Greek with Professor Ariel Lazcano and later with Javier Alvarez, who holds a degree in Classical Philology from the University of Seville.

Two great masters contributed to Prabhuji's retroprogressive process. In 1976, he met his first guru, H.D.G Bhakti-kavi Atulānanda Ācārya Swami, whom he called Gurudeva. In those days, Gurudeva was a young *brahmacārī* who held the position of president of the ISKCON temple at Eyzaguirre 2404, Puente Alto, Santiago, Chile. Years later, he gave Prabhuji his first initiation, Brahminical initiation, and finally, Prabhuji formally accepted the sacraments of the holy order of *sannyāsa*, becoming a monk of the Brahma Gauḍīya Sampradāya. Gurudeva connected him to the devotion to Kṛṣṇa. He imparted to him the wisdom of bhakti yoga and instructed him in the practice of the *māhā-mantra* and the study of the holy scriptures.

In 1996, Prabhuji met his second guru, H.D.G. Avadhūta Śrī Brahmānanda Bābājī Mahārāja, in Rishikesh, India. Guru Mahārāja, as Prabhuji would call him, revealed that his own master, H.D.G. Avadhūta Śrī Mastarāma Bābājī Mahārāja, had told him years before he died that a person would come from the West and request to be his disciple. He commanded him to accept only that particular seeker. When he asked how he would identify this person, Mastarāma Bābājī replied, "You will recognize him by his eyes. You must accept him because he will be the continuation of the lineage." From his first meeting with young Prabhuji, Guru Mahārāja recognized him and officially initiated him as his disciple. For Prabhuji, this initiation marked the beginning of the most intense and mature stage of his retroprogressive process. Under the guidance of Guru Mahārāja, he studied Advaita Vedanta and deepened his meditation. Since his guru was a great devotee of Śrī Rāmakṛṣṇa Paramahamsa and Śāradā Devī, Prabhuji desired to be initiated into this disciplic lineage. He sought initiation from Swami Swahananda (1921–2012), minister and spiritual leader of the Vedanta Society of Southern California from 1976 to 2012. Swami Swahananda was a disciple of Swami Vijñānānanda, a direct disciple of Rāmakṛṣṇa. In 2008, Swami Swahananda initiated him, granting him both *dīkṣā* and the blessings of Śrī Rāmakṛṣṇa and the Divine Mother.

Guru Mahārāja guided Prabhuji until he officially bestowed upon him the sacraments of the sacred order of *avadhūtas*. In March 2011, H.D.G. Avadhūta Śrī Brahmānanda Bābājī Mahārāja ordered Prabhuji, on behalf of his own master, to accept the responsibility of continuing the lineage of *avadhūtas*. With this title, Prabhuji is the official representative of the line of this disciplic succession for the present generation.

Besides his *dikṣā-gurus*, Prabhuji studied with important spiritual and religious personalities, such as H.H. Swami Yajñavālkyānanda, H.H. Swami Dayānanda Sarasvatī, H.H. Swami Viṣṇu Devānanda Sarasvatī, H.H. Swami Jyotirmayānanda Sarasvatī, H.H. Swami Kṛṣṇānanda Sarasvatī from the Divine Life Society, H.H. Ma Yoga Śakti, H.H. Swami Pratyagbodhānanda, H.H. Swami Mahādevānanda, H.H. Swami Swahānanda of the Ramakrishna Mission, H.H. Swami Adhyātmānanda, H.H. Swami Svarūpanānda, and H.H. Swami Viditātmānanda of the Arsha Vidya Gurukulam, while the wisdom of tantra was awakened in Prabhuji by H.G. Mātājī Rīnā Śarmā in India.

In Vrindavan, he studied the bhakti yoga path in depth with H.H. Narahari Dāsa Bābājī Mahārāja, disciple of H.H. Nityānanda Dāsa Bābājī Mahārāja of Vraja. He also studied bhakti yoga with various disciples of His Divine Grace A.C. Bhaktivedānta Swami Prabhupāda: H.H. Kapīndra Swami, H.H. Paramadvaiti Mahārāja, H.H. Jagajīvana Dāsa, H.H. Tamāla Kṛṣṇa Gosvāmī, H.H. Bhagavān Dāsa Mahārāja, and H.H. Kīrtanānanda Swami, among others.

In 1980, Prabhuji received the blessings of H.G. Mother Krishnabai, the famous disciple of H.D.G. Swami Rāmdās. In 1984, he learned and began to practice Maharishi Mahesh Yogi's Transcendental Meditation technique. In 1988, he took the *kriyā-yoga* course on Paramahamsa Yogānanda. After two years, he was officially initiated into the technique of *kriyā-yoga* by the Self-Realization Fellowship. In 1982 he received *dikṣā* from H.H. Kīrtanānanda Swami, disciple of Śrīla Prabhupāda, who also gave him his second initiation in 1991 and *sannyāsa* initiation in 1993.

Prabhuji wanted to confirm the sacraments of the holy order of *sannyāsa* also within the Advaita Vedanta lineage. His *sannyāsa-dīkṣā* was confirmed on August 11, 1995, by H.H. Swami Jyotirmayānanda Sarasvatī, founder of the Yoga Research Foundation and disciple of H.H. Swami Śivānanda Sarasvatī of Rishikesh.

Prabhuji has been honored with various titles and diplomas by many leaders of prestigious religious and spiritual institutions in India. He was given the honorable title Kṛṣṇa Bhakta by H.H. Swami Viṣṇu Devānanda (the only title of Bhakti Yoga given by Swami Viṣṇu), disciple of H.H. Swami Śivānanda Sarasvatī and the founder of the Sivananda Organization. He was given the title Bhaktivedānta by H.H. B.A. Paramadvaiti Mahārāja, the founder of Vrinda. He was given the title Yogācārya by H.H. Swami Viṣṇu Devānanda, the Paramanand Institute of Yoga Sciences and Research of Indore, India, the International Yoga Federation, the Indian Association of Yoga, and the Śrī Shankarananda Yogashram of Mysore, India. He received the respectable title Śrī Śrī Rādhā Śyam Sunder Pāda-Padma Bhakta Śiromaṇi directly from H.H. Satyanārāyaṇa Dāsa Bābājī Mahant of the Chatu Vaiṣṇava Saṁpradāya.

Prabhuji dedicated more than forty years to studying hatha yoga with prestigious masters of classical and traditional yoga, such as H.H. Bapuji, H.H. Swami Viṣṇu Devānanda Sarasvatī, H.H. Swami Jyotirmayānanda Sarasvatī, H.H. Swami Satchidānanda Sarasvatī, H.H. Swami Vignānānanda Sarasvatī, and Śrī Madana-mohana.

He attended several systematic hatha yoga teacher training courses at prestigious institutions until he achieved the level of Master Ācārya. He has completed studies at the following institutions: World Yoga University, the Sivananda Yoga Vedanta, the Ananda Ashram, the Yoga Research Foundation, the Integral Yoga Academy, the Patanjala Yoga Kendra, the Ma Yoga Shakti International Mission, the Prana Yoga Organization, the Rishikesh Yoga Peeth, the Swami Sivananda Yoga Research Center, and the Swami Sivananda Yogasana Research Center.

Prabhuji is a member of the Indian Association of Yoga, Yoga Alliance ERYT 500 and YACEP, the International Association of Yoga Therapists, and the International Yoga Federation. In 2014, the International Yoga Federation honored him with the position of Honorary Member of the World Yoga Council.

His interest in the complex anatomy of the human body led him to study chiropractic at the prestigious Institute of Health of the Back and Extremities in Tel Aviv, Israel. In 1993, he received a diploma from Dr. Sheinerman, the founder and director of the institute. Later, he earned a massage therapy diploma at the Academy of Western Galilee. The knowledge he acquired in this field deepened his understanding of hatha yoga and contributed to the creation of his own method.

Retroprogressive Yoga is the result of Prabhuji's efforts to improve his practice and teaching methods. It is a system based especially on the teachings of his gurus and the sacred scriptures. Prabhuji has systematized various traditional yoga techniques to create a methodology suitable for Western audiences. Retroprogressive Yoga aspires to the experience of our authentic nature, promoting balance, health, and flexibility through proper diet, cleansing techniques, preparations (*āyojanas*), sequences (*vinyāsas*), postures (*āsanas*), breathing exercises (*prāṇayama*), relaxation (*śavāsana*), meditation (*dhyāna*), and exercises with locks (*bandhas*) and seals (*mudras*) to direct and empower *prāṇa*.

Since his childhood and throughout his life, Prabhuji has been an enthusiastic admirer, student, and practitioner of classic karate-do. From the age of 13, he studied different styles in Chile, such as kenpo with Sensei Arturo Petit and kung-fu, but specialized in the most traditional Japanese style of shotokan. He received the rank of black belt (third dan) from Shihan Kenneth Funakoshi (ninth dan). He also learned from Sensei Takahashi (seventh dan) and Sensei Masataka Mori (ninth dan). Additionally, he practiced shorin ryu style with Sensei Enrique Daniel Welcher (seventh dan), who granted him the rank of black belt (second dan). Through karate-do, he delved into Buddhism and gained additional knowledge about the physics of motion. He is a member of Funakoshi's Shotokan Karate Association.

Prabhuji grew up in an artistic environment and his love of painting began to develop in his childhood. His father, the renowned Chilean painter Yosef Har-Zion ZT"L, motivated him to devote himself to art. He learned painting from both his father and the famous Chilean painter Marcelo Cuevas. Prabhuji's abstract paintings reflect the depths of the spirit.

Since he was a young boy, Prabhuji has been especially drawn to postal stamps, postcards, mailboxes, postal transportation systems, and all mail-related activities. He has taken every opportunity to visit post offices in different cities and countries. He has delved into the study of philately, the field of collecting, sorting, and studying postage stamps. This passion led him to become a professional philatelist, a stamp distributor authorized by the American Philatelic Society, and a member of the following societies: the Royal Philatelic Society London, the Royal Philatelic Society of Victoria, the United States Stamp Society, the Great Britain Philatelic Society, the American Philatelic Society, the Society of Israel Philatelists, the Society for Hungarian Philately, the National Philatelic Society UK, the Fort Orange Stamp Club, the American Stamp Dealers Association, the US Philatelic Classics Society, Filabras - Associação dos Filatelistas Brasileiros, and the Collectors Club of NYC.

Based on his extensive knowledge of philately, theology, and Eastern philosophy, Prabhuji created "Meditative Philately" or "Philatelic Yoga," a spiritual practice that uses philately as the basis for practicing attention, concentration, observation, and meditation. It is inspired by the ancient Hindu mandala meditation and it can lead the practitioner to elevated states of consciousness, deep relaxation, and concentration that fosters the recognition of consciousness. Prabhuji wrote his thesis on this new type of yoga, "Meditative Philately," attracting the interest of the Indian academic community due to its innovative way of connecting meditation with different hobbies and activities. For this thesis, he was honored with a PhD in Yogic Philosophy from Yoga-Samskrutham University.

For more than 20 years, Prabhuji lived in Israel, where he furthered his studies of Judaism. One of his main teachers and sources of inspiration was Rabbi Shalom Dov Lifshitz ZT"L, whom he met in 1997. This great saint guided him for several years along the intricate paths of the Torah and Hassidism. He personally taught him Tanakh, Talmud, Midrash, Shulchan Aruch, Mishneh Torah, Tanya, Kabbalah and Zohar. The two developed a very close relationship. Prabhuji also studied the Talmud with Rabbi Raphael Rapaport Shlit"a (Ponovich), Hassidism with Rabbi Israel

Lifshitz Shlit"a, and the Torah with Rabbi Daniel Sandler Shlit"a. Prabhuji is a great devotee of Rabbi Mordechai Eliyahu ZT"L, who personally blessed him.

Prabhuji visited the United States in 2000 and during his stay in New York, he realized that it was the most appropriate place to found a religious organization. He was particularly attracted by the pluralism and respectful attitude of American society toward freedom of religion. He was impressed by the deep respect of both the public and the government for religious minorities. After consulting his masters and requesting their blessings, Prabhuji relocated to the United States. In 2003, the Prabhuji Mission was born, a Hindu church aimed at preserving Prabhuji's universal and pluralistic vision of Hinduism and his "Retroprogressive Path."

Although he did not seek to attract followers, for 15 years (1995–2010), Prabhuji considered the requests of a few people who approached him asking to become his monastic disciples. Those who chose to see him as their spiritual master voluntarily accepted vows of poverty and life-long dedication to spiritual practice (*sadhāna*), religious devotion (*bhakti*), and selfless service (*seva*). Although he no longer accepts new disciples, he continues to guide the small group of monastic disciples of the contemplative Ramakrishnananda Monastic Order that he founded.

In 2011, Prabhuji founded the Avadhutashram (monastery) in the Catskills Mountains in upstate New York, USA. The Avadhutashram is his hermitage, the residence of the monastic disciples of the Ramakrishnananda Order, and the headquarters of the Prabhuji Mission. He operates various humanitarian projects, inspired in his experience that "serving the part is serving the Whole." The ashram organizes humanitarian projects such as the Prabhuji Food Distribution Program and the Prabhuji Toy Distribution Program.

According to Prabhuji, the quest for the Self is individual, solitary, personal, private, and intimate. It is not a collective endeavor to be undertaken through organized, institutional, or communitarian religiosity. Nowadays, he disagrees with spirituality practiced in a social, communal, or collective manner. Therefore, he does not proselytize or preach, nor does he try to persuade, convince, or make anyone change their perspective, philosophy, or religion. His message does not promote collective spirituality, but individual inner search.

Prabhuji has delegated the choice to his disciples between keeping his teachings exclusively within the monastic order or spreading his message to the public. Upon the explicit request of his disciples, he has agreed to have his books published and his lectures disseminated, as long as this does not compromise his privacy and his life as a hermit.

In 2022, Prabhuji founded the Retroprogressive Institute. Here, his most senior disciples can systematically share his teachings and message through video conferences. The institute offers support and help for a deeper understanding of his teachings.

In 2025, he established the Retroprogressive Yoga Academy, where he personally transmits his yoga method to disciples and students without departing from his hermitic life. That same year, he founded the Retroprogressive Karate Academy, through which he shares his knowledge of the martial arts as a path toward the expansion of consciousness.

Prabhuji is a respected member of the American Philosophical Association, the American Association of Philosophy Teachers, the American Association of University Professors, the Southwestern Philosophical Society, the Authors Guild, the National Writers Union, PEN America, the International Writers Association, the National Association of Independent Writers and Editors, the National Writers Association, the Alliance Independent Authors, and the Independent Book Publishers Association.

Prabhuji's vast literary contribution includes books in Spanish, English, and Hebrew, such as *Kundalini Yoga: The Power is in you*, *What is, as it is*, *Bhakti Yoga: The Path of Love*, *Tantra: Liberation in the World*, *Experimenting with the Truth*, *Advaita Vedanta: Being the Self*, *Yoga: Union with reality*, commentaries on the *Īśāvāsya Upanishad* and the *Diamond Sūtra*, *I am that I am*, *The Symbolic Turn*, *Being*, *Questioning your Answers: Philosophy as a Question*, *Beyond Answers: Philosophy in the Eternal Search*, *Phenomenology of the Sacred: Foundations for a Retroprogressive Phenomenology*, *Discovering the Last God*, and *Mapuche Spirituality*.

The term *Prabhuji*
by Swami Ramananda

Several years ago, some disciples, followers and friends of His Holiness Avadhūta Bhaktivedānta Yogācārya Śrī Ramakrishnananda Bābājī Mahārāja, opted to refer to him as Prabhuji. In this article, I would like to clarify the deep meaning of this Sanskrit term. The word *prabhu* in Sanskrit means "a master, lord or a king" and it is applied in the scriptures to God and to the Guru.

Like many words in the Sanskrit language, the word is actually made of some components, and understanding its etymology will lead us to discover its various meanings. The word *prabhu* is a combination of the root *bhu* which means "to become, to exist, to be, to live" and the prefix *pra*, which can mean "forth, or forward" and which then, when attached to *bhu* would mean "one who causes to exist, who gives life, from whom life emanates, that which sustains or maintains."

The prefix *pra* can also mean "very much, or supremacy," and then when attached to the root *bhu* would mean "to be the master, to rule over."

The suffix *jī* is an honorific title in Hindi and other Indian languages. It is added after the names of Gods and esteemed personalities to show respect and reverence.

As manifestations of the Divine, great *ṛṣis*, or 'seers' and gurus are also called *prabhus*. For example, the sage Nārada is addressing the *ṛṣi* Vyasadeva as *prabhu*:

जिज्ञासितमधीतं च ब्रह्म यत्तत्सनातनम् ।
तथापि शोचस्यात्मानमकृतार्थ इव प्रभो ॥

jijñāsitam adhītaṁ ca
brahma yat tat sanātanam
tathāpi śocasy ātmānam
akṛtārtha iva prabho

You have fully delineated the subject of impersonal Brahman as well as the knowledge derived therefrom. Why should you be despondent in spite of all this, thinking that you are undone, my dear master (*prabhu*)?

(*Bhāgavata Purāṇa*, 1.5.4)

Mahārāja Parīkṣit addresses Śukadeva as *prabhu* when he approaches the sage to seek spiritual guidance, thus accepting him as his guru.

यच्छ्रोतव्यमथो जप्यं यत्कर्तव्यं नृभिः प्रभो ।
स्मर्तव्यं भजनीयं वा ब्रूहि यद्वा विपर्ययम् ॥

yac chrotavyam atho japyaṁ
yat kartavyaṁ nṛbhiḥ prabho
smartavyaṁ bhajanīyaṁ vā
brūhi yad vā viparyayam

O prabhu, please let me know what a man should hear, chant, remember and worship, and also what he should not do. Please explain all this to me.

(*Bhāgavata Purāṇa*, 1.19.38)

The term *avadhūta*

This is an excerpt from the book *Sannyāsa Darśana* by Swami Niranjanānanda Sarasvatī, a disciple of Paramahaṁsa Swami Satyānanda.

Stages of *sannyāsāvadhūta*

"The *avadhūta* represents the pinnacle of spiritual evolution; none is superior to him. *Avadhūta* means 'one who is immortal' (*akṣara*) and who has totally discarded worldly ties. He is really Brahman itself. He has realized he is pure intelligence and is not concerned about the six frailties of human birth, namely: sorrow, delusion, old age, death, hunger, and thirst. He has shaken off all bondage of the experimental world and roams freely like a child, a madman or one possessed by spirits.

He may be with or without clothes. He wears no distinctive emblem of any order. He has no desire to sleep, beg, or bathe. He views his body as a corpse and subsists on the food that comes to him from all classes. He does not interpret the *śāstras* or the Vedas. For him, nothing is righteous or unrighteous, holy or unholy.

He is free from karma. The karmas of this life and past lives are all burned out, and due to the absence of *kartṛtva* (the doer) and *bhoktṛtva* (the desire for enjoyment), no future karmas are created. Only the *prārabdha-karmas* (unalterable) that have already begun to operate will affect his body, helping to sustain it, but his mind will remain unaffected. He will live in this world until the *prārabdha-karmas* are extinguished, and then his body will fall. Then he is said to attain *videhamukti* (the state beyond body consciousness).

Such a liberated soul never returns to the embodied state. He is not born again; he is immortal. He has achieved the final aim of being born in this world."

The *Bṛhad-avadhūta Upaniṣad* reads as follows: "The *avadhūta* is so called because he is immortal; he is the greatest; he has discarded worldly ties, and he is alluded to in the meaning of the sentence 'Thou art That.'"

His Divine Grace Śrīla Bhakti Ballabh Tīrtha Mahārāja in his article entitled "*Pariṣads*: Śrīla Vaṁśi das Bābājī" wrote: "He was a Paramahaṁsa Vaiṣṇava who acted in the manner of an *avadhūta*. The word *avadhūta* refers to one who has shaken off from himself all worldly feelings and obligations. He does not care for social conventions, especially the *varṇāśrama-dharma*, that is, he is quite eccentric in his behavior. Nityānanda Prabhu is often characterized as an *avadhūta*."

From the foreword to Dattātreya's *Avadhūta-gītā*, translated and annotated by Swami Aśokānanda: "The *Avadhūta-gītā* is a Vedanta text representing extreme Advaita or non-dualism. It is attributed to Dattātreya, who is looked upon as an Incarnation of God. Unfortunately, we possess no historical data concerning when or where he was born, how long he lived, or how he arrived at the knowledge disclosed in the text.

Avadhūta means a liberated soul, one who has 'passed away from' or 'shaken off' all worldly attachments and cares and has attained a spiritual state equivalent to the existence of God. Although *avadhūta* naturally implies renunciation, it includes an additional and even higher state that is neither attachment nor detachment, but is beyond both. An *avadhūta* feels no need to observe any rules, whether secular or religious. He seeks nothing and avoids nothing. He has neither knowledge nor ignorance. Having realized that he is the infinite Self, he lives in that vivid realization."

Swami Vivekānanda, one of the greatest advaitins of all times, often quoted this *Gītā*. He once said, "Men like the one who wrote this song keep religion alive. They have experienced. They care for nothing, and feel nothing done to the body; they don't care for heat, cold, danger, or anything else. They sit still, enjoying the bliss of the Ātman, and even if embers burn their bodies, they do not feel them."

The *Avadhūta Upanishad* is number 79 in the *Muktikā* canon of Upanishads. It is a *Sannyāsa Upanishad* associated with the Black (Kṛṣṇa) Yajur-veda: "One who has transcended the *varṇāśrama* system and has always established in himself, that yogi, who is above the *varṇāśrama* divisions, is called *avadhūta*." (*Avadhūta Upanishad*, 2).

The *Brahma-nirvāṇa Tantra* book describes how to identify *avadhūtas* of the following types:

- *Bramhāvadhūta*: An *avadhūta* by birth, who appears in any cast of society and is completely indifferent to the world or worldly matters.
- *Śaivāvadhūta*: *Avadhūtas* who have taken to the renounced order of life or *sannyāsa*, often with long matted hair (*jaṭa*), or who dress in the manner of Shaivites and spend almost all of their time in trance *samādhi*, or meditation.
- *Virāvadhūta*: This person looks like a *sadhū* who has put red-colored sandal paste on his body and wears saffron-colored clothes. His hair is very well grown and is normally furling in the wind. They wear around their necks a *rudrākṣa-mālā* or a chain of bones. They carry a wooden stick, or *daṇḍa*, in their hand, and additionally always carry an axe (*paraśu*) or an *ḍamaru* (small drum) with them.
- *Kulāvadhūta*: These people are supposed to have taken the Kaul *Sampradāya* initiation. It is very difficult to recognize these people as they do not wear any outward signs that can identify them from others. The specialty of these people is that they stay and live like normal people. They may show themselves in the form of kings or family men.

The *Nātha Sampradāya* is a form of *Avadhūta-pantha* (sect). In this *Sampradāya*, Guru and yoga are of extreme importance. Therefore, the most important book of this *Sampradāya* is the *Avadhūta-gītā*. Śrī Gorakṣanāth is considered the highest form of the *avadhūta* state.

The nature of *avadhūta* is the subject of the *Avadhūta-gītā*, traditionally attributed to Dattātreya.

According to Bipin Joshi, the main characteristics of an *avadhūta* are: "He who is a sinless philosopher and has cast off the shackles of ignorance (*ajñāna*). He who lives in a stateless state and relishes the experience all the time. He revels in this blissful state, unperturbed by the material world. In this unique state, the *avadhūta* is neither awake nor in deep sleep; there is no sign of life or death. It is a state defying all descriptions. It is the state of infinite bliss, which a finite language is incapable of describing. It can only be intuited purely by our intellect. A state that is neither truth nor non-truth, neither existence nor nonexistence. He who has realized his identity with the imperishable, who possesses incomparable excellence, who has shaken off the bonds of *saṁsāra* and never deviates from his goal. That thou art (*tat tvam asi*), and other upanishadic statements, are ever present in the mind of such an enlightened soul. That sage who is rooted in the plenary experience of 'Verily, I am Brahman (*ahaṁ Brahmāsmi*)', 'All this is Brahman (*sarvaṁ khalvidaṁ brahma*)', and that '…there is no plurality, I and God are one and the same…', etc. Supported by the personal experience of such Vedic statements, he moves freely in a state of total bliss. Such a person is a renunciant, liberated, *avadhūta*, yogi, paramahamsa, *brāhmaṇa*."

From Wikipedia, the free encyclopedia:

Avadhūta is a Sanskrit term used in Indian religions to refer to mystics or antinomian saints who are beyond ego-consciousness, duality, and common worldly concerns, and act without consideration of standard social etiquette. Such personalities "roam free as a child on the face of the Earth." An *avadhūta* does not identify with his mind or body or 'names and forms' (Sanskrit: *nāma-rūpa*). Such a person is considered pure consciousness (Sanskrit: *caitanya*) in human form.

Avadhūtas play a significant role in the history, origins, and rejuvenation of a number of traditions such as yoga, Advaita Vedanta, Buddhist, and bhakti *paramparās* even as they are released from standard observances. *Avadhūtas* are the voice of the *avadhūti*, the channel that resolves the dichotomy of *Vāmācāra* and *Dakṣiṇācāra* or "left and right-handed traditions." An *avadhūta* may or may not continue to practice religious rites as long as they are free from sectarian ritual observance and affiliation. The Monier Williams Sanskrit dictionary defines the term *avadhūta* as follows: "अवधूत / अव-धूत — one who has shaken off from himself worldly feelings and obligations."

From *Hinduism, an alphabetical guide* by Roshen Dalal

Avadhūta: A term for a liberated soul, one who has renounced the world. Totally beyond all that is, an *avadhūta* follows no rules, no fixed practices, and has no need to follow conventional norms. There are several texts dealing with the life and nature of an *avadhūta*. In the *Avadhūta Upanishad*, the Ṛṣi Dattātreya describes the nature of the *avadhūta*. Such a person is immortal, has discarded all worldly ties, and is always full of bliss. One of its verses states: "Let thought contemplate Viṣṇu, or let it be dissolved in the bliss of Brahman. I, the witness, do nothing, nor do I cause anything to be done." (v.28)

The *Turīyātīta Avadhūta Upanishad* contains a description of the *avadhūta* who has reached the state of consciousness beyond the *turīya*. In this state, a person is pure, detached and totally free. An *avadhūta* who has reached this level does not chant mantras or practice rituals, wears no caste marks, and is finished with all religious and secular duties. He wears no clothes and eats whatever comes his way. He wanders alone, observing silence, and is totally absorbed in non-duality. The *Avadhūta-gītā* has similar descriptions.

The *Uddhava-gītā*, which is part of the *Bhāgavata Purāṇa*, describes an *avadhūta* who learned from all aspects of life and was at home anywhere in the world. The term *avadhūta* can be applied to any liberated person, but it also refers specifically to a *sannyāsa* sect.

Avadhūta Upanishad

Avadhūta Upanishad is a small Upanishad consisting of about 32 mantras. It falls under the category of the *Sannyāsa Upanishads* and is a part of Kṛṣṇa Yajurveda. The *Avadhūta Upanishad* takes the form of a dialogue between Dattātreya and Ṛṣi Saṁkṛti.

One day Ṛṣi Saṁkṛti asks Dattātreya the following questions: "Who is an *avadhūta*?; What is his state?; What are the signs of the *avadhūta*?; How does he live?"

The following are the answers given by the compassionate Dattātreya.

Who is an *avadhūta*?

The *avadhūta* is so called because he is beyond any decay; he lives freely according to his will, he destroys the bondage of worldly desires, and his only goal is That thou Art (*tat tvam asi*).

The *avadhūta* goes far beyond all the castes (such as *brāhmaṇa, vaiśya, kṣatrya,* and *śūdra*) and *Āśramas* (such as *brāmhacaryā, gṛhastha, vānaprastha,* and *sannyāsa*). He is the highest Yogi who is established in a constant state of self-realization.

What is his state?

An *avadhūta* always enjoys supreme bliss. The divine joy represents his head, happiness is his right wing, ecstasy represents his left wing, and bliss is his very nature. The life of an *avadhūta* shows extreme detachment.

What are the signs of *avadhūta*? How does he live?

An *avadhūta* lives according to his own will. He may wear clothes or go naked. For him, there is no difference between *dharma* or *adharma*, sacrifice or non-sacrifice, because he is beyond these aspects. He performs inner sacrifice and that forms their *aśvamedha-yajña*. He is a great yogi who remains unaffected even when engaged in worldly objects. He remains pure.

The ocean accepts water from all the rivers but remains unchanged. Similarly, an *avadhūta* is unaffected by worldly objects. He is always at peace and (like the ocean), all his desires are absorbed in this supreme peace.

For an *avadhūta* there is no birth or death, no bondage or liberation. He may have performed various actions for the sake of liberation, but they become history once he becomes an *avadhūta*. He is always satisfied. Others wander to fulfill their desires. But an *avadhūta*, being already satisfied, does not run after any desire. Others perform various rituals for the sake of heaven, but an *avadhūta* is already established in the omnipresent state and hence needs no rituals.

Other qualified teachers spend time teaching the scriptures (Vedas) but *avadhūta* goes beyond those activities, because he has no actions. He doesn't have any desire to sleep, beg (*bhikṣa*), bathe, or clean.

An *avadhūta* is always free from doubt, and since he is always in union with the supreme reality, he does not even need to meditate. Meditation is for those people who are not yet one with God, but an *avadhūta* is always in the state of union and therefore does not need to meditate.

Those who are after *karmas* (actions) are filled with *vāsanās*. These *vāsanās* haunt them even when they finish their *prārabdha-karma*. Ordinary men meditate because they wish to fulfill their desires. However, an *avadhūta* always stays away from that trap. His mind is beyond mental destruction and *samādhi*. Mental destruction as well as *samādhi* are possibly modifications of the mind. The *avadhūta* is already eternal and hence, there is nothing to attain for him.

Following worldly duties is like an arrow released from a bow, i.e. it cannot be stopped from giving good or bad fruits causing a cycle of action-reaction. However, an *avadhūta* is not a doer at any level and is not engaged in any action.

Having attained such a stage of detachment, an *avadhūta* remains unaffected even if he follows a way of life as prescribed by the scriptures. Even if he engages in *actions* such as worshipping God, bathing, begging, etc., he remains unattached to them. He lives as a witness and therefore does not perform any action.

An *avadhūta* can clearly see Brahman before his eyes. He is free from ignorance or *māyā*. He has no actions left to be performed and nothing left to achieve. He is totally satisfied and there is no one else with whom he can be compared.

नलिनी नालिनी नासे गन्धः सौरभ उच्यते ।
घ्राणोऽवधूतो मुख्यास्यं विपणो वाग्रसविद्रसः ॥

> *nalinī nālinī nāse*
> *gandhaḥ saurabha ucyate*
> *ghrāṇo 'vadhūto mukhyāsyaṁ*
> *vipaṇo vāg rasavid rasaḥ*

The two doors called Nalinī and Nālinī are to be known as the two nostrils, and the city named Saurabha represents the aroma. The companion spoken of as *avadhūta* is the sense of smell. The door called Mukhyā is the mouth, and Vipaṇa is the faculty of speech. Rasajña is the sense of taste.

(*Bhāgavata Purana*, 4.29.11)

Purport of H.D.G. A.C. Bhaktivedanta Swami Prabhupada:

The word *avadhūta* means "most free." A person is not under the rules and regulations of any injunction when he has attained the stage of *avadhūta*. In other words, he can act as he likes. This stage of *avadhūta* is exactly like air, which does not care for any obstruction. In the Bhagavad Gita (6.34) it is said:

चञ्चलं हि मनः कृष्ण प्रमाथि बलवद्दृढम् ।
तस्याहं निग्रहं मन्ये वायोरिव सुदुष्करम् ॥

> *cañcalaṁ hi manaḥ kṛṣṇa*
> *pramāthi balavad dṛḍham*
> *tasyāhaṁ nigrahaṁ manye*
> *vāyor iva suduṣkaram*

The mind is restless, turbulent, obstinate, and very strong, O Kṛṣṇa, and to subdue it is, it seems to me, more difficult than controlling the wind.

(Bhagavad Gita, 6.34)

Just as air or wind cannot be stopped by anyone, the two nostrils, situated in one place, enjoy the sense of smell without impediment. With the tongue, the mouth continuously tastes all kinds of tasty foods.

अक्षरत्वाद्वरेण्यत्वाद्धूतसंसारबन्धनात् ।
तत्त्वमस्यर्थसिद्धत्वात् अवधूतोऽभिधीयते ॥

aksaratvād varenyatvād
dhūta-saṁsāra-bandhanāt
tat tvam asy-artha siddhatvāt
avadhūto 'bhidhīyate

Since he is immutable (*akṣara*), the most excellent (*varenya*), since he has removed the worldly attachments (*dhūta-saṁsāra-bandanāt*) and he has realized the meaning of *tat tvam asi* (That thou art), he is called *avadhūta*.

(*Kulārṇava Tantra*, 17.24)

From Yogapedia: What does *avadhūta* mean?

Avadhūta is a Sanskrit term used to refer to a person who has reached a stage in their spiritual development in which they are beyond worldly concerns. People who have reached the stage of *avadhūta* may act without considering common social etiquette or their own ego. This term is often used in the cases of mystics or saints.

Advanced yoga practitioners may find inspiration in the idea of reaching this stage through further sustained meditation and asana practice.

Avadhūta is often associated with some sort of eccentric and spontaneous behavior from a holy person. This comes partly from the fact that mystics who have achieved this level of spiritual enlightenment may forget wearing clothes or other normal social behavior.

About the Prabhuji Mission

Prabhuji Mission is a Hindu religious, spiritual, and charitable organization founded by H.H. Avadhūta Bhaktivedānta Yogācārya Śrī Ramakrishnananda Bābājī Mahārāja. Its purpose is to preserve the "Retroprogressive Path," which reflects Prabhuji's vision of *Sanātana-dharma* and advocates for the global awakening of consciousness as the radical solution to humanity's problems.

Apart from imparting religious and spiritual teachings, the organization carries out extensive philanthropic work in the USA, based on the principles of karma yoga, selfless work performed with dedication to God.

Prabhuji Mission was established in 2003 in the USA as a Hindu church aimed at preserving its founder's universal and pluralistic vision of Hinduism.

The Prabhuji Mission operates a Hindu temple called Śrī Śrī Bhagavān Yeshua Jagat Jananī Miriam Premānanda Mandir, which offers worship and religious ceremonies to parishioners.

The extensive library of the Retroprogressive Institute provides its teachers with abundant study materials to research the various theologies and philosophies explored by Prabhuji in his books and lectures.

The Avadhutashram monastery educates monastic disciples on various aspects of Prabhuji's approach to Hinduism and offers them the opportunity to express devotion to God through devotional service by selflessly contributing their skills and training to the Mission's programs.

The Mission publishes and distributes Prabhuji's books and lectures and operates humanitarian projects such as the "Prabhuji Food Distribution Program," a weekly event in which dozens of families in need from Upstate New York receive fresh and nutritious food and the "Prabhuji Toy Distribution Program," which provides the less privileged kids with abundance of Christmas gifts.

Avadhutashram
Round Top, New York, USA

About the Avadhutashram

The Avadhutashram (monastery) was founded by Prabhuji. It is the headquarters of the Prabhuji Mission and the hermitage of H.H. Avadhūta Bhaktivedānta Yogācārya Śrī Ramakrishnananda Bābājī Mahārāja and his monastic disciples of the Ramakrishnananda Contemplative Monastic Order.

The ideals of the Avadhutashram are love and selfless service, based on the universal vision that God is in everything and everyone. Its mission is to distribute spiritual books and organize humanitarian projects such as the Prabhuji Food Distribution Program and the Prabhuji Toy Distribution Program.

The Avadhutashram is not commercial and operates without soliciting donations. Its activities are funded by Prabhuji's Gifts, a non-profit company founded by Prabhuji, which sells esoteric items from different traditions that he himself has used for spiritual practices during his evolutionary process. Its mission is to preserve and disseminate traditional religious, mystical, and ancestral crafts.

The Retroprogressive Path

The Retroprogressive Path does not require you to be part of a group or a member of an organization, institution, society, congregation, club, or exclusive community. Living in a temple, monastery, or *āśram* is not mandatory, because it is not about a change of residence, but of consciousness. It does not urge you to believe, but to doubt. It does not demand you to accept something, but to explore, investigate, examine, inquire, and question everything. It does not suggest being what you should be but being what you really are.

The Retroprogressive Path supports freedom of expression but not proselytizing. This route does not promise answers to our questions but induces us to question our answers. It does not promise to be what we are not or to attain what we have not already achieved. It is a retro-evolutionary path of self-discovery that leads us from what we think we are to what we really are. It is not the only way, nor the best, the simplest, or the most direct. It is an involutionary process par excellence that shows what is obvious and undeniable but usually goes unnoticed: that which is simple, innocent, and natural. It is a path that begins and ends in you.

The Retroprogressive Path is a continuous revelation that expands eternally. It delves into consciousness from an ontological perspective, transcending all religion and spiritual paths. It is the discovery of diversity as a unique and inclusive reality. It is the encounter of consciousness with itself, aware of itself and its own reality. In fact, this path is a simple invitation to dance in the now, to love the present moment, and to celebrate our authenticity. It is an unconditional proposal to stop living as a victim of circumstance and to live as a passionate adventurer. It is a call to return to the place we have never left, without offering us anything we do not already possess or teaching us anything we do not already know. It is a call for an inner revolution and to enter the fire of life that only consumes dreams, illusions, and fantasies but does not touch what we are. It does not help us reach our desired goal, but instead prepares us for the unexpected miracle.

This path was nurtured over a lifetime dedicated to the search for Truth. It is a grateful offering to existence for what I have received. But remember, do not look for me. Look for yourself. It is not me you need, because you are the only one who really matters. This life is just a wonderful parenthesis in eternity to know and love. What you yearn for lies in you, here and now, as what you really are.

Your unconditional well-wisher,
Prabhuji

Prabhuji today

Prabhuji has retired from public life

Prabhuji is the sole disciple of H.D.G. Avadhūta Śrī Brahmānanda Bābājī Mahārāja, who is himself one of the closest and most intimate disciples of H.D.G. Avadhūta Śrī Mastarāma Bābājī Mahārāja.

Guru Mahārāja guided Prabhuji until he officially bestowed upon him the sacraments of the sacred order of *avadhūtas*. Prabhuji was appointed as the successor of the lineage by his master, who conferred upon him the responsibility of continuing the line of disciplic succession of *avadhūtas*, or the sacred *paramparā*, officially designating him as guru and commanding him to serve as the successor Ācārya under the name H.H. Avadhūta Bhaktivedānta Yogācārya Śrī Ramakrishnananda Bābājī Mahārāja.

Prabhuji is also a disciple of H.D.G. Bhakti-kavi Atulānanda Ācārya Mahārāja, who is a direct disciple of H.D.G. A.C. Bhaktivedānta Swami Prabhupāda.

In 2011, with the blessings of his Gurudeva, he adopted the path of a secluded *bhajanānandī* and withdrew from society to lead the contemplative life of a hermit. Since then, he has been living as an independent Christian-Marian Hindu religious hermit. His days have been spent in solitude, praying, writing, painting, and meditating in silence and contemplation.

He no longer participates in *sat-saṅgs*, lectures, gatherings, meetings, retreats, seminars, study groups, or courses. We ask everyone to respect his privacy and do not try to contact him by any means for gatherings, meetings, interviews, blessings, *śaktipāta*, initiations, or personal visits.

Prabhuji's teachings

As an *avadhūta* and a realized master, Prabhuji has always appreciated the essence and wisdom of a wide variety of religious practices from around the world. Although many see him as an enlightened being, Prabhuji has no intention of presenting himself as a public figure, preacher, propagator of beliefs, promoter of philosophies, guide, coach, content creator, influencer, preceptor, mentor, counselor, consultant, monitor, tutor, teacher, instructor, educator, enlightener, pedagogue, evangelist, rabbi, *posek halacha*, healer, therapist, satsangist, pointer, psychic, leader, medium, savior, New Age guru, or authority of any kind, whether spiritual or material. According to Prabhuji, the quest for the Self is individual, solitary, personal, private, and intimate. It is not a collective endeavor to be undertaken through organized, institutional, or community religiosity. Since 2011, Prabhuji has disagreed with spirituality practiced in a social, communal, or collective manner. Therefore, he does not proselytize or preach, nor does he try to persuade, convince, or make anyone change their perspective, philosophy, or religion. Many may find his insights valuable and apply them partially or fully to their own development, but Prabhuji's teachings should not be interpreted as personal advice, direction, counseling, instruction, guidance, tutoring, self-help methods, or techniques for spiritual, physical, emotional, or psychological development. The proposed teachings do not aspire to be definitive solutions for life's spiritual, material, financial, psychological, emotional, romantic, family, social, or physical problems. Prabhuji does not promise miracles, mystical experiences, astral journeys, healings of any kind, connections with spirits, angels or extraterrestrials, astral travel to other planets, supernatural powers, or spiritual salvation.

Service and glorification of the guru are fundamental spiritual principles in Hinduism. The Prabhuji Mission, as a traditional Hindu church, practices the millenary *guru-bhakti* tradition of reverence to the master.

Some disciples and friends of the Prabhuji Mission, on their own initiative, help to preserve Prabhuji's legacy and his interfaith teachings for future generations by disseminating his books, videos of his internal talks, and websites.

The sacred way

Some time ago, on the sacred journey toward transcendence, Prabhuji reaffirmed his resolve not to disturb those who showed no interest in joining him on this path. This decision is not simple detachment, but instead, a deliberate choice to preserve the essence of this migratory route: a commitment to authenticity and deepening self-inquiry. Such a decision, far from being an abandonment, is a respectful recognition of individual autonomy and divergent destinies and aspirations. On this journey, choosing fellow travelers is not a mere whim, but an exercise in critical discernment and alignment with those whose vision intertwines with own own in the search for our home within our own house.

Public services

Even though the monastery does not accept new residents, volunteers, donations, collaborations, or sponsorships, the public is invited to participate in daily religious services and devotional festivals at the Śrī Śrī Bhagavān Yeshua Jagat Jananī Miriam Premānanda Mandir.

Titles by Prabhuji

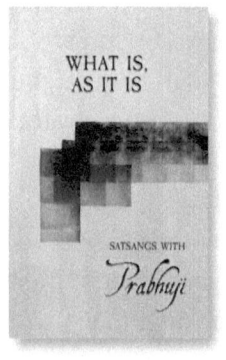

What is, as it is: Satsangs with Prabhuji (English)
ISBN-13: 978-1-945894-26-8

Lo que es, tal como es: *Sat-saṅgas* con Prabhuji (Spanish)
ISBN-13: 978-1-945894-27-5

Russian: ISBN-13: 978-1-945894-18-3
Hebrew: ISBN-13: 978-1-945894-24-4

Kundalini Yoga: The Power is in you (English)
ISBN-13: 978-1-945894-30-5

***Kuṇḍalinī-yoga*: El poder está en ti (Spanish)**
ISBN-13: 978-1-945894-31-2

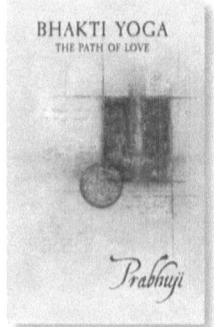

Bhakti Yoga: The Path of Love (English)
ISBN-13: 978-1-945894-28-2

***Bhakti-yoga*: El sendero del amor (Spanish)**
ISBN-13: 978-1-945894-29-9

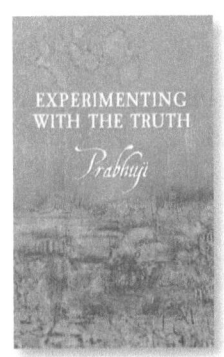

Experimenting with the Truth (English)
ISBN-13: 978-1-945894-32-9

Experimentando con la Verdad (Spanish)
ISBN-13: 978-1-945894-33-6

Hebrew
ISBN-13: 978-1-945894-93-0

Tantra: Liberation in the World (English)
ISBN-13: 978-1-945894-36-7

Tantra: La liberación en el mundo (Spanish)
ISBN-13: 978-1-945894-37-4

Advaita Vedanta: Being the Self (English)
ISBN-13: 978-1-945894-34-3

Advaita Vedānta: **Ser el Ser (Spanish)**
ISBN-13: 978-1-945894-35-0

Beyond Answers: Philosophy
in the Eternal Search (English)
ISBN-13: 978-1-945894-91-6

Más allá de las respuestas:
La filosofía en la búsqueda
eterna (Spanish)
ISBN-13: 978-1-945894-88-6

Discovering the Last God
(English)
ISBN-13: 978-1-945894-71-8

Descubriendo al Último Dios
(Spanish)
ISBN-13: 978-1-945894-89-3

Questioning your Answers:
Philosophy as a Question
(English)
ISBN-13: 978-1-945894-80-0

Cuestionando tus respuestas:
La filosofía como pregunta
(Spanish)
ISBN-13: 978-1-945894-77-0

Īśāvāsya Upanishad
commented by Prabhuji
(English)
ISBN-13: 978-1-945894-38-1

Īśāvāsya Upaniṣad
comentado por Prabhuji
(Spanish)
ISBN-13: 978-1-945894-40-4

The Diamond Sūtra
commented by Prabhuji
(English)
ISBN-13: 978-1-945894-51-0

El Sūtra del Diamante
comentado por Prabhuji
(Spanish)
ISBN-13: 978-1-945894-54-1

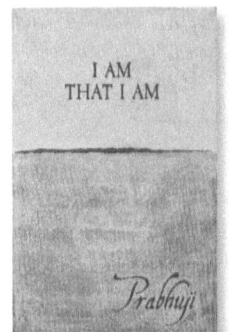

I am that I am
(English)
ISBN-13: 978-1-945894-78-7

Soy el que soy
(Spanish)
ISBN-13: 978-1-945894-48-0

Being (English)
Vol I: 978-1-945894-73-2
Vol II: 978-1-945894-74-9
Vol III: 978-1-945894-55-8
Ser (Spanish)
Vol I: 978-1-945894-70-1
Vol II: 978-1-945894-94-7
Vol III: 978-1-945894-56-5

The Symbolic Turn (English)
ISBN-13: 978-1-945894-62-6

El giro simbólico (Spanish)
ISBN-13: 978-1-945894-59-6

Phenomenology of the Sacred: Foundations for a Retroprogressive Phenomenology (English)
ISBN-13: 978-1-945894-68-8

La fenomenología de lo sagrado: Fundamentos para una Fenomenología Retroprogresiva (Spanish)
ISBN-13: 978-1-945894-65-7

**Mapuche Spirituality
(English)**
ISBN-13: 978-1-945894-92-3

**La espiritualidad mapuche
(Spanish)**
ISBN-13: 978-1-945894-95-4

www.ingramcontent.com/pod-product-compliance
Lightning Source LLC
Chambersburg PA
CBHW021129230426
43667CB00005B/73